MASCULINE
INTERESTS

FILM AND CULTURE

A series of Columbia University Press

Edited by John Belton

What Made Pistachio Nuts? Early Sound Comedy and the Vaudeville Aesthetic
Henry Jenkins

Showstoppers: Busby Berkeley and the Tradition of Spectacle
Martin Rubin

Projections of War: Hollywood, American Culture, and World War II
Thomas Doherty

Laughing Screaming: Modern Hollywood Horror and Comedy
William Paul

Laughing Hysterically: American Screen Comedy of the 1950s
Ed Sikov

Primitive Passions: Visuality, Sexuality, Ethnography, and Contemporary Chinese Cinema
Rey Chow

The Cinema of Max Ophuls: Magisterial Vision and the Figure of Woman
Susan M. White

Black Women as Cultural Readers
Jacqueline Bobo

Picturing Japaneseness: Monumental Style, National Identity, Japanese Film
Darrell William Davis

MASCULINE
INTERESTS

HOMOEROTICS IN
HOLLYWOOD FILM

ROBERT LANG

COLUMBIA
UNIVERSITY
PRESS
NEW YORK

Columbia University Press
Publishers Since 1893
New York   Chichester, West Sussex
Copyright © 2002 Columbia University Press

Library of Congress Cataloging-in-Publication Data

Lang, Robert, 1957–
Masculine interests : homoerotics in Hollywood film / Robert Lang.
p.   cm.—(Film and culture)
Includes bibliographical references and index.
Contents: Masculine interests—Oedipus in Africa: The lion king—To "have known ectasy": hunting men in The most dangerous game—Friendship and its discontents: The outlaw—Looking for the "great whatsit": Kiss me deadly and film noir— Midnight cowboy's backstory—Innerspace—Batman and Robin—My own private Idaho and the new new queer road movies—"The things we think and do not say": Jerry Maguire and the business of personal relationships.
ISBN 0-231-11300-5 (alk. paper)—ISBN 0-231-11301-3 (pbk.: alk. paper)
1. Homosexuality in motion pictures   2. Men in motion pictures.   I. Title.   II. Series.
PN1995.9.H55 L37 2002
791.43'653—dc21
2002024705

Columbia University Press books are printed on permanent and durable acid-free paper.
Printed in the United States of America
c 10 9 8 7 6 5 4 3 2 1
p 10 9 8 7 6 5 4 3 2 1

CREDITS: Portions of this book have appeared in different form in the following publications: *The Road Movie Book* (New York: Routledge, 1997); *Perspectives on Film Noir* (New York: G. K. Hall, 1996); *American Imago* 52.2 (Summer 1995); *American Imago* 47.3–4 (Fall-Winter 1990); and *Cinema Journal* 27.3 (Spring 1988). The illustrations on pages 92, 103, 108, 115, 129, 131, 135, 136, 141, 145, 148, 152, 178, 196, 201, 270, and 290 courtesy of Photofest (New York). All other illustrations are from the author's collection.

To my brother, Gordon

CONTENTS

PREFACE

Those of us who are born male must at some point early in our lives start figuring out what it means to be male. Although we are inscribed within culture from birth, and there is the question of the roles played by genetics and biology, there is a sense in which we also make choices about how to inhabit our maleness. To become gendered, as one of the first requirements of becoming socialized, we both consciously and unconsciously learn the codes of masculinity available to us—by observing Mom and Dad, brothers and sisters, friends, strangers on the street, teachers, magazine advertising, television, movies, and so on.

For a long time, after the advent of cinema as a mass form of entertainment, movies played a significant role in the shaping of masculine behavior and identity in American culture. They still do, even though television has taken over as the dominant medium through which masculine subjectivities are forged in the United States and the industrialized countries of the West. The American feature film nevertheless remains, directly or indirectly, one of the most powerful producers of images of what it means to be a man in late capitalist society. The implications of this fact are central to the themes of this book, in which I examine some contemporary masculinities in a handful of American genre films.

I begin with the uncontroversial observation that a mass cultural artifact like the American genre film (particularly with its excessive sexual stereotyping) can tell us a great deal about the ideological underpinnings of the society which produces (me as) a masculine subject, and I have chosen my films for analysis accordingly. To be(come) a man involves looking at other men, seeing them in dramatic, narrative contexts, *identifying* with them—which is why I limit my investigation to films in which a male-male relationship is central in the construction of a masculine identity. Although I look at movies from almost every decade of the cinema, this is not a survey or history of the

American sound film nor even a study of American film genres, but a set of critical essays in which I consider masculinity in social and psychoanalytic terms as an ideological-generic construction, and explore some of the ways in which men engender men. The constraints imposed by my methods of psycho/textual analysis notwithstanding, there are many genres (and literally hundreds of films) I wish could have been included, and which the reader could easily argue might have been better suited to the book's purpose. In the end, however, I have been guided by my desire, and my habit of queer reading, to discover how Hollywood—insofar as it positions the spectator—owns up to some contradictory dissatisfactions with the norms of masculinity implied by its representations, particularly in those genres and films that privilege the troublesome terrain represented by male-male relationships.[1]

Among the many people who have given me help during the writing of this book I particularly acknowledge my gratitude to the following: Richard Allen, Nemanja Bala, Marta Balletbò-Coll, Jennifer Barager, Maher Ben Moussa, Jean-Pierre Bertin-Maghit, Sherry Buckberrough, Ellen Carey, David Chenkin, Candace Clements, Steve Cohan, Paul Dambowic, David Galef, Roy Grundmann, Julian Halliday, Ina Rae Hark, Cora Harris, Sumiko Higashi, Henry Jenkins, Ann Kaplan, Alex Keller, George Lechner, Peter Lehman, Mark Lilly, Susan LoBello, Greg Martino, Paula Massood, Laurent Odde, Fred Pfeil, Tony Pipolo, Dana Polan, Jean Prescott, Susannah Radstone, Peggy Roalf, Phil Rosen, Ed Sikov, Charles Silver, Candace Skorupa, Bill Stull, Marge Sullivan, Roy Thomas (my superb manuscript editor), Randolph Trumbach, Kitty Tynan, Michael Walsh, Tom Waugh, Estela Welldon, and Patrick Woodcock.

I thank my wonderful and wise publisher at Columbia University Press, Jennifer Crewe, who knew how to get a manuscript out of me without seeming to apply the slightest pressure. And for his confidence in the project, I sincerely thank John Belton, editor of the Film and Culture series at Columbia. I feel it an honor to be included in the series and am grateful to have received encouragement and good counsel from him at several crucial stages during the writing of the book.

To my family, scattered across three continents—June and Vic, Lesli-Sharon, Alison, and Helen—I offer my love. Finally, my profoundest gratitude to Paul Scovill, whose love and understanding make it all possible.

MASCULINE
INTERESTS

1

MASCULINE INTERESTS

In his memoir *Screening History*, Gore Vidal describes his childhood desire to be a twin, which he remembers experiencing when he watched *The Prince and the Pauper* for the first time.[1] The prince and the pauper were played by Billy and Bobby Mauch, identical twins who were the same age as Vidal, twelve: "I thought [they] were cute as a pair of bug's ears, and I wished I were either one of them, *one* of them, mind you. I certainly did not want to be two of *me*."[2] Although an only child, Vidal was not a lonely one; rather, he was solitary, wanting no company at all other than books and movies, and his own imagination. Vidal notes that the star of the film was Errol Flynn, a swashbuckling actor at the height of his beauty, and that although Flynn "is charming as an ideal older brother," Vidal had completely forgotten that he was in the movie: "Plainly, I didn't want an older brother. I was fixated on the twins themselves. On the changing of clothes, and the reversal of roles" (25).

Vidal goes on to comment that this desire to be a twin does not seem to him to be narcissistic in the vulgar sense: "After all, one is oneself; and the other other. It is the sort of likeness that makes for wholeness, and is not that search for likeness, that desire and pursuit of the whole—as Plato has Aristophanes remark—that is the basis of all love?" (24). Elsewhere in his memoir, Vidal reveals that as a boy he had for a fleeting moment once been a newsreel personage, but what he really wanted to be was a movie star: "specifically, I wanted to be Mickey Rooney, and to play Puck, as he had done in *A Midsummer Night's Dream*. . . . He was my role model, though he must have been all of fourteen when I was only ten."[3]

Much in these recollections and in Vidal's assessment of their significance is relevant to the themes of this book. And in case the reader objects that Gore Vidal is a famously singular case and not emblematic of the norms of masculine identity formation against which I read the films discussed in the following pages, I hasten to point out that I might just as appropriately have begun my investigation with the example of Chuck Norris, who watched John Wayne movies as a child and dreamed of becoming a screen hero such as Wayne.[4]

Here we have the basic elements of what I call masculine interest—a male interest in what it means to be male; an interest in masculinity—accomplished through looking at another male, in an act of identification.[5] Vidal's remarks reveal that among the reasons people watch movies is the opportunity the experience offers to observe and evaluate the possibilities of how to "be" masculine or feminine. But he also insists that one enters the movie theater as an already constituted ego ("After all, one is oneself; and the other other"). Mickey Rooney/Puck may have been his "role model," and the Mauch twins were quite understandably objects of erotic identification, but Vidal's *desire* remains radically free—free to pursue the whole, wherever it may take him.

While there is something to be said for the cinema's powerfully reassuring ability to confirm or encode the viewer's sense of self, it must also be recognized that the conscious ego, which is formed mimetically (via models), can be the enemy of desire, which is formed unconsciously. One of my chief aims in writing this book is to put into play a number of analytical tools to help the reader experience Hollywood cinema not only as a means of developing the ego self-consciously or critically through a series of imaginary identifications or "role models"—if only to learn from the movies how to perform gendered identities that are at least not misogynist or homophobic—but as a means of achieving what Tim Dean calls "maximum subjective and sexual freedom."[6] To the extent that this is possible, we need to understand desire and sexuality both in terms of the unconscious and as a (self-)conscious play within the symbolic—not, for example, in dominant culture's polarizing terms of gay or straight identities. Like the boy who wanted no company at all other than books and movies and his own imagination,[7] I believe in the power and value of fantasy, in the productive sense in which the spectator constructs and is constituted by fantasy as the mise-en-scène of desire.[8] By becoming active, cinematically literate viewers, we can better equip ourselves to create the conditions in which we might find happiness. If, like Vidal, it occurs to me that the only thing I ever really liked to do was go to the movies, I might analyze and tap into that desire, for desire is the unconscious of all social productions and is behind every investment of time and interest and capital, and vice versa.[9] I am motivated first by the radical insight of psychoanalysis, elaborated by Lacan, that desire springs from the relation between language and one's own body. As Dean puts it:

One desires what he or she does not have, and the loss that initiates desire involves not gender (or the imaginary other) but something more fundamental, namely, the way language (what Lacan calls the symbolic Other) violates bodily integrity, thereby thwarting the sense of bodily wholeness conferred by the ego, one's sense of self. Although the capture of the human body by culture's symbolic networks functions differently for different subjects, in all cases that symbolic impact entails a *dis*embodiment that no amount of theory or activism can restore. Yet it is also this disembodiment that creates desire.[10]

This representation of desire as grounded in loss need not be viewed as tragic; rather, the contrary. As Dean implies, every subject's relation to the symbolic order is different, and that matrix of identification, desire, and the Law in which subjectivity is forged is an infinitely flexible structure. To participate actively in the dialectic of embodiment and disembodiment that creates desire is but a question of learning the language—and using it with imagination. What follows, then, are readings of some of those models for identification offered to us by the cinema which I hope will challenge the notion that sexuality—and the "masculinity" which gives that sexuality a discursive identity—is a regime involving notions of adaptation, maturity, and cure.

The title of this book was suggested by a reiterated phrase in Henning Bech's original and stimulating work about homosexuality and modernity, *When Men Meet*: "*the interest between men in what men can do with one another.*"[11] In a chapter titled "Absent Homosexuality," Bech writes that "being or wanting to be a man implies an interested relation from man to man. This *male interest* includes the pleasures of mirroring and comparing, as well as of companionship and apprenticeship. . . . The interest between men in what men can do with one another is a specification of this" (44; emphasis in original). Although Bech quite rightly insists that male homosexual attraction is intimately and inextricably entwined with attraction to masculinity, he is at pains—as I should be—not to imply that "the social relations inherent in the wish to be a man and in the experience of being a man [are] at bottom 'homosexual' relations" (54–55). Indeed Bech is interested in the *specificity* of these relations, their unique and distinctive character: "But the connections between wish, longing, body, male images, togetherness, sharing, security, excitement, equality and difference in relation to other men which are intrinsic to identification make it impossible to keep it apart from eroticism" (55). It is precisely this eroticism that is narrativized as a problematic in each of the films I discuss, where the male-male eroticism as a symbolically fraught aspect of relations between men in our culture is given a generic articulation.

As "systems of orientations, expectations, and conventions that circulate between industry, text, and subject,"[12] cinematic genres offer the critic a uniquely accessible approach to a large and complicated object of study. And as Frank Krutnik observes, they function as "intertextual systems which assert a forceful pressure upon the channels and the limits of readability"[13]—which is also how ideology operates generally, to persuade the subject that in the matter of masculine identity formation, for example, there is some variety and choice, but there are also norms to be respected.

Genres, however, are never "pure," a fact we seem to have become more conscious of since the collapse of the Hollywood studio system in the late 1950s.[14] The idea of genre, and the paradoxes of genre-mixing, are central to the controlling thesis of this book—that masculinity itself is a genre formation. Gender, like genre, is a performative accomplishment. As Judith Butler puts it in *Gender Trouble*, "the various acts of gender create the idea of gender."[15] Just as a film *genre* has no content until a number of genre *films* render it visible, gender, we may say, echoing Butler, is "an identity tenuously constituted in time, instituted in an exterior space through a *stylized repetition of acts*. The effect of gender is produced through the stylization of the body and, hence, must be understood as the mundane way in which bodily gestures, movements, and styles of various kinds constitute the illusion of an abiding gendered self."[16] And so it is that we recognize types of masculinity; but as soon as we come closer, to identify the type, we find a surprising degree of contradiction in our model of the genre of masculinity it supposedly represents. Gender, thus, as a regulatory, cultural fiction, is a norm that can never be fully internalized. In Butler's phrase: "gender norms are finally phantasmatic, impossible to embody."[17]

This paradox notwithstanding, I have chosen the self-reflexive trope of men looking at men in some recognizably generic ways as a point of entry for my exploration of how males become masculine subjects and how that subjectivity is maintained, for it is the subversive potential of the eroticism intrinsic to identification (the homoerotic variations of which highlight the discursive rather than essential character of gender) that engages me in the first place.

I start with *The Lion King* because the film proposes itself as a retelling of an ur-story of how we are all formed within the familial matrix that produces and ensures the norms of gender identity. Whether or not the Oedipus complex is universal, *The Lion King* would have it be so, particularly to the extent that it encodes the way in which boys become men in patriarchal societies. The generic power of the oedipal drama is such that Disney's CEO can call the film's story "archetypal" and assume that we (the readers of his autobiography, where he makes this comment, and the tens of millions of people who saw and enjoyed the movie) will know what he means. The film shows males (and females) working in the interests of masculinity, with masculinity as a metaphor, or code, that helps to hold in place patriarchal structures that, among their more baleful effects, keep women and gays in positions of subordination.

Where the key relationship in *The Lion King* is between father and son, acknowledged as the productive nexus of the son's correct identity as a properly masculine subject, the relationship between the two men in *The Most Dangerous Game*, a "classic" jungle-adventure/horror film of the 1930s, is meant to show what can go wrong when a boy's identification with his father is overeroticized and is transformed into a perversion by a trauma of some kind. Through the metaphor of the hunt, the risk, or temptation—which is to say, the ever-present possibility—of a perversion of the norm is expressed by showing a hunter being hunted. Count Zaroff and Bob Rainsford can be seen as two players in a perverse scenario in which each man's identification with the other and the masculinity the other represents is overdetermined, resulting in a compulsively repeated enactment of a sadomasochistic dialectic. The woman's presence in the movie is a reminder of a possible earlier attachment (the boy's love for his mother and/or an ancient memory of pre-oedipal plenitude) that indirectly helps to explain why the male-male relationship is surrounded by an aura of dread and desire that usually characterizes incest fantasies.

Unlike the horror film, the western—frequently described as the cinema's most "American" genre—might be expected to deliver mainstream images of masculine norms. More than most, it seems to deal in conservative, iconographically ritualized representations of masculinity, and seeks to articulate in the western hero a specifically American style of manliness. Robert Warshow and others have observed that although the westerner lives in a world of violence (the gun he wears on his thigh tells us this), "really, it is not violence at all which is the 'point' of the western movie, but a certain image of man, a style, which expresses itself most clearly in violence." Our eyes are focused, above all, on "the deportment of the hero": "Watch a child with his toy guns and you will see: what most interests him is not (as we so much fear) the fantasy of hurting others, but to work out how a man might look when he shoots or is shot. A hero is one who looks like a hero."[18] This invitation to look at the hero, to *gaze* at him, is offered not only to the film viewer but to characters within the film—usually other men.

In *The Outlaw*, the homoeroticism intrinsic to this look is developed by the narrative in such a way that the nominally heterosexual identity of the main male characters—usually no more than perfunctorily asserted in the western, and rarely very persuasively demonstrated—is revealed to be a function, or effect, of "Civilization" (of which "the woman" in this genre is a chief representative)—which is to say, of the conscious ego. The woman (Rio, played by Jane Russell) can offer the hero nothing, not even her sexuality, that he might want or need. She is not a schoolteacher from the East, who might teach him how to read and write (or dance!),[19] or how to behave in a drawing room. Nor is she proposed as the future mother of his children. She is, more than is usually so in the western, almost irrelevant to the action and the film's deeper meanings: embedded in the film is a nonheterosexual model of desire which has implications for the genre as a whole, suggesting that by the 1940s, when *The Outlaw* was made, it has become possible to propose the male homosexual as a figure of modernity.

In the film noir detective story, as in few other genres (certain types of horror film come to mind), a perverse and seductive sexuality dominates the mise-en-scène. The invariably troubled sexuality of the hero is partly revealed or explained by his quest, which often involves an obsessive curiosity about another man. In *Kiss Me Deadly*, a late film noir from the noir detective story's classic period, Mike Hammer's search for "the great whatsit" leads him to the mysterious Dr. Soberin and to Carl Evello, the vaguely homosexual "Mafia King," by whom he is clearly fascinated. Soberin and Evello are behind the murder of Christina, the sexy tomboy who makes a fatal pass at Mike at the beginning of the film. Mike's interest in Evello is personal, but in his role as a private investigator he is able to justify it as a professional one, which also allows him, in effect, to act out fantasies of sadism and tenderness that cannot be expressed in his uneasy friendship with Pat (who, with apt symbolism, is an officer of the law), and with Nick, his garage mechanic.

The mark of perversion also dominates the film I discuss in chapter 6, *Midnight Cowboy*. Starting with a screenwriters' term, *backstory*, I examine how the film tries to answer its own question of why the protagonist, Joe Buck, leaves his small town in Texas to become a "cowboy hustler" in New York City. I focus on the film's use of flashbacks, which render the unique complexity of Joe's point of view, and which are central to the film's discursive strategy whereby, in effect, Joe tells his "story" in the hope that the viewer/analyst will help establish the significance of past events as a key to unlock the meanings of the present situation, which the protagonist himself finds somewhat baffling.

While flashbacks of one kind or another have long been a part of the cinema's vocabulary, the use of this technique in *Midnight Cowboy* turns out to be metonymic, or emblematic, of the very question that sustains the narrative—the question of where and how to locate the "truth." For example, we are given images of Joe being raped by a gang of teenage boys, but we cannot know, from these images alone—which are presented as Joe's nightmare—whether they represent a wish-fulfillment, in the complex manner of dream distortions, or whether they represent something that really did happen to Joe, but which is unrepresentable (except as a false memory) because profoundly traumatic; *or* whether the filmmaker is merely using a cinematic convention that would render an "explanation" (for Joe's decision to become a hustler) that is orderly but psychoanalytically false.

The two questions—Whose story is it? *and* Who is telling the story?—are precisely ones that must be decided, but which cannot really be answered. If we say it is Joe who recalls, or fantasizes, this "event," we must also acknowledge that this story is being told by a filmmaker (who, furthermore, is not really the sole creator but rather a signifier for the many forces that come together to make a film). The film is clearly concerned with the question of the main character's identity, and understands sexuality to be the mainstay of identity. But the film does not easily capitulate to those questions that were important to the gay liberation movement in full swing at the time the film was made: Is Joe gay? Can we know *why* some people are gay, and others are not? The movie is the first scandalously queer film to come out of Hollywood, and as such poses questions about sexual-identity formation that seem more relevant than ever to our own "postmodern" moment in which some of us have come to see gender as "performative."

At the height of the so-called sexual revolution of the 1960s, the kind of self-consciousness that infects *Midnight Cowboy* around questions of intimacy between men becomes increasingly exacerbated in the genre of the buddy film, and by 1987, with *Innerspace*, reaches the limit of its own logic as a genre founded on the sublimation of homosexual desire. As a science-fiction comedy and buddy film about a man who is miniaturized in an experiment and accidentally injected into another man's body, *Innerspace* seems pressed to ask (but reluctant to answer) the question put by Eve Sedgwick in *Epistemology of the*

Closet: "Is men's desire for other men the great preservative of the masculinist hierarchies of Western culture, or is it among the most potent of the threats against them?"[20] The film becomes hysterical in its attempts, on the one hand, to acknowledge that the homosocial desire which provides the buddy film with its erotic energies exists in a continuum with homosexuality, while seeking on the other hand to affirm a determinedly active and heterosexual masculinity rooted in biology.

Innerspace's strategies of narration, a giddy mix of comedy, fantasy, parody, pastiche, allusion, irony, and sentiment, attempt simultaneously to acknowledge and disavow that homosexuality is the issue at the heart of the film's meanings. It is an attempt that in many ways recalls the Jerry Lewis–Dean Martin comedies of the 1950s in which, as Ed Sikov puts it, "Lewis and Martin play the sexual side of buddyism for dangerous comic effect, turning a kind of vicarious homosexual panic on the part of audiences into pleasure by way of nervous laughter."[21] Needless to say, as it comes too close to openly interpreting the "hom(m)o-sexual"[22] laws according to which the buddy film operates, the cycle of the genre which began in 1969 with *Midnight Cowboy*, *Easy Rider*, and *Butch Cassidy and the Sundance Kid*, and flourished in the 1970s with movies like *Scarecrow*, *Thunderbolt and Lightfoot*, and *California Split*, more or less comes to an end with *Innerspace*. Other genres, or variants of the buddy film, start to emerge, like the queer road movie.[23]

Throughout the 1980s, the live-action movie based on established cartoon characters, and movies devoted to the display of the spectacular bodies of certain male stars, such as Chuck Norris, Arnold Schwarzenegger, and Sylvester Stallone, proliferate on American screens, signaling a desire to engage overtly with contemporary anxieties about how men might behave "as men," through parodic performances of muscular masculinity which both enact and call into question the qualities they embody.[24]

Among the most publicized movies of this trend have been the *Batman* films, starting with the Warner Bros., live-action *Batman* released in 1989, which was made to celebrate and cash in on the fiftieth anniversary of the DC Comics cartoon character created by Bob Kane in 1939.[25] One of the reasons for the enduring and widespread appeal of Batman and his sidekick Robin is the fact that the two men are clearly fascinated by each other—indeed they *love* each other—but never "come out" as gay. For many, Batman's mystique is precisely his queerness. He is unquestionably "masculine," and yet—according to popular morality and the laws of desire—his erotic attractiveness as an embodiment of heroic masculinity must exist in a powerful dialectical relation to his loneliness, which has its origin in a childhood trauma.

Close examination of Batman's provenance reveals the character to be a function of the "family romance," described by Freud as a (child's) neurotic fantasy, in which he frees himself of his parents, so that he might create a more glamorous story of his origins. In the *Batman* comics and movies, the narrator's fantasy of Bruce Wayne as a rich and handsome man who lives with his young ward Dick Grayson in an enormous, baronial mansion, and of how they disguise themselves as Batman and Robin during their crime-fighting adventures together in Gotham City, can be read as an elaborate family romance which permits an endless replay of favorite themes, chief among them being the emotional bond between the older and the younger man. In the first decades of Dick/Robin's existence, he is depicted as a boy of about twelve. Later, he is presented as a college-age teenager, which frequently generates "adult," homoerotic currents in his relationship with Bruce/Batman. Contemporary homophobia renders Robin's presence in the *Batman* universe increasingly problematic, and a variety of attempts have been made in recent years to "heterosexualize" or efface his role.

Whether or not Robin appears in a *Batman* story, however, the perverse scenario is always essentially the same: the masked hero "saves" someone in danger, or must battle the forces of evil which threaten to overwhelm him. (In psychoanalytic terms, these forces represent the threat of castration, which are shown to originate in a moment of oedipal trauma.) The dominant ideological reading insists that Batman and Robin are not gay lovers, because neither of them will, or is able, to make an object-choice that would resolve his Oedipus complex. And yet . . . they might be lovers—the texts invite *other* readings. Despite the widespread notion that *Batman* stories are made for adolescent males (i.e., for boys experiencing a crisis of identification, like the one in which Batman and Robin are permanently inscribed), these stories can be read as acts of resistance to some of the masculinist and patriarchal structures they ostensibly celebrate. In this way, precisely—as a strategy of subversion from within—the *Batman*-text can function as an inspiriting challenge to hetero-patriarchal assumptions about whom we might choose to love and how we might choose to live.

The serial nature of the *Batman* narrative, which mobilizes fantasies that need never be foreclosed by an ending, is inscribed in the structure of the road movie genre also; and echoing Félix Guattari's contention that once there's marriage, there's no more desire, no more sexuality, I analyze *My Own Private Idaho* as an example of the queer road movie cycle that flourished in the 1990s—a cycle that understands that the opposite of homosexuality is not heterosexuality but marriage. Marriage does not function along a line of desire, whereas queer (homo)sexuality does. With its "quasi-gay themes and big stars" (which is how filmmaker Gregg Araki defined its crossover status), *My Own Private Idaho* is a watershed film in the (quasi-mainstream) American cinema for the way in which it deals with the affective bonds between men, and refuses "marriage" as the telos of its conception of desire. Like *Midnight Cowboy*, and like the *Batman* comics and films, *My Own Private Idaho* flirts with the possibility that its protagonists are gay, but will not, in Amy Taubin's phrase, "[turn] sexuality into a soundbite." Taubin wrote in her *Village Voice* review of the film that, while Gus Van Sant is one of the few openly gay directors in Hollywood, he is attracted to "the liminal, to barely perceptible thresholds between identification and desire."[26]

If the queer road movie is epistemologically not very different from the contemporary straight road movie (at least, not so different from one like Richard Linklater's *Before Sunrise*, 1995), or from the buddy film, it announces its radical aspiration in a unique way. The road movie genre came into its own after the collapse of classical cinema, but the queer road movie, in a sense launched by *Midnight Cowboy*, challenges traditional notions of desire as a libidinal force that must find its "proper" (heterosexual) object and be contained by "marriage."[27]

As the queer road movie that seemed to officially announce the arrival of the new genre, or cycle, *My Own Private Idaho* explores the truth of Roland Barthes's observation that every narrative leads back to Oedipus: "Isn't storytelling always a way of searching for one's origin, speaking one's conflicts with the Law, entering into the dialectic of tenderness and hatred?" The Death of the Father, Barthes writes, would deprive literature of many of its pleasures: "If there is no longer a Father, why tell stories?"[28] In *Idaho*, Mike (River Phoenix) does not, structurally speaking, have a father (in an incestuous twist of the plot, Mike's father is his brother), and Scott (Keanu Reeves) is in flight from his. By the end of the film, Scott has married and taken his place in the hetero-patriarchal, bourgeois society that is his birthright or "destiny," while Mike is still on the road, hustling for love, much as he was at the beginning. As a truly queer road movie, the film offers no easy answers, but gestures toward the "impossibility" of desire—toward the problem, as Guattari puts it, of how to "sexualize the body," the impossibility of becoming a "totally sexed body"—at the same time that it insists on the powerful reality of desire as a formation of the unconscious.

Seemingly as a desperate bid to reassert the "norms" of masculine desire that the independent cinema and films like *My Own Private Idaho* were doing so much to upset, *Jerry Maguire* (1996) is premised on the notion that it is possible to realize or recover a "true [masculine] self," and—indicative perhaps of the decline of Hollywood's cultural authority in the representational struggles over hegemonic masculinity—it was the only film in the 1997 lineup of Academy Award nominations for Best Picture that was produced by a major studio.

Jerry Maguire presents its eponymous hero as a man who feels alienated by modernity, and who hates "[his] place in the world." Despite his very successful career as a sports agent, and his numerous girlfriends, he is lonely. "I [have] so much to say, and no one to listen," he laments. On some level, he understands that what he wants is an intimate friendship with a man—but a form of homophobia (inherited from the Father), and his narcissism (as a defensive response to his inability to construct a secure and stable self), prevent him from developing what sociologists call a "pure friendship" with another man. Jerry (Tom Cruise) tries to forge an intimate friendship with one of his clients, Rod Tidwell (Cuba Gooding Jr.), but they both continually suffer confusions over where to draw the line between friendship and business. It becomes clear very quickly that the bond that develops between them is only possible because it is safely inscribed within their professional relationship as agent and client, which supposedly has them both after the same thing, "the money." ("Show me the money!" is the film's catch-phrase and mantra.) But the "money," quite obviously, is a metaphor for the "love" that both men want and need from each other.

As for the question of Jerry's narcissism—of which all his girlfriends complain—it is interesting to note that among the American and British theorists of narcissism, there are only rare mentions of fathers. Stephen Frosh observes:

> All is maternity: the security of the self, the modification of exhibitionism, the establishment of a realistic position in the world, these all derive from the mother's ability to support and contain her child's needs. It is in the maternal twosome that mental health or ill-health has its source; moreover, the perfect meeting of a subject's demand, the perfect union and relationship—the perfect primary narcissism—is a simple self-other absorption.[29]

And so it is that *Jerry Maguire* tries to convince the viewer that Jerry's salvation must come in the form of a woman: whatever problems Jerry has with intimacy, and so on, will be resolved by his relationship with Dorothy (Renée

Zellweger), who will provide him with a "second chance," as it were, for ide-alization. But Jerry's relationship with Rod is as much at the heart of the film as his romance with Dorothy. The two relationships are dialectically linked, but not in the way the film explains it. The film acknowledges that Rod rep-resents much more than a 4 percent commission to Jerry, yet it cannot open-ly acknowledge the extent to which Jerry's profound loneliness might be re-solved by certain kinds of interaction with a man. The film, according to patriarchal logic and convention, posits that what Jerry needs is a woman's love (and what he needs to love is a woman); and that what he needs from a man is empathy. What we actually see on the screen, however, is more com-plicated (and impossible to resolve, except in an illogical "happy ending"), as his relationship with Dorothy founders and fails, and his exclusive contract with Rod comes inevitably to an end.

In a discussion of therapeutic interventions with narcissistic patients, Frosh weighs the "relative worth of transference versus empathy modes" (119), asking, in effect, what psychotherapy can offer—i.e., "on the extent to which early deprivation can be made good by an accepting and maternal an-alyst" (119). It is the same question we find ourselves asking about Jerry, a question about the meaning of analytic "cure"—which, as noted earlier, must eventually be answered by the film. Can Dorothy, as "an accepting and maternal analyst" (although the film says it is *love* between them, i.e., trans-ference), ever be able truly to make good on whatever early deprivations have made Jerry incapable of experiencing intimacy with another human being?

The conclusions of *Jerry Maguire* notwithstanding, this is a question that will in one way or another haunt all the pages of this book, as I explore some "barely perceptible thresholds between identification and desire"—for, as Frosh reminds us, "something outside the merger of self and other is need-ed if narcissism is to be surpassed—something paternal, in family terms" (118). Kaja Silverman makes the same point when she writes that she is no longer as certain as she once was that the primary function of the Oedipus complex is social normalization. It now seems that its imperative is "to in-duct the subject into the speaking of his or her language of desire."[30] By forc-ing us to give up the one we love for a series of substitute love objects, and the fact that we pay "this exorbitant price" early in our lives, the Oedipus complex opens up the world for us. Indeed, as Silverman insists, "only inso-far as we are thrown into a kinship structure, for the effectuation of which the Oedipus complex is one possible vehicle, can there *be* a world" (151) She points out that the terms *mother* and *father* do not designate "encompassable entities": "Nor do they represent fixed symbolic constructs that largely transcend the actuality of the persons so designated. Rather, *mother* and *father* constitute complex discursive events that can take very different forms from one subject to another, and even from one moment to another" (151).

The chapters that follow, then, and the experience of watching the movies that have occasioned their writing, constitute a form of dialogue with the Other, to find or make a world in which we may satisfactorily take our place. Like Vidal's account of his childhood desire to be a twin, and his experience of "the shock, as it were, of twinship"[31] when he saw *The Prince and the Pauper*, they are offered as one way we can actively assume our particular language of desire.

OEDIPUS IN AFRICA

THE LION KING

In his 1998 autobiography, Michael Eisner, chairman and chief executive officer of the Walt Disney Company, proudly records that *The Lion King* (1994) would ultimately earn nearly $1 billion worldwide, "making it by far [Disney's] most popular animated film and probably the most profitable film ever made."[1] Oddly, considering this remarkable fact, Eisner shows no curiosity about why the film quickly became so successful, nor does his explanation offer much insight: *The Lion King* is "one of those magical films in which everything comes together," he writes. "It was visually stunning. The story of a son trying to live up to his father's legacy had a powerful archetypal resonance, and so did the simple themes of betrayal and retribution, responsibility and honor" (341).

What I wish to explore in this chapter are some of the more obvious themes of *The Lion King* arising from its self-consciously oedipal cast, which are revealed as anything but "simple," and to examine the part the father plays in the formation of the male child's sense of self.[2]

"From the day we arrive on the planet," sings the narrator in the film's opening shots, "the sun rolling high through the sapphire sky keeps great and small on the endless round . . . 'til we find our place in . . . the circle of life." And in *Three Essays on the Theory of Sexuality*, Freud wrote: "Every new arrival on this planet is faced by the task of mastering the Oedipus complex," adding that "anyone who fails to do so falls a victim to neurosis."[3] The song and the film's opening shots, we recognize immediately, announce that this will be the story of how Simba masters his Oedipus complex—how his personality will be structured, and how his desire will be oriented in relation to the loving and hostile wishes he experiences toward his parents (although in some ways Simba more closely resembles Hamlet, a later version of Oedipus). The Oedipus complex is a Freudian "story" about human psychic development that has taken hold of the popular imagination, to become, as one theorist has put it, "the special law of the modern psyche."[4] Indeed, we could say it has colonized the contemporary unconscious; and *The Lion King* does everything within its considerable power as cinema and as storytelling apparatus to naturalize and consolidate the patriarchal project, of which the Oedipus complex can be seen as the key instrument, producing a kind of template for the complicated *détour* called life, which leads back to death—or, in Peter Brooks's phrase, "Freud's masterplot,"[5] according to which the beginning foretells the end and the end speaks to the beginning (a father announcing the birth of his son: a king presenting his subjects with their future king).

"THE CIRCLE OF LIFE"

The film's four-minute prologue—which begins with an image of the sun, a gorgeous orange disk rising over the African savanna, and ends with all the creatures of the kingdom paying hommage to the king's newborn heir, whom even the heavens acknowledge with a benedictory shaft of light—is striking for its proliferation of phallic imagery and the overdetermination of the themes of timelessness and the existence of a natural and harmonious, hierarchical order. It makes a series of connections that all say something about the origins and order of things (a big concern to young viewers, for whom the film was ostensibly made). The ideological power of *The Lion King* is overwhelming. The movie says, in effect—before the narrative proper has even begun—that yes, mothers are important (they are the child's reality in the domestic sphere); but fathers are perhaps even more important, and they are certainly more glamorous, for fathers are the link to the public sphere, where a male child's destiny will be played out (to the sound of trumpeting elephants, in this instance). By making the social order reflect the natural order, the film blurs distinctions that young viewers do not consciously make—between simile, metaphor, and metonymy (for example, Mufasa later instructs Simba: "A king's time as ruler rises and falls like the sun. One day the sun will set on my time here and will rise with you as the new king"). The result is a film that children *love*, a film that Katha Pollitt in the *Nation* noted is "a weirdly sincere defense of feudalism, primogeniture, and the divine right of kings," in addition to being—as we shall see—"vaguely racist," "sexist," and "anti-intellectual."[6]

For our purposes, *The Lion King* is interesting not only for the way in which it seeks so brazenly to affirm male privilege, but for its "textbook" articulation of popular culture's ideal father-son relationship. It is obviously a film of its time, and as such tells us what a great many people think the father-son relationship should, or can, be—its impossible contradictions notwithstanding. It attempts to do essentially the same thing Robert Bly's bestselling book *Iron John* did at the beginning of the decade—explain what, in Eisner's phrase, a "father's legacy" should be, and how sons might live up to that legacy. Although Bly denies that his book advocates a return of traditional patriarchy (or to the state of relative grace he imagines prevailed in the United States prior to World War II),[7] the net effect of his project would do just that. Bly thinks mythologically— much as Disney sought to be "archetypal" in its approach to *The Lion King* (by setting the action in a timeless Africa, using cartoon animals as characters, etc.)—and his symbology is similar to *The Lion King*'s. For example, in a chapter titled "The Hunger for the King in a Time with No Father," he writes:

> The genuine patriarchy brings down the sun through the Sacred King, into every man and woman in the culture. . . . The death of the Sacred King . . . means that we live now in a system of industrial domination, which is not patriarchy. The system we live in gives no honor to the male mode of feeling. . . . The system of industrial domination determines how things go with us in the world of resources, values, and allegiances; what animals live and what animals die; how children are treated. And in the mode of industrial domination there is neither king nor queen. (98)

Like *Iron John*, *The Lion King* is a reaction against the kind of undermining of father-son bonding that began when the Industrial Revolution moved into high gear in the mid-nineteenth century. Susan Faludi's *Stiffed: The Betrayal of the American Man* (1999) similarly indicates what many men in our rampantly consumer-oriented culture feel they have lost, and to which it seems clear *The Lion King* is a response: a meaningful social world. Humans do not intrude into the world of *The Lion King*, which is safely set in some preindustrial Eden. And in the ideal world Bly imagines, men and their sons spend long hours together (like the "fathers and sons in most tribal cultures [who] live in an amused tolerance of each other" [93]), while the son's "cells receive some knowledge of what an adult masculine body is. The younger body learns at what frequency the masculine body vibrates" (93). What quickly emerges from reading Bly's book is that he has a very clear vision of what "the masculine" is. It is a "mode" or "frequency," which the boy learns from his father this way:

> Now, standing next to the father, as they repair arrowheads, or repair plows, or wash pistons in gasoline, or care for birthing animals, the son's body has the chance to retune. Slowly, over months or years, that son's body-strings begin to resonate to the harsh, sometimes demanding, testily humorous, irreverent, impatient, opinionated, forward-driving, silence-loving older masculine body. Both male and female cells carry marvelous music, but the son needs to resonate to the masculine frequency as well as the female frequency. (94)

Bly's prescription, or fantasy, is equal parts absurd, valid, and distressing. Absurd, not for its vocabulary of "body-strings" and so on, but for its embrace of a popular ideology of masculinity as if it were the one "true" masculinity, and for its bonding activities that most boys living in American cities today would have no access to—and would probably have no interest in, even if they did. We appreciate that Bly does not necessarily mean the reader to take his proposed father-son bonding activities literally, and that they perhaps only reflect the class background (sexist, anti-intellectual) of Bly's imagined readership, but we note their gendered quality, according to which it becomes a *truth* that men "wash pistons in gasoline," but do not, for example, bake cookies or do laundry, just as it might be seen as *natural* that men are "harsh" or "silence-loving" rather than warm or conversational.[8]

  The Lion King, too, attempts to offer a clear vision of "the masculine" (Mufasa and the adult Simba are meant to embody this correct masculinity, which is probably why they are among the film's less vivid characters—strictly two-dimensional). But more interesting than its representation of various ways of performing masculinity (Mufasa, Scar, Pumbaa, Timon, Zazu, and so on) is the way the film illustrates the process—with an emphasis on the father's role, or function, in that process—whereby Simba, as a normal male infant, grows up to be, *inevitably*, a monogamous, heterosexual patriarch. This chapter seeks to decenter the culturally dominant notion guiding the narrative that identity follows a developmental trajectory resulting in heterosexual complementarity. By focusing on what Jessica Benjamin calls "the identificatory, homoerotic bond between toddler son and father," which she sees as the prototype of ideal love, "a love in which the person seeks to find in the other an ideal image of himself,"[9] this chapter tries to identify the part played by the Oedipus complex as an ideologically determined structure that enables society to enforce its norm of heterosexuality. As elaborated by Freud, and as played out in *The Lion King*, the oedipal scenario turns on a dynamic of renunciation: the child abandons hope of fulfilling identificatory love of the parent of the opposite sex, and renounces object love of the parent of the same sex. This normative goal of sexual identity appears to be achieved quite happily by Simba and Nala in the film, but we observe how it also reproduces patriarchal structures that encourage the viewer to accept male dominance as a social fact.

Lynn Hunt's description of the social order in France before the revolution of 1789, which resulted in the king's execution, summarizes the ideology of deference that underpins *The Lion King*:

> The king had been the head of a social body held together by bonds of deference; peasants deferred to their landlords, journeymen to their masters, great magnates to their king, wives to their husbands, and children to their parents. Authority in the state was explicitly modeled on authority in the family. A royal declaration of 1639 had explained, "The natural reverence of children for their parents is linked to the legitimate obedience of subjects to their sovereign."[10]

Hunt then asks: "Once the king had been eliminated, what was to be the model that ensured the citizens' obedience?" (3). This question is important for our analysis because we live in a republic from which the king was eliminated a long time ago.

While the improbable "message" of *The Lion King* is that the world would be a better place if it were a kingdom or genuine patriarchy of some other kind, what we face in our society is no longer patriarchy itself, as John MacInnes points out in *The End of Masculinity*, but patriarchy's material and ideological legacy. *The Lion King*, with its family model of politics, makes a fetish of gender, which MacInnes sees as "the last vestige of enchantment, an attempt, in a godless and chaotic world, to 'worship' [sexual difference] as an anchor for social relations and thus defend men's privilege against the corrosive logic of modernity."[11] The film encourages the viewer to think of masculinity as an empirically existing form of identity, which is the legitimating cornerstone of patriarchy. The "correct" masculinity toward which Simba moves—"through despair and hope, through faith and love, on a path unwinding"—will at the very least be heterosexual. And Zazu can inform Simba and Nala, when they are no more than four years old, that they have been "betrothed" since birth. The hornbill insists they "have no choice"[12] in the

FIGURE 2.1 The *Lion King*'s family model of politics makes a fetish of gender: Simba's "destiny" as the first-born son of King Mufasa (voiced by James Earl Jones) and Queen Sarabi (voiced by Madge Sinclair) is confirmed and sanctioned by the shaman mandrill Rafiki (voiced by Robert Guillaume). (Copyright © The Walt Disney Company. All rights reserved)

matter: "One day you two are going to be married!" he assures them. Simba and Nala are horrified. "I can't marry her. She's my *friend*," he protests. "Yeah. It'd be too weird," she agrees. But Zazu is confident: "It's a tradition going back generations."

As Juliet Mitchell clarifies in *Psychoanalysis and Feminism*, "The myth that Freud rewrote as the Oedipus complex epitomizes man's entry into culture itself. . . . It is *not* about the nuclear family, but about the institution of culture." And culture—all human civilization, according to Freud—is patriarchal.[13] What Zazu is telling the cubs is that they will not be able to resist the imperatives of [their patriarchal] culture, the "tradition" that goes back *generations*.[14] Society will seek to enforce its cultural norms of gender relations and heterosexuality in the two cubs, regardless of the relative strengths of the masculine and feminine dispositions in the psyche of each. Thus, while the oedipal struggles of every individual are in reality fraught with contingency, contradiction, and a great variety of possible outcomes, the film conceives of Simba's story as "a path unwinding" and is structured as a melodrama (with claims to the grandeur of tragedy, but with a happy ending), which organizes everything into binary terms, the first and most comprehensive being the binarism of gender.

"Life's Not Fair"

These are the first words of the film after the prologue, spoken by Scar, Simba's scheming, green-eyed uncle. Scar explains: "Yes. You see, I shall never be king." His dictum refers of course to much more than the law of primogeniture in the lions' kingdom. First of all, it is ideology's way of offering an "explanation" for the overall subordination of women in society (and also, quite consciously in the film, of gays), and is meant to discourage analysis. It is pronounced as a truism, as incontestable as the Darwinian fact that cats eat mice, and lions eat antelope. *The Lion King* offers an explicit argument for masculinity and femininity as socially reproduced behaviors, but as MacInnes reminds us, "to the extent that we become aware that gender is something that is socially constructed and not naturally ordained, then we must also become aware that it is not determined by sex."[15] The film, however, would have us believe that, mysterious as it may be, gender *is*, in the final analysis, determined by sex—that (regardless of how Freud may have intended his aphorism to be understood): *Anatomy is Destiny*—and little girls, among others, should just accept that "life's not fair."

According to patriarchy's gender logic, the world is divided into masculine and feminine spheres. Thus, when Simba early one morning bounds energetically over to his sleeping parents and urges his father to wake up, Mufasa half-jokingly grumbles to Sarabi: "Before sunrise, he's *your* son." In the division of labor required by capitalism, the mother is relegated to the private sphere.[16] Not only does the mother in bourgeois, patriarchal-capitalist society feed, bathe, and toilet-train the child, she is expected to make the home a haven from the workplace. As in Bly's cosmology, where the "sacred King" is associated with the sun, and the "sacred Queen" with the moon, Sarabi here is identified with "home," the shadowy cave where the lions sleep at night.

Mufasa gets up and (Sarabi a few steps behind) leads Simba out toward the promontory of Pride Rock. As they reach the exit to the cave, Simba turns back toward his mother, in a moment of anxiety about separation from her, and excitedly weaves in and out of her front legs. Sarabi gives her son a gentle but firm push toward his father, who takes him to the edge of the rock. There follows a shot of Sarabi holding back at the entrance of the cave, a look of maternal pride and regret on her face, as father and son walk toward the spot that offers the best view of the sun rising over the Pride Lands. This image of the abject mother is followed by the most dramatically phallic shot in the entire film: Pride Rock shooting straight up (as seen from the plain below), its impossibly sheer face dominating the screen. At the top, barely visible, Mufasa and Simba sit side by side, looking out.

"When a son goes off with his father," writes Dorothy Dinnerstein in *The Mermaid and the Minotaur*, "his mother's regret is more bearable; the father cannot replace her in a son's feelings as he can in a daughter's."[17] Sarabi senses that her job is done, and that Simba is ready to start learning what he will need to know in order to command in the public (masculine) sphere. And this learning about masculinity is best learned from the father. "The mother supports the active project," Dinnerstein continues, "but she is also on hand to be melted into when it is abandoned. She may, indeed, even encourage the child's lapses from selfhood, for she as well as the child has mixed feelings about [his] increasing separateness from her."[18]

"Simba, look! Everything the light touches is our kingdom," Mufasa tells his son. Simba is thrilled ("Wow!"), and Mufasa explains that one day he will inherit the kingdom. "This will all be mine?" the cub asks incredulously. "Everything," the father confirms. Simba, in awe, tries to absorb what he has just been told: "Everything the light touches . . . What about that shadowy place?" Clearly, the mechanism by which Simba will learn what it means to be male in his culture—i.e., to be properly masculine—is *identification*. Mufasa is saying, "See what I see." And in patriarchal/oedipal terms, the father is telling the son that one day, when he takes his father's place, the son will inherit everything the father has, including the mother. (As we can predict, it will be Nala, who, in an appropriately incestuous twist, appears to be Simba's half-sister.) The "shadowy place" ("You must *never* go there," Mufasa warns) is the threat of symbolic castration posed by Mufasa, whose primary claim to Sarabi is indicated in the shot of the two of them sleeping together in the cave, apart from the other lions.

Later, after Simba and Nala have visited "that shadowy place," Mufasa becomes angry with Simba, and instructs Zazu: "Take Nala home. I have to teach my *son* a lesson." The "lesson" for Nala is that females do not participate in the public sphere as males do. She will, if the patriarchal strategy succeeds, always be kept slightly helpless and in need of male protection. And yet several times in the movie Nala succeeds in "pinning" Simba, which, among other things, suggests that she is a stronger or more skilled fighter than he is. When they succeed in giving Zazu the slip, so that they can visit the elephant graveyard, Simba takes credit for "ditching the dodo":

Simba: I am a genius!
Nala: Hey, genius, it was *my* idea!

Simba: Yeah, but *I* pulled it off!
Nala: With me.
Simba: Oh, yeah?

When they playfully tussle, Nala flips Simba onto his back. He tries to get up, but she holds him there. "Pinned ya!" she exults. "Hey, let me up!" he protests. She does. He tries to flip her, but she flips him again.

Obviously, at this stage in their young lives, the cubs are equals. They are in that period of parallel development between the sexes that Freud sees as masculine, or phallic, for both boys and girls. The engendering process that will result in his becoming a leader (father/protector/patriarch) and her taking the role of helpmeet (mother/homemaker/ornament) is just beginning. Nala's libido, or sense of self (ego), will shortly be made to succumb, in Freud's phrase, "to the momentous process of repression whose outcome, as has so often been shown, determines the fortunes of a woman's femininity."[19] The substance of Mufasa's "lesson" for Simba is that if he wants to be king (and he certainly does), he must understand how power works, and what the basis of his authority will be. He must learn not to "go looking for trouble," which might reveal the real limits of his power; and as a male, Simba must accept the responsibility of protecting the female ("And what's worse, you put Nala in danger!"), who will be persuaded that the price she pays for giving up her independence is worth the compensation of male protection.[20] This "masculine" responsibility is usually felt by males in patriarchal societies to be worth it. In Simba's words: "I just can't wait to be king!" He sings in Broadway showstopping style:

> No-one saying "Do this!"
> No-one saying "Be there!"
> No-one saying "Stop that!"
> No-one saying "See here!"
> Free to run around all day.
> Free to do it all my way!

Above all, it is the male's dependence on the mother in infancy (we see how Simba hates to be bathed by Sarabi) that he wants to forget, as he attempts to gain physical and psychological mastery of himself and the world around him. Adult masculinity holds out the promise of being able to "do it all my way." But successful adult masculinity can only be achieved if the male child absorbs the lesson of "castration" and later resolves his Oedipus complex (integrates into the symbolic). Simba's feeling of phallic, narcissistic omnipotence, expressed so exuberantly in his song, is bound to crash. It is a feeling, Freud remarks in "Creative Writers and Day-Dreaming," that is best expressed in the phrase: "Nothing can happen to *me!*" Freud adds: "It seems to me, however, that through this revealing characteristic of invulnerability we can immediately recognize His Majesty the Ego, the hero alike of every daydream and of every story."[21] Simba's daydream, or fantasy, will come abruptly to an end when he and Nala arrive at the elephant graveyard.

Simba is humbled by his experience there, and unconsciously resolves to keep a check on his desires. In psychoanalytic terms, what happens at the elephant graveyard gives rise to the formation of his superego.[22] He will subject himself to its internal authority, not only because he fears retribution in the form of the loss of his father's love (for desiring the mother; for his competitive, aggressive feelings toward the father), but because the powerful economy of the superego produces conscience and guilt, whereby action and desire can no longer be distinguished. The superego constitutes an agency whose function is to prohibit wishes from being fulfilled or becoming conscious, and is constructed on the model of the child's parents' superego. Freud writes: "The contents which fill it are the same and it becomes the vehicle of tradition and of all the time-resisting judgements of value which have propagated themselves in this manner from generation to generation."[23] (Zazu will be proven right—according to the "tradition going back generations," Simba will eventually obey the dictates of his superego and return to Pride Rock.)

THE ELEPHANT GRAVEYARD

There is an important intertext for *The Lion King* in a much earlier film, *Tarzan, the Ape Man* (1932), of a strikingly symbolic use of an elephant graveyard. When Jane Parker (Maureen O'Sullivan) arrives at a port in Africa to meet up with her old father (C. Aubrey Smith), who is about to depart on an expedition into the interior with a young man called Harry Holt (Neil Hamilton), her curiosity is piqued by references to "the Mutea Escarpment." She asks her father what it is, but at first he is unwilling to say. When she persists, he relents—

> *Father:* Somewhere to the east, there's a mysterious barrier of mountains called the Mutea Escarpment—and the natives won't say where that Mutea Escarpment is. It's sacred. Taboo. If one of them

is found even to have looked at it, he is put to death by the witch-men of the tribe. Now, Holt and I believe that beyond that Mutea Escarpment somewhere lies the burial place of the elephants.[24]

Jane: You do? But, why? Oh, of course, *ivory!*

Father: Enough ivory to supply the world! There's a million pounds for the man who finds it!

Jane: And how much do I get for helping you?

Father: Huh! You're not going to help! You can't. ·

Like Nala, Jane is not invited to join the men in their world of action and adventure, and like Nala when she pins Simba, Jane is revealed to be the equal of any man in the use of a rifle (she shoots "like an angel"), before she succumbs to "the momentous process of repression" that will have her screaming for male protection throughout much of the remainder of the movie.

Jane of course does go on the expedition with her father and the handsome young Harry (who believes he is falling in love with her). With single-minded determination, Jane's father pushes on through every danger, in his quest to reach the trove of ivory, as if, and paradoxically, to outrun death, which he feels is fast approaching. Jane is abducted by Tarzan (Johnny Weissmuller); and on the very morning after Tarzan lures her to his bower and makes love to her, Jane's weakened and haggard-looking father stumbles and falls to the ground.

Later, when the expedition party (including Jane) is captured by a hostile tribe of pygmies, Tarzan calls for his elephant friends to help them. The elephants succeed in routing the pygmies, and then, guided by Tarzan, they bear the expedition party away from the scene. Jane and Harry notice that the elephant carrying Tarzan and her sick father has been wounded. Still, the old man insists they go on: "[He's] our only chance! The elephants' graveyard . . . If he's dying, he'll take us there." Tarzan jumps down from the dying elephant, and Parker, slumped forward and clutching at his chest, leads the somber procession. Upon arriving at the graveyard, Jane's father collapses and dies, as does the elephant that has borne him to this "sacred" and "taboo" place. Parker's death has coincided with his half-conscious recognition of Tarzan's claim to Jane, and her acceptance of it.

The graveyard represents both death and life, in a dialectical relation.[25] It is the phallus ("enough ivory to supply the world"), which is to say, it stands here for the libido as phallic/masculine. Jane's father has clearly been a vigorous and glamorous embodiment of the phallic principle all his adult life; but as he approaches the end of his life (he describes himself as now "a bit more grizzled and moth-eaten"), and as Jane seeks to gain access to the phallic principle herself—i.e., resolve her Oedipus complex—she must, in the master metaphor of *The Lion King*, take her place in the circle of life, or wither and die ("Listen, Dad, from now on I'm through with civilization; I'm going to be a savage, just like you," she tells her father at the beginning of the film). As a woman in a patriarchal world, Jane's only means of access to the phallus is through a man. In choosing whom to desire, she must turn away from her father. "But the conscious object of desire is always a red herring," Victor Burgin reminds us. "The object is only the representative, in the real, of a psychical representative, in the unconscious."[26] Obeying society's taboo on incest, and rejecting Harry as a possible love object, she chooses Tarzan. But as Burgin observes, "The real object, present—most poignantly, the 'love-object'—is 'chosen' (does *choice* ever really come into it?—'*coup de foudre*') because something about it allows it to represent the lost object, which is *irretrievably* absent" (32).

FIGURE 2.2 "Listen, Dad, from now on I'm through with civilization—I'm going to be a savage, just like you," Jane (Maureen O'Sullivan) tells her father (C. Aubrey Smith) in *Tarzan, the Ape Man* (1932).

We see that Tarzan is closely associated throughout the movie with the elephants (with their almost-human intelligence and their "post-oedipal" acceptance of their mortality), and that Parker is associated with the elephant graveyard. The cultural taboo on incest—represented by the graveyard as incest's deadly consequence—forces Jane to take her exogamous journey beyond the Mutea Escarpment, to that same shadowy place *The Lion King* describes as "beyond our borders." There, in unfamiliar and dangerous territory, she will find something familiar—a *man*. That Tarzan is able in Jane's unconscious to psychically represent both her father *and* the irretrievably lost object—the maternal body—is suggested not only by the obvious ways in which he is *like* Parker (and Harry), but by the ways in which he is *different* from Parker and Harry: Tarzan's smooth, nearly naked body; his (as it were) pre-mirror phase/pre-oedipal muteness; his lack of conventional signifiers of "masculinity" (he wears no mustache, for example, as both Parker and Harry do); his association with water (he and Jane frolic and swim together in the river); his "primal" connections to the natural world around him—these

FIGURE 2.3 Tarzan (Johnny Weissmuller) is associated with the elephants, whose knowledge of their mortality paradoxically renders them phallic.

are all things that allow Tarzan to psychically represent the original "lost object," Jane's mother, whom we never see.[27] As Jonathan Rutherford explains in *Men's Silences*, Lacan describes the phallus as the register of desire. It is a symbol of plenitude and completeness: "[Lacan] recognizes that the infant's perception of this register originates in the mother but moves to the third term of the father and becomes consolidated in the symbolic as the signifier of gendered meaning."[28] Though Jane may identify the "father" as possessing the phallus, Lacan would remind us that (in Rutherford's phrasing): "The phallus is a symbolic and idealized substitute for the unity of mother and child which can never reoccur. It stands for the oneness or wholeness that is denied to human subjectivity in the castration complex" (147).

Some of the meanings of the elephant graveyard in *The Lion King* become very clear when we observe where it appears in the narrative. When Simba asks his father what the dark spot on the horizon is, a shadow falls symbolically across Mufasa's face as he replies—which in itself answers Simba's next question ("But I thought a king can do anything he wants!"). In other words, even kings are subject to the law of castration. Simba first learns of the elephant graveyard's existence during a conversation with his uncle Scar, who concedes that Simba "would have found out sooner or later." Scar, whose very name refers to symbolic castration, calls it "that *dreadful* place." As the second son, and more acutely since his nephew "the little hairball" was born, Scar is painfully reminded every day of the lesson Simba is about to learn—which Freud put this way: "[A] young man has to learn to suppress the excess of self-regard which he brings with him from the spoilt days of his childhood, so that he may find his place in a society which is full of other individuals making equally strong demands."[29]

When Simba and Nala tumble down into the graveyard, they are thrilled by the strangeness of what they see, and are quite unaware of the real danger they are in. "Danger? Hah!" Simba brags to Zazu and Nala, "I walk on the wild side! I laugh in the face of danger—ha, ha, ha!" As soon as the three sinister, wisecracking hyenas emerge from the giant elephant skull, the precise nature of the danger becomes frighteningly apparent. The hyenas, with their mocking, mad laughter and snapping teeth, intend to humiliate, torture, then eat the two cubs. *This* is the meaning of "castration"—and its hideous reality dawns on Simba (and Nala) for the first time in their young lives.

There is no doubt that the elephant graveyard in both films is an overdetermined site that admits a range of negotiated readings.[30] In Lacanian terms, it signifies above all the individual's confrontation with the Real—the fact of [his] mortality. The films choose an elephant graveyard to give textual reality

FIGURE 2.4 The final shots of *Tarzan, the Ape Man* are strikingly similar to those that conclude *The Lion King.*

to what is unsymbolizable: *Death.* As far as we know—the purported existence of "elephant graveyards" notwithstanding—human beings are the only animals that know they will die. In *The Lion King,* as in *Tarzan, the Ape Man,* the existence of the graveyard, which implies that elephants have knowledge of their mortality, is analogous to Simba's fearful discovery that not only will his father die (the very thought of which—because he has unconsciously wished it—is doubly traumatic), but that he will die also. Moreover, as Dinnerstein remarks, echoing Freud, "the adult's grief at mortality is preceded and preformed by the infant's grief at its lost sense of oneness with the first parent: The later knowledge that we will die resonates with the pain of our earliest discovery of helplessness, vulnerability, isolation; with the terrified sorrow of the first, and worst, separation."[31] The whole movie, in a sense, is a response to our terrible knowledge that the world existed before we entered it, and that it will carry on after we leave it. But there is some consolation in knowing that we are participating in a collective enterprise—that, in the conceit of the film, we are all part of "the circle of life" (which of course includes death). And for those of us who have children, we can feel that we never really die.[32] Not only do we leave a genetic legacy, we exist in the psyches of our children—are lodged in their superegos—or in Mufasa's formulation, become stars in the night sky.

"We're Pals, Right?"

From Simba's song, "I Can't Wait to be King," we can infer how the cub sees his father:

> I'm gonna be a mighty king, so enemies beware!
> I'm gonna be the mane event, like no king was before.
> I'm brushing up on looking down, I'm working on my roar!

Mufasa is obviously perceived by his son as impressive and intimidating, a glamorous figure "standing in the spotlight." The king/father is identified by the son as possessing the phallus—which the movie shows this father and son as each having the means to represent as an integral part of his body, in the form of the mane (the G-rated stand-in for the penis).[33] Simba reveals that he understands phallic masculinity to be a matter of *domination*, achieved through superior strength and will, and signified by his "roar." Indeed, nothing will ever again be as impressive to Simba as Mufasa's rescue of the two cubs from their mortally dangerous situation in the elephant graveyard. Cornered and desperate, Simba tries to scare off the hyenas by roaring at them, when suddenly—as if by magic—his puny roar is thunderously amplified by Mufasa, who seems to appear from nowhere, to reduce the hyenas to a state of blithering terror.

This spectacularly frightening display of masculine wrath is a form of power that is available to Simba as an inheritance, and he wisely chooses to align himself with it, to become like his father, rather than his mother. As in "Reaganite entertainment" generally (to borrow a phrase from a well-known essay by Andrew Britton), we see in *The Lion King* that "with unremitting insistence and stridency, it is the status and function of the father and their inheritance by the son that are at stake."[34] Moreover, as Britton notes about a significant number of American films since the early 1980s, "the exclusion of the mother is always the essence of the project" (24). Pollitt wryly observes that while Simba's father is "powerful, heroic, strong, brave, and sententious," his mother is "a gentle nobody." But "at least he's got a mother; in most Disney cartoons she's dead before the story opens."[35]

While there is no doubt that *The Lion King* seeks to make the father look impressive, the movie from the beginning also shows the radical instability of the paternal signifier. In his very first conversation with his son, for example, Mufasa warns Simba that he [Mufasa] will one day die. The sturdiness of the mother-infant bond, meanwhile, is emphasized, and on a connotative level it is even suggested that the earth itself is a maternal body (i.e., that Simba's origins are autochthonous), a body into which we all sink back when we die, to become the grass, which the antelope eat, etc. But there is only one father in the film. Although Simba may be in awe of his father—as few viewers can fail to be also when, in the scene described above, he saves the cubs from the hyenas—Disney in fact seems to have trouble with Mufasa's "performance." He is, paradoxically, one of the least convincing characters in the film, in part because of James Earl Jones's familiar and widely admired—but for all that, stilted and pompous—way of reading his lines; and because, it would seem, we have no idea in the United States at the end of the twentieth century how a king would "act." Mufasa strains to look regal (Simba thinks of a monarch's performance as one of "looking down"), and to the extent that his status as a king is meant for viewers to denote his status as a father, Mufasa's performance makes Dinnerstein's comment about our contemporary sexual arrangements entirely apt: "What we have worked out is a masquerade, in which generation after generation of childishly self-important men on the one hand, and childishly play-acting women on the other, solemnly re-create a child's-eye view of what adult life must be like."[36]

Nevertheless, Mufasa does stand for something significant in the child's psychic development. The two historically important ideals of fatherhood, the father as ruler and the father as educator, are combined in the film; and in his relation to Simba, Mufasa has basically two modes, or roles—he oscillates between the roles of stern patriarch and loving father—which will inevitably (which is to say, oedipally) result in the son having ambivalent feelings toward him. Simba has already been told by his father that he will inherit "everything the light touches," and he is impatient to incorporate awesome adult power. Mufasa explains to Simba that "there's more to being king than getting your way all the time," and proceeds to describe the "delicate balance" that requires lions to "respect all the creatures, from the crawling ant to the leaping antelope," and which permits them at the same time to "eat the antelope." He teaches Simba how to "pounce"; and Simba sees his father respond with dutiful alacrity to "news from 'the underground'" (reported by a mole) that there are hyenas in the Pride Lands that need to be driven out—a royal task that Zazu promises Simba he will inherit: "Oh, young master! One day *you* will be King. Then you can chase those slobbering, mangy, stupid poachers from dawn to dusk!"

As a figure of separation and agency, this father is one that no cub can resist. Quite properly, Simba loves him narcissistically, that is, as an interiorized ego ideal, as that which he would like to be. The "father-son love affair," as Benjamin calls it, is the model for later, ideal love. The scene following the cubs' rescue from the elephant graveyard is remarkable for the way it handles the impossible tension so many sons in the contemporary oedipal scenario must negotiate between their perception of the father as a playful and exciting figure of liberation and as a forbidding and frightening figure of discipline. It would appear that in the late 1990s we no longer insist, as Bruno Bettelheim did in 1956, that the relationship between father and child be built principally "around a man's function in society: moral, economic, political."[37] Fathers now are expected to be more nurturing. Mufasa is meant to be a "kinder, gentler" father, but one who still "[carries] a big stick."[38]

At first, and only for an instant, Mufasa is angry with Simba ("You *deliberately* disobeyed me!"), and as Simba approaches his father for his "lesson," he thinks he will be punished. Instead, as we have noted, he gets a very reasonable, and mercifully brief, lecture about not "looking for trouble" and about taking responsibility for Nala's safety. When he steps into one of Mufasa's giant paw-prints in the damp soil, the cub is nearly overwhelmed by the enormity of it in relation to his own tiny paw. But when Simba says he was just "trying to be brave" like his father, whom he believes is "not scared of anything," Mufasa immediately softens, and says: "I was today . . . I thought I might lose you." This slightly disingenuous response—in which something is implied and glossed over at the same time—allows Simba to misunderstand the full meaning of castration (i.e., that even a father knows mortal fear, for *himself,* as opposed to fear for another), which he will have to learn if he is to master his Oedipus complex and not fall victim to neurosis. To paraphrase Lacan, Mufasa tries to teach Simba the secret of the power of the phallus, while keeping the phallus veiled. Mufasa's reply becomes a lesson in paternal love, which has the effect of restoring Simba's self-esteem. Thus, somewhat incongruously, Simba perks up his ears and smiles: "I guess even kings get scared, huh?" The real lesson of castration is postponed (until Mufasa's death), for Simba immediately becomes complicit. Leaning toward his father's ear, he whispers: "But you know what? I think those hyenas were even scareder!" Mufasa responds by reaching for his son in a roughhousing embrace and chuckling with mock-ferocity: "Because *nobody messes with your Dad!*" The two playfully chase each other and tumble about in the grass, until Simba, perched on his father's massive head, says: "Dad, we're pals, right?"

The kind of assurance Simba seeks from his father is structurally impossible, according to the logic of Oedipus. Bly remarks that "it is interesting that we find very few examples of close or chummy father-son relationships in mythological literature," and he concludes that it is very possible that "we will never have the closeness we want from our fathers."[39] He says this to the "many young men who want from the father a repetition of the mother's affection, or a female nurturing they haven't gotten enough of. Whatever the father gives us, it will not be the same kind of closeness that our mother offered" (121). Bly, of course, is working firmly within oedipal epistemology, unlike Dinnerstein, Benjamin, and others who acknowledge that the meaning of sexual difference is, precisely, a process of production, "something mutable, something historical, and therefore something we can do *something* about."[40]

Simba is at the point where, as Dinnerstein puts it, "Ideally, the little boy manages to find some provisional balance between the old, jealous, aggrieved erotic tug toward the mother and the new feeling of friendship with the father."[41] His task is to find a balance between two contrasting varieties of love, "one that provides primitive emotional sustenance, and another that promises—if rivalry over the first can be handled—to offer membership in the wider community where prowess is displayed, enterprise planned, public event organized" (48). Benjamin insists that the wish to be like the father is not merely "a defensive attempt to defeat the mother," and, as has been noted, suggests we call it *identificatory love.*[42] Simba in this scene is poised on the threshold, or caught, between his identification with the idealized father as mirror of desire and his apprehension of the oedipal authority figure who institutes the superego that demands prohibition, conscience, and self-control.[43] When Simba asks his father, "And we'll always be together, right?" Mufasa switches gears and says: "Simba, let me tell you something my father told me: Look at the stars. The great kings of the past look down on us from those stars. . . . So, whenever you feel alone, just remember that those kings will always be there to guide you. And so will I." Years later, when he is living with Pumbaa and Timon, Simba will remember these words and understand, finally, that a father is, and will always be, much more than a pal.

"Hakuna Matata"

A father's death, wrote Freud, is "the most important event, the most poignant loss of a man's life"[44]—and for Simba, it is in addition spectacularly traumatic. Mufasa is trampled to death in the great, dry canyon that slices through the lush Pride Lands like a wound in the landscape. There is even a sense, conveyed by the overdetermined mise-en-scène, that the cub experiences the two fundamental terrors construed by psychoanalysis—merging (the drowning wave of stampeding wildebeests) and absolute loss (Simba utterly alone in a flat, baking-hot desert). And to make matters worse, Scar will exploit Simba's inevitable feelings of self-reproach.

The solution to Simba's suffering, according to Pumbaa and Timon, the warthog and meerkat who find him, is to "put your past behind you." They call it "Hakuna Matata. It means: 'No Worries.'" They tell him, "It's our problem-free philosophy" and insist that it "ain't no passing craze!"

This next period of Simba's life, which he spends with the "outcast" couple, corresponds in psychoanalysis to the "latency period," which Freud described as having its origin in the dissolution of the Oedipus complex. It is a period that "represents an intensification of repression which brings about an amnesia affecting the earliest years, a transformation of object-cathexes into identifications with parents, and a development of sublimations."[45] As in the psychological situation presented at the beginning of *Hamlet*, where the son's protective identification with his father has been jeopardized by the father's death, we may also see Simba's flight from the Pride Lands after Mufasa's death as a strategy to save himself from the potentially engulfing mother at a decisively vulnerable moment in his development toward selfhood.

Pumbaa and Timon are represented as a gay couple, which is why the film, with its heterosexist assumptions, can in effect explain their "lifestyle" as a case of permanently arrested development. Thus, while the couple can offer Simba their philosophy of "Hakuna Matata," the viewer—who assumes a heterosexual destiny for the cub—will see his time with them as a period of recovery, a respite from the turbulence of his recent past. In keeping with the vocabulary of psychoanalysis, the time it takes Simba to grow into a young adult (which, in a montage sequence, takes as long as the "Hakuna Matata" song) is not a *stage*, but a *period*—the significance of this distinction being that, as Laplanche and Pontalis point out, "during the period in question, although manifestations of a sexual nature are to be observed, there is strictly speaking no new *organization* of sexuality" (235). For Simba, then (but not Pumbaa and Timon), it will be, precisely, a "passing craze."[46]

With characteristic camp humor, Pumbaa and Timon introduce Simba to their "humble home"—a green and pleasant Eden of sparkling waterfalls and exotic, leafy trees, reminiscent of certain Maxfield Parrish idylls, and of Frederick Church's jungle landscapes that were made to entertain.[47] Their "bachelor pad," as the screenplay calls this jungle paradise, is purged of all of Nature's threatening elements. Food is plentiful, and the only hunting they do is done in play, like Pumbaa's comically exaggerated and inept stalking of a bright blue dung beetle. Unlike the Pride Lands, where violence is the hidden engine of the "circle of life," Pumbaa and Timon's world is designed for fun and leisure—where they swing on vines, swim, sing, and eat. "You're gonna love it here," Pumbaa assures Simba. "This is the great life," Timon explains: "No rules, no responsibilities . . ."

As a gay couple (the "unnaturalness" of which is signaled in a number of ways, such as their being of two different animal species), Pumbaa and Timon are not tied to "home" as a place where children are raised, or as an estate that is passed on to the next generation. "We live wherever we want," Timon tells Simba. "Yup! Home is where your rump rests," echoes the plump pig. They are a happy couple, who appear not to miss "home" in the sense that Simba will. For them, home is a playground decorated in jungle-froufrou—a place, some would say, that represents a radical *denial* of castration (all snakes have been removed).[48]

In a scene that offers a lesson about the relative mutability of desire, Pumbaa and Timon introduce a skeptical Simba to their diet of insects. When Simba announces that he is so hungry he "could eat a whole zebra," Timon explains: "Listen, kid: If you live with us, you have to eat like us." The implication—which is consistent with the notion that Simba is entering a latency period with regard to his sexual appetites—is that as a "motto" to live by, "Hakuna Matata" can only deliver on its promise of happiness if Simba will sublimate his desire.[49] For a life of "No Worries," he will have to give up his carnivorous habit. Adam Phillips notes in his essay, "Worrying and Its Discontents," that the semantic history of *worrying* includes among its meanings a "devouring, a particularly intense, ravenous form of eating,"[50] and in *worry* Phillips finds elements of pursuit and persecution: "two things that in psychoanalysis tend to be associated with desire" (51). Pumbaa and Timon make eating look like a *pleasure* ("These are rare delicacies," Timon remarks as he bites into a small, brown beetle, then murmurs appreciatively: "Piquant, with a very pleasant crunch"), rather than as an act that has something to do with *desire* (a hunger that demands to be satisfied). Pumbaa's gesture of slurping down a worm can even be seen as an allusion to fellatio—especially when Simba tries it with an enormously fat grub and agrees that it is "slimy, yet satisfying." When Timon presents Simba with a colorful tray of wriggling and fluttering snacks, there is an element of promiscuous fun implied by the sheer variety and number of insects available; and for the time being, Simba is persuaded that "this is the great life."

Unlike Pumbaa and Timon, however, Simba has a *destiny*. The warthog and meerkat are a mere sideshow to "the mane event," and there is a hint of reproof in the film's attitude toward their "philosophy" of "No Worries." When Timon tells Simba: "When the world turns its back on you, you turn your back on the world," Simba replies: "Well, that's not what I was taught." The gay couple are not taken seriously, except as an example of the use-value of humor and wit in hard times. "Worrying implies a future, a way of looking forward to things," Phillips observes. "It is a conscious conviction that a future exists, one in which something terrible might happen, which is of course ultimately true. So worrying is an ironic form of hope" (56). According to the movie, Pumbaa and Timon—and by implication, all gay people—have no future. The film, quite literally, locates them outside the "circle of life" (until, that is, the couple decide to join Simba in his decision to return to Pride Rock, whereupon they become his courtiers), for it can only understand the future in oedipal-familial terms of reproduction, the limiting, constricting features of which Mark Poster describes this way:

Oedipus reduces and shrinks the individual to the family. The internalization of the father as super-ego prevents the individual from participating in collective myth. Oedipus privatizes myth, emotion, fantasy and the unconscious, centering the psyche forever on Mama/Papa. . . . Far from a general law, Oedipus is the special law of the modern psyche. It is bound up with the nuclear family, not with kinship, and it goes far in revealing the psychic dynamics of modern families. The neuroses analyzed by Freud are private myths, individual religions; they are the fetishism, the magic of the nuclear family, the myth of people without collective fetishes to relieve guilt. As long as Freud maintains the universality of Oedipus there can be no real history of the family since this requires above all an account of the change from kinship to private families.[51]

Pumbaa and Timon are self-described "outcasts" whose relationship has no status in the comprehensively familial order of the Pride Lands. In the style of a Negro spiritual, they sing the story of how, "when he was a young warthog," Pumbaa discovered he was different from all the other animals. Timon gets to the point: "He found his aroma lacked a certain appeal; he could clear the savanna after every meal." And in his rejoinder, Pumbaa painfully recalls: "I'm a sensitive soul—though I seem thick-skinned—and it hurt that my friends never stood downwind. And, *oh!* The *shame . . .* !" Then, just as Pumbaa is about to describe how, "Every time that I . . . ," Timon claps a hand over his mouth and says: "Pumbaa! Not in front of the kids!"

Pumbaa's problem, of course, is that he suffers from chronic flatulence—but the universal issue here that every small viewer of the film recognizes is that of identity, and the problem of "fitting in." Identity (the making of a "self"), we know, is first a question of borders and boundaries—the line between inside and outside, the difference between "self" and "other"—and Pumbaa, as a recognizably gay character, does not "fit in." His transgression is figured as a problem concerning a corporeal boundary. With the forging of (sexual) identity conceived as a Freudian narrative that progresses through a series of stages toward the ultimate goal of a stable heterosexual genitality, Pumbaa's development is understood to be arrested in the anal stage. The filmmakers give him the problem of experiencing difficulty controlling his anal sphincter, that *écluse*, the successful sublimation of which (as an erotic zone) is the first step toward proper socialization. The message to viewers is that as Simba takes the "path unwinding" to adulthood and his proper place in the "circle of life," he will meet all kinds of people (i.e., potential role models), and he may learn something from each of them—but if he "chooses" the homosexual life ("Hakuna Matata"), he must expect to live forever as an outcast, beyond society's borders.

There is no doubt that Pumbaa's "shame" refers to homosexuality as sodomy, with its associations of uncleanness which consequently inspire homophobia. In *Homosexual Desire*, Guy Hocquenghem observes that "there is a certain 'kind of affection'—or rather a desiring relation as opposed to its sublimated form, friendship—which anal cleanliness does not permit, 'anal cleanliness' being the formation in the child of the small responsible person; and there is a relation between 'private cleanliness' and 'private ownership' [*propreté privée* and *propriété privée*] which is not merely an association of words but something inevitable."[52] Echoing Freud, Hocquenghem notes that "the ability to 'hold back' or to evacuate the faeces is the necessary moment of the constitution of the self" (99), and in a spin on Deleuze and Guattari, he explains why "control of the anus is the precondition of taking responsibility for property" (99) (Pumbaa and Timon, we have observed, are not property-owners—they sleep wherever they want). As an organ with no social desiring function, the anus in capitalist society expresses privatization (that is to say, sublimation) itself: "Money, which must be privately owned in order to circulate, is indeed connected with the anus, in so far as the anus is the most private part of the individual" (97). *The Lion King* celebrates the private ownership of property and capitalism (the Pride Lands as Mufasa's estate; the "circle of life" as the circulation of goods and money), and all the jokes in the film, both verbal and visual, about Pumbaa's "backside" (as Scar calls it), are meant unconsciously to steer Simba, and the viewer who identifies with him, toward the norm of bourgeois/feudal, capitalist heterosexuality.

"Can You Feel the Love Tonight?"

When Nala is formally introduced to the warthog and meerkat, she is polite, but no more than that (for she cannot figure out why Simba would be friends with them); and by way of apologetic explanation, Simba says to her: "Timon and Pumbaa: You learn to love 'em." His remark is quite startlingly homophobic, but it is consistent with Freud's insight that the latency period does not represent, or result in, a new organization of sexuality. Simba identifies with Timon and Pumbaa, but they do not, psychoanalytically speaking, represent object-cathexes. With the reappearance of Nala, however, Simba falls in love. Appropriately, it is when she pins him during the fight in which he saves Pumbaa, that he realizes she is his childhood "friend" (which is how he introduces her to the confused couple), and we recall Zazu's prediction that one day they will marry. This old memory of being pinned by her as a child unconsciously recalls the ancient memory of being on his back, in this same position, in his mother's arms.[53] When later she allows herself to be pinned by Simba, and with a gimlet eye that signals her conscious attempt to seduce him, Nala licks his cheek—in lion lingo, a kiss—he is surprised to realize that her feelings for him have undergone a transformation since they were children. Again, the kiss recalls those first kisses he received from his mother as an infant. It is not surprising, in view of the film's patriarchal project, that an attempt is made to represent Simba as fundamentally innocent. As in the Book of Genesis, where it is Eve who persuades Adam to eat of the forbidden fruit of knowledge, Nala is the one who focuses Simba's libido and leads in the process of finding an object (shows Simba whom to desire). She seems to know, as Freud put it, that "the finding of an object is in fact a refinding of it."[54]

Timon understands immediately that they are falling in love, and explains "the bottom line" to Pumbaa: "Our trio's down to two." It's a "disaster," he sings. Their pal is "doomed," they agree. The narrator, however, sings that "the world, for once, [is] in perfect harmony with all its living things."[55] (I find this moment in the film especially offensive, for its blatant assertion of the traditional heterosexual relation as the one *true* and *natural* emblem of [a] comprehensive, global harmony—just as it is offensive when the first in-tertitle of Griffith's *The Birth of a Nation* suggests that the American South was an Eden, before "The bringing of the African to America planted the first seed of disunion.") In Poster's phrase, Oedipus centers the psyche forever on Mama/Papa—and Nala, we understand, will finally "have" the "father" she loved as a child, if only Simba will "be the king I know he is, the king I see inside." She leads him down beside a cataract (the downward movement suggesting Simba's "fall" from sexual innocence; just as their tumble down a hillside a few minutes later, and their landing in an embrace on the soft, grassy plain below recalls the oedipally encoded moment in their childhood when they tumbled down together into the elephant graveyard) to a pool, where their reflections in the water create a metaphorical corollary to their attempts to get to know each other.

FIGURE 2.5 Timon (voiced by Nathan Lane) tries to make his buddy Pumbaa (voiced by Ernie Sabella) understand "the bottom line": their happy trio with Simba is now down to two. (Copyright © The Walt Disney Company. All rights reserved)

According to patriarchy's rule of dividing the world into public and private spheres, with the public sphere dominated by men and the prerogatives of masculinity, and the private sphere by women and functions construed as feminine, Nala—like Simba's mother before her—has come to represent the sphere of affect and emotion ("Can You Feel the Love Tonight?"), and she urges Simba to take up his (masculine) "responsibility" to challenge his uncle to take his place as *king*.

When Simba does finally return to his now gray and desolate birthplace, it is, in a sense, to "save" his mother, who has had to endure the humiliation of living as Mufasa's widow under Scar's illegitimate rule. We may see Simba's stake in returning to Pride Rock as similar to that of Hamlet when he seeks to avenge his father's death, as argued by Janet Adelman: "Despite his ostensible agenda of revenge, the main psychological task that Hamlet seems to set himself is not to avenge his father's death but to remake his mother: to remake her in the image of the Virgin Mother who could guarantee his father's purity and his own, repairing the boundaries of his selfhood."[56]

When Scar violently knocks Sarabi unconscious, for making an invidious comparison between him and her late husband, Simba leaps forward from the shadows where he has been hiding and rushes to her side. He nuzzles his mother's cheek, and as she returns to consciousness, she mistakes him for Mufasa. Simba's reply is anxious, tender, apologetic: "No, it's me." It is a telling moment, which reveals the oedipal truth of Adelman's insight into the origins and objects of love, and the way the self is formed within desire's familial imperatives.

SCAR

Simba's unconscious jealousy of Mufasa is displaced by the narrative onto Scar's character, as in *Hamlet*, where the son's oedipal rivalry with his father is displaced into a conflict with his usurping uncle:

Literalized in the plot, the splitting of the father thus evokes the ordinary psychological crisis in which the son discovers the sexuality of his parents, but with the blame handily shifted from father onto another man as unlike father as possible—and yet as like, hence his brother; in effect, the plot itself serves as a cover-up, legitimizing disgust at paternal sexuality without implicating the idealized father.[57]

And although *The Lion King* is the kind of movie that would be content to present Scar simply as an "evil" character, it in fact offers a psychologically plausible and convincing explanation for Scar's jealousy and discontent.

When Scar reveals in the opening shots of the film that he is envious of his older brother, this both is and is not the whole story.[58] While it is a truism that, as David Gutmann observes, within families "siblings are routinely, even necessarily envious, begrudging the rations of love and attention that the parents mete out to their 'rivals,'"[59] Scar's envy is a signal of thwarted identification and, like the envy that has been attributed to women, is the longing for a homoerotic bond as boys may achieve with their fathers.[60] We understand early on that Scar's ideological function in the film is to represent everything that Simba—and the viewer who would identify with him—should reject. Catherine R. Stimpson has observed that "to be 'masculine' is to have a particular psychological identity, social role, cultural script, place in the labor force, and sense of the sacred";[61] and it is clear that, according to Stimpson's identification of the criteria by which "real men" are defined in secular, modern industrial societies, Scar emerges as a figure of thoroughly compromised masculinity: "First, they earn money in the public labor force and support their families through that effort. Next, they have formal power over women and the children in those families. . . . Finally, they are heterosexual" (xii). We see that Scar is an unemployed bachelor; he is disrespectful toward his king; he is sarcastic, ironic, and witty; he is sexually ambiguous; he refuses to accept his "place" in the kingdom's social hierarchy and harbors seditious ambitions—all in all, a dangerously untrustworthy member of the family and society.

On the afternoon of his planned murder of Mufasa and Simba, Scar takes his nephew down to the dry riverbed in which Mufasa is to be trampled to death by the herd of wildebeests. He tells Simba: "Now, you wait here. Your father has a marvelous surprise for you. . . . This is just for you and your Daddy—you know, a sort of father-son . . . thing." Scar instructs Simba not to move from the rock on which he is seated ("You wouldn't want to end up in another mess, like you did with the hyenas? . . . Lucky Daddy was there to save you, eh?"). Jeremy Irons's insinuating delivery of these lines, and the complex, shifting looks on Scar's face, reveal that in adulthood Scar is envious and bitter because he did not establish the kind of identificatory bond with his father that he believes Mufasa did, and that Simba enjoys with his father. Scar's envy is deeply rooted in familial feeling and provides the film's strongest argument for fathers to love (*all*) their sons and to *show* their love. The (human) personality quite literally is formed by parental love or its ab-

FIGURE 2.6 Scar (voiced by Jeremy Irons) lays the trap which he hopes will remove his nephew Simba (voiced by Jonathan Taylor Thomas) from his place in line of succession to the throne.

sence, and Scar, we realize, felt unloved as a cub—for if he had known paternal love, he would not (could not) do what he is doing now.

Like many films before it, especially westerns—and, most famously, John Ford's *The Man Who Shot Liberty Valance*—*The Lion King* acknowledges that in (human) society physical prowess and violence will invariably find themselves pitted against intelligence and reason, and it stages the struggle between these opposing forces in a typically contradictory fashion. When Zazu wants to know why Scar will not challenge Mufasa to a fight (the only means of resolving their differences that Mufasa can propose), Scar says: "Well, as far as brains go, *I* got the lion's share; but when it comes to *brute strength*, I'm afraid I'm at the shallow end of the gene pool." Much later, when Simba returns to Pride Rock as an adult, to challenge Scar's right to rule as king, Scar sighs melodramatically: "Oh, *must* this all end in violence?" (The answer, apparently, is *yes*.)[62]

Mufasa is clearly perplexed. "What am I going to do with him?" he asks Zazu rhetorically. Zazu's remark is coded to make the viewer think Scar might be homosexual: "[*Sigh*] There's one in every family, sire—*two* in mine, actually—and they always manage to ruin special occasions."[63] The point is that special occasions, like the one Scar has just avoided (the presentation of Simba to all the creatures of the Pride Lands), are always *family* occasions. And as a confirmed bachelor, Scar has no obvious role to play in the hetero-familial order.[64] Zazu's observation nevertheless acknowledges that the Scars of the world are the exception that proves the rule: they are a contradiction in the system. There is nothing that can be done about such individuals who always ruin the picture of "perfect harmony"—except, as Zazu jokes about Scar, to eliminate them: "He'd make a very handsome throw-rug. And just think—whenever he gets dirty, you can take him out and *beat* him!"

"Hey, Uncle Scar!" Simba asks. "When I'm king, what'll that make you?" To which Scar replies: "A monkey's uncle." The cub laughs uncomprehendingly: "You're so weird!" he says. Scar looks him straight in the eye and deadpans: "*You have no idea!*"[65] Scar's subversive wit is meant to signal his dishonesty (as in: his relationship to language is not simple, direct, *honest*), and his campy theatricality is meant to suggest that he is not *the real thing* (we note that Mufasa never performs a musical number; nor does the adult Simba). Pumbaa and Timon—the "happy" homosexuals, to Scar's unhappy homosexual—live their lives as musical theater, the most emblematic moment of which, for this theme of authenticity and the idea of the existence of a "true" masculinity, being Timon's Hawaiian hula dance in drag to distract the hyenas. Timon pretends to be something he is not, and he and Pumbaa offer the hyenas something they have no intention of delivering. Marjorie Garber writes that as a theoretical intervention, the transvestite is the equivalent of Lacan's third term, "not 'having,' or 'being,' the phallus, but 'seeming,' or 'appearing.'"[66] In Lacan's words: "the intervention of a 'to seem' that replaces the 'to have,' in order to protect it on the one side, and mask its lack in the other."[67] On the one hand, Timon in drag is a confirmation of his maleness; and on the other, it allows Simba (who is not wearing a skirt) to appear to "be" or to "have" the phallus (the idea of "lack," for the moment, having been projected onto Timon). Similarly, Scar's performance of the languid and witty uncle—with his upper-class English accent; his speaking in riddles—can only make him seem "weird," compared to Mufasa, who is relatively transparent (his American accent is meant to make him "one of us"; he may resort to the occasional metaphor, as befits a king, but generally speaks in simple, declarative sentences).

The film's most interesting articulation of Scar's difference from the other lions is played out in his alliance with the hyenas. After Mufasa's death, Scar informs the grieving pride that "it is with a heavy heart that I assume the throne. Yet out of the ashes of this tragedy, we shall rise to greet the dawning of a new era, in which lion and hyena come together in a great and glorious future!" For the viewer who has been persuaded that hyenas are "stinky," "hairy," and "ugly" (the very words the hyenas use to describe the lions), Scar's vision is almost unthinkable.[68] But as the hyena Banzai says, "Now *you*, Scar—you're one of *us*." Scar does not exactly deny it, for he knows what the hyenas mean. He does not fully embody the phallic principle ("Ooh, I like that!" the hyena Shenzi teases him. "He's not king, but he's still so proper"), just as Simba doesn't when he is living with Pumbaa and Timon as an adolescent outcast. When Nala finds Simba, she insists that he is the legitimate heir to the throne; and Timon turns to his feline friend: "Let me get this straight. You're the king . . . and you never told us?" Simba tries to explain: "Look, Timon, I'm still the same guy," to which—grasping immediately the significance of this new information—Timon says: "*But with power!*"

The hyenas are obviously fascinated and disgusted by the lions. They like to believe, as Shenzi says, that "if it weren't for those lions, we'd be running the joint." Shenzi tells Scar that she gets a thrill every time she even hears Mufasa's name, because Mufasa is "somebody *important*." Banzai agrees: "Now *that's* power!" As perpetually hungry scavengers, the hyenas are "dangling at the bottom of the food chain," and so Scar is able to persuade them that they will get a better deal with him as king. He promises: "Stick with me, and you'll never go hungry again." His proposal is pitched in a spectacular musical number, in which he sings: "[But] the point that I must emphasize is, *you won't get a sniff, without me!*"

Scar's song is accompanied by a kaleidoscopically shifting series of images that include: volcanic eruptions of sulfurous, green gases; battalions of jack-booted, goose-stepping storm-trooper hyenas; tremendous, rock-cracking earthquakes; and the motif of skeletal remains, as we saw them in the earlier, elephant-graveyard scene.[69] The visual allusions of his song are primarily to Leni Riefenstahl's *Triumph of the Will* (1935), which documents the Sixth Nazi Party Congress in 1934, at Nuremberg, and to *Pink Floyd: The Wall* (Alan Parker, 1982), which is about a rock star's descent into madness.[70] There would seem to be little doubt, as Mitchell observes in her review of Wilhelm Reich's *The Mass Psychology of Fascism*, that "Nazism appeals to and diverts sexuality: the erotic goose-stepping and the exhibitionism of parades show that militarism is based on libidinous mechanisms"[71] (although this scene serves to deflect attention away from the revelation that the real fascist of the film is Mufasa).[72] The song ends on an image of Scar perched high on a pillar of rock, in the style of a fascist dictator or godhead surrounded by his blindly obedient followers, as a crescent moon rises in the night sky behind him—evoking one of Islamic culture's best-known symbols and alluding, no doubt, to various Muslim countries in which there have been spectacular incidents of social unrest, violent displays of religious extremism, or acts of terrorism and war sponsored by leaders radically opposed to the interests of the (Judeo-Christian) West.

When Scar assumes the throne after Mufasa's death, the Pride Lands decline dramatically—and with Mufasa's explanation of the kingdom's economy still in mind ("When we die, our bodies become the grass, and the antelope eat the grass. And so we are all connected in the great Circle of Life")—the viewer understands that what Scar has done is wrong, on every level. He has broken the most sacred natural orders: not only has he killed the "father," he has taken the father's place beside the mother and, in the oedipal sense, has defiled the marriage bed (the Pride Lands, which become sterile and ashen). When Sarabi tells him that by refusing to leave Pride Rock he is "sentencing us to death," he screams: "*I am the king, and I can do whatever I want!*"

At the beginning of *Oedipus the King*, we learn that Thebes is suffering from a terrible plague because, according to the oracle at Delphi, a defiler, the murderer of their former king, Laius, is being harbored within the city and must be removed before Thebes can return to health. This is the same situation that overtakes the Pride Lands, and by making an explicit connection between Scar's action and the famine that follows, the film invites a psychoanalytic reading that makes the oedipal nature of Scar's transgression very clear, in much the same way that Anthony Burgess makes the link between the riddle of the Sphinx and incest:

> If Oedipus had read his Lévi-Strauss, he would have known [after solving the riddle of the Sphinx] that incest was on its way. The man who solves the insoluble puzzle has, symbolically, disrupted nature. Since incest is the ultimate perversion of nature, nature is shocked to death. To the "primitive" mind, the puzzle and the sexual taboo have an essential factor in common—the knot that it is dangerous to untie since, untying it, you are magically untying the knot that holds the natural order together.[73]

Whereas Simba sublimates and defers his desire, Scar acts on his. Scar represents nothing less than desire itself, in that desire turns on a perpetual metonymy (the memory trace of a previous gratification which can never be attained), described by Jean Laplanche and Serge Leclaire as that which "designates, covers, or masks the gaping abyss of the subject . . . this metonymy like a scar, by its inexhaustible power of displacement, is made precisely to mark and mask the gap through which desire originates and into which it perpetually plunges on the bedrock of the death drive."[74] Scar wants to be king—his "teeth and ambitions are bared." But what he wants goes back further—to childhood, or infancy, to a dream of omnipotence, a dream that offers proof that one is loved, that one is, in the words of his song, "[love's] main addressee." Scar believes he will find, at last, what he thinks he has always wanted: "I'll be king undisputed, respected, saluted, and seen for the wonder I am."

"Remember Who You Are!"

"Who are you?" Nala asks Simba, when she discovers him in the jungle. This is the question that the film seeks to answer for its young viewers. In effect, the movie is that "conversation" children have with their parents (or more broadly, with culture), in which they find out where they came from and who they are. "From the day we arrive on the planet," to that day "the sun will set on [my] time here," the quest for identity persists, and—though the film will not go so far as to admit it—this quest can never be completely realized or attained. But there is, in Stimpson's phrase, a "cultural script" to follow (or resist, as the case may be). The short answer to Nala's question, then, is this: Simba is his father's son. From the moment of his baptism—when he is named, and he enters History—Simba will be, as Rafiki later calls him, "Mufasa's boy," inscribed in a universal story "going back generations."

There is an allusion to the specifically oedipal character of this story in Rafiki's first appearance, on the day of Simba's birth.[75] When all the animals of the kingdom have gathered at the foot of Pride Rock, we see in a low-angle shot a phallic-looking stick, to which two gourds are attached, making its way through a group of kudu and buffalo. In the following shot, we see that the stick is being carried by a mandrill solemnly approaching his king on three feet (two feet and one hand, and carrying the stick in his other hand), and we are reminded of the famous riddle put to Oedipus by the Sphinx at Thebes.[76] That Rafiki should be the only animal in the kingdom that (or who) actually resembles a human being, has its own logic. Just as the Sphinx of legend is a composite creature—part man, part woman, part animal (usually a lion, and often with wings and a conspicuous tail)[77]— Rafiki not only belongs to a physically intermediate species, who in a sense mediates between the human viewer and the animal world on the screen, but is a figure who mediates between the earthly world of the Pride Lands and a spiritual/mystical world represented by shafts of light that beam from the heavens at opportune moments, and by his knowledge of when "it is time," and so on.

The Lion King's representation of identity formation is ruthlessly deterministic. The viewer is forced to agree that Simba should return to Pride Rock because, as Nala insists, it is his "responsibility." She informs him that Scar has let the hyenas take over the Pride Lands, and that everything is destroyed. She quickly resorts to emotional blackmail: "We've really needed you at home. . . . You're the king. . . . Simba, if you don't do something soon, everyone will starve! . . . *You're our only hope!*"

To make Simba look selfish and irresponsible for thinking he might always live the "Hakuna Matata" life, the film shows him on his back, swinging in a hammock of vines, as he tries to explain to Nala why he did not return to Pride Rock after his father's death: "I just needed to get out on my own, live my own life. And I did! And it's great!" Although we know the real reason Simba fled from home, we nevertheless feel the force of the film's ideological message: proper, adult masculinity requires the male of the species to support a family. In Nala's exhortations, everything Simba ever learned from his father comes back to him. The film says: We have no choice. Our identities are fixed. Whether I am a Pumbaa or a Timon, a Mufasa or a Scar, a Nala or a Simba, it is only a question of knowing, and remembering who I am.

In its guise as a movie about an animal kingdom, set in no particular time period, the ideological message of *The Lion King* manages to be a clear throwback to the United States in the 1950s when, as Barbara Ehrenreich summarizes it, "there was a firm expectation (or as we would now say, 'role') that required men to grow up, marry, and support their wives. To do anything else was less than grown-up, and the man who willfully deviated was judged to be somehow 'less than a man.'"[78] The film tells us that we can be all that we can be (as a recruitment slogan for the U.S. Army promises), so long as we conform strictly to at least four laws of the cultural script (disguised as laws of nature)—the laws of race (species), gender, class, and place.

By living with Pumbaa and Timon, Simba learns that he is a lion, and not a (gay) warthog or meerkat—he may learn to eat insects instead of antelope, for example, but will eventually start craving meat again; he can adopt a "problem-free philosophy" for a while, but knows it is "not what [he] was taught." And when he meets Nala in adulthood, Simba learns that he is heterosexual. He also finds that it is impossible to avoid his class destiny—like an English prince, who is sent abroad for a high-school term in Canada or Australia, to learn how to rough and tumble with "ordinary" (i.e., ostensibly middle-class) boys in a "natural" (i.e., rural) landscape, before returning to the palace to take up his royal duties. Finally, like Dorothy in *The Wizard of Oz* (1939), or the brutally coerced young woman in *Holy Smoke* (Jane Campion, 1999),[79] Simba is persuaded that "there's no place like home." (When Timon sees the Pride Lands for the first time, he says: "Uh . . . we're going to fight your uncle, for *this*?" To which Simba replies: "Yes, Timon, this is my *home*.")

These laws of identity are fixed early in life, if not at birth. "What's happened to you? You're not the Simba I remember," Nala accuses him. "You're right, I'm not!" he shoots back, "Now, are you satisfied?" Simba becomes angry and defensive: "Listen! You think you can just show up and tell me how to live my life?" The answer, of course, is: Yes.

When Simba runs into Rafiki, the old ape reiterates this theme of identity. He is a link between the past and the present, between historical reality and Simba's superego. As Simba struggles with the issues that have been stirred up by his reunion with Nala, Rafiki chatters and dances around him until, annoyed and exasperated by the distraction, Simba demands to know:

FIGURE 2.7 After a long absence, an adult Simba (voiced by Matthew Broderick) returns to find his Uncle Scar king of the Pride Lands.

"Who *are* you?" Quick as a flash, and drawing his face to within an inch of Simba's own, Rafiki replies: "The question is, *who* are *you*?" To help Simba figure out the answer, he whispers something unintelligible in his ear, and when Simba asks, "What's that supposed to mean, anyway?" Rafiki says: "It means you're a baboon and I'm not!" It is perfectly true, of course, that Simba is genetically a lion— and Rafiki's method of leading Simba to some conclusions about his identity is off to a good start—but how much of a lion is he *culturally*? As we saw in Simba's confrontation with Nala, both Simba and the viewer are expected to proceed on a number of firmly held assumptions about lions—who have, to echo Stimpson, a particular psychological identity, social role, cultural script, place in the labor force, and sense of the sacred—if Rafiki's riddling game is to yield a satisfactory result.

Rafiki insists that Mufasa is still alive. "I'll show him to you!" he exults. "You follow old Rafiki, he knows the way." He leads a frightened and curious Simba through a mass of dark, tangled undergrowth, representing Simba's unconscious, and they come, finally, to a small pool, nestled at the center of the jungle. In a gesture charged with distinctly sexual connotations, Rafiki gently parts the luxurious grasses that grow around the pool, and invites Simba to step forward and look into its surface.

Simba stares at his reflection, and as he stares harder, he sees his father's image reflected back at him. "You see? He *lives* in *you*!" Rafiki says. This notion of identity being illustrated is Lacanian in its simplicity: the subject is formed through the image of the self as an other. To be more precise, the moment recalls Christian Metz's description in *The Imaginary Signifier* of the subject who enters the movie theater seeking to have subjectivity confirmed. For Metz, the film image is coded as analogy. It reenacts an already completed phase of the subject's formation. Simba is an "already constituted ego," which is why his father now (as Simba's superego) reconfigures himself as a ghostly presence in the night sky and tells the young lion: "Simba, you have forgotten who you are, and so have forgotten me!"

Mufasa's ghost (for that is surely what he is, in the spirit of *Hamlet*) is very specific about what Simba should do: "You *must* take your place in the Circle of Life. . . . Remember who you are! You are the one true king. Remember . . ."

After Simba's confrontation with Scar, he can properly be said to have successfully resolved his Oedipus complex. Simba ascends Pride Rock and roars mightily; and in a single dissolve, the Pride Lands are restored to lush, green health. When, in the final shots of the film, Rafiki holds up Simba and

Nala's newborn cub for all the kingdom to see and pay homage to, we recall the film's opening shots, in which the same ritual marked Simba's birth. As in Freud's masterplot, the narrative has come full circle. These last shots are almost the same as those first shots, yet different—precisely according to a model of narrative transformation elaborated by Tzvetan Todorov, whereby plot is constituted in the tension between resemblance and difference.[80]

This time, the proud parents do not stand alone behind the baboon shaman holding the baby, but are accompanied by their two new courtiers, Pumbaa and Timon, who take up a supportive and deferential position on Simba's right. It is implied that the errant sexuality they represent will be accommodated under the new regime. As the song on the sound track confirms, the warthog and meerkat are now included in the "Circle of Life"—but at the cost, we realize, of their "Hakuna Matata" lifestyle. "Home" is no longer "where your rump rests," but at King Simba's court, and the ideological implications of this bargain (for gay viewers especially) are far from clear.

According to Lévi-Strauss, the Oedipus myth functioned in the classical Greek context as a means of exploring a contradiction between a traditional, or "theoretical," belief in autochthony (born of the earth)[81] and an experientially grounded belief in the origins of man in sexual procreation.[82] Henry Krips argues that the contradiction—"*I know that* man is the product of intercourse between husband and wife, *but even so* he is born of earth-woman-wife alone"—functions as a disavowal concerning woman's lack of reproductive self-sufficiency. The mother's lack, he writes, "filled the role of fetish." And as in fetishism generally, "the object of desire must reside somewhere other than the fetish" (69). In the classical as well as Hellenic Greek context, a man's object of desire was the *eromenos*, the young male lover, "relations with whom were in uneasy tension with the adult male's responsibility to the *oikos*, that is, the household and its attendant women embodied in the figure of the mother and wife" (69).

We see a version of these contradictions and their resolutions in *The Lion King*, when Simba is persuaded to give up his bachelor life with his gay buddies in order to marry Nala: he brings Pumbaa and Timon with him to Pride Rock, where they will enjoy an uneasy status as Simba's best friends (surrounded by carnivores—Nala chief among them—who would eat the gay couple, were it not for Simba's protection). The Oedipus myth provides a means of coping with the contradiction of whether man is autochthonous or the result of sexual reproduction, by showing it to be equivalent to a "real contradiction" (Lévi-Strauss) negotiated in social life between two marital strategies: endogamy (marrying in) and exogamy (marrying out). As a film ostensibly for small children, *The Lion King* is preoccupied with the question of the origins of humanity and man's place in the universe. Which is why the Oedipus myth is so useful in providing an answer. It implies that settling upon a marriage partner (Simba choosing to go back to Pride Rock with Nala) involves more than a private arrangement of who lives with whom. The question of Simba's origins in an act of sexual reproduction can on some level be disavowed, while a practical contradiction is resolved. Echoing Lévi-Strauss, Krips suggests that the Oedipus myth provides a kind of "logical tool" which relates the original problem—born from one or born from two—to the derivative problem: born from different or born from same? The Oedipus myth stages both the disavowal ("but even so man comes from woman/earth alone") and the avowal ("woman is lacking/needs a man"). Indeed, it goes further "by inflecting the resultant contradiction out of the domain of cosmological schemes into the domain of marital strategies" (69). The tension, finally, is not the result of an opposition between homosexuality and heterosexuality or between love of boys and an ethic of marital fidelity, but arises from a conception of the adult male as one who must exercise self-control, which is the cornerstone of society and civilization. If Simba were to continue to live with Pumbaa and Timon, the riddle of the origins of humanity would not be confronted (and there would be no community to speak of).

In the triangular composition of the grouping in the final shots, Simba of course is at the apex. Nala's place—slightly behind and to Simba's left—recalls the strangely coded wording of the description of her character in the Disney press kit: "Simba's playmate is always in top form when it comes to childhood adventures, but as an adult she gets the lion's share of his attention."[83] Like the gay couple, she has found a place in the social-sexual-familial hierarchy, but at a certain price to her subjectivity—and, although one is not encouraged by the film to do so, it is up to the viewer to decide for him- or herself whether such a price is worth paying.

When Disney proudly announces in the promotional materials for the film that *The Lion King* is the studio's first animated feature "to be based on original source material and set in a naturalistic environment populated entirely by animals and untouched by man,"[84] the message is clear: *The Lion King* is meant to be taken as Disney's spin on an ur-text, or on truths that have organized themselves into myths, legends, plays, short stories, novels, and movies, which all say the same thing, whether articulated by Sophocles, Shakespeare, Freud, Kipling, or Disney. In being "original," it manages, in a sense, to be entirely unoriginal: a totally generic text constructed out of allusions, references, homages—everything recycled, borrowed, or plagiarized (but, for the most part, not intended to be postmodern in its resonances). Its setting, "untouched by man," suggests that, while human culture produces the particularities of individual authorship, "nature" and the animals who live in it embody eternal truths. These "truths," as I have attempted to examine them here, partly explain why, in Eisner's words, this story of a son trying to live up to his father's legacy had a powerful archetypal resonance; they also help to explain why *The Lion King* has been embraced by viewers on a massive scale, making it Disney's most popular animated film and one of the most profitable films ever made.

3

TO "HAVE KNOWN ECSTASY"
HUNTING MEN IN *THE MOST DANGEROUS GAME*

Since its beginnings as a commercial enterprise based on the concept of mass entertainment, the Hollywood film has put a girl in the picture because—as the director says in *King Kong* (1933), that famous movie about Hollywood filmmaking—the public "must have a pretty face to look at." The dialogue in *King Kong*'s opening scene is in fact very explicit about the ways in which mainstream filmmaking practices seek to cash in on the dominant sexual ideology of the day. The conversation between Carl Denham, the film director, and Weston, the theatrical agent, goes as follows:

> *Weston:* You never had a woman in any of your other pictures. Why do you want one in this?
> *Denham:* Holy Mackerel! Do you think I want to haul a woman around?
> *Weston:* Then, why?
> *Denham:* Because the public, Weston, must have a pretty face to look at.
> *Weston:* Sure! Everybody likes romance!
> *Denham:* Well, isn't there any romance or adventure in the world, without having a flapper in it?
> *Captain:* Mr. Denham, why not make a picture in a monastery!
> *Denham:* Makes me sore! I go out and sweat blood to make a swell picture, and then the critics and the exhibitors all say, "If this picture had love interest, it would gross twice as much." All right! The public wants a girl, and this time I'm gonna give them what they want!

Although made at the same time as *King Kong*—and sharing the same codirector (Ernest B. Schoedsack), the same female star (Fay Wray), and the same jungle sets—*The Most Dangerous Game* (1932) might seem at first to be only incidentally, or occasionally, driven by a concern to define and demonstrate the prevailing Hollywood formula of what Virginia Wright Wexman calls the "socially sanctioned ways of falling in love" and of "creating the couple."[1] However, The Most Dangerous Game is based on a short story that contains not a single female character. And like King Kong, the film's ideological imperatives are absolutely conventional: to confirm, at the very least, a norm of heterosexual desire. The Most Dangerous Game's producers have tried to channel the short story's sadistic homoeroticism into a conventional romantic subplot by introducing a woman, in an attempt, presumably, to be more commercially successful in a mass market.

While Denham's attitude could be seen as misogynistic, one understands his exasperation at having to acknowledge that, in Hollywood, there is really only one story to be told, and it must be told over and over again, in every genre. For all its vaunted success as an entertainment industry, Hollywood during the studio era was a vast and ideologically powerful apparatus that can be said to have ultimately had a warping effect on the sexuality of a great many men and women, for whom the heterosexual romance is not the only romance.

If, as Freud maintains, "a closer investigation of a man's day-dreams generally shows that all his heroic exploits are carried out and all his successes achieved only in order to please a woman and to be preferred by her to other men,"[2] there is much to be said about "The Most Dangerous Game" (the short story by Richard Connell)[3] as a man's daydream, in which the hero does not rescue a heroine, as in the film, but is hunted by the villain and his hounds; and then, when the villain believes him to have died in his attempt to avoid capture, the hero surprises him in his bedroom that night (by "hiding in the curtains of the bed").[4] Presumably, a struggle ensues, and the villain dies, for the story rather abruptly ends here. The last line, following an unusually provocative ellipsis in the text, is the hero's pronouncement that, "He had never slept in a better bed"! Like the fade/dissolve in cinema—so often used by filmmakers to cover a sexual embrace not represented on the screen—this ellipsis vaguely suggests, by connotation, that something illicit has occurred between the two men.

ADVENTURE AND HORROR

The Most Dangerous Game is first of all an adventure story, one in which, according to John G. Cawelti's typology of literary formulas, the central fantasy is that of the hero "overcoming obstacles and dangers and accomplishing some important and moral mission." This is the simplest of story types, in which "the hero frequently receives, as a kind of side benefit, the favors of one or more attractive young ladies."[5] Cawelti goes on to observe that the (super)hero of the adventure story, who usually triumphs over death, against all odds, "frequently embodies the most blatant kind of sexual symbolism," and the principle of identification between hero and audience is "like that between child and parent and involves the complex feelings of envious submission and ambiguous love characteristic of that relationship" (40). But *The Most Dangerous Game* is also a horror film, with Count Zaroff (Leslie Banks) as the Monster.[6] And to the extent that, in Robin Wood's formulation, the relationship between normality and the Monster constitutes the essential subject of the horror film, *The Most Dangerous Game* articulates its horror in the genre's privileged form: the figure of the doppelgänger, alter ego, or double, with the hero driven by a desire to destroy the doppelgänger, who embodies his repressed self.[7]

"A good horror film," Bruce Kawin has written, "takes you down into the depths and shows you something about the landscape. . . . The seeker, who is often the survivor, confronts his or her own fallibility, vulnerability, and culpability as an aspect of confronting the horror object, and either matures or dies. ("Matures" in this sense refers to the adult act of making peace with the discrepancy between self and self-image.)"[8] Bob Rainsford (Joel McCrea), the hero of *The Most Dangerous Game*, sees himself as a hunter. But on Zaroff's island, he is forced to confront his own vulnerability when he is hunted like an animal. As a complex psychosexual metaphor, the hunt describes Rainsford's experience in oedipal terms; and when he survives the hunt, with Eve Trowbridge (Fay Wray) at his side, we are meant to understand that he has "matured" in a sexual sense. The "castration crisis" that we might identify at the heart of *The Most Dangerous Game* is, as Kawin notes, a relatively consistent pattern in the horror films of the twenties, thirties, and forties. In horror movies of this kind, according to Kawin, the boy, the girl, and the monster are structurally linked in a perverse love triangle, and the happy pairing of the surviving couple only becomes possible when they come to some kind of understanding with the forces the monster represents. In order for the film to end, this romantic resolution must "bode well for the society at large" (239).

BONDING, TRANSGRESSION, AND DEATH

What is it that Rainsford confronts when he meets Zaroff, and what kind of "understanding" does Rainsford gain about himself? Thierry Kuntzel has noted in his landmark essay on *The Most Dangerous Game* that the film deploys as its major figure "the reversal of the code" and that "on the distant horizon of the question of deviation and the norm, there is the issue of sexuality and Rainsford's opposition to Zaroff's deviance."[9] What follows is a discussion of the film and short story that foregrounds precisely this issue of sexuality and the hero's opposition to the villain's deviance—for there is something to be gained from an analysis of the movie as an adaptation of the short story, in which the hero's "opposition" becomes a rather more complex matter than the melodrama of the story would suggest.[10] By introducing a female character into the text, a triangle is set up in the film (linking Rainsford, Eve, and Zaroff) that—to borrow Marty Roth's evocation of Eve Sedgwick's phrasing—works as "a dynamic shuttle for containing, distributing, displacing, and confusing homosexual and heterosexual energies because 'in any erotic rivalry, the bond that links the two rivals is as intense and potent as the bond that links either of the rivals to the beloved.'"[11]

And as Phyllis Chesler would remind us about "the complicated love-play among men"[12] in a society that insists on universal heterosexuality, male bonding is perhaps only an attempt to deny or at least to survive the fact that men "are the deadliest killers of men on earth": "Male-bonding is about the lengths to which men are willing to go to gain male approval, or rather, to avoid male violence; male-bonding is about the male craving to inherit power from real or surrogate father-figures—power at least over women, if not over other men" (243–44).

When Zaroff, in a male-bonding attempt, invites Rainsford to hunt men with him, Rainsford recoils in horror and disgust. What Zaroff wants him to do is perverse. Chief among the perversions implied by the hunt is a sadistic homosexuality, which is very much present in both the short story and the film but always coded in cross-writing, displacement, or erasure.

Kawin notes that so many horror films are "psychoanalyzable" because they often "map out the terrain of the unconscious, and in that connection they often deal with fantasies of brutality, sexuality, victimization, repression, and so on."[13] While this observation is certainly true of *The Most Dangerous Game*, it reminds us that we are not dealing with the unconscious of a single character but of a narrator/text. Rainsford's desire is dialectically linked to and bound up with that of all the other characters, particularly Zaroff's desire, and this desire is legible everywhere in the mise-en-scène.

Kuntzel describes the successive opening of doors—one of the film's most privileged hermeneutic figures—and the final escape to the sea as "a sort of voyage of initiation: light, liberty, and love can be found only after having descended into the heart of darkness and captivity, after having risked the loss of the loved one and the loss of self."[14] What I wish to analyze here is the nature of this "heart of darkness" that Kuntzel refers to, and what he might mean by "the loss of self." Kuntzel's conclusion is that the film tells us, "in a word, *transgression* generally leads to death" (10). Thus heterosexual ideology tries to frighten us. As Deleuze and Guattari have put it, the oedipal scenario informs us that "if you don't follow the lines of differentiation daddy-mommy-me, and the exclusive alternatives that delineate them, you will fall back into the black night of the undifferentiated."[15] That which lies outside of difference is unimaginable, horrible. It is the undifferentiated, first of all, of incest. In *The Most Dangerous Game*, it is primarily homosexuality that is being alluded to: "Oh, Rainsford, you'll find this game worth playing!" urges Zaroff. "When the next ship arrives, we'll have *gorgeous* sport together! . . . Come, Rainsford, say you'll hunt with me!" To which, with proper indignation, Rainsford protests: "What? Hunt men?" Somewhere, on some level of his consciousness, he also knows that this kind of hunt probably ends in rape.

"What Do You Think I Am?"

Heterosexual ideology—and its frequently concomitant masculinism and homophobia—always, in the final analysis, pits men against each other. Although presented in sometimes startlingly direct terms, Chesler's insights into the consequences for men of "compulsory heterosexuality" (to use Adrienne Rich's term for the hegemonic structure of mainstream opinion and representation)[16] certainly ring true for Zaroff's character. He so desperately needs a male friend, "because [male friendship] is yearned for as ardently as men yearn for their fathers to love them, protect them, and name them heir to some legacy"[17]—but he is too competitive (not to mention narcissistic) for male friendship. He is a lonely figure, and like Rainsford, who hunts big game so obsessively, he is looking for something that has been lost—and we begin to understand what it is when Rainsford describes the men on the ship that went down as "the swellest crowd on earth, my best friends." When Zaroff finally offers to show Eve's brother Martin his "trophy room," Trowbridge's response—in ordinary language and conventional terms—is another indication of the male intimacy which all the men in *The Most Dangerous Game* seek: "Say, that's a great idea! Now we're pals. No more secrets now, huh? We'll make a night of it! Just you and I . . . pals. We'll have fun together . . ."

These men want to feel an emotional closeness to other men, or to another man, and yet are caught in a deadly game of rivalry over a woman. We may think that if they were not so committed to conventional (homophobic) heterosexuality, they would not so quickly find themselves trying to kill each other. But the short story, in which the third term is not a female character but appears to be Zaroff's dead father, suggests that the dynamic at play need not be heterosexual in nature. Indeed, Freud observes that it would be tempting, as a theoretical explanation, to say that "the behavior towards men in general of a man who sees in other men potential love objects must be different from that of a man who looks upon other men in the first instance as rivals in regard to women," when, in fact, "jealousy and rivalry play their part in homosexual love as well, and . . . the community of men also includes these potential rivals."[18]

Zaroff, Rainsford, and Trowbridge provide a spectrum for the issue of masculinity that the film treats, and all of them are identified and measured by that yardstick of the patriarchy—their relation to the woman: Martin Trowbridge, as Eve's brother, is somewhat epicene, the taboo on incest removing him as a player in any conventional competition for the woman (his heavy drinking, however, suggesting an unresolved attraction to his sister); Zaroff, living alone on his island, without companion, lover, or spouse, is a study in frustrated, perverse sexuality; and Rainsford is presented as the desirable norm (which is confirmed at the end of the film when he escapes the island with Eve). But Rainsford's identity wavers at the edge of what contemporary mainstream opinion would consider normal. When Zaroff tries to make him acknowledge that he experiences the hunt as something sexual, Rainsford responds uncertainly, "Oh, I don't know." Zaroff scoffs: "You Americans! One passion builds upon another. *Kill, then love!* When you have known that, you have known ecstasy!"

The "edge" that Rainsford is tempted by is nicely literalized in the film's last shot, when the fatally wounded Zaroff—trying to shoot at the fleeing couple with his Tartar war bow from a window of his fortress—falls slowly, voluptuously, off the window ledge to his death. Rainsford throughout the film is on the threshold of confirming an identity, but must repress a number of possibilities in order to claim a single coherent and conventional identity. When Zaroff—lit by the filmmakers to look like the Devil himself—tries to tempt Rainsford by urging him, "Say you'll hunt with me!" Rainsford replies with the film's big question: *"What do you think I am?"* And the ambiguous answer: "One, I fear, who dare not follow his own convictions to their logical conclusion." This exchange does not, of course, necessarily refer to a repressed homosexual identity, or to any other identity that can be specified exactly. As a fiction and as a work of art, *The Most Dangerous Game* allows the viewer to see in it what he or she will. But in the spirit of Freud, we can say that the movie encourages a kind of reading that enacts a symbolic daydream. The answer to Rainsford's (rhetorical) question—"What do you think I am?"—is meant to be revealed by his response to Eve.

HUNTER AND HUNTED

The question of what is put at stake by including the female character in *The Most Dangerous Game* has been summarized by Rhona Berenstein:

> [Eve's] participation in the hunt signifies a heterosexual safety net in which the woman is the representative of the animal-world, and the figure who prevents the men from falling irreversibly into a monstrous jungle in which there are no women, in which there are only the pursuit and display of (or hunt and hunger for) homosocial desires. She is civilization in the form of the promise of heterosexuality.[19]

Eve's presence in the film allows Rainsford (and the viewer) to flirt with another side of his sexuality, while maintaining his role as a conventionally masculine man, and offering him a solution to his dilemma in the form of a legitimate heterosexual object-choice.

The central metaphor of *The Most Dangerous Game* is articulated by Rainsford toward the beginning of the film, when the ship's doctor asks him "if there'd be as much sport in the game if you were the tiger instead of the hunter." Rainsford replies complacently: "Well, that's something I'll never have to decide. Listen here you fellows, the world's divided into two kinds of people: the hunter and the hunted. Well, luckily, I'm a hunter. And nothing could ever change that." This theme of hunter and hunted is clearly a discourse on masculinity and manhood, and Rainsford as a hunter is identified above all as a man. With the hunter posited as the supremely masculine man, the one who is hunted is understood, therefore, to be not-masculine, i.e., a woman, a feminized man, or an animal.

Whether or not the story contains a woman, the controlling discourse on manhood is the same. What cannot be disguised by the inclusion of a female character in the film are the narrator's fears and desires, which are organized around an obsession with manhood. In *Manhood and the American Renais-*

sance, David Leverenz proposes that "manhood functions to preserve self-control and, more profoundly, to transform fears of vulnerability or inadequacy into a desire for dominance;"[20] and, as we can see is the case in *The Most Dangerous Game*, he suggests there is a "basic connection between manhood and humiliation" (74). The issue of manhood is crucial for both Rainsford, the handsome, famous hunter, and Count Zaroff, the seductive and dangerous aristocrat. Both short story and film establish Rainsford's manhood in generic terms as an impressive and attractive fact; and Zaroff's masculinity—while ambiguous—is no less emphatically presented as something to be reckoned with. When Rainsford's manhood is challenged by Zaroff, the possibility of humiliation is guaranteed by the presence of the woman, who is witness to and the ostensible prize in the contest between the two men. It is from this matrix, then, that the short story and film derive their perverse eroticism. Leverenz writes:

> Anyone preoccupied with manhood, in whatever time or culture, harbors fears of being humiliated, usually by other men. The sources of humiliation may be diverse, in parents or the loss of class position, in marketplace competition or other fears of being dominated. A preoccupation with manhood becomes a compensatory response. (73)

Leverenz goes on to explain that manhood becomes a way of minimizing loss: "While the loss may be symbolized as castration, its emotional roots lie in a man's fear that other men will see him as weak and therefore vulnerable to attack" (73).[21] The idea of the hunt, of course, mobilizes these terms and throws into sharp relief the issues at stake.

It is the trope of deviance that makes it possible to clarify the main thrust of the narrative, which is consonant with the narrative logic of classical cinema: "to establish, by the end of the film, the nature of masculinity, the nature of femininity, and the way in which those two can be complementary rather than antagonistic."[22] Kuntzel is right to stress that "two related paradigms are insistently repeated: savage/civilized; hunter/hunted . . . [and that] *The Most Dangerous Game* plays indefatigably on the fragility of the barrier that separates the two."[23] But what animates the film with perversely erotic resonances, giving the mise-en-scène its interest, are the corresponding subtextual paradigms—homosexual/heterosexual, sadism/masochism, mastery/humiliation.

In the film, Rainsford's prerogative as a man to be always the hunter is challenged. He discovers what it is like, as it were, to be a woman, or—as some of the dialogue and mise-en-scène would suggest—what it is like to be a passive

FIGURE 3.1 *The Most Dangerous Game* (1932): Count Zaroff (Leslie Banks) insists that he and Bob Rainsford (Joel McCrea) are "kindred spirits." On Zaroff's island, however, Rainsford will be forced to confront his own vulnerability, when the count hunts him like an animal.

homosexual. As figuration of the narrator's desire, the film makes sense as a fantasy of Rainsford's unconscious wish to be hunted—to be possessed, ravished, and beaten. And this desire corresponds to his fear of the female sex, and his attraction (which is more apparent in the short story) to his masculine "other." A curious consequence of the ingenious adaptation of the short story to include a woman is the link between Rainsford's fear of female sexuality and his unconscious homosexual desire. Just as Leverenz observes that there is a basic connection between manhood and humiliation, the hunt in which Zaroff pursues Rainsford reveals that the desires of these two men are dialectically linked. Rainsford (or rather, the narrator who invents both his and Zaroff's character) wants to be hunted. He unconsciously wants to find himself bound and helpless, at the mercy of this man (whom the short story describes as "singularly handsome"), who functions as a feared and desired father figure. The woman, as pointed out earlier, serves to displace and disguise this desire, to bring the film within Hollywood's code of sexual norms.

Rainsford's unconscious sense of guilt about being a hunter, translated into psychoanalytic terms, reveals a need for punishment at the hands of a parental power. According to Freud, the wish "which so frequently appears in phantasies, to be beaten by the father, stands very close to the other wish, to have a passive (feminine) sexual relation to him and is only a regressive distortion of it."[24] The short story makes all this fairly obvious. How Rainsford lands on the island, for example, tells us a great deal.

Unconscious Desire and the Primal Scene

In his analysis of the movie, Kuntzel wishes to make it clear that "even if I can point out, here and there, that the text is played out on the side of perversion, perversion in no way constitutes the vanishing point with respect to which my analysis, like a painting, attempts to make all its lines of perspective converge."[25] I shall attempt, however, to do precisely what Kuntzel seeks to avoid, by examining the way in which perversion does in fact constitute a sort of vanishing point with respect to an understanding of what is significant about the changes made in the short story's adaptation for the screen.

We may begin by attempting to answer a question Kuntzel rhetorically puts to "positivists." He asks: "Why is Rainsford's fall, pure chance in the short story by Richard Connell, transformed in the film into a *necessary* accident?" (51–52). The answer becomes obvious when we look closely at the text of the short story. In the movie, it is Zaroff who moves the channel lights, which causes the ship Rainsford is on to smash into the coral reef (in the world's most shark-infested waters). The hero, in other words, is innocent. He appears to bear no responsibility of unconscious desire motivating the action that deposits him on the beach of Zaroff's island. All villainy is figured in the character of the Count, and Rainsford is meant to be seen as a victim of circumstance (for the moral code of Hollywood would discourage the sort of reading that the short story begs).

In the short story, Rainsford's fall—hardly a matter of "pure chance"—assumes a dream logic, and reads like an unconscious yielding to something feared and forbidden. For this scene, Connell makes it a "dank tropical night that was palpable as it pressed its thick warm blackness in upon the yacht" (71). The night, and the island, are figured in terms that connote an oppressive, claustrophobic female sexuality. "Ugh! It's like moist black velvet," Rainsford complains (71). The third line of dialogue in the short story has Rainsford's fellow hunter Whitney explaining to him that "sailors have a curious dread" of the island marked on "the old charts" as 'ship-Trap Island," and a page later, Whitney describes how once before, passing the island, he felt "a sort of sudden dread."[26] During their discussion about hunting, Whitney remarks that while hunting may be for Rainsford "the best sport in the world," he rather thinks that animals being hunted "understand one thing—fear. The fear of pain and the fear of death" (71). Rainsford laughingly rejects out of hand Whitney's line of thinking: "Nonsense. . . . This hot weather is making you soft, Whitney. Be a realist. The world is made up of two classes—the hunters and the huntees. Luckily, you and I are hunters. Do you think we've passed that island yet?" (72). The island obviously intrigues Rainsford. When Whitney says he is going to bed, Rainsford says, "I'm not sleepy. I'm going to smoke another pipe up on the after deck" (72). Rainsford's pipe—certainly a phallic signifier in this context—will play a crucial role (because it functions as a fetish) in his fall from the boat:

> Rainsford, reclining in a steamer chair, indolently puffed on his favorite brier. The sensuous drowsiness of the night was on him. "It's so dark," he thought, "that I could sleep without closing my eyes; the night would be my eyelids." (73)

Connell is creating a sort of dream-reality for the scene, and Rainsford, no longer experiencing the enveloping night air as disgusting, slips into a state of wakeful receptiveness, as he listens to the sounds of "the muffled throb of the engine that drove the yacht swiftly through the darkness, and the swish and ripple of the wash of the propeller" (72–73).

What follows can be described as a *primal scene*. While he believes he recognizes what he hears, he cannot *see* it; he has no visual proof:

> An abrupt sound startled him. Off to the right he heard it, and his ears, expert in such matters, could not be mistaken. Again he heard the sound, and again. Somewhere, off in the blackness, someone had fired a gun three times.
>
> Rainsford sprang up and moved quickly to the rail, mystified. He strained his eyes in the direction from which the reports had come, but it was like trying to see through a blanket. He leaped upon the rail and balanced himself there, to get greater elevation; his pipe, striking a rope, was knocked from his mouth. He lunged for it; a short, hoarse cry came from his lips as he realized he had reached too far and had

lost his balance. The cry was pinched off short as the blood-warm waters of the Caribbean Sea closed over his head.

He struggled up to the surface and tried to cry out, but the wash from the speeding yacht slapped him in the face and the salt water in his open mouth made him gag and strangle. (73)

In other words, there is an area in which he is expert (he is a hunter who knows all about hunting), but in his phallic narcissism, there is something he does not know about (the "other"/the woman/the hunted/the jaguar Whitney talks about). He is quite unable to imagine what it is like to be hunted, to put himself in the jaguar's position. He is arrested in the phallic phase (Freud), which is characterized by the opposition phallic/castrated. In that phase there is no representation of an other sex.

This primal scene functions *après coup*. When he hears the report of a gun, and he hears a scream, he imagines what is happening. While he believes that his ears cannot be mistaken, he cannot quite credit what must be happening, for absolute verification can only come from seeing. The fetish that makes it possible for him to experience the dark night as a "sensuous drowsiness" is knocked out of his mouth by his reaction to something heard. As a child might hear his parents making love, and strain to see what is happening, but finds that it is "like trying to see through a blanket," Rainsford is traumatized by something he knows but does not know (knows but does not *want* to know).[27] That pipe stands between him and knowing. Without its support, he is forced to see, and to know (when he later learns what Zaroff keeps in his trophy room). In the film, the woman takes the place of the pipe. At the end of the film, with Eve at his side, Rainsford steers a safe passage away from the island through the very coral reefs that wrecked his ship at the beginning of the film.

As Kuntzel says, the film plays on the fragility of the barrier that separates the terms of the two related and insistently repeated paradigms (savage/civilized; hunter/hunted), and here in the short story we see Rainsford, on the threshold of his adventure, balanced upon the rail that would prevent him from falling into the "blood-warm waters" of oedipal self-knowledge.

THE BODY

In the short story, Rainsford wrestles himself out of his clothes and swims in the direction the sounds came from. Propelled by the suspense of the narrative, the reader may not fully register that Rainsford is now naked; but the logic of why he should be so becomes clearer when we read about the island, which is described in terms that evoke the garden of Eden, or a maternal body that is simultaneously protective and dangerous. "On a night less calm he would have been shattered" against the rocky shore:

> Dense jungle came down to the very edge of the cliffs. What perils that tangle of trees and underbrush might hold for him did not concern Rainsford just then. All he knew was that he was safe from his enemy, the sea, and that utter weariness was on him. He flung himself down at the jungle edge and tumbled headlong into the deepest sleep of his life. (74)

His sleep on the beach invigorates him and he looks about calmly. "But what kind of men," he wonders, live "in so forbidding a place?" He looks at the shore and finds a spot "where the jungle weeds were crushed down and the moss was lacerated; one patch of weeds was stained crimson. A small, glittering object not far away caught Rainsford's eye and he picked it up. It was an empty cartridge" (74).

Rarely does one read a passage that so vividly, yet unconsciously, describes a scene that corresponds to the small child's belief that when he sees his parents making love, something violent—involving blood, even—is taking place. The narrative nature of this tableau is confirmed by the fetishistic presence of the spent cartridge.

Bodily metaphors abound. When Rainsford sees Zaroff's fortress set high on a bluff, he notices that "on three sides of it cliffs dived down to where the sea licked greedy lips in the shadows" (75). Indeed, we are encouraged to read the dream-logic of Rainsford's experience when the narrator remarks, "yet about it all hung an air of unreality" (75).

In the film, a smile flickers across Rainsford's face when he sees Zaroff's fortress, little suspecting that it might as well be the castle in the Black Forest described by the Marquis de Sade in *120 Days of Sodom*. That Rainsford's unconscious desire has something to do with the body can be inferred from the language Connell uses in the short story to describe the impression (General) Zaroff and his castle make upon Rainsford. The servant, Ivan, is described as "the largest man Rainsford had ever seen—a gigantic creature, solidly made and black-bearded to the waist. In his hand the man held a long-barreled revolver, and he was pointing it straight at Rainsford's heart" (75). Rainsford's first impression of Zaroff, "an erect, slender man in evening clothes," is that he is "singularly handsome," with "the face of an aristocrat." When Zaroff smiles, Rainsford notices his "red lips and pointed teeth" (76).[28]

Zaroff offers the naked Rainsford some of his own clothes to wear: "You'll find that my clothes will fit you, I think" (77). This is the beginning of an identification between the two men that resonates homoerotically throughout the story. Rainsford is given a bedroom with "a canopied bed big enough for six men." A few sentences on, the motif of size, measured in numbers of men, is repeated: in the dining room is a "vast refectory table where twoscore men could sit down to eat" (77). The General and Rainsford sit at this table and eat a "rich red soup." Rainsford finds him to be "a most thoughtful and affable host, a true cosmopolite"—he is clearly being seduced by Zaroff— "but there was one small trait of the general's that made Rainsford uncomfortable. Whenever he looked up from his plate he found the general studying him, appraising him narrowly" (77).

In the film, this scene is handled slightly differently, but with hardly any less homoerotic resonance. After a conversation that includes Zaroff's observation that, "Death is for others, not for ourselves," the Count suddenly looks at Rainsford's naked shoulder, visible through his torn shirt (much like Count Dracula seeing the blood on Jonathan Harker's pierced finger), and says to Rainsford, as he touches the young man's arm: "Oh, by the way, you'll be wanting to change those wet rags immediately." The Count seems slightly agitated, and he laughs awkwardly when Rainsford says, "They look about the way I feel!" As they start to mount the steps of an enormous staircase, Zaroff stops, looks at Rainsford's forearm and says, "I have some loose hunting clothes which I keep for my guests that you can possibly get into." The dialogue is a little less revealing than it is in the short story, but what has been repressed returns in the mise-en-scène. As Rainsford turns to go up the stairs with Ivan, Zaroff stares for a moment, quite unambiguously, at Rainsford's behind. When Rainsford pauses farther up the stairs to thank his host for the "stiff" drink Zaroff says he'll find in his room, Zaroff's reply—"*All pleasure is mine!*"—is said with such feeling that Rainsford, in countershot, looks perturbed.

Rainsford, the erstwhile predator, feels vulnerable. The hunter's prerogatives (to fix his prey within the sights of a gun) are being challenged by Zaroff's calculating look. When Zaroff in the film asks Rainsford to "assume a cheerfulness you may not feel," because "our feminine guest is easily perturbed," we have already seen that it is actually the Count's emotions that have been perturbed—by Rainsford's (sexual) presence. Their small exchange on the stairs, as Rainsford comes down to meet Zaroff's other guests—agreeing to put on a show of confidence for Eve—reveals the patriarchal strategy of displacing male fears onto the woman, to keep the woman in her position of subordination to male desire. Indeed, the whole business of the hunt, which will require Rainsford to protect and later rescue Eve, is but a way for Rainsford and us to play out a rescue fantasy that masks a desire to be rescued.[29] Moreover, Eve might rescue Rainsford from his unconscious homosexual impulses—save him through, and for, heterosexuality.

ABJECTION AND THE "FEMININE"

At the beginning of the film, as the ship's doctor is asking Rainsford if he thinks "there'd be as much sport in the game if you were the tiger instead of the hunter," the cardplayer seated nearby mutters to himself: "Hmm, here comes that bad-luck lady again, third time tonight." Rainsford immediately turns to the player and offers to shuffle the cards (suggesting that he knows how to avoid danger when it presents itself in the form of a woman). But the doctor says: "Wait a minute, don't evade the issue. Now, *I asked you a question!*" It is fairly clear that the real issue being evaded is the question of sexual difference. As earlier noted, the "woman" is absent in Connell's story but appears in the film. Kuntzel writes: "Whereas the other figures are displaced, transformed, and inverted in the course of the narrative, there is one which remains strangely constant: that of the woman."[30] He notes that whereas the hunter/hunted paradigm may be perturbed where men are concerned, that of sexual difference remains intact. Eve may not take part in the game because she is the object at stake; she is the ultimate prey.

There is a sense in which we can say that the woman is the "structuring absence" of the short story, for it becomes apparent early on that Rainsford's crisis of identification and desire is an answer to the question put by Julia Kristeva in *Powers of Horror*: How does one "confront the feminine"? Kristeva notes that what we designate as "feminine," far from being a primeval essence, "will be seen as an 'other' without a name."[31] She is speaking of that which is coded as "abject," and remarks on the "abject or demoniacal potential of the feminine," which "threatens one's own and clean self, which is the underpinning of any organization constituted by exclusions and hierarchies" (65). Rainsford's story (which is every bit as much Zaroff's story) is a story of abjection, or "the journey to the end of the night."[32] It begins when Rainsford is thrown from the ship—*ab-jected*—and tossed up onto the beach of Zaroff's island; and we know Rainsford will survive, when he shows himself willing—

against Zaroff's advice—to enter Fog Hollow (where Zaroff's rifle will be rendered "useless"). Like the rocky ravine below the waterfall into which he later plunges in order to save his life, the alligator-infested swamp is symbolic of female sexuality as a nightmare of drowning or being torn to pieces.

When the captain's mate says, "But two light buoys mean a safe channel between the world over," and the captain shoots back, "'Safe between the world over' doesn't go in these waters!" a double meaning can be read. One understands that heterosexuality is anxiously being defined as normal, and that there should be nothing to be afraid of. We all ("the world over") passed through this passage when we came into the world. And everybody knows it is safe to enter between (the two lights). But the captain is warning his young mate that their safety cannot be guaranteed. No man is ever completely safe—from the *vagina dentata*, the threat of homosexual rape, or worse.

But, in a metaphorical register, the narrator of *The Most Dangerous Game* proves not only that heterosexuality can be dangerous—when the ship is

FIGURE 3.2 Rainsford is advised against entering Fog Hollow, where Zaroff's rifle will be rendered "useless." (Note how the threat of homosexual rape to the hero, and the notion of female sexuality as potentially engulfing, are suggested in the mise-en-scène.) (Fay Wray as Eve Trowbridge)

wrecked while attempting to enter the passage indicated by the buoys—but that homosexuality is dangerous, too (Martin Trowbridge's mortal encounter with Zaroff in the dead of night is the first indication). In the short story, Zaroff's description of what can happen to a ship seeking access to the island resonates with sexual terror: the lights "indicate a channel where there's none: giant rocks with razor edges crouch like a sea monster with wide-open jaws. They can crush a ship as easily as I crush this nut" (82).

If the film, like the short story, begins with the assertion that the world is divided into hunters and the hunted, and then proves that a hunter can be hunted, what is really being said about those crucially important underpinnings of social organization, masculinity and femininity? The symbolic field on which the whole story is charted is turned upside down—like the wrecked ship in the film. Signs are revealed to be deceiving—like the falsely positioned buoys that cause the shipwreck (deception, as we know, is crucial to perversion).[33] While it is easy to sense the subversive power of *The Most Dangerous Game* and to identify the hunt as a metaphorical crisis of desire and identification, we might nuance our reading of its logic of metaphor and hallucination by paraphrasing Kristeva: the hunt gives a language to unnameable states of fear. Rainsford and Zaroff are inscribed in "*a drive economy in want of an object*—that conglomerate of fear, deprivation, and nameless frustration." The hunt is a "metaphor that is taxed with representing want itself."[34]

RULES OF THE GAME

Although he approvingly cites an old "Ogandi" saying, "Hunt first the enemy, then the woman," Zaroff is not really interested in the woman at all. His mastery of Rainsford, in the metaphor of the successful hunt, might give Zaroff the sexual confidence to approach Eve; but winning the hunt is the key thing: it is phallicizing. Zaroff's rape of Eve would be only a symbolic proof of his victory. It would prove that he is a man, in a narrative that worships the masculine and defines true manhood as heterosexual. The short story is perhaps more subversive of patriarchal masculinity than the film, because it offers no proof of this kind. *The Most Dangerous Game*'s screenwriter understood that if you show that a man can be hunted—i.e., penetrated (by an arrow) = "fucked"—the only way to level the symbolic field is to introduce a woman into the narrative. The task of the hero becomes, then, to protect *her*, to save *her* (from being raped by the villain). Rape and/or whatever

FIGURE 3.3   The hero's role is to protect the woman.

it is Zaroff does to his victims in his trophy room is not really the point of it all. The hunt—the game itself—is the point.

The very ordinariness of these metaphors—the field, the game—signals the pervasiveness in everyday life of the dangerous game implied by the title. The most dangerous game of all is a metaphysical and psychological one that is played out behind masks, in metaphor and disguise. In a curious acknowledgment of the blatantly metaphorical nature of the hunt, Zaroff in the film says to Rainsford: "You do not excuse what needs no excuse." He goes on to quote from one of Rainsford's books: "'Hunting is as much a game as stud poker, only the limits are higher.' You have put our case perfectly, Mr. Rainsford!" This is a subtle invitation to the viewer to interpret and experience the hunt sexually. Indeed, the inherent sexuality of both the story and film is everywhere except in what we normally call sex.

What Mark Simpson writes in *Male Impersonators* about the ground rule of football applies to the hunt in *The Most Dangerous Game*, namely, that the game gives men ways to reconcile homoerotic desire with the need to be manly: "Interest in men is permitted, indeed encouraged, but must always be expressed *through the game*":

Boys discover that football places them in a masculine universe where they can enjoy the company of men and the spectacle of their bodies—as long as it is framed within competition, a struggle for dominance: to be "a fucker"; love is once again circumscribed by hate. The game itself becomes the phallus, something to be forever pursued and worshipped, something that bestows manhood: "I fell in love with football as I was later to fall in love with women."[35]

But Zaroff does not later fall in love with women. Indeed, even the hunt ceases to interest him. As he says to Rainsford, hunting had ceased to be a sporting proposition (79–80); he explains that it was a tragic moment when he realized that instinct is no match for reason. Zaroff's desire is arrested in the "mirror phase" described by Lacan.[36] His tragic moment corresponds to the sense of loss a child experiences when—upon seeing its reflection in a mirror—understands for the first time that it is alone in the world. Zaroff falls in love with his mirror image and spends a lifetime pursuing that image. The tragedy is that he can never *become* that ideal image, although he certainly tries. As Zaroff's dying word in the film describes it, this desire is "*impossible*." It can only be experienced as a moment of ecstasy—of *jouissance*, as Lacan would describe it—in death. When Rainsford asks what the Count's most dangerous game is, Martin Trowbridge's comment will echo with a kind of poignancy, as it evokes the elusiveness of the object of Zaroff's desire: "It's no use, Rainsford, he won't tell. He won't even let you see his trophy room 'til he gets ready to take you on the hunt of the great whatsit!"[37]

"I wanted the ideal animal to hunt," Zaroff in the short story explains. Then he asks rhetorically: "What are the attributes of an ideal quarry?" He answers by describing a version of himself: "The answer was, of course: 'It must have courage, cunning, and, above all, it must be able to reason'" (80). Physically, too, the prey must be a splendid specimen, like the man Zaroff tries to tempt Rainsford with, describing him as a "rather promising prospect . . . a big strong black" (83).

Zaroff is of course describing his oedipal crisis, which is structurally similar to the earlier crisis the infant experiences in the mirror phase. When he says that hunting animals "had become too easy," he is describing his realization that, in a patriarchy, the Father himself is the biggest challenge. Ultimately, only the Father really matters.[38] Zaroff wishes to go directly to the biggest challenge of all: he wants to confront the symbolic phallus. What he learned from his actual father—and, no doubt, from the Russian Revolution—was that "life is for the strong, to be lived by the strong, and, if need be, taken by the strong" (81). It is the lesson all little boys in a patriarchy are encouraged to learn: renounce the mother and identify with the values of the father. The mother comes to represent everything weak and abjected. This is why there is no mention of her in the text. Instead, Zaroff pretends to have a philosophy of love, in which the woman does play a role: "[Trowbridge] talks of wine and women as a prelude to the hunt," he says. "We barbarians know that it is after the chase, and then only, that man revels! . . . It is the natural instinct. What is woman? Even such a woman as this? [*He gestures dismissively toward Eve*] Until the blood is quickened by the kill."

Betrayal and Loss

Zaroff was raised to worship masculinity and becomes, in Leverenz's phrase, a man "preoccupied with manhood." The difficulty of being a man is exacerbated when he loses his actual father; he loses his "Great White Tsar" (83),

FIGURE 3.4 "We barbarians know that it is after the chase, and then only, that man revels! . . . It is the natural instinct. What is woman? Even such a woman as this?" Zaroff designates Eve as the survivor's prize in the hunt he is proposing.

his country, and his domain in the Crimea.[39] His sense of betrayal and loss is enormous, because these losses compound the original loss nothing can replace: the mother and the sense of pre-oedipal attachment that all infants experience.

As Louise Kaplan's study of perversions amply confirms, Zaroff's perverse attachment to the hunt is an "enactment, or performance [that] is designed to help [him] to survive, moreover to survive with a sense of triumph over the traumas of [his] childhood."[40] What distinguishes perversion, Kaplan notes, is "its quality of desperation and fixity. A perversion is performed by a person who has no other choices, a person who would otherwise be overwhelmed by anxieties or depression or psychosis" (10). Although "an appeasement of personal demons," the perverse strategy is unconscious: "The protagonist does not know that the performance is designed to master 'events' that were once too exciting, too frightening, too mortifying, to master in childhood" (10–11).

Zaroff can acknowledge that the Russian Revolution was a catastrophe for his social class, but he cannot think of it as a personal trauma, or as being linked in any way to a trauma in his childhood. He will not see himself as a victim; the humiliation would be unbearable. He will rebuild his subjectivity as a fortress on the "ruins"[41] of a structure that once stood firm and impregnable—before castration and all its effects threatened it with dissolution.

In the film, when Martin Trowbridge says of himself and his sister, "We are victims of circumstance, same as Mr. Rainsford, and if anyone has a right to his liquor, it's a victim of circumstance," he is acknowledging that we are all—in the psychoanalytic metaphor—subject to the law of castration. But it is this law that Zaroff cannot accept. His denial is radical and violent. He tries to free himself from the constraints of patriarchal law—to "dethrone God the Father"[42] and create a new kind of reality.

Zaroff attempts at first to mitigate the perversity of his desire by asking Rainsford to hunt *with* him. When Rainsford refuses, he becomes Zaroff's prey. Zaroff does not wish merely to *be* Rainsford (by identifying with the famous hunter), but wants to possess him. Like the late and infamous serial killer Jeffrey Dahmer, Zaroff takes the bodies of his victims down into the cellar of his fortress, where—it is implied—he does unspeakable things to them.

In the short story, the roots of Zaroff's mania for hunting—the way in which he has transformed his fears of vulnerability or inadequacy into a desire for dominance—are offered in a monologue to Rainsford:

"My hand was made for the trigger, my father said. . . . I killed my first bear in the Caucasus when I was ten. My whole life has been one prolonged hunt. I went into the army—it was expected of noblemen's sons—and for a time commanded a division of Cossack cavalry, but my real interest was always the hunt." (78–79)

There are elements of what Freud calls the "family romance" in Zaroff's description of his childhood,[43] and Leverenz's analysis of why some men are preoccupied with manhood—they harbor fears of being humiliated or dominated by their parents, or through failure at work, or loss of social status—offers the key to Zaroff's character. "Many noble Russians lost everything," Zaroff reminds Rainsford. But: "I, luckily, had invested heavily in American securities, so I shall never have to open a tea room in Monte Carlo or drive a taxi in Paris" (79).[44] Zaroff is saved, at least, from financial embarrassment. But the trauma of his other losses have twisted his aristocratic pride into a pathological narcissism.[45]

Zaroff's narcissism, as his little speech makes obvious, is a compound of love for what he once was, love for what he would like to be, love for someone who was once part of himself, and—quite simply—self-love. He seeks to impress Rainsford with the credentials of his manhood; he knows Rainsford is a world-famous hunter, and he will not be outclassed. And Rainsford is impressed by the mounted trophies of the heads of lions, tigers, elephants, moose, and bears lining the Count's library—until his regard for Zaroff starts turning into fear.

THE TROPHY ROOM

Rainsford declines his host's invitation to view his newest collection of heads, with the excuse that he is feeling unwell. Zaroff's "trophy room" certainly stands as gruesome testimony of Leverenz's observation that *there can never be enough* evidence of power, where power is felt as narcissistic compensation.[46] There, in the dank bowels of his fortress, Zaroff keeps the bodies of the men he has killed in his pursuit of manhood.

In an article on "Trophy-Hunting as a Trope of Manhood in Ernest Hemingway's *Green Hills of Africa*," Thomas Strychacz explains the function of the hunter's trophy. The hunter's manhood is not of an essence, but rather must be represented in a theater of signs: "Trophy-display reveals manhood to be a performance created out of the relationship between the hunter, his display, and his audience, rather than a permanent characteristic of special men."[47]

When Zaroff mentions his career as a Cossack cavalry officer, he implies his mastery of the horse and authority over men. "Manhood begins," Leverenz reminds us, "as a battlefield code, to make men think twice before turning and running, as any sensible man would do."[48] As a short-term defensive strategy in competitive situations, it is useful. But as Zaroff's example illustrates, when manhood becomes an ideology designed to control fear, it can become a way of magnifying and repressing fear so deeply as to create a monstrous passion to dominate.[49]

As a narrator's fantasy, Zaroff's passion for mastery, fused with sexuality, is pornographic. (To paraphrase Gore Vidal: the one theme that recurs throughout all pornography is that of the man or woman who manages to capture another human being for use as an unwilling sexual object.)[50] The fantasy of *The Most Dangerous Game* is predicated on its remote setting,

FIGURE 3.5 The one theme that recurs throughout all pornography is that of the man or woman who manages to capture another human being for use as an unwilling sexual object. (Zaroff locks Rainsford in a restraining brace.)

where even the island's sole landowner has heard of Rainsford, the legendary hunter, and where Zaroff, for his part in the narrator's fantasy of feudal absolutes, has almost total control over the island's small society. It is perhaps inevitable that Zaroff's game should become sadistic.

When Leverenz writes that manhood functions to preserve self-control, we recall in the short story Zaroff's remark to Rainsford: "I have heard that in America business men often go to pieces when they give up the business that has been their life. . . . I had no wish to go to pieces" (79). Zaroff's scar is a reminder of the fragility of subjectivity (as even a fortress—like the one Zaroff lives in—can fall or be battered to pieces, and must be rebuilt); of how easy it is for a man to be maimed or die (as the sailors are torn to pieces by sharks at the beginning of the film). When Rainsford in the short story admires a particularly impressive Cape buffalo head mounted in the library, Zaroff describes how the animal "hurled me against a tree . . . fractured my skull" (78). The reader may wonder what it is that Zaroff, as a hunter of men, unconsciously hopes a man will do to him in a hunt. The scene in the film in which he explains how he was scarred is extraordinarily revealing of the nature and origins of Zaroff's desire. While the scar on Zaroff's left temple is proposed consciously as a symbol of his madness, it serves as a reminder that oedipal subjectivity is predicated on a fear of castration.[51]

KINDRED SPIRITS

When Zaroff in the film reveals that he is a hunter, Rainsford's response is diffident, almost insulting. Zaroff replies more forcefully: "We are kindred spirits! It is my one passion!" Zaroff wants desperately for Rainsford to acknowledge that they are alike; but only when Rainsford finally discovers what is in his host's trophy room does he understand what the stakes are, and why Zaroff finds him fascinating. As Strychacz observes, "Acquiring and displaying trophies . . . creates a relationship with other men that is profoundly sexual in the sense that it informs the construction of the masculine self accurately measurable against the other's 'manhood.'" The hunter's trophies, as complex tropes for masculine identity, represent the inner man's toughness and authority. They are meant to signify his phallic power.[52]

And, as in the pornographic style which resonates with unintended double meanings, the dialogue that follows Zaroff's assertion that he and Rainsford are "kindred spirits" sounds rather like an invitation from a vampire or homosexual to go cruising. Martin Trowbridge warns Rainsford: "He sleeps all day and hunts all night. And what's more, Rainsford, he'll have you doing the same thing!"

"We'll have capital sport together, I hope!" says the Count.

"Don't encourage him!" says Trowbridge.

The Count won't be stopped. He wants to tell Rainsford about the scar: "It was in Africa that the Cape buffalo gave me this . . . " (he draws his hand tenderly across the scar). "It still bothers me sometimes," he growls. "One night, as I lay in my tent with this . . . this head of mine, a terrible thought crept like a snake into my brain: *hunting was beginning to bore me!*" Looking steadily at her agitated host, Eve asks, "Is that such a terrible thought, Count?" It is significant that a woman should ask this question. She is asking, in effect, why he could not direct his libidinal energies toward women, the conventional object-choice for a man.

Zaroff is pacing about the room now: "It *is* [a terrible thought], my dear lady, when hunting has been the whip for all other passions. When I lost my love of hunting, I lost my love of life, . . . of *love!*"

Contrary to the implications of his remark, hunting is not merely the "whip" (i.e., the fetish) for all Zaroff's other passions. It *is* his passion. As Neal King contends in *Heroes in Hard Times*, his lively study of the cop action movie genre, repression/displacement arguments tell of "homoerotic currents diverted into a violence supposedly less sexy," when really that violence itself is the "erotic rush."[53] Cop action movies should not be viewed as "panicked engines of repressed desire," he tells us, and the "sodomite violence" and "deviant male bonding" that characterize the genre should not be seen as standing in for something else: "If Martin of *Lethal Weapon 2* says that he will fuck a man's ass, later takes it in the thigh with a large knife, rams the blade back into his opponent's chest, and then drops a trailer on him with a happy smile, then maybe that's the sort of fucking Martin likes to do" (177). King notes that one finds conventional "sex" in cop action movies, to be sure, although not often, "and viewers so inclined might find pleasure in either the domestic caresses between male cop and female lover or the gentler moments between sidekick and cop," but this does not mean we should interpret the genre as antihomosexual at heart: "If we take them at their words, then most of the 'fucking' takes place between male couples. This is their sexuality. This is what they want. This is how they live and die hard" (177).

And so it is with Zaroff and Rainsford's desire in *The Most Dangerous Game*—the hunt *is* their sexuality: which is why the viewer who takes seriously Eve's function in *The Most Dangerous Game* as the ultimate prize, the hero's reward (what Zaroff rather incongruously calls "love"), has it all wrong. "Love"—even when the word is used by the Count, as one of the attempts to heterosexualize the film's logic—is presumably meant to denote heterosexual, romantic love(making), but it is nowise an appropriate term to describe the desire that fuels the narrative.

What Zaroff has lost is the ability to see himself in the eyes of a woman. His sense of self is in perpetual danger of fragmenting. Only a strenuous effort of control—figured as a sadistic hunt—keeps him from falling apart. There are several indications that Eve doesn't much interest Zaroff. What clearly interests him is Rainsford: he sees in the younger man his ideal self. When Zaroff suddenly stops playing the piano, it is because he feels that Rainsford is paying Eve too much attention, so he sends her off to bed. He may be trying to get Rainsford alone, but he is left with Martin Trowbridge, who only wants yet another drink.

Trowbridge's flabby heterosexuality is disgusting to Zaroff, who is more excited by Rainsford, for reasons acknowledged by the narrative, and for other reasons unconsciously expressed. Trowbridge invites the Count to his camp in the Adirondacks, where they'll "have a private car, liquor and girls on the trip, and the guys will make the deers behave!" Zaroff pulls away, saying, "I think we'd better change the subject." Later, when Eve encounters Zaroff in his trophy room with her brother's dead body, Zaroff again has her removed from the scene, in order—it would seem—to be alone with Rainsford, who is this time strapped helplessly in a brace that would render him powerless to prevent Zaroff from using him as an unwilling sexual victim. Here, as Freud reminds us, we see how *man is a wolf to man*. He is an aggressive creature who will use his neighbor: "to exploit his capacity for work without compensation, to use him sexually without his consent, to seize his possessions, to humiliate him, to cause him pain, to torture and to kill him. *Homo homini lupus*."[54]

That Zaroff's drive for mastery has been fused with sexuality is very clear in the scene of his final confrontation with Rainsford. Zaroff believes him to be dead, but he reappears—in the Freudian analogy, like a "return of the repressed"—at the very spot where Zaroff first saw him and asked him, with barely suppressed excitement, if he was the sole survivor of the shipwreck. This time, the Count exclaims in surprise, "Why, you're not even wounded!" As a fantasy of phallic potency, Rainsford lives up to Zaroff's unconscious desire for what follows.

The final scene of the short story occurs, as earlier noted, in a bedroom. It appears that Rainsford confronts Zaroff just as he is about to get into bed, and that Zaroff dies in the struggle that presumably ensues. Earlier, when

Zaroff had been so sure that Rainsford would not prevail in the hunt, he made Rainsford promise—should he win—"to say nothing of your visit here" (85). The illicit quality that this phrase lends Zaroff's proposal is, we see, confirmed and amplified at the end.

In the movie, the struggle between Rainsford and Zaroff is visually extraordinary, confirming the homoerotic implications abundantly present in the short story. Zaroff tries to shoot Rainsford with his Tartar bow, but Rainsford lunges forward and grabs the Count's arm. They writhe for a few moments in a sort of macabre parody of a tango, Zaroff clutching the arrow in his right hand. Rainsford twists Zaroff's right arm around, and Zaroff is stabbed in the back with his own arrow. They are pressed against each other at the groin; Zaroff places his left hand on Rainsford's right shoulder and throws back his head, as if in ecstasy. The camera cuts to a medium close-up of Zaroff's sweating face, and for a moment he stops struggling, as he looks into Rainsford's eyes. For a moment longer, they hold each other in this deadly embrace. Then Zaroff goes limp, and he falls to the floor.

FIGURE 3.6 Zaroff is stabbed by his own arrow in this mortal embrace.

If, as Kristeva writes, "abjection is nothing more than a flaw in Oedipus' impossible sovereignty, a flaw in his knowledge,"[55] we might see Rainsford's experience of abjection on Zaroff's island as the flaw in the impossible identity he claims when he announces that, "Luckily, I'm a hunter, and nothing can ever change that." He is forced by the hunt to recognize himself as mortal, and becomes subject to the symbolic order. Zaroff's mortal lesson is the same: while he might call himself a hunter, he can also be hunted. Furthermore, his homosexuality becomes exemplary of the truth of desire itself. As in one of Lacan's formulations, the homosexual subject

> exhausts himself in pursuing the desire of the other, which he will never be able to grasp as his own desire, because his own desire is the desire of the other. It is himself whom he pursues. . . . The intersubjective relation which subtends perverse desire is only sustained by the annihilation either of the desire of the other, or of the desire of the subject. It can only be grasped at the limit. . . . In the one as in the other, this relation dissolves the being of the subject.[56]

The paradox is this: if Zaroff hunts his own image in the mirror, he is both hunter *and* hunted. And if he "wins" this deadly game, he will at last—to use his own word—have known *ecstasy*.

4

FRIENDSHIP AND ITS DISCONTENTS
The Outlaw

Outlaw, The (1943), 115m. *** Dir: Howard Hughes. Jane Russell, Jack Beutel, Walter Huston, Thomas Mitchell, Mimi Aguglia, Joe Sawyer. Notorious "sex western" (and Russell's ballyhooed screen debut) is actually compelling—if offbeat—story of Billy the Kid, with principal honors going to Huston as Doc Holliday. Filmed in 1941 and directed mostly by Howard Hawks, though Hughes' interest in Russell's bosom is more than evident. Some prints run 95m. and 103m., but no one seems to have uncensored 117m. version.[1]

Sixty years after it was made, *The Outlaw* is still described in film dictionaries as a notorious "sex western," and always with a reference to Jane Russell's bosom. And yet it is overwhelmingly obvious that the movie is scarcely about Russell's bosom at all, in the sense that her character's sexuality is integral to the plot. Rather, it is about the complications that arise when Doc Holliday (Walter Huston) falls in love with Billy the Kid (Jack Beutel), and Pat Garrett (Thomas Mitchell) becomes jealous of the bond that develops between the two men. What Leonard Maltin describes as the offbeat quality of the story derives from the homoerotic dynamics of the narrative, which are displaced and contained by a number of strategies that attempt, contradictorily, to celebrate and deny the nature of the passionate interest the men take in each other.

Edward Buscombe in *The BFI Companion to the Western* acknowledges that *The Outlaw* is "generally credited with introducing sex into the western,"[2] but only Parker Tyler, among major critics, has ever pointed out that the proper locus of the film's sexuality is not embodied in Jane Russell as Rio MacDonald, but is played out in the relationship between the two men (and their horse);[3] and only David Thomson, who describes *The Outlaw* as "that mistreated vagrant," has identified the movie as "the first American film to suggest that homosexuality might be pleasant."[4] Thomson does allow that "the cinematography of breasts was thrust forward by *The Outlaw*, as was the medium's creative teasing of prudery and censorship," and suggests that Russell was "a very amiable, amused woman," whose tongue-in-cheek sexiness redounds to the film's considerable charm. But he also tells us: "Hughes's record shows that he endorsed Russell's blatant and honest reckoning of sexual pleasure, and at the same time looked on it as a joke" (356)—which possibly accounts, at least in part, for the film's decidedly mixed tone, which is on the whole frank and sexy, sometimes camp, occasionally irritating in its attempts to be funny, and finally very moving.

The Outlaw is famous in the history of film exhibition for its prolonged and salacious publicity campaign, which was masterminded, at Hughes's behest, by Russell Birdwell, who had designed and handled a similarly over-the-top publicity campaign for *Gone with the Wind*.[5] The campaign for *The Outlaw* included a variety of billboards and posters of a "mean . . . moody . . . magnificent" Jane Russell lying in a seductive pose on a mound of hay, a leather whip (or gun) in her hand, with a tag line asking the viewer: "How would you like to tussle with Russell?" Even today, the film is advertised in such a way as to intentionally obscure what it is about; and publicists, who appear not to have seen the film before writing their copy, still blatantly misrepresent the plot. For example, on the box of the videotape released in 1993 by Front Row Entertainment, Inc., Jane Russell is described as being "the main interest of [Billy, Doc, and Pat]. When they meet at a way station they quarrel over the beautiful half-breed."

Although it was Hughes's stated intention to make a sexy superwestern, it is not clear how conscious he and his collaborators were during the making of the film of the extent to which its main interest is not the fragile subplot of heterosexual attraction between Billy and Rio, but the one articulated by the themes of male friendship and homosexual infatuation. George Fenin and William Everson note in their landmark book *The Western* that, at the time of *The Outlaw*'s release, many opponents of the film were angered not so much by its "obtrusive eroticism" (i.e., the part played by "Russell's bosom . . . enhanced by an ingenious 'heaving' brassière designed by Howard Hughes"), but by "the minimal *importance of the woman*, even on a sexual level."[6] They note that "there is no sincerely motivated love story" in the film, but judge that its "long trail of censorship hassles and the fact that it *did* deliver the goods it advertised tended to obscure the fact that it was really a good western in its own right."[7]

FIGURE 4.1 One of the posters used in *The Outlaw*'s prolonged and salacious publicity campaign.

The Outlaw, however, is an unusual western because all the ways in which, as J. Hoberman has put it, the cowboy movie was used as the typical vehicle for America "to explain itself to itself" are questions posed and answered by the film *in a psychological register*: "Who makes the law? What is the order? Where is the frontier? Which ones are the good guys? Why is it that a man's gotta do what a man's gotta do—and how does he do it?"[8]

"A Man's Gotta Settle Down Sometime"

Although Rio is not the main interest of Billy, Doc, and Pat, as the film's advertising would have us believe, the desire of the three men is indeed triangulated. In most films in which these historical figures appear as characters (Doc Holliday the gambler and former dentist, Pat Garrett the sheriff, and Billy the Kid, aka William Bonney, the cowboy and outlaw), it is in fact the friendship between Doc Holliday and lawman Wyatt Earp that is inflected with homoerotic tensions, and that is centrally important among the films' themes and strands of plot, leading to the gunfight at the O.K. Corral (the best of these films being John Ford's *My Darling Clementine*, 1946; John Sturges's *Gunfight at the O.K. Corral*, 1957; and George P. Cosmatos's *Tombstone*, 1993; with the most recent major film to treat the friendship between Holliday and Earp being Lawrence Kasdan's *Wyatt Earp*, 1994).

In movies that focus on Billy the Kid, however, Doc Holliday does not appear, and the central relationship is between Garrett, as sheriff of Lincoln County, and Billy, the convicted outlaw. The two most well-known and interesting among these films are still Arthur Penn's first feature, *The Left-Handed Gun*, 1958 (based on a 1955 *Philco Playhouse* TV play by Gore Vidal),[9] which portrays Billy as a charismatic, misunderstood teenager in need of love, who seeks eye-for-an-eye justice for the murder of his kind and fatherly cattle-boss John Tunstall; and Sam Peckinpah's *Pat Garrett and Billy the Kid* (1973). Both accounts of Billy the Kid's life, as the title of Peckinpah's film suggests, focus on the (ambiguous and ambivalent) friendship between the young outlaw and the lawman charged with bringing him in. *The Outlaw* is thus additionally unusual in its pairing of Billy the Kid and Doc Holliday.

In *The Outlaw*, the theme of friendship is announced immediately, as are the questions of who makes the law, what is the order, and where is the frontier. When Pat Garrett, recently made sheriff, hears that Doc Holliday has arrived in town, he dismisses his deputy's suggestion that he not go alone to meet the eccentric and famously erratic, sharp-shooting gambler: "I'm not going to make any trouble for Doc Holliday. *He's my best friend!* As long as I'm sheriff around here, the place is his!"

Doc is surprised to learn that Pat has become a sheriff—"You're the last man I ever thought would be so easily satisfied," he says; to which Pat replies: "Well, a man's gotta settle down sometime." Their exchange, like the film's title, refers to an insistently repeated paradigm concerning the law and its transgression. Not only will the plot be motivated by Pat's official duty to arrest and try Billy for the killing of a man in a brawl (Rio's brother, as it turns out), it becomes obvious—when Doc falls in love with Billy—that Pat's "set-tling down" also refers to his sexual complacency, which Doc finds intolera-ble. Doc's outlaw desire finds an object in Billy, and the main drama of the narrative will turn on this question of whether the sexual frontier is still open for Doc, or whether advancing age and the commitments and responsibili-ties of old friendship will be experienced as a closing of the frontier, a relin-quishing of any stake in its youthful promise of polymorphous possibilities.

"The western doesn't have anything to do with the West as such," Jane Tompkins argues in *West of Everything*: "It isn't about the encounter be-tween civilization and the frontier. It is about men's fear of losing their mas-tery, and hence their identity, both of which the western tirelessly rein-vents."[10] Certainly this is true of *The Outlaw* and the character of Doc Holliday, whose sense of his masculine identity is tied up with his attrac-tiveness to other men, and who admits that he is terrified of "dying in bed." Although I would agree with Douglas Pye that Tompkins's "desire to make the western monolithically about gender pushes a brilliant argument to a polemical extreme," and that "the cultural meanings of the western cannot be restricted to a single theme,"[11] I nevertheless intend in the following pages to focus on gender in a similarly exclusive manner, to argue that *The Outlaw* is the first major western to acknowledge the sexuality and subjec-tivity of its heroes as the film's dominant themes, articulating them in terms of melodrama.

The transgressive potential of the intimate bond that develops between Doc and Billy (outlaws both) comes into conflict with the conception of friendship held by Pat (the official representative of civil law at the frontier), in a way that strongly resembles the central conflict in that ur-text of the twentieth-century western, Owen Wister's *The Virginian* (the novel was pub-lished in 1902, and film adaptations were made in 1914, 1923, 1929, 1946, and 2000).[12] In the 1914 film, the Virginian is described in an intertitle as "fear-less and strong," and as having "for his best friend the easily led, lovable Steve." Further along in the narrative, we are told that "Steve, the weakling, falls into bad habits," namely cattle rustling; and when the Virginian is made to confront the fact that his best friend is an outlaw, he is asked by the men who will form the posse to capture the rustlers: "You ain't goin' to let friend-ship for Steve stand in the way of Justice, are you?"

In the 1929 version of *The Virginian*, starring Gary Cooper, the Virginian runs into Steve after not having seen him for four years, and during their conversation over a drink in a saloon, asks his old friend: "Ain't you ever gonna settle down?" Steve replies: "Me? Quit your laughing! Why should I?"

A saloon dancer appears at this point in the scene and throws herself in a provocative manner across the bar counter, suggesting that Steve intends to remain heterosexually promiscuous; but the trajectory of the Virginian's evolving (sexual) subjectivity will be revealed to entail a dire form of repression, according to which he must kill the wild and free sexuality in himself (represented by Steve), if he is to achieve the proper, adult—i.e., monogamously heterosexual—identity that will enable him to marry Molly Wood, the newly arrived schoolteacher from Vermont.

When the Virginian discovers Steve putting the villain Trampas's brand on a calf that does not belong to him, he tries to explain to his old friend that there is a difference between what is "loco" and what is "plain wrong," and that, "Times, they are a-changin'": "I reckon I couldn't be sore at you, no matter what you did. But listen, Steve, you and I have been friends too long to find ourselves lined up on opposite sides in anything like this. Don't put me in any hole like that!" Steve responds by complaining that "this country is getting too civilized!"

When Steve is eventually caught and hanged for his cattle-rustling, the Virginian's grief is overwhelming. Shortly after the hanging, which is overseen by the Virginian as leader of the posse, the Virginian is shot by Trampas, and—in a delayed displacement of the emotion he could not admit he feels about his friend's death—he falls unconscious. During his convalescence, which Molly insists on supervising, even though she has been implacably opposed to the frontier justice that requires Steve's death, the Virginian slips into a delirium and can be heard moaning: "I warned you, Steve! I warned you! How could you have done this to me?"

Molly's anguished attempts in this scene to soothe the unhappy hero are perhaps even more telling than his delirium, of the sense that something passionate, almost carnal, and illicit, is being repressed in order that the couple might have a future as man and wife: "It's all right, darling! It's all right! I'm trying to understand. Let's never talk about it . . . never let it come between us . . . *forget it ever happened!*"

When the Virginian recovers (Molly having thus decided she will stay in Wyoming and marry him after all), a scene follows which confirms the notion that the drama involving Steve represented a struggle in the hero between homosexual and heterosexual impulses. We see the Virginian's friends come to inform him that Trampas is back, and when they find him with Molly, they ask her permission to talk to him privately. The Virginian turns to Molly and asks: "You don't mind my goin' with them, do you, honey?" To which she replies: "Of course not. The boys have their right to you just as much as I have."

My interpretation of the emotional-sexual logic of Steve's role in *The Virginian* (the films) is the same one made by Tompkins in her elegant psycho-biographical analysis of Wister's novel:

> The death of Steve is the price the hero pays for becoming successful, being foreman, getting money for a ranch, acquiring authority. His own legitimation and Steve's death are inseparable. Everything Steve stands for is forbidden—same-sex love, breaking the laws of property, being physical and devil-may-care—so in killing Steve, Wister is stamping out something in himself. Not a desire to steal or to have sex with other men, necessarily, but the courage to transgress, whatever form it might take.[13]

The marriage of the frontier hero to the heroine from the East is the novel's way of resolving East-West tensions in the modernizing of America, and after *The Virginian* this figure becomes one of the mainstays of the western genre. In *The Outlaw*, Billy does ride off with Rio in the final shots of the film, but the meanings produced by this heterosexual coupling (for whatever such a "tacked-on" ending is worth) are radically different, not least because Rio represents "sexuality," unlike Molly and all heroines from "Back East" who follow her and who tend to represent the values of Christianity and Civilization.

When Leslie Fiedler wrote in *Love and Death in the American Novel* of "the pure marriage of males" that can be found so often in American literature, he was referring to a union in which the male is bound "in life-long loyalty to a help-meet, without the sacrifice of his freedom."[14] It is "sexless and holy, a kind of counter-matrimony": "The very end of the pure love of male for male is to *outwit* woman, that is, to keep her from trapping the male through marriage into civilization and Christianity. The wilderness Eros is, in short, not merely an anti-cultural, but an anti-Christian, a Satanic Eros" (210).

But there is a sense in which we cannot assert unequivocally that the developing bond between Doc and Billy is, or will be, a sexless and holy thing. The energizing subtexts of *The Outlaw* are precisely what give the film its interest; and when Pat describes Doc as "my best friend," we are encouraged to consider the possibility that their friendship (at least during its early years, when they were young men Billy's age) included a sexual element. There is, as Pam Cook observes, "a potential perversity at the heart of the [western] genre, [a] regressive drive to elude the law of the father, to play forbidden games,"[15] and there is no doubt that *The Outlaw* is the first film in the genre to have done so in a flamboyant, self-conscious manner, confirming with outrageous directness what westerns have always implied—"that relation-ships between men are more satisfying or at least more worthy of narrative attention than relationships between men and women."[16]

As the first *modern* western, *The Outlaw* grapples with the notion that, while the friendship between Pat and Doc was undoubtedly a powerful thing, Doc—in falling in love with Billy—undergoes some sort of change of value. He appears to exchange a "best friend" for a lover, which would make *The Outlaw* Hollywood's first "coming out" story. But the film does not *neces-sarily* mean to suggest that Doc is a latent homosexual, who discovers the "truth" of his desire during a desublimating midlife crisis. Rather, the ho-mosexual motif seems to occur almost by default because the filmmakers no longer know how to represent a great friendship between men.

By the 1940s in America, romantic love (outside of agonistic settings, like war) begins to be the only form of male-male intimacy possible—which is to say, an impossibility.[17] There are several reasons for this—as Peter Murphy observes in a useful essay entitled, "Friendship's Eu-topia": "Moderns un-derstand the intimacy of love but not the amity of friendship":

> Friendship is not a trope of the modern world. It fits at best uneasily into a modernity created by Northern Europe—a North whose hand-maidens (the Protestant Reformation, the sovereign nation-state, the Industrial Revolution, and the reach of global communications) ush-ered in an unprecedented social formation. For sure, "friendship" is part of the vocabulary of moderns, who pirated the idea . . . for their own purposes. But moderns have used the word as shorthand for a multitude of relationships with only a passing similarity to true friend-ship. A friend in modern times might be an acquaintance, a colleague, a buddy, a mate, an amicable neighbor, a love interest, or a patron. While not all of these relationships are utilitarian (in Aristotle's sense), neither are they true friendships. They are just relationships that have a certain casual amity about them.[18]

The Outlaw is shot through with nostalgia and a sense of yearning for "the lost possibility of friendship in a deracinated world"[19] (for all his limitations as an actor, Jack Beutel vividly conveys this in his eyes). Friendship, Murphy reminds us, "takes time," and in the modern world, time is costly.

One imagines that *The Outlaw*'s director—a strange, "lonely" figure who became legendarily reclusive toward the end of his life—was drawn to filmmaking in Hollywood partly because it offered the possibility of a sense of community. (There is a scene in the 1998 film *Gods and Monsters*, in which the young man who has befriended James Whale in old age asks the former director if he misses working in the film business, and Whale replies: "Making movies is the most wonderful thing in the world—*working with friends*, entertaining people. Yes, I suppose I miss it.")[20] And yet we know that production of *The Outlaw* frequently languished because Hughes spent most of his time and energies at his aircraft plant, developing military aircraft with the object of winning government contracts.[21]

Murphy suggests that friendship involves the sharing of a cause:

> Friends stand to each other not directly but through the medium of the Great Idea. They are not *two halves*; they are not *equals*. They do not look at one another and see their "other half" matching them eye to eye, with each one finishing the other's sentences, enjoying the same tastes, coming from the same sort of background, and searching through life for the same sort of outcomes. No, friendship is a more subtle, and at the same time more powerful, relationship than that of equals. Friends are often quite different, yet in one important respect they are "equalized" (made the same), namely, by their relationship to the Great Idea.[22]

The cause, or Great Idea, shared by Doc and Pat can only be inferred—as having had something to do with their youth (as we see it projected in the aura surrounding Billy)—in much the same way that, twenty years after *The Outlaw*, the "cause" uniting the two friends in *One-Eyed Jacks* (1961; directed by and starring Marlon Brando) must be inferred, *après coup*. The theme in both films of lost friendship/youth is the same: "Rio" (Brando) and "Dad" Longworth (Karl Malden) are best friends, until they have a falling out. Years later, when they meet up again in Monterey, where Dad is now sheriff, Dad invites Rio to have dinner with him and his wife and stepdaughter, Louisa:

> *Rio:* Dad and I go way back. I wasn't anything more than a kid when Dad picked me up . . . We was kinda hairy in them days . . .
> *Dad:* Oh, that's all right kid—everybody around here knows I used to be on the other side of the law. Yeah! We were a couple of cockleburs, we were, huh? We had a lot of fun, didn't we!
> *Rio:* Always full of laughs, Dad!
> [. . .]

Dad: Of course, that was a long time ago . . .
Louisa: You were a bank robber, Mr. Rio?
Rio: Yes, ma'am—me and your Dad, here.
Louisa: But, no more?
Dad: No more.

On the simplest level of interpretation, these films suggest that the great friendship breaks up because one of the men changes (evolves or regresses) and the other does not. Or that a man's character does not fully reveal itself until youth is past; and friendships formed in youth may not survive a man's maturity. Or that the Great Idea lacked flexibility. In any event, as movies they allow viewers to have it both ways—to see their ideological convictions both confirmed and subverted—for it is not Pat Garrett or "Dad" Longworth whom we are invited to admire (for becoming sheriffs and ostensibly moving to the right side of the law), but rather Doc Holliday (and Billy), and the Ringo Kid ("Rio"). As Philip French succinctly puts it in his description of *One-Eyed Jacks* (a study of the relationship between two former friends, with its "suggestions of homosexuality"), one "retained his integrity as an outlaw" and the other "revealed his weakness and hypocrisy through taking a job as lawman in a settled community."[23]

THE "CUTEST LITTLE FELLAH YOU EVER SAW"

When Pat Garrett comes to the hotel to meet his old friend Doc Holliday, the scene begins in a shot that is characteristic of Gregg Toland's deep-focus cinematography. Doc is in the foreground, completing his toilette at a mirror, as Pat enters the frame in the far background of the shot, pushes open the swing doors to the saloon, and strides forward past the bar, through an antechamber, and into Doc's room—the modulated sound perspective of "Camptown Races" playing somewhere on a piano in the saloon, and the enfilade giving Pat's entry a blustering, erotic energy appropriate to the occasion.

It is immediately obvious that Doc is a dandy. The historical Doc Holliday would have been a relatively young man at this point in his life, since he lived only to the age of thirty-five. But as played by fifty-six-year-old Walter Huston, he is a man accustomed to getting what he wants (by a combination of bold charm, cunning, and skill with a gun), but perhaps experiencing for the first time—and not without anxiety—a certain diminution of his sex appeal.

Thomson's description of Huston as "one of those actors who seem to hide most of their feelings and thoughts," and his insight that "as a cinematic method it has no equal,"[24] suggest an apt match of actor and role in *The Outlaw*, particularly in the presentation of Doc as a gambler.

Buscombe quotes Bernard Eisenschitz in *Le Western* as saying the gambler "introduces into a heroic cinema the possibilities of the anti-hero, the attraction of vice and corruption, presented under the fascinating cover of the seducer."[25] Buscombe also notes that the gambler in western fiction is usually fastidious about his clothes, "but the fancy waistcoat and bootlace tie will not immediately gain him respect as a real man; he has to earn the title" (127). And so it is in the articulation of Doc's character, who sets himself the challenge of seducing Billy without forfeiting his right to be called a man (in a world that would define the homosexual as not-masculine).

Doc apparently has a formidable reputation, which we infer from a comment made by Pat's deputy during the movie's first exchange of dialogue ("Well, I certainly wouldn't want to fool around with him alone!"), but his theatricality—and in other movies, his intellectuality, consumptive cough, or alcoholism—suggests a deviation from the classic codes of ideal western masculinity, some hidden fracture in his psyche, which the actor serves well in the role: "Huston lacked the raw material to be a star," Thomson observes: "He was not beautiful; he was forty-six before he made his first film; he never entirely gave up Broadway for Hollywood. [And] above all, he was never ingratiating." But he is, Thomson adds, "a constantly interesting actor."[26]

The two friends, grinning broadly, are clearly delighted to see each other. "You're lookin' plenty sassy!" Doc says, as he pinches Pat's cheek: "You wintered kind of fat, didn't you?" Doc's remark signals a dominant theme, or motif, of all westerns—masculine display: that the genre is essentially about men looking at men. Much has been written about this aspect of the western—"a genre that ever denies it is doing what it does: gazing at the male body"[27]—but the film stands out as the genre's first in which the male look at another male is explicitly acknowledged (in a sustained motif) as an index of his sexual viability vis-à-vis other men.

That our first look at Doc should find him standing in front of a mirror—we see a tall, handsome man wearing a white shirt with silver cufflinks, plaid pants, a gun at each hip, and sporting a bootlace tie; he has thick, luxuriant hair—is a hint that he, not the Kid, may turn out to be the real outlaw of the film. Dandyism, Martin Pumphrey says, is a sign of potential threat, an indicator of a "dangerous otherness" that implies "the essential weakness of the urban villain" and "gives warning of his erratic selfishness":[28]

For a man to betray a desire to be looked at (to make himself a willing object of the gaze) is to transgress the natural order of the genre. Though the hero may be distinguished by style, cleanliness and appearance, he cannot be seen to invite the pleasure-seeking gaze of other characters. Equally, although he is the focus of narrative attention, he cannot be explicitly transformed into an object for the spectator's (potentially erotic) contemplation. Thus conflicting imperatives make the two extremes of bodily display, nakedness and dandyism, sources of confusion and anxiety. (54)

It comes as a surprise, nonetheless, that officially Doc will be the villain of the story. Indeed, there remains throughout the film an uneasy sense that the moral occult is in trouble—that basic moral imperatives are never properly clarified (in a film driven by emotional imperatives)—because hero and villain, if they can be so called, are constructed not so much in opposition but as versions of each other; and Pat, the unjustly treated lawman, starts to seem like the bad guy. The historical Pat Garrett, contrary to the ending of *The Outlaw*, shot Billy the Kid at Fort Sumner, New Mexico, on July 14, 1881— and as Buscombe points out, "since almost all films about Billy the Kid have made the Kid a hero, Garrett's pursuit of him has been viewed with, at best, mixed feelings."[29]

Doc is on the prowl, as it were. He tells Pat that somebody has stolen his horse, "a little strawberry roan . . . cutest little fellah you ever saw. Mean as mean . . . but I dote on him, like he was pure rock candy!" (There is no question that this dialogue has a sexual meaning, just as—when Doc asks him what he'll have to drink—Pat says, with odd gravity: "Well, I started with rye, and I don't see no cause to change!") Doc invites Pat to join him in a deal, and Pat responds by revealing, in a rather curious gesture, that now he is a sheriff—to indicate that his days of doing anything illegal, or joining Doc in search of the cutest little fellah you ever saw, are over: he looks Doc in the eye and slowly pulls his leather vest aside, to show the sheriff's badge pinned to his belt. The camera cuts to a close-up of the area just above his groin, and Doc bends down ostentatiously to get a closer look. The film thus establishes that the two men (and Billy, when he is introduced into the narrative a few moments later) have an overdetermined relationship to the law, not just the law of the frontier, exercised by guns or sheriffs, but also the law in its various registers of sexual connotation.

The scene in which Doc meets Billy is extraordinary. For Doc, certainly, it is love at first sight. Finding his horse in front of "the dentist's place" (a reference to Doc's former profession), he goes up to it, as Billy just then emerges from the building. We know immediately—from Robert Warshow's dictum that "a hero is one who looks like a hero"[30]—that Billy, the outlaw of the film's title, is the hero: he appears like a dream figure, a slender, beautiful young man in full cowboy rig, the answer to Doc's search for the horse he has just described as "about thirteen hands high, and cute as a bug's ear."

FIGURE 4.2 "About thirteen hands high, and cute as a bug's ear." Billy the Kid (Jack Beutel) and his horse in *The Outlaw*. (Courtesy Photofest)

One of the first critics to acknowledge that "contemplation of the male hero [might] in itself be a substantial source of gratification for a male viewer—as is demonstrated time and time again in the contemporary American cinema's celebration of male couples,"[31] is Paul Willemen, who describes the "fundamentally homosexual voyeurism" (of Anthony Mann's cinema, in which, as in *Man of the West*) "the viewer's experience is predicated on the pleasure of seeing the male 'exist' (that is, walk, move, ride, fight) in or through cityscapes, landscapes or, more abstractly, history."[32] In his 1980 book *Genre*, Stephen Neale takes up Willemen's point, suggesting that the western's invitation is essentially to a male viewer, since its conventions seem to function precisely "to privilege, examine, and celebrate the body of the male."[33] The genre is obsessed with definitions of masculinity, and "the erotic component of the look at the male is caught in a dialectical movement between the male as ideal father on the one hand and the male as symbolic father on the other, these functions being either mapped onto the hero himself or distributed variously across a series of male roles" (59). *The Outlaw*, as if to announce the end of the traditionally "innocent" address of the western and to acknowledge the homosexual voyeurism at the heart of the genre, presents Billy as the object of Doc's gaze, a pinup for which we have been prepared by the narrative's overdetermined identification of him with his horse. And Billy, although he tries to conceal it, is quite obviously dazzled by the older man.

If, as Pye asserts (echoing Neale), the postwar western derives much of its intensity from the constant negotiation of the opposition between two conceptions of the hero, "the ahistorical or mythic and the historical and human,"[34] Billy stands out as a fantasy figure, an ideal ego for the vain, aging, all-too-human Doc Holliday. Moreover, Jane Gaines and Charlotte Herzog have it right when they comment that

> It is difficult to imagine a male costume that lends itself more to eroticization than that of the western gunfighter, and it is not surprising that the iconography of the low-slung, skin-tight trousers and the cocked hat, the texturing of raw and smooth cowhide, is one of the favorite costume repertoires of gay male pornography, lending itself to fantasies of soft flesh concealed and protected by leather.[35]

Doc squints up at Billy, who is bathed in the strong light of late afternoon.[36] They introduce themselves to each other, exchanging compliments and signaling their mutual attraction in the encoded style of the masculine challenge:

Doc: Nice little horse you got here, sonny.
Billy: I think so.
[. . .]
Doc: My name's Holliday.
Billy: Doc Holliday?
Doc: Yeah.
Billy: I've heard of you.
Doc: Thanks. I don't want to take advantage of you . . .
Billy: Thanks, for a while I thought it'd be the other way 'round.
Doc: What's your name, son?
Billy: Bonney. William Bonney.
Doc: Billy the Kid, huh?
Billy: Still think I stole your horse?
[. . .]
Doc: Now, look, son . . . !
Billy: I hear you're pretty good, Doc.
Doc: That's what I hear about you.

Doc, too, cuts a glamorous figure, and Billy will become enamored of him in equal proportion as Doc reveals his emotional-erotic interest in the Kid. Doc will frequently call him "son," and Billy's friendship with Doc will be marked, according to the oedipal logic of the western, by a dialectical movement between his (erotic) identification with Doc as the ideal father on the one hand, and his wary view of him as the symbolic father on the other.

Throughout the film, the complicated love-play between the two men will revolve around the horse, to which more meanings accrue with every scene in which it appears or is mentioned. What is at stake is each man's masculinity defined and measured by the horse's value, which shifts according to the discourse in play—whether it turns on the man's cunning, his physical prowess, sexual attractiveness, wit, ability to be decisive, flexible, heartless, or kind. Billy is flattered by Doc's interest in him; but he also knows how to bargain with Doc, to get what he wants (a man he can trust; a man he can love). He knows he has what Doc wants (youth, beauty; the possibility of love returned), and knows that until they can finally trust each other and commit themselves to each other in freedom and reciprocity, he must never let Doc forget it. Therefore, when Pat appears on the scene and says rhetorically to Doc: "It's *your* horse, ain't it?" Billy promptly corrects him: "It *was*."

The "Old Stand-by"

As I have suggested, Pat cannot help Doc get back what he has lost. And he does not realize that the friendship he offers Doc has lost the aura it presumably once had of being something special that gave the two friends an endlessly renewed sense of discovery. Doc, however, remains true to his desire; and we will see him abandon his middle-aged friend for the twenty-something cowboy and a chance to relive his youth.

There is a brief scene in the saloon involving a drunk patron waving a gun, and how Pat disarms him is meant to explain how Pat gets by in the world, and why he loses everything in the end. It is offered as an implicit criticism of Pat's political style, and as a comment on the problem of an ill-defined code of friendship as the basis of civil society on the frontier. Pat approaches the drunk man and extends his hand in greeting, and as the man turns to offer his own hand, Pat punches him in the face. A surprised Doc remarks: "You're still using that one, huh?" and Pat replies: "My old stand-by—never has failed, yet."

Of course, it fails Pat in the very next scene, when he tries the ruse on Billy, and Billy punches him first. Pat falls to the ground; and in a gallant attempt to help his friend recover his dignity, Doc quips: "You want to use that only on your friends!" The film, like most westerns, is obsessed with this question of trust between men, and we understand right away (since his handshake cannot be trusted) why Pat will be the loser in the high-stakes contest of first friendship. Although the film glories in the idea of the best friend, it is attracted to and understands more intuitively the sexual-romantic bond that Doc and Billy will forge.

The ideal of first friendship between heroes that the film celebrates is essentially Athenian in its fifth-century simplicity, but as Louis Ruprecht remarks in an article entitled "Homeric Wisdom and Heroic Friendship," the heroic code's simplicity was ultimately its undoing, "since nothing human could ever be so simple."[37] Pat, who has "wintered kind of fat," is no longer a hero in Doc's eyes (assuming he once was). He may remain a friend but cannot expect to be the special friend, the *best* friend. Apparently a subscriber to the principle of "helping friends and harming enemies," Pat offers Doc help against Billy, not realizing that his friend is falling in love with the young man. The situation—because it is emotional rather than moral—is far from simple, and not one that is comprehended by a heroic code of friendship that has its origins in fifth-century Athenian popular morality.

In his discussion of the Ancient Greek term *philia* (usually translated as "friendship"), Ruprecht remarks that *philia* differs from *erôs* in its range and multiplicity, its application to more than one person: "In fact, it would have been unwise to commit oneself too narrowly in one's friendships, particularly in fifth-century Athens, where ostracism and litigation were both complex *social* rituals. In such a setting, one needed friends—lots of friends" (31–32). The frontier setting of the western, at least for those participating in the politics of settlement and the establishment of civil law, is essentially the same in this regard. "Helping friends and harming enemies," in other words, is a radically inadequate credo for a sheriff.

Pat unwisely commits himself too narrowly in his friendships—indeed, not only does Doc appear to be his *only* friend, the two men have not seen each other in quite some time. Moreover, there are hints that his relationship with Doc is marked by sublimation and thwarted desire, and that he lives truly neither by the one code (*philia*) nor the other (*erôs*), which is why he ends up friendless and alone. Despite his being a sheriff (i.e., a member of the settled community, a political person), his capacity for friendship is limited. The film implies, finally, that Pat ought to cultivate the honest handshake; and that as a friend or (would-be) lover, he ought to come clean about his desire. When Pat lectures Billy at the end of the film about the importance of trust, it is really himself that he is talking about: "There you go again, Billy, distrusting a person who's trying to be decent to you! Don't you realize that's your whole trouble? . . . How do you expect to get along with people, when you think every man who holds his hand out to you has a knife behind his back!"

Pat and Doc create an ambivalent and ambiguous ideological tension in the film between two sets of meanings and attitudes, in a way that is typical of the western—which, as Jim Kitses has formulated it, offers a philosophical dialectic through a series of antinomies that cluster thematically under the opposing signs of Civilization and the Wilderness.[38] Like Karl Malden's sheriff in *One-Eyed Jacks*, Pat's character is marked by forms of hypocrisy and compromise associated with Civilization (although Pat is not evil, nor even a villain); whereas Doc is shown refusing to forswear his (homosexual) desire, which is associated with the "mean as mean" (i.e., wild) strawberry roan, and which finds its proper object in Billy, the untamable, sexy, young outlaw.

Pat thinks he is Doc's "best friend," and he believes that friendship's the thing. But, evidently, the causes and ideas to which his friendship with Doc is party are not inexhaustible. When Pat uses his "old stand-by"—first, on the drunk man in the saloon, and then on Billy—Doc's response both times is ironic. To use the terminology of the identity politics of our age, it would seem that Pat, not Doc, is the latent homosexual, the one who lacks the hero's courage to act on his desire (i.e., to be Doc's lover).[39] He substitutes an idea of friendship for the romantic bond that would be more honest and rewarding. If he had a real talent for friendship—if he *understood* friendship—he would be a better sheriff, and his handshake could be trusted. And as for his friendship with Doc, it is just that—a friendship. It is not the passionate and noble thing he would like to think it is. Their friendship has lost its *milieu*, in this sense that Murphy means it when he describes friendship as a relationship "not between two but among three."[40]

The film, however, does not treat Pat merely as a narrative device that keeps the plot moving, nor does it dismiss him as irrelevant to the main drama of the Doc-and-Billy story. We admire him for his dogged fidelity, which in itself can be seen as a form of heroic virtue. Ruprecht discusses Aristotle's description in book 3 of the *Nicomachean Ethics* of the (fifth-century Athenian) virtue of "manliness," or "heroism," or "skill at being a man," and of another virtue he describes as "temperance," or "moderation," or the "skill at being human." Quoting William Arrowsmith, Ruprecht suggests that Sophocles' tragic vision (like Aristotle's moral vision) gives us a "modal contrast" between "the hero (untamable, intransigent, committed to total freedom, even to defying the apparent laws of the world)" and the character who "knows who he is and accepts his metaphysical and even social limitation." Following Aristotle, Ruprecht suggests that to ask which man is more heroic is senseless, for "they embody different, but by no means mutually exclusive, modes of heroic virtue—and our moral task . . . is to celebrate them both."[41]

The Outlaw does not really ask us to choose between Pat and Doc, although, for reasons having to do with mid-twentieth-century popular morality, and for ideological reasons enshrined in Hollywood's Production Code, Pat will live and Doc must die. The film allows that each man's struggle to remain committed to a principle, or code, is heroic in its own way. Doc is not being merely selfish when he goes off with Billy toward the end of the film, but is attempting to remain true to the western's *manly* ideal of total freedom.

"You've Got the Right to Choose Your Friends"

In the typical western plot, Tompkins tells us, "the hero frequently forms a bond with another man—sometimes his rival, more often a comrade—a bond that is more important than any relationship he has with a woman and is frequently tinged with homoeroticism."[42]

The Outlaw, as noted previously, takes this homoerotic element further than any Hollywood western before or since (including *The Hi-Lo Country*, 1998; and discounting spoofs like *Son of Paleface*, 1952). The film represents the developing bond between Doc and Billy as a homosexual romance (in the encoded manner of the Hollywood of its time), and it scarcely bothers to pretend that, in Fiedler's words, it is about a "pure love of male for male," or that "the very end" of their bonding is to "outwit" the woman who would trap one of them through marriage into "civilization and Christianity."

Whether or not the movie wishes us to read the interplay between Doc and Billy as "erotic" or "sexual" (i.e., how we decide, in Eve Sedgwick's phrase, what *counts* as the sexual)[43] is largely beside the point, because it hardly matters in the end—from the point of view of the relation of sexual desire to power—whether a gambler and an outlaw actually do something "sexual" together (or want to, or would, or will, and how often, and how, etc., within the limits of what the film can imagine). The passionate interest between the two men is amply and unambiguously conveyed, and whether we are witnessing the beginning of a great friendship, or a grand romance, or *both*, is—happily—undecidable. The answer to the question, "what difference does the inclusion of sex make"[44] to the relationship between Doc and Billy—now, sixty years after the film was made—is, I think, "not much."

Agnes Heller's remarks in "The Beauty of Friendship" about Aristotle's conception of *prote philia* (i.e., *special* friendship, *first* friendship, *best* friendship) are worth quoting here for the way in which they suggest (to me, at least) how fine the line is between the erotic and the sexual in what becomes first friendship:

> Erotic attraction can occur in an instant, but friendship takes time to develop. . . . [Yet] friends normally also accord significance to the moment of their first meeting, their initial enchantment. This is not yet friendship but something like falling in love. Friendship, after all, develops out of love. Love may not yet be friendship, but first friendship is always love. How else could it be desire? Friendship without erotic attraction (though not in the sense of sexual attraction) is just camaraderie, which has very little to do with first friendship.[45]

When Heller describes the first meeting between friends in terms of erotic attraction, and as something like falling in love, she obviously has a clear idea of what counts as the sexual. We could debate the question, or offer our own definition—as Bill Clinton and the nation did in 1998 when it was discovered that the President of the United States had had some sort of sexual relation(ship) with a twenty-three-year-old White House intern—but I think it is enough to say that *The Outlaw* represents the meeting between Doc and Billy, and the friendship that develops out of it, according to the contemporary Hollywood conventions of representing romance.

Doc follows Billy to the stable where he is putting his horse up for the night. To his delight, Billy learns from Doc that the horse can do tricks. However, the moment Billy begins to feel at ease with Doc, he discovers he has been ambushed. Doc tells him to back up, while he makes the horse walk over and "take those gloves right out of your belt!" (In a gesture that seems sexually threatening, Doc leans forward and flips at the soft, leather gloves tucked into the Kid's pants above his groin.) We watch Billy confidently follow Doc's directive—until he feels Pat's gun pressing into the small of his back. Pat tells him to put his hands up, and as Billy does so, Doc takes the two guns out of the Kid's holsters and fondles them appreciatively. The dialogue seems to thicken the sexually charged atmosphere: "This is something new for you . . . ain't it?" Pat says.

Billy decides to humiliate the two men in return, by casting a slur on Doc's sense of honor, and alluding to their age: "This is something new for you, too, isn't it Doc? . . . The great Doc Holliday . . . getting someone else to help him—and a policeman, at that! [*The smile fades from Doc's lips*] I can hardly believe it! And after the way I've heard people talk about you! Ever since I was in short pants!"

The scene is sexually coded. Although Billy is saying that entrapment is not worthy of Doc, and that he would have thought Doc could get his man on his own, he is covertly trying to flatter Doc, by hinting—in the implicit comparison he makes between the two men (contemptuously calling Pat a "policeman")—that he thinks Doc is still attractive and sexually viable. An embarrassed Pat says gruffly: "That's enough of that!" But Doc's vanity is hurt, and he identifies the hint of flirtation in Billy's jibe. He rushes forward: "Ah, wait a minute, Pat! Well . . . [*He looks at Billy's gun in his hand*]. This thing don't seem to sit right on my stomach no-how."

Pat is incredulous. "What? Doc! You're not going to back out on me!" Doc replies: "I'm afraid I am, Pat. I'd never hear the end of this." The shot is framed in such way that Billy, with his back to Pat and facing Doc, is tightly sandwiched between the two men. Doc places Billy's guns back in his holsters; but as Billy slowly brings down his hands, Pat—still very tense and upset—barks at him: "Hold on! I'm not through with you, yet!"

"Step aside, Doc, he may shoot me in the back," Billy says half seriously, as he brings his hand up to Doc's shoulder in a protective gesture. And then, in one of the film's most shocking sexual allusions, Pat says in a low, strangled voice: "They tell me that's the way you've given it to some of the boys!"

This will mark a major turning point in the relationship between Doc and Billy. Doc defends Billy, saying: "Now, Pat, that's a pretty strong thing to say. I never heard anything like that." (If we go along with the sexual reading: Doc is saying, in effect, that if the rumors of the Kid's homosexuality are true, it's all right with him.) Pat looks at Doc quizzically, wondering whether Doc is really abandoning their alliance. Billy says over his shoulder: "Well, Mr. Garrett, if you believe that, here's your chance to do the same to me." He starts to walk away from the sheriff, pauses, then turns toward Doc. The camera cuts to a close-up of the young man's face. His expression signals his gratitude but also seems to contain elements of desire and fear. Billy is not completely sure if Doc meant what he said, and now *everything* depends on Doc's response. Trying to sound casual, he says: "Coming, Doc?"

Catching the flicker of yearning in Billy's eyes, Doc suddenly realizes that Billy's invitation to join him is genuine. He looks questioningly at Billy, then at Pat—who is rigid with humiliation. Doc looks back at Billy, pauses for a moment, and slowly gives his answer: "Yeah, I think I will."

As the two men walk out of the barn together, the film's music track falls uncharacteristically silent. The scene represents the collapse of Pat's world. What has just happened is nothing short of catastrophic—a divorce: the end of everything he thought he believed in. The camera cuts back to Pat, then returns to Doc and Billy. In a gesture that suggests the older man is gallantly escorting the younger man to safety, Doc falls a step behind Billy, and they walk out into the sunshine of the late afternoon. They pause under a tree, and Billy, turning to face his new friend, reaches into Doc's breast pocket for his tobacco pouch.

As Billy begins to roll a cigarette, Pat marches angrily out of the barn, staring fixedly in front of him, refusing to look at his former friend and the young man who has stolen his heart. He suddenly stops, swings around, and orders them: "I want the two of you out of this town by sundown!" Doc pretends not to understand: "Well, what did *I* do?" Pat looks Doc in the eye and says gravely: "That's all right, Doc. You've got the right to choose your friends."

The *best* friendship, Heller tells us, is a relationship founded on mutual free choice:

> The irresistible drive or desire to be together, to live together, to see each other constantly and never to be separated from one another—in short, everything that Aristotle enumerates among the manifestations of *prote philia*—results from that free and mutual choice. *Desire enters the world and the works of friendship through freedom.* It still remains irresistible. But since this desire grows out of freedom, neither of the two friends wants to resist it, so in this sense it is not irresistible. (11)

The reason Billy and Doc spend most of the movie testing one another, and why each man endeavors with deadly seriousness to prove that he is the other's equal, is that they both understand—notwithstanding Murphy's claim that friends are not equals—that their binding cause is western manliness itself. This is what gives their developing friendship its homosexual or narcissistic dimension, and explains why their flirting is fraught with danger. They are both western "legends," as they acknowledge in their first conversation, and although different (the disparity in age being perhaps the only potentially significant difference between them), they must prove that their legendary reputations are justified. They sense that they are "equalized" by their erotic investment in the same image of masculinity, but before they can trust each other enough to become lovers, they must be assured that they are equals in terms of how their desire positions them in relation to power. The fact that Doc is old enough to be Billy's father, although in itself irrelevant to the conditions of friendship, gives their relationship its oedipal quality and is a possible obstacle to their desire to be both friends *and* lovers. Murphy does concede that friends may be true lovers, but only if they are "coincidentally" equals—otherwise, the relationship will have a doomed and tragic dimension, or "the fiery ice of eroticism will scorch rather than meld them."[46]

"YOU MUST HAVE A GIRL SOMEWHERE!"

Doc and Billy spend their first evening together playing cards. Even though Billy knows Doc is cheating him, he allows it; and when Doc learns that Billy knew he was playing with a false hand, he is encouraged, taking it as a sign that Billy is willing to meet him half way (is willing to gamble on the friendship, as it were). Doc then offers to walk the Kid back to his hotel; and what follows is one of the movie's most intensely romantic scenes, in which Billy all but confesses his desire. But Doc is still afraid. He wants to spend the night with Billy, but fears the Kid might be using his sexuality to entrap him, as he himself had entrapped Billy earlier, in the barn.

The music on the sound track is conventionally romantic, as the two men approach the hotel. When they reach the front door, they pause:

> *Billy:* Doc, if you're not already fixed up, you can bunk with me tonight.
> *Doc:* No thanks, Billy—I've got a girl. She and her aunt just moved into town.
> *Billy:* Yeah?
> *Doc:* You got a girl, Billy?
> *Billy:* Nah, I ain't got nothin' . . . 'cept that horse.
> *Doc:* You can't fool me—good-looking boy like you! You must have a girl somewhere!
> *Billy:* No . . . I don't trust 'em.
> *Doc:* Hey, you're pretty young to talk like that.
> *Billy:* Well, I've known quite a few.
> *Doc:* And they all did you dirt? Every one of them?
> *Billy:* Every one of them!

This exchange recalls Pye's observation that in postwar westerns "two themes constantly intertwine—emotional damage (as in 'trusted a woman once' or a murdered loved one) and social change."[47] *The Outlaw*, however, only invokes this conceit of the cowboy who doesn't trust women as a way of enhancing Billy's status as a figure of homosexual fantasy. Like a Victorian melodramatic stage heroine "whose helpless perfections attract disaster like a magnet,"[48] or like Melville's Billy Budd, whose beauty and grace inspire an unconsciously erotic obsession in his antagonist, Billy (the Kid) brings out the best or the worst in those around him. Unlike Doc, he is presented as having virtually no history—which adds to the impression he gives of being a dream figure. And to the extent that the movie is concerned with the theme of social change, it is articulated in the private-sphere terms of melodrama, embodied primarily in Doc, as a character facing the universal problem of aging—particularly the question of sexual viability as a precarious mainstay of identity—of when, for example, if ever, it is appropriate or necessary to "settle down."

Laura Mulvey notes in her "Afterthoughts on 'Visual Pleasure and Narrative Cinema' Inspired by *Duel in the Sun* (King Vidor, 1946)"[49] that an essential aspect of the kind of folktale analyzed by Vladimir Propp is the social integration of the hero represented by marriage.[50] But in the western, she ob-

FIGURE 4.3 Doc Holliday (Walter Huston) takes a gamble on Billy—the highest stakes he has ever played in his life. (Courtesy Photofest)

serves, the hero can choose "not marriage." Indeed, a hero can gain in stature by "refusing the princess and remaining alone." Mulvey describes the resolution of the Proppian tale in "marriage" as representing the resolution of the Oedipus complex, and sees the rejection of marriage in the western as personifying "a nostalgic celebration of phallic, narcissistic omnipotence," which as "a phase of play and fantasy [is] difficult to integrate exactly into the Oedipal drama."[51] Mulvey notes that the tension between these two points of attraction often generates a splitting of the hero into two (something unknown in the Proppian tale): "Here two functions emerge, one celebrating integration into society through marriage, the *other* celebrating resistance to social demands and responsibilities, above all those of marriage and the family, the sphere represented by woman" (14).

We observe at once, however, that these two functions identified by Mulvey as common in the western are not forcefully articulated in *The Outlaw*, or rather, are recast in a homosexual configuration. Like Pearl Chavez (Jennifer Jones) in *Duel in the Sun*, Rio MacDonald is a "half-breed," and like Pearl, she is shown caught (although not with much narrative conviction) between two conflicting desires—first, between her desire to kill Billy and her desire to make love to him; and then, in a vaguely parallel structure, between her fidelity to Doc as his "girl" and her love for Billy. But it comes as a surprise to the viewer to realize that nothing essential in *The Outlaw* would change if Rio were removed from the narrative altogether. Unlike Pearl, she is not at the center of the story, and the two men do not acquire their meaning from her. Unlike Lewt (Gregory Peck) and Jesse (Joseph Cotten) (in *Duel in the Sun*), who have different attributes and represent different things, Doc and Billy are very similar, almost mirror images of each other. The splitting of the hero, as earlier suggested, is manifested in the opposition between the differing attributes and values ascribed to Doc and Pat. But since Pat is not shown to have opted for the sex-specific convention of "marriage" (he only talks of "settling down," i.e., entering politics, that analog of friendship), the tension between the film's two points of attraction is shown to be (homo)sexual. Billy is at the center of the story, and the two older men acquire their meaning from him. The hero's choice of "not marriage," in other words, is a homosexual one. This truth is revealed by the fact that none of the men in the film wants Rio, and it would seem to be confirmed by Rio's very excessiveness as a signifier of female sexuality.[52]

Anthony Mann's dictum that "a woman is always added to the story because without a woman the western wouldn't work"[53] is only true if the woman authentically signifies male heterosexual desire and if all the film's assumptions are heterosexual. Mann's phrasing is interesting in that it identifies the woman as something *added* (a supplement, a fetish) to "the story" (which is presumably about men). Budd Boetticher (another well-known director of westerns), on the other hand, makes the woman in the western sound like Hitchcock's MacGuffin: "What counts is what the heroine provokes, or rather what she represents. She is the one . . . who makes him act the way he does. In herself the woman has not the slightest importance."[54]

In *The Outlaw*, as has been noted, the woman is not important to the narrative in the ways Mann and Boetticher (or Raymond Bellour)[55] insist she is in the western. But their remarks reveal that Billy is the "woman" in the film. What counts is what *he* provokes, what *he* represents. *He* is the one who makes Doc and Pat (and Rio) behave the way they do. It is nevertheless interesting to see how the filmmakers attempt to integrate Rio into the narrative, and how (unconsciously and unintentionally) her presence always refers us back to Doc's and Billy's homosexuality. Rio is what Tompkins would call a "'screen' character" (like Laura Dembo [Rhonda Fleming] in *Gunfight at the O.K. Corral*, who "is a screen for Doc Holliday, an alibi the movie supplies Wyatt Earp with so that his love for Doc won't mark him as 'queer'"): "Female 'screen' characters, who are really extensions of the men they are paired with, perform this alibi function all the time, masking the fact that what the men are really interested in is one another."[56]

Thus, when Rio ambushes Billy in the barn as he is preparing for bed, we recognize that she represents the film's half-hearted attempt to give Billy (and Doc) a heterosexual identity, and that she appears in the narrative at precisely this moment to mask the fact that in the fantasy controlling the logic of the scene it is Doc, not she, who would rape or be raped by Billy. Moments before, Doc had tried to seize Billy's horse, but Billy surprised him in mid-theft (the third time he has betrayed Billy's trust). It is not difficult to see that every time Doc tries to take possession of the horse, he is trying to possess Billy; but the fact that he is willing to use force—as we see it displaced into Rio's attack on Billy in the darkened barn—inflects our reading of Doc's sexuality as having a potentially unpleasant, sadistic edge.

In the event, it is Billy who is threatened with "rape" in the barn (although Rio will be raped by him, as the only way to end the scene, and to explain the conversion of her feelings from hate to love). She shoots at the Kid, and lunges at him with a pitchfork. But he is able to subdue her, and we discover—in the first interesting twist of her identity—that she is the sister of the man Billy killed in Socorro (the second revelation of interest, which comes later, being that she is Doc's "girl"). Billy tells Rio that if he had known the man was her brother, "maybe I wouldn't have tried so hard to get the other girl." Their dialogue by now seems full of ambiguities, as Billy has also told her (and we recall Pat's slur about how Billy has "given it to some of the boys"): "Well, he shouldn't have taken so much tequila. . . . It was him or me . . . and I didn't wait for him in no barn, neither."

Although Doc and Billy have confronted each other twice in the barn over the horse, the outcome of their second confrontation is complicated by Doc's inhibitions. He is certainly not sentimental (a fact of which the film seems critical), as we see when he bids the horse goodnight:

Doc: Good night, Red, see you tomorrow!
Billy (sarcastically): What, no kiss?
Doc: No, they don't like mush!

At this point, Billy is as fed up with Doc for his evasions as Doc is humiliated about not getting what he wants. As he turns to leave, Doc notices his tobacco pouch in Billy's breast pocket, and snaps irritably: "Hey, that's my tobacco, isn't it? . . . You don't mind if I take *that*, do you?"

The truth, however, is that the only thing Doc will not mind Billy taking from him is Rio. When Billy in a later scene is shot and wounded by Pat, and he falls unconscious, Doc takes him to his girl, who is, as noted, living with her Aunt Guadalupe. In an extraordinarily charged, homosocial (and erotic) gesture, Doc tells Rio to cut Billy's clothes off, and to keep him warm and dry. And before departing, he instructs her: "Now, do your best for this boy!" The camera fades out on the scene, as Rio starts removing Billy's clothes with a knife. Later, when Billy starts moaning in a fevered delirium (like the Virginian after he has been shot by Trampas), it is highly ambiguous as to whether he is calling after Doc, or someone else: "Where are you? Don't go away! . . . I'm so cold. You're mad at me . . . sure. Why do you hide from me?" Rio instructs her aunt to leave the room, and begins to undress.

The scene is daringly erotic in its implications, especially as it functions in a register of displaced desire. It is during this period, when Billy is lying naked and helpless on (possibly) Doc's bed, that Doc is able finally to take possession of the horse. The first thing Billy wants to know, when he returns

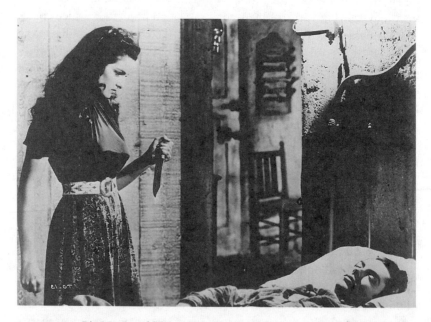

FIGURE 4.4 Rio MacDonald (Jane Russell) prepares to remove the clothes from a comatose Billy.

to full health nearly a month later, is whether Rio has been taking good care of Red. Indeed, Rio's value is not rated very highly by the film—but since her sexuality is revealed not to have a very secure hold on the male characters, her character is given the traditional female skills of a nurse and cook, and Billy will eventually take her with him into the sunset because he "can't stand ranch cooking."

When Doc returns and discovers that Billy and Rio have slept together, he is momentarily furious. Guadalupe, trying to defend Rio, blames Billy: "He's a devil! He did the same to me! He can charm a bird right out of a bush!" In a rather bizarre twist of logic (no doubt created by the requirements of the Production Code), Rio explains that she is married to Billy, although he does not know it. She married him when he was "out of his mind," as Guadalupe puts it. Billy seems thus to have been violated, and at the same time to have kept his virginity/innocence—which also explains how he can borrow $40 from Doc to pay Rio (for her services as a nurse), and will insouciantly offer to "return" Rio to Doc if Doc will return Red to him. "You mean, you'd trade *me* for a *horse*?" Rio asks incredulously. "And after all she did for you?" Guadalupe chimes in. Billy's response, like most of the dialogue concerning the horse, sounds as though it is referring to something *else*—this time, masturbation: "Say, you should have seen what that little horse did for me!"

The scene demonstrates that desire circulates, and no commodity has value except in the movement of its exchange. The horse, the forty dollars, and the woman are all meant to disguise the fact that the real object of value is Billy. All the characters "want" Billy (Pat, Doc, Rio, even Aunt Guadalupe), although Billy is determined to be an agent—not an object—of exchange.

During Billy's delirium, Rio steals the ring from his finger and puts it on her own, signifying on some level that he has lost his "virginity" to her. But there is more to the meaning of this ring. When he returns to consciousness, he is distressed about its disappearance, and explains to Rio that he got it from another man. It has been lucky for him—"belonged to a fellow who's supposed to have had a charmed life." We never learn who that fellow was, but infer the possibility—extraordinary in its implications—that it was Rio's brother, which would confirm the film's thesis that the oedipal scenario, as producer of desire and identity, is not limited to the child's relation to parental figures, but extends to siblings. Rio instinctively understands that the obscurely homoerotic attachment which the ring represents is a threat to the heterosexual bond she is trying to forge with Billy. She also recognizes that Doc is her immediate rival for Billy's affections—as the film symbolically acknowledges when it shows her repeatedly throwing out the

FIGURE 4.5 Billy and Doc both become outlaws when they must flee a vengeful Pat Garrett and his posse. (Courtesy Photofest)

rooster that makes its way into Billy's room when he is asleep. The lengths to which she will go to realize her deadly heterosexual imperative (as we understand it on this symbolic level) are shocking: Rio finally kills the bird and serves him for dinner.[57]

Later, when Doc and Billy are on the run from Pat and his posse, they discover that, in her anger and humiliation over having been traded for a horse, Rio has put sand in their canteens. Unable to divine Rio's motives, however, and also wondering why she would have betrayed them to the sheriff, Billy looks to Doc for an explanation. "Well," says Doc, as he chews on his newly rolled cigarette, "women are funny." That evening, sitting beside their campfire, Doc says he knows that Billy is thinking of "killing that woman," but urges him not do it: "They're all alike—there isn't anything they wouldn't do for you [*Doc spits into the fire*] . . . or *to* you." (He spits again.)

When Billy steals away during the night to confront Rio, his motives and plan of action are murky, and what happens between them is rendered in an ambiguous manner. The mood is distinctly weird. He surprises her in her room, and the camera begins to cut back and forth in a series of portentous close-ups, suggesting their conflicting emotions. Rio becomes frightened when it becomes clear that, despite the dialogue, Billy has not come to make love to her. The lighting and the framing of the scene create a hostile environment around Rio, and suggest that Billy's anger is real. He says to her: "Will you keep your eyes open? Will you look right at me while I do it?"[58]

Billy will tie up Rio as bait, to get Pat, who in the meantime has caught Doc. And when Pat and Doc come upon Rio, Doc says to her: "You know, I think he's in love with you! The crazier a man is about a woman, the crazier he thinks, and the crazier he does." At this point in the movie, the viewer may not be so convinced. The narrative itself seems to be unraveling—as it comes under ever greater pressure to make sense in heterosexual terms of what will only make sense in homosexual terms. Rio is perhaps correct when she responds: "He's only crazy about one thing—himself!" And Doc pronounces: "If he's fool enough to come back, he ought to get himself caught."

Whether the filmmakers really believe that this test of Billy's feelings for Rio can overturn the homosexual logic of the film is moot. After all, if he returns, it may really be for Doc, not Rio. Billy of course does return, and as he is untying Rio he is inevitably caught by the sheriff. "Say, why didn't you tip me off?" Billy asks Rio—as the camera fades out on the scene.

Indeed, the film's very engine of suspense turns on baffled questions such as this. The film attempts to make Rio—the woman—inscrutable, when in fact her motives are not at all mysterious. The only character whose desire is represented as being not yet fixed upon an object (other than himself or his horse) is Billy, and this, as has been noted, is because he is not so much a character as a projection of the viewer's and characters' fantasies.

"A Purely Personal Matter"

Following a scene in which Billy shoots a young man in self-defense (the man asks to talk to Billy alone in the back room of the saloon, suggesting—again, on a level of connotation and fantasy—that the effect Billy has on other men is erotic), Pat tries to arrest Billy on charges of murder. As he and his men surround the Kid, Doc intervenes, and Pat is forced to ask his (former) friend: "Are you throwing off on me again?" Doc replies: "Well . . . since I figure this is purely a personal matter between you and Billy, and don't think you ought to bring in all this . . . uh, hired help . . ." Pat, furious and humiliated yet again, clarifies the moral and emotional stakes of the situation in the absolute terms of melodrama: "You're making a big mistake, Doc, turning on an old friend—all because of a little snip, who's never given anybody nothin' except the back of his hand!" (The camera then cuts to a close-up of Pat's crotch, as he rearranges his belt and holster, in readiness for the anticipated shoot-out.)

This will be the turning point in the friendship between Pat and Doc, because Doc indicates that he would rather stick with Billy. The gambler and the outlaw start cautiously backing out of the saloon together, but as they get to the swing doors, a cowboy bolts into the room and inadvertently knocks Billy off balance. Pat shoots, and Billy falls to the floor, clutching at his groin. Doc shoots the gun out of Pat's hand and kills two of the hired men. "Take it easy, Pat," he says gravely. With slow deliberation, Pat replies: "Doc! This finishes you and me for good and all." Quietly, and with absolute sincerity, Doc says simply: "I'm sorry." And then, to Billy: "Can you get up, son? . . . Can you make it to the horse?" Billy, in a remarkable gesture, reaches for Doc's belt at his groin, and pulls himself up off the floor. And the two men ride off together.

The theme of revenge, so common in the western, is thus officially launched in *The Outlaw*. And, unusual for the genre, the reason given is quite openly what divorce lawyers call "alienation of affection." Pat will pursue Billy halfway across New Mexico to avenge his masculine pride as a man who has lost his best friend to a "little snip" of a cowboy on a pretty horse.

"You're the Only Partner I Ever Had"

As soon as Billy is well enough to ride again, after Pat's shooting, Doc buys him a new horse, but the horse is still "a little wild," and Billy is thrown to the ground trying to mount him. Doc offers to lend him Red until he gets his strength back, but Billy jumps to his feet, protesting: "Say, you're not going to do me any favors! I don't want to be obligated to you about Red. Because I haven't given up getting back Red, yet . . ."

Again, the question of Red's ownership defines the relationship between the two men. If they will be friends/lovers, Billy wants them to come to the relationship as equals. The taming of the wild horse will test Billy's mettle and be a sign to Doc of Billy's worth, with Billy deciding his own value. Each man wants to prove himself worthy of the other—to be the kind of man he wants the other man to fall in love with; to be the kind of man he would himself fall in love with. (Appropriately, the two horses take to each other immediately, and Red is able to calm down the wild one when it is panicked.)

The next day, the two fugitives stop to rest, Billy admitting that he is very tired. Doc decides to smoke a cigarette, but realizes that Billy has taken his tobacco pouch again. He reaches for the pouch in Billy's breast pocket and snatches it back. This, we realize, is how cowboys conduct a courtship:

Doc: Say, is there anything of mine you don't cotton to?
Billy: I guess I forgot.
Doc: Yeah, it's a bad habit you've got.
Billy: What?
Doc: Forgetting what belongs to other people.
Billy: You think I do it on purpose?
Doc: Yes!
Billy: Listen, mister, I don't feel too good as it is!
Doc: Neither do I!
Billy (struggling to his feet): You want to make something out of it?
Doc (looking at Billy's two guns): That's a big advantage you're taking!
Billy: I can't help it—I'm so plumb beat out, I'd be lucky if I could draw 'em clear!
Doc: I don't want to crowd a sick man.
Billy: I'm all right! Just give me forty winks, and I'll take you on with both hands free!
Doc: Well, I guess this is as good a place as any to make a camp.

The poignant absurdity of Billy's attempt to challenge Doc has a witty visual counterpoint in the two horses behind them, who nuzzle each other affectionately throughout the exchange. As the two men talk about Pat, and turn to look anxiously out at the valley through which they have just traveled, Billy stands directly behind Doc, looking over his shoulder, their bodies almost touching. As they speculate about who put the sheriff on their trail, Billy comes around to face Doc, their hips and shoulders aligning, as if the younger man were about to lead the older man in a dance—except that both men continue to look out at the valley, in half-conscious acknowledgment of the conflict raging within them between their homosexual desires and the heterosexual code of western manly conduct that always makes the expression of intimacy between men such a fraught matter.

The emotional climax of the film—in which Doc and Billy in effect declare their love for each other, and Pat gives full vent to his anger, jealousy, and grief—is rendered in an appropriately intense and dramatic fashion. To borrow Peter Brooks's description of this kind of melodramatic culmination, the scene "represents a victory over repression, a climactic moment at which the characters are able to confront one another with full expressivity, to fix in large gestures the meaning of their relations and existence."[59] This *necessary* moment is driven by a desire to "express all" and is a fundamental characteristic of the melodramatic mode:

> Nothing is spared because nothing is left unsaid; the characters stand
> on stage and utter the unspeakable, give voice to their deepest feelings,
> dramatize through their heightened and polarized words and gestures
> the whole lesson of their relationship. They assume primary psychic
> roles, father, mother, child, and express basic psychic conditions. (4)

During a dangerous confrontation with some Mescalero Indians, Pat reluctantly returns Doc and Billy their guns. When they reach safety, however, it becomes obvious that Doc has no intention of giving up his gun again to the sheriff, and that he intends to escape—alone. Realizing that Doc will take Red, the disputed and hyper-signifying horse, Billy challenges the wily gambler at gunpoint.

FIGURE 4.6 Only the threat of some Mescalero Indians will briefly unite the jealous group: Pat Garrett (Thomas Mitchell), Doc, Rio, and Billy.

The situation is complicated. Billy first asks if Doc thinks Pat will leave them alone, or whether they should "pull his teeth" before they "start." Pat gives the answer to this question: "Don't worry about me! I wouldn't lift a finger, Doc, to keep you from killing him. *You and me never had any trouble until he came along!*" Rio tries to intervene, telling Billy that Doc will kill him, and suggesting that he can always get another horse. "I want *this* one!" he says tensely.

He decides to let the chiming of the cuckoo clock be their countdown. Doc agrees, and proceeds to give a final speech. His summation is very moving, because it is tragic in its implications, and reveals that for all the wisdom of what he is saying, Doc cannot help himself. He cannot prevent what seems about to happen, such is his masculine code of honor, his habit of emotional restraint, his inability to trust another man:

> *Doc:* Well, Billy, I guess this is it. Men are pretty much like children, after all. Have you ever seen two kids wrestling in the yard? They push and tussle, and maybe look like they're fighting, but they're not. They're really friends, and everything's in fun. Then, pretty soon, they play a little too rough. One of them gets mad. And in the end, somebody always gets hurt. So, for you and me, this is where somebody gets hurt. But when it's over—and however it turns out, son—no hard feelings.

"Doc!" Billy blurts out, as the clock just then begins chiming. There is a pained and anxious expression on his face. There are repeated close-ups of Doc and Billy from the waist down, of their faces, of Pat, the cuckoo clock, and Rio.[60] On the last "cuckoo," Billy does not draw.

"Why didn't you draw?" Doc demands to know. "I changed my mind," Billy says simply. Pat suggests that Billy lost his nerve, adding: "I always knew you were nothing but a show-off!" Doc becomes angry. He shakes his head sadly:

> *Doc:* That's no good, Billy. If you and I are bound to fight sooner or later, I'd rather do it now and have it over with. You've been ready to pull on me every day since I met you. I never wanted it, but I've waited and let you pick your own time and place. You've done that tonight. Are you going to draw it, or do I have to make you?

Doc pulls out his gun, aims at Billy's right hand, and shoots, grazing it. He fires two more shots, nicking both of Billy's ears. Rio screams: "Doc, have you gone *loco*?" Doc is puzzled, frustrated, angry, perhaps also embarrassed:

Doc: What's the matter with you, Billy? I didn't think you'd take this
   off anybody!
Billy (quietly): Maybe I wouldn't off anybody else.
Doc: What do you mean by that?
Pat: Doc, don't listen to that kind of talk! Haven't you ever seen a case
   of cold feet before?
Doc: He never had cold feet in his life! . . . What is it, Billy?
Billy: I guess that idea about the cuckoo clock wasn't so good.
Doc: Why?
Billy: Well, it gave me time to think, and remember a few things . . .
   You're the only partner I ever had.

The sadism of Doc's nicking Billy's ears makes for an unusually charged scene
of suppressed erotic energies. And the idea of the "partner," while almost fundamental to the genre, is stretched here to comprehend the relationship between Doc and Billy in a way that is not quite traditional. As in film noir, cop
movies, and other genres in which two men will work together—whether they
be detectives solving a crime, a superhero and his sidekick saving the world
from destruction, or outlaws robbing a bank—partners in the western are
paired in a safe zone provided by a shared cause that is outside themselves.
But Doc and Billy have not really partnered their skills or collaborated in the
name of a cause or for a specified outcome except, briefly, to avoid being captured by Pat, and, possibly, to "outwit" the woman (cf. Fiedler). Their cause,
in the sense Murphy gives the term, is essentially a private one, which binds
them for all the possibilities of friendship, with or without a sexual dimension. (It is interesting that nowadays many gay couples refer to themselves as
"partners," although many others think the term too businesslike and rooted
in the public sphere, and too often deployed disingenuously in an attempt to
remove any element of the erotic in the aura surrounding the relationship.)

   Doc, at last, is convinced of Billy's love. "Gosh, do you really feel that way,
son?" he says with emotion, as he strides forward, takes Billy by the shoulders, and looks into his eyes. Apologetically, and awkwardly, Billy says: "And
I treated you worse than anyone!" Doc wants all to be forgiven as quickly as
possible: "Nah! It was all my fault. I had no business getting sore and . . . cutting you up this way. C'mon, let's get out of here!"

   There is one last reference to the horse, and a final bit of play involving the
tobacco pouch, both indicating that from now on such "fighting" is in fun and
that they're really friends. The camera cuts to Rio, smiling, but it is obvious to
the viewer—if not to Rio—that this declaration of friendship between the two

FIGURE 4.7 When Pat forces Doc to "choose" between him and Billy, Doc chooses the young outlaw. (Courtesy Photofest)

men signals her exclusion from their orbit. Doc's repeated recommendation that they "get out of here" has more to do with what Pye calls "the dream of male separateness and escape" that haunts the twentieth-century western, than with the immediate necessity of fleeing Pat Garrett's vengeful wrath.[61] As the camera cuts to Pat, his face contorted with emotion, we hear Doc saying: "I ain't worried about you and me ever fighting now, Billy. Because one thing is certain—if we didn't do it tonight, we never will. Come on, let's go!"

"I Was Always the Best Friend You Ever Had!"

Pat, stunned by the outcome of the confrontation between Doc and Billy over the horse, starts to approach his former friend. But Doc seems to have forgotten that Pat is in the room, for he takes Billy's elbow, and they walk toward the door. Just as they reach the door, Doc becomes aware that Pat is behind him. He turns and says with exaggerated lightness and a wave of his hand: "Uh . . . so long, Pat! Don't take any wooden nickels!"

Thomas Mitchell's performance in the film is accomplished and professional, and what follows is his finest scene:

Pat (incredulous): You're not going with him!
Doc: Now, look here, you ain't goin' to start something with the two of us, are you?
Pat: I might have known you would do this to me! Ever since you met him, you've treated me like a dog! The very first day, you sided with him against me! That made me the laughingstock of the town!
Doc: Take it easy!
Pat: I gave you your guns, so you'd have a chance for your life. And now you tell me I got to fight the two of you to get them back! [He seems about to burst into tears. His voice is tight, and rising with extreme emotion.] You stand there . . . side by side with that little snip of a kid . . . against me! Me! [He thumps his chest with his fist.] I was always the best friend you ever had. And I still would be . . . if it wasn't for him!
Billy: Say, Mister, that's about enough out of you for one night.
Doc: Wait a minute, Billy, you let me handle this. Pat is a friend of mine! I don't want to kill him, and I don't want you to kill him. Is that clear? . . . Pat, you're just getting yourself all steamed up. I'll be seeing you one of these days, and we'll have a good laugh about all this . . . So long!

As Pat reaches for his gun, Doc urges him to be careful: "You know you haven't got a chance against me," he says. And then, simply: "Goodbye. Goodbye, Pat." Pat shoots, and Doc staggers.

This is the moment toward which the narrative has been moving inexorably—yet it is still shocking. As Charles Ford observes in his book, *Histoire du Western* (1964), Doc Holliday in western mythology is not only "an unscrupulous killer," but "the very illustration of corruption and degeneracy,"[62] and in *The Outlaw* his character is "made wise by the onset of old age" (147). We see him, finally, as a poignant symbol of the westerner's constant struggle with the threat of castration—his fear, as Tompkins puts it, of losing his mastery. The fear of bodily decay and dying may be universal, but Doc's willingness to risk everything for a last chance at happiness—in the *physical* terms of the western: of emotional freedom (represented by the Wilderness, in all its aspects) and sensual pleasure (a vigorous, bodily enjoyment of life)—gives the film its emotional center, its existential *gravitas*.

In the confusion that follows the shooting, Doc begs Billy not to kill Pat. Rio tries to get Doc to lie down, but he refuses: "No," he says, "that's one thing I've always been afraid of . . . dying in bed." Pat rushes to Doc's side as he falls to the floor. "Why didn't you shoot?" he asks despairingly—"You had me beat a mile. You had me *cold*!" Doc's last words are: "Maybe I don't like cold meat, Pat."[63]

Death is everywhere in the western, but as several critics have observed, it is not the fact of death that matters so much in the genre as *how* you die. From his first appearance in the film—which indirectly refers to his abject fear of dying (his grooming himself in front of the mirror)—to his last moments as a warm and living body, Doc insists on the here and now. He is animated by the gambler's impatient, utopian desire to find a shortcut to happiness, before it is too late. In the psychoanalytic metaphor, he wants unmediated access to the phallus, which explains why in the western his character is often coded as homosexual (and/or as alcoholic and tubercular). He wants a finer, keener, more vivid experience of life than, say, Pat, and is willing to transgress the "law" to attain it. Among the genre's handful of recurring characters based on historical figures, he is perhaps the most "subtle and elusive, despite appearances" (to use Charles Ford's description of Victor Mature's Doc Holliday in *My Darling Clementine*)[64]. He has glimpsed happiness and wants it for himself, even as he knows the impossible truth about desire: that it cannot be seized or grasped as such. He is a questing, yearning figure, which is what makes him so appealing. Like a road-movie character, he is a searcher and will never "settle down," which is to say, he will not settle for *less*. His courage and daring, in making a bid for Billy's love, is what makes him a quintessentially "American" character, the very embodiment of the right that Americans claim to "life, liberty, and the pursuit of happiness."

As the first "modern" western, *The Outlaw* responds in a psychological register to mutations of the gender system wrought by modernity. As traditional divisions of labor are undermined and the old distinctions between masculinity and femininity are blurred, we see a certain intensification and exaggeration of difference—for example, in the prominence given to Jane Russell's bosom, or in the excessiveness of Billy's emotional taciturnity—reflecting a tenacious desire in culture for a fixed relation to the symbolic. The film's misogyny reflects some of the potential "costs" of these shifts in the relations between the sexes, although on the positive side, modernity is understood to liberate the individual. Moreover—to borrow an image popularized by Gilles Deleuze and Félix Guattari in *Anti-Oedipus*—modernity to a degree enables the subject to resist or escape the "colonizing" effects of the oedipal scenario. The subject's desire might even cease to be a matter of object relations; but if not, he is at least freer on the range, where he may prefer his horse, or his friend, to the woman. His best friend, the film suggests, might also be his lover—but such a relationship, we see, is not easily forged. The problem, as the fluctuations of power and desire are reordered in modernity, is that between men who are equals–who are free agents; whose access, or relation to power is essentially the same—the question of trust is recast in terms that are different from those that traditionally underpin the heterosexual encounter. The territory is relatively unfamiliar, and according to the conventions of the western genre, it is conceived as a frontier. As such, it is nothing less than a representation of desire itself: anything is possible—there is everything to gain, and everything to lose.

A FINAL WORD ABOUT TRUST

After they finish burying Doc, Billy tells Pat that he is sincerely sorry about the way things have turned out: "You and Doc have been friends for years—if I hadn't come between you, none of this would have happened." Pat reflects for a moment, and replies: "It sure is funny . . . how two or three trails can cross, and get all tangled up." They are obviously reconciled on some level, but as they start to leave Doc's grave, Billy shows himself reluctant to walk ahead of Pat, for fear of being shot in the back. Pat is (or pretends to be) incredulous: "You *never* trust *anybody*, do you?"

Shortly afterwards, however, as he is preparing to quit Lincoln County, Billy's doubts about Pat's trustworthiness will appear to have been justified. Pat offers Billy Doc's guns "as a keepsake," and Billy accepts them with gratitude. "Do you think they'll suit you?" asks the sheriff. "If the barrels ain't too long!" Billy replies, as he measures them against his own. He is delighted to discover that they are just the same and concludes that Doc's guns are even better balanced than his own. This posthumous proof at last that Billy is Doc's equal, coded in the specifically masculine terms of a phallic comparison, confirms the oedipal underpinnings of their relationship—and perhaps of all such relationships, grounded in mutual attraction, admiration, and competitive fear.

Pat suggests Billy give him his own guns in exchange, so that he can tell people it is Billy's body in the grave outside, not Doc's. With some difficulty, Billy is persuaded to give up his guns, but as soon as he does so, Pat points a gun at the Kid and reveals that he has taken the firing pins out of Doc's guns. But, in a final reversal of fortune, it turns out that the gun Pat is aiming at Billy is one of Doc's, and Billy has kept one of his own guns after all. Pat has been outwitted one last time—because, despite the pretty speech he gives about how Billy needs to trust people, he will not himself trust (or forgive) Billy, and nor will Billy ever completely trust another man.

The film acknowledges that trust is indispensable in modern societies, but reveals that the necessary conditions of trust are disappearing. From our late modern perspective, we may see *The Outlaw* as an unconscious response— possibly triggered by the start of World War II—to the steady eroding of relations of trust in American society and among nations in the world. On the one hand, certain changes in material conditions in the United States, such as the increasing mobility of labor and the impact of new technologies, has had the effect of releasing the modern subject from the constraints of traditional roles and diminishing the authority of social groups over him or her. The individual, now free to move between roles, is free (at least theoretically; and this freedom can be costly) to pursue his or her own opportunities and possibilities for happiness. On the other hand, with trust depending on people seeing themselves and others as individual agents having responsibility for their actions, the problem of maintaining order in society is exacerbated in proportion as this moral self-understanding wavers or wanes.[65]

As the conditions of modernity undermine the superego, the internal norms and sanctions of conscience are experienced as constraints on personal freedom, a hampering of the individual's autonomy. Trust has little place in late modern societies, and individual subjects are left to make alliances with one another, or with groups, and to seal those alliances with legal contracts. Doc is impervious to Pat's moral claim of old friendship because he sees his first responsibility as being to himself—to his own happiness. The western's equivalent of the force that backs up the legal contract is the individual's ability to use a gun. And so, while Doc is free to choose his own friends (as Pat points out), he is also risking death when he makes his choice. Doc dies at the end of the film because he trusts Pat not to kill him, even as he callously explains that the old rules—according to which partners remain loyal for life—no longer apply ("Pat, you're just getting yourself all steamed up. I'll be seeing you one of these days, and we'll have a good laugh about all this").

The Outlaw grapples with a moment in the ethical life of modern individuality by articulating a struggle between what Pat represents (the community, "settling down," the law) and what Doc represents (individuality, social and sexual mobility, transgression). As noted earlier, the western as a genre is particularly well suited to explore problems confronting a society that feels itself to be on a frontier of some kind, facing something new, requiring new modes of thought, new attitudes and ideas, new ways of relating to others. To make Pat and Doc (and Billy) homosexual, then, is apt—for the "frontier" that the film explores is one where it seems necessary to rethink the individual's place within a network of ties and responsibilities to kin and community. The homosexual is seen as a modern, even utopian, figure: dyadic, committed to personal freedom, and—as Mulvey notes about the western hero who "[refuses] the princess"—not constrained by the social demands and responsibilities of marriage and the family, the sphere represented by woman.

The final scenes showing Pat and Billy still not trusting each other nevertheless make for a strange conclusion to the film—but they suggest that the specificity of masculinity (the thing about masculinity that gives the mode its specific charm) is this wariness. Such are the dangers involved in trusting another man (the film in effect says), that when first friendship or a romantic bond is achieved between two men, it has more value than the bond between a man and a woman, where the power differential generally lowers the stakes.[66] We are meant to believe that if Doc had lived, he and Billy would have become totally trusting partners. They would then have had *everything*; in a word, they would have found happiness.

5

LOOKING FOR THE "GREAT WHATSIT"
Kiss Me Deadly and Film Noir

There is a scene near the beginning of *Kiss Me Deadly*[1] in which the unconscious logic of the movie suddenly becomes clear to me, a logic that permeates much of film noir and explains in part what is so compelling about the film noir detective genre.

Mike Hammer (Ralph Meeker) parks his car on a deserted city street late at night and gets out. As he starts walking, a man follows him. We get a shot of the man's look, which indicates that Hammer is the man he has been waiting for.[2] When Hammer stops at a newsstand, the man stops, too, at a discreet distance and lights a cigarette. Hammer continues his walk down the street, and the man follows. The tempo of the cutting increases perceptibly as the sound of their footsteps increases in volume and the uneasy music on the sound track becomes more insistent. When Hammer stops to buy some popcorn from a street vendor, he casually steals a glance at his pursuer. He resumes his stroll, and then stops again—at a vending machine, in the shiny surface of which he is able to see the reflected figure of the man who is now only a few paces behind. Hammer resumes his walk, and so does the man, who walks a little faster. Cut to a close-up of the man withdrawing a switchblade from his pocket. He flicks the switchblade open.

Just then Hammer turns and flings his popcorn into the man's face and grabs his arms in a wrestler's embrace. "Drop the knife!" he barks. The man drops the knife, they struggle, and Hammer punches his assailant violently in the face. He falls, and Hammer pulls him to his feet, to punch him again. Hammer pounds the man's head against a wall, again and again—his lip curling with sadistic pleasure. The man slumps to the ground. (The graffiti on the wall behind includes in large letters the words NOSE and RIPPER.)

Hammer turns slowly, picks up the man's knife, closes it, puts it in his pocket, and starts to walk away. The man struggles to his feet and lunges toward Hammer, who turns just in time to protect himself. Hammer punches him with fantastic violence, and the blow catapults the man down a long flight of steps. Cut to Hammer's calm face, watching, and then to the falling man, and back to Hammer, and back again to the man—still falling—in an extreme low-angle shot, this time from the bottom of the steps. Hammer smiles, turns, and walks away from the camera.

My description of this scene makes the point that, as in so much film noir (*The Big Sleep*, 1946, is a supreme example), story is less important than iconography, gesture, the play of signs within a *sexual* logic. There is more going on here, in other words, than simply one of the bad guys trying to do in the hero, Mike Hammer. This is a kind of disguised homosexual fantasy, a sadomasochistic scene in which Hammer is out cruising for a homosexual encounter—expressed here in violent form by the knife (rather than the usual gun) that can be extended and retracted, the insistent beating of the man's head against the wall, and the man's subsequent orgasmic fall down an impossibly long flight of steps.

"I Don't Know Whether to Fight Him or Fuck Him"[3]

The film is homophobic as well as misogynistic.[4] It is so *extreme* that it reveals heterosexuality working in a way that can be described as, paradoxically, "hom(m)o-sexual."[5] Luce Irigaray comes up with this neologism to designate the structural reality of heterosexuality: "Reigning everywhere, although prohibited in practice, hom(m)o-sexuality is played out through the bodies of women, matter, or sign, and heterosexuality has been up to now just an alibi for the smooth workings of man's relations with himself, of relations among men" (172). It is more or less homologous with Eve Sedgwick's phrase, "male homosocial desire," which also refers not only to the transactions between men concerning the possession of women but to a continuum that includes mentorship, rivalry, homosexuality, and such other activities as male bonding, "which may, as in our society, be characterized by intense homophobia, fear and hatred of homosexuality."[6]

Homophobia, as Robin Wood defines it, "is the inability to accept one's own bisexuality." Wood's remarks on homophobia (his representation of the Freudian paradigm) are worth quoting here, for they succinctly get me to the main point I wish to make about *Kiss Me Deadly*, and by implication, much of film noir:

Homophobia . . . can be explained only in psychoanalytic terms. Freud's investigations proved . . . that the human individual is innately bisexual and that the homosexual side of that bisexuality has to be repressed in order to construct the successfully "socialized" adult. . . . Homophobia results when that repression is less than completely successful—when, that is, one's homosexuality is experienced as a constant, if unconscious, threat. . . . Masculine violence in our culture (the construction of the male *as* violent) must be read as the result of the repression of bisexuality. Violence against women: the woman represents the threat of the man's repressed femininity. Violence against other men: the man represents the threat of the arousal of homosexual desire.[7]

As Wood goes on to say, the relationship between repression and sublimation is obscure. By definition, however, what is repressed is inaccessible to consciousness, "manifesting itself only in dreams, jokes (Jake La Motta in *Raging Bull*: 'I don't know whether to fuck him or fight him') and fantasies" (41).

The status, then, of the brief scene from *Kiss Me Deadly* that I have described should be clear. Read as a fantasy—as figuration of the film's unconscious, in traces of what is repressed by the narrating sensibility—*Kiss Me Deadly* (most especially in scenes like the one described above) reveals its perverse nature.

ANXIETIES ABOUT MASCULINITY

"Hard-boiled" detective novels, like the *films noirs* that were made from them in the 1940s and 1950s, often simmer with an explosive sexuality. The action moves fast. In the movies, the elaborate mise-en-scène and vivid graphic movement within the frame and between shots preserve the distinctive energy that we find in the books. Love, in the novels and films, is never a simple or benign matter. In fact, the word is scarcely ever appropriate. Although treated by critics as a theme in film noir—one that sometimes becomes "the focus of psychotic behavior, the catalyst for crime"[8]—love as a theme signifies sexuality itself,[9] or more specifically, a kind of sexual paranoia that animates the genre.

From the film's opening shots, and relentlessly to the end, *Kiss Me Deadly* is driven by a weirdly erotic verve. In the figure of Mike Hammer particularly, and also in *Kiss Me Deadly*'s style, in its plot, in all its narrative assumptions, heterosexuality is revealed, as I have suggested, on a foundation of repressed homosexuality. Homosexuality is repressed because, as Irigaray has put it, masculine homosexual relations "openly interpret the law according to which society operates." Heterosexuality, we find, is an organization (economic and desiring) in which "woman exists only as an occasion for mediation, transaction, transition, transference, between man and his fellow man, indeed between man and himself."[10]

Both the novel and the film push at the limits of the tradition to which they belong, and what was always there in the genre is made extreme, almost to the point of self-parody, making the semantic-symbolic code fairly obvious. What follows is an examination of *Kiss Me Deadly* (novel and film) in terms of the energy that drives the narrative and, in particular, the cinematic signifier that transforms the mode of narration in the film.[11] As a melodrama, *Kiss Me Deadly* has at its heart the sublimation of desire, with the problem of individual identity written in phallic terms, but the film is possibly also something else: among other things, it may be a Cold War movie, a nightmare dream-wish that will not come directly to terms with politics. It displaces fears about the Soviet Union and nuclear annihilation, and the threatening nature of mass society that was rising in the 1950s, into a sadosexualized narrative about a search (for a box of radioactive material).

These other anxieties are translated into anxieties about masculinity and fears of passive homosexuality, and yet there is a paradox: the obsession with strength and potency, with mastery and knowledge—signified in *Kiss Me Deadly* by the search for the "great whatsit"—draws the hero toward the very signifier that will homosexualize his position because he will not mediate his relation to it. The fear of homosexuality in American culture generally is so great that it is denied to the point of conversion into symptoms, and those symptoms, as they can be read in *Kiss Me Deadly*, give the film and the book their perverse tenor. In her 1986 article, "Sound, Woman, and the Bomb: Dismembering the 'Great Whatsit' in *Kiss Me Deadly*," Carol Flinn argues that there are "some strong reasons to consider [*Kiss Me Deadly*] as some kind of response to the cold war—not the least of which is the atomic explosion that concludes the film."

Like Flinn, I do not question the importance of Cold War issues in critical interpretations of fifties' cinema, and also believe that "it would be a gross disservice to the film to approach it merely as a response to cold war Fifties politics." Where Flinn, however, chooses to examine "the ways femininity has been figured into this political and cultural preoccupation," I am interested more in how the film has trouble (or *I* have trouble) with its definition of masculinity, and with the logic of "normal" heterosexuality that the film as a limit-text dramatizes. There is no question that, "to analyze a film like *Kiss Me Deadly* as a product of only cold war politics deflects and ultimately obscures the fear of feminine sexuality which displays itself so lavishly across this and other examples of film noir." But where Flinn calls that fear a fear of *feminine* sexuality—in the sense, presumably, of a sexuality that only women can possess—I would elaborate on her designation to include, or even stress, the fear of passive homosexuality, which in our culture is understood to be feminine in nature.

Mike Hammer's fear, then, is not just a fear of women, but of the woman (the feminine) in himself, and of the feminine position that (he perceives) homosexual desire puts him in. Femininity, passivity, and homosexuality are often synonymously linked in our culture, and although this linking is a cultural fact, *Kiss Me Deadly* uses its female characters and the elements associated with them (as Flinn so interestingly points out) "in ways that sidestep film theory's routine claims to femininity's passivity." Flinn's attention to the film's sound track—her "reading against the grain of, and as a critique of, the visually oriented criticism of film noir"—supports her counterclaim, although it does not, given its rather different emphasis, contradict my own in any essential respects.[12]

RESISTING HETEROSEXUAL NORMATIVITY

In their perversion of the sexual norm of society, Mike Hammer and Lily Carver offer a critique of conventional heterosexuality and dramatize the crucial question of how subjects are formed within its repressive terms. They are positioned in a relation to the phallus,[13] which is the linchpin of the system in which the film and the spectator are inscribed. In Freudian terms, their sexuality is arrested in the phallic stage, as it were, and we see how they must accede to an organization around the phallus, to the law of the signifier, if they are to gain an identity. Velda is the one who first suggests that it is more than the story-level box of radioactive material that everybody is looking for, calling it the "great whatsit," and in *Kiss Me Deadly* the main characters look with deadly need (literally, to death), and with such urgency, that a curious homosexualization of the means of access to the symbolic—that realm in which meaning and value are articulated—takes place.

Mike Hammer and Lily Carver could be seen as martyrs in a struggle against Oedipus, for they are caught within its mortal coils without any awareness that there is no escape, and that there is no finding the "great whatsit." To be free, one can only destroy. Otherwise there will be psychosis or death. In the film, Mike Hammer and Lily Carver do gain the box/phallus in the end, through total destruction, in death, which ironically (in a Lacanian sense) is how they are at last constituted as subjects—unified, made whole, no longer lacking.[14] Like all melodramas, *Kiss Me Deadly* offers the viewer simultaneously and contradictorily not just a critique (of heterosexual norms), but a moral lesson to be learned: Follow the script. This field has been laid for you. This drama, this universal story that we might call Oedipus, has been written for you. Learn your lines and moves well, and you will not get hurt (which means of course that only the usual damage will be done).

A steady weakening of the professional identity of the detective—observable, for example, in such noir films as *The Maltese Falcon* (1941), *Murder My Sweet* (1944), and *Out of the Past* (1947)—ends in the figure of Mike Hammer who, as neither cop nor crook, appears in both the film and the novel to have lost all traces of a professional code by which he operates as a detective. Unlike the character in the book, Mike Hammer in the film is not presented as the narrating source, and Ralph Meeker's cool, restrained acting style, his perfectly regular features, opaque gaze, and high, clear forehead discourage access to the Hammer psyche. Hammer's sexuality is dramatized in the novel through his own narration, language, and interior aspects, while the film shows his outside and detaches his sexuality from this body to a style of narration outside of him. The perverse and ambivalent sexual identity of Mike Hammer, which so strongly pervades the book, characterizes the film on the level of the cinematic signifier because it would be too gross to have the Mike Hammer of the film signify this sadistic, obsessive sexuality entirely through his characterization. Meeker, therefore, cuts a less excessive figure, and the graphic depiction of specific acts of violence is less explicit in the film than in the novel, even as the film's cutting style and camera angles are consistently lurid.[15] This sexuality of the controlling sensibility is the essentially noir element that, although transformed, is most successfully preserved in the adaptation.

In the film we learn that Hammer is a private investigator who precipitates divorce cases by generating false evidence for his clients, and that he is prompted to follow up the Christina Bailey case because he senses that there is "something big" behind it. His curiosity to decode Christina's cryptic message ("Remember me!"), against the advice of his friends and the warnings of the enemy, launches Hammer on an adventure of extreme danger. In the novel, Hammer's pretext for conducting his own investigation (against the law and after his license to carry a gun is revoked) is one of personal vengeance for the wrecking of his car, and because he was beaten up by men he soon finds out to be Mafia agents. Although his own code of professional behavior is almost nonexistent, Hammer is impressed nevertheless by the tight organization of the Mafia. "There's a code they work by, a fixed unbreakable code," he says in the book, and the person "someplace at the top of the heap" evidently impresses him most of all.[16]

SADISM/MASOCHISM

Hammer's fascination with personal power, his sadistic impulse to destroy what he fears (the sexuality of powerful men, and the women who are associated with them) is what drives him in the novel to an obsessive contemplation of female sexuality, and to the humiliation and destruction of men who embody extremes of his own self-hatred or fantasies of personal power. His hatred of the feminine in himself accounts for his problematic feelings for Velda, Gabrielle/Lily, and Friday, and he hates the men whom he would love, or whose power is enviable (Carl Evello, Dr. Soberin), or whose relative powerlessness and littleness is disgusting to him (Evello's bodyguards and hit men, the man at the health club, the man at the morgue). In the book, even before he has left the hospital (chapter 5), Hammer imagines with sadistic relish, in an act of thinly disguised identification, what he will do with the biggest prize of all, the Mafia "king":

> From him the fear radiated like from the center of a spiderweb. He sat on his throne and made a motion of his hand and somebody died. He made another motion and somebody was twisted until they screamed. A nod of his head did something that sent a guy leaping from a roof because he couldn't take it any more.
>
> Just one person did that. One soft, pulpy person.
>
> I started to grin a little thinking how he'd act stripped of his weapons and his power for a minute or so in a closed room with someone who didn't like him. I could almost see his face behind the glass and my grin got bigger because I was pretty sure of what I was going to do now. (38)

The perverse energy of such writing is largely conveyed in the film, as I have noted, by the pursuit of the "whatsit" and in the film's style of narration.

Pursuit of the man is replaced by object-fetishism in the film's effort to disguise the homosexual nature of Hammer's desire. His essential desire is to rape and be ravished by such a man—a man worthy of his fantasies of power/vulnerability—a man like himself, only better. The desire is impossible, of course, for he wants to realize his mirror image, as the Narcissus of myth does. While Hammer seeks to inscribe himself in action, and is propelled forward by his desire to find the "whatsit," his desire to *know* Michael Friday's mouth (Friday is Carl Evello's sister and is a more developed character in the book), to discover reflections of himself in contacts with men and women in a world of extreme situations, more revealingly describes his desire and explains his quest. He is inscribed in a phallic sexuality, "caught in the reign of the One, obsessively trying to tame otherness in a mirror-image of sameness."[17]

GOING BEYOND REPRESENTATION

Although the book and the film are similar in their equation of sex and knowledge, the film attempts to locate "the truth" in something graphically representable: knowledge comes from seeing something. In novelistic fiction, generally, knowledge is not pressured in the same way to predicate itself on vision. Jean Mitry writes, "In the cinema . . . we gain access to the idea through emotion and because of this emotion, while in verbal language we gain access to emotion by means of ideas and through them."[18] What is missing in this quotation, of course, is how that emotion is generated, but Charles Affron has followed up on Mitry's observation by noting that "this is, in part, due to that aspect of the cinematic image (and sound) that must remain unmediated, its *non*symbolic relationship to its reference—that which was filmed—a characteristic of all cinema, from its art films to its most popular, 'bathetic,' tearjerkers" (5). What Affron's remark reveals is the extent to which film is still bound to the notion of image-as-truth, that the image is not coded, that it is immediate and of the imaginary (that great storehouse of truth in image-based data). The ending of *Kiss Me Deadly*, probably for this reason, seems somewhat inadequate.

No graphic signifier can possibly be found for that which is signified by the "great whatsit." Although the exploding beach house is an impressive image, it can still only be an image, where what is sought is a going-beyond-representation. It represents nothing less than the end of the world and must mean, therefore, even more than those other (inadequate) words with which Pat attempts to impress Mike Hammer: "Manhattan Project. Los Alamos.

Trinity." When, for example, Lily Carver (compared to Pandora just a few moments earlier) insists on looking into the lethally irradiating box, the source of light/truth, she actually sees nothing. The screen is filled with a blinding white light. There is no image, no representation. An empty space, a lack—indeed, death is here.[19] The more that is revealed, the less there is to see. The exploding beach house attests that the truth cannot be present-ed *im*mediately, but must be *re*presented. Truth destroys the visual signifi-er that would convey it. Truth must exist in that space between signifier and signified. In other words (because there is no reality apart from its rep-resentation), Aldrich has made a film that is not primarily about what it would appear to be about—a story about an investigator's effort to find out who the bad guys are and what they are up to—and so, by the end, when *Kiss Me Deadly* has filmed itself into a corner, it has to show us *some-thing*: *a* "whatsit" where it cannot show us *the* "whatsit." As a film about a crisis of representation, *Kiss Me Deadly* must be about Cold War fears (or

FIGURE 5.1 *Kiss Me Deadly* (1955): Pat (Wesley Addy) warns Mike Hammer (Ralph Meeker) to stop his investigation by cryptically alluding to: "Manhattan Project. Los Alamos. Trinity." Velda (Maxine Cooper) looks on. (Courtesy Photofest. Copyright © 1955 United Artists Corporation)

a fear of feminine sexuality, or homosexuality, or whatever) displaced into a hermeneutic involving a box of radioactive nuclear material.

A Text of Sexual Obsession

Spillane makes spatial and temporal transitions in his novel that are as rapid and as transparent as the straight film cut, which accounts in part for the novel's eminent adaptability to film. As Noël Burch has pointed out, "Aside from its greater technological simplicity, the cut proved from the outset to be the *ideally transparent signifier*; its invisibility—through editing procedures such as eyeline matching or cutting on movement—was such that 'meaning,' the message, seemed to issue forth naturally from the context as a whole, from the flow of images itself."[20] Spillane gives us a flow of rapidly drawn, cartoonlike images. His book is meant to be read rapidly—the narrative is all-important. He scarcely bothers with description that does not propel the narrative. And where Spillane charges his narrative with a sadosexuality through the voice of his narrator-protagonist Mike Hammer, Aldrich achieves the same effect of sexual, sadistic propulsion primarily through framing that fragments the human body, and an editing style and mise-en-scène that startle in a way that has come to be recognized as typically noir. Editing and framing that convolute narrative and fragment space (particularity the human body) arouse in the viewer a primitive sense of the cinema. Such editing and framing is sadistically erotic, for these operations on the body of the film and the film of the human body, not least among the myriad flows and fractures of desire unleashed by film, are read subconsciously as dismemberment.

The opening sequence of the film includes several of the most potent signifiers that are to be used throughout the film: the shot of the human body from the waist down; the fast car; the blonde, boyish woman; the kiss; the bed; the cigarette; of course all names; all dialogue; and a cutting that disorients rather than clarifies. As a text of sexual obsession, *Kiss Me Deadly* (both novel and film) abounds in fetish objects, and its main source of power derives from the attempts to suppress what is so clearly illustrated for the reader and the viewer. Hammer's compulsion to assert his masculine self accounts for the privileged status of the cigarette as phallic signifier in his world and explains his obsession with guns and fast cars, his narcissistic attraction to strength, action, and power, his identification with masculine/dangerous/athletic or Junoesque women, and his relations with men, which arouse in him an erotic response that he fiercely represses.

Mike Hammer's sexual ambivalence is announced in an extraordinarily explicit way. From the disturbing sound in aural close-up of (Christina's) prolonged and heavy breathing, to the disorienting spectacle of the film's opening credits scrolling in reverse down the road—suggesting a subjective journey into the past, and launching the sodomitical motif of things ass-backwards—the movie sucks the viewer into a vortex of sexual connotation that redounds to Hammer's character. Christina, naked under her trench coat, positions herself squarely in the beam of his headlights, causing Mike to swerve off the highway. His car is temporarily disabled, and he is furious with her: "You almost wrecked my car! . . . Thumb isn't good enough for you? You've got to use your whole body?" She replies with the obvious question: "Would you have stopped if I had used my thumb?" His answer, emphatic and disgusted, is "No!"

On his car radio, we hear Nat "King" Cole singing, "*I'd rather have the blues, than what I got . . . ,*" which speaks directly, if ambiguously, to Mike's

FIGURE 5.2   Mike becomes angry when he is stopped by a young woman (Cloris Leachman) on the highway in the middle of the night: "You almost wrecked my car! . . . Thumb isn't good enough for you? You've got to use your whole body?" (Courtesy Photofest. Copyright © 1955 United Artists Corporation)

mood, which is strangely unforgiving. The notion that Mike Hammer is not much interested in women sexually (Christina's thumb would go unnoticed or ignored; whereas her "whole body"—because more visible/phallic—jolts him out of his narcissistic self-absorption) would seem to be confirmed in the scenes that immediately follow. When they are stopped by the police, Mike pretends—for appearances' sake (and of course plot reasons), that Christina is his wife. But the moment they are safely beyond the roadblock, he gruffly demands: "May I have my hand back, now?"

He decides to stop at a gas station because, as he explains to Christina, "This wheel doesn't feel right—it keeps pulling over." The element of erotic domination (which we later observe colors Mike's friendship with Nick) appears in this scene, too, when Mike orders the station attendant to check the right front wheel. While the young man jacks up the front of the car (the sexual symbolism of the action is explicit), Mike looks on; and when he pulls a small branch from beneath the car, Mike explains, as if unconsciously guilty: "We must have picked it up when we went off the road back there." The young man replies complicitly: "The only thing I ever pick up when I go off the road is poison ivy!" For both men, it seems, going "off the road" is an error with unpleasant consequences. With Christina out of the picture for the moment, the two men seem to be flirting. When Mike hands the young man some money and says, "Thanks, kid" (to which the young man enthusiastically replies, "Thank *you!*"), the atmosphere of the scene suggests, finally, that Mike has received a roadside blow job, and that we have been given an explanation for Mike's surly attitude toward Christina. Her sexuality is clearly disturbing to his narcissism (heterosexuality "doesn't feel right") and—as he has done many times before, and as we will see him do again—he goes to an auto-mechanic for realignment, or (as the garage signs advertise) for "repairs" and "lubrication."

After Mike and Christina are ambushed by Evello's men and tortured, the unconscious couple are placed back in Mike's car—and in an image that is highly suggestive of Mike's latent wishes, the sportscar is pushed from behind by an enormous, black car (belonging either to Evello or Soberin), over a cliff and into fiery oblivion.

"THE LIAR'S KISS"

The men in the Interstate Commissioner's Office who hold Mike for questioning after Christina's murder are contemptuous and distrustful of Mike, accusing him of "playing both ends against the middle"—an allusion, within the film's sexual logic, to his bisexuality (the homosexual side of which, we come to realize, has been neither successfully repressed nor accommodated). Mike moves in a number of worlds but is an outsider in all of them. "I think it's a good thing to speak a lot of languages," he tells Evello when he finally meets him. "Any country you go to, you can take care of yourself." Evello's response—"Yeah, well maybe you can speak my language"—refers not only to his world of organized crime (the language of intimidation, bribes, and so on) but to the mysterious undercurrents of homosexual feeling that seem to characterize Evello's relationships with other men.

Mike Hammer dips in and out of various demimondes with ease. He obviously knows Eddy, for example, who runs a corrupt boxing club. When, following a trail he hopes will lead to the "great whatsit," Mike visits his black, cigar-chewing friend, the boxers' agent proudly shows Mike his latest acquisition: "How do you like my new boy? 'Kid' Nino. Isn't he pretty? Doesn't he *move* pretty?" Mike replies: "Sure, just like all your fighters, Eddy!" With his cigar sticking out of his mouth at a 45-degree angle, Eddy instructs the young man: "All right, Kid, shadowbox around—I'm showing you off to a friend!" And, apparently unable to take his eyes off the young boxer, repeats rhetorically to Mike, "Isn't he beautiful? Isn't he *lovely?* Look at the way he moves!" Mike agrees, "Sure, he's great, Eddy!" but goes on to complain cynically that Eddy sells out all his fighters in rigged matches. Aside from telling us some potentially significant things about Mike Hammer (in the same way that, as Christina remarks, "You can tell [a great deal] about a person from such simple things—[Mike's] car, for instance"), the scene also functions on a connotative level to suggest that Mike is familiar with the world of organized male prostitution.

Mike Hammer is in some way incomplete, and other characters are parts of him. Velda is like his own mirror image dancing around him, which he never quite sees or only catches glimpses of. No genuine sexual feeling can ignite between them because she is on the one hand too much like him and, on the other hand, still only a woman (i.e., not the thing itself but—in heterosexual culture—the means of exchanges between men, the medium of access to the phallus). She is his business partner; she does physical exercises to keep in good physical shape—for professional and, no doubt, personal reasons—as it is suggested by Christina Bailey that Mike Hammer does also, to "keep [his] belly hard"; she embodies traces of his feminine self that he avoids acknowledging, but is not his complement so much as his double, his double in female form. While this notion suggests itself strongly in the film's motifs and thematic content, it is also conveyed cinematically, with subtlety and economy. For example, the dissolve of Mike Hammer alone, thinking of Velda, to a shot of their embrace, might be seen as a fluid answer to his thoughts of the "other" and to the sense of absence that pervades his apartment (he stalks it, only to find that it is empty; the answering machine feigns his absence). The *image* of Mike Hammer is the image of Velda and Mike Hammer standing in the middle of Hammer's living room, kissing, when Pat enters the apartment to announce that Hammer's license to carry a gun has been rescinded.[21] But the image includes Pat's entry. Pat apparently has *his own key* to Mike's apartment: when Mike and Velda fail to answer his knock, we hear the sound of the door being unlocked and see Pat let himself in. His entry breaks up their embrace and gives the lie to the phallic, "hom(m)osexual" nature of Mike Hammer's heterosexuality; and the scene's subtexts of sexual ambiguity are reinforced when Pat delivers his announcement in a taunting and vaguely "swishy" manner, suggesting that Pat is unconsciously jealous of Velda and irritated by what he sees as Mike's *charade* of heterosexuality. The phallic phase, in Freud's story of sexuality, "is characterized by the opposition phallic/castrated. In that phase there is no representation of an other sex—the vagina, for example, is 'unknown.'"[22]

Hammer's attempts to be free of an essential feminine side of his character prevents him from following through completely with any conventional heterosexual impulse. In the words of Lily Carver in the final scene of the film, he gives "the liar's kiss, the kiss that says, 'I love you' but means something else," (which, I have suggested, means, "I love myself"). He wants direct access to the phallic principle, unmediated through women. He is, as Lily Carver notes, "good at giving such kisses." In the novel, a persistent image is the mouth of Michael Friday, the one woman by whom he is truly sexually fascinated: "The wetness glistened on her lips. They were firm lips, large, ripe, parted slightly over the even lines of her teeth. There was fire there that grew hotter as I came closer. I could see her mouth open even more, the tip of her tongue impatiently waiting, then the impatience broke and it met me before lips did" (130).

RAPE FANTASIES

Michael Friday, with her masculine name and her "sleekness like a well-fed muscular cat, an athletic squareness to her shoulders, a sensual curve to her hips, and antagonizing play of motion across her stomach that seemed un-

FIGURE 5.3 Mike uses the Mafia "king" Evello's half-sister Michael Friday (Marian Carr) to get him closer to the "something big" behind Chistina's death. (Courtesy Photofest)

consciously deliberate," is the kind of woman (who may in fact be a man—she is a "lovely phony") who excites Mike Hammer's imagination most. What is more, she is incestuously attracted to her brother, Carl Evello, whose humiliation and death in a violent parody of sexual contact Hammer imagines and later acts out. In that scene, spread-eagled on a bed, face down, bound—much as he was in the opening sequence while Christina is being tortured—Mike Hammer experiences/Spillane "dreams" a rape fantasy, repeated also in several verbal variations throughout the book: "They must have known how it felt because the guy in the back bored the rod into me every time I tightened up and laughed when he did it" (91).

The film makes little of the Michael Friday character[23] but instead makes Lily Carver and Christina Bailey imaginatively interchangeable (boyish with short blonde hair, dangerous) and masculinizes Velda in the way that Friday is in the book. The visual motif of the bedstead is just one of several bridging devices connecting Mike Hammer with these various women in the film. Hammer is physically abused (quite how, we do not know) and left on a bed in the opening sequence; at the former apartment of Lily Carver and Christina Bailey, Hammer pauses beside Christina's bed and sees on the wall a painting of a human figure stretched out as if on a rack; Hammer finds Lily at her new apartment, lying on a bed in a seductive way, with a gun in her hand; the bed to which Hammer is tied, face down and legs apart, at Evello's beach house (the same bed on which Hammer lays out Evello's unconscious body) is, like all the other beds, clearly an object of perversely sexual, violent, deadly connotation.

With a syringe, Soberin injects the prostrate Mike Hammer with a delirium-inducing drug, while on the radio we hear snatches of commentary on a boxing match: "He has him up against the ropes . . . McCoy's eyes have a glazed look . . . Jim Wenders is on top . . ." This scenario, by way of connotative reference to sodomy, is an expression of the humiliation of the weaker by the stronger. The act, one might say, defines Mike Hammer's relation to the world and adds a sadistic edge to his professional role as an investigator. But this is happening *to* Hammer. The blackouts that the noir hero in

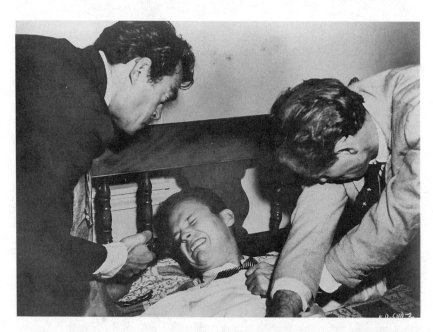

FIGURE 5.4 Carl Evello's hit men, Sugar Smallhouse (Jack Lambert) and Charlie Max (Jack Elam), spread-eagle Mike and tie him to the bed so that Dr. Soberin can inject him with a "truth-telling" drug. (Courtesy Photofest. Copyright © 1955 United Artists Corporation)

many films often experiences when he is beaten up or drugged function like a forgetting of and yielding to the desired, impossible contact with the phallic other.[24]

Mike Hammer is most at ease with Nick, the Greek automechanic who so admires him, but their kind of homosociability is only possible because it is understood that Nick is Hammer's social inferior. When Nick is killed, Velda is jealous that Mike—after an alcoholic binge of inconsolable grief—wants to avenge his death. She understands instinctively the connection (which excludes her) between Hammer's relationship with Nick and his efforts to discover the "something big" behind Christina's note. "How nicely it justifies your quest for the great whatsit," she says. "Everyone everywhere is searching for it. For what?" Soberin later asks the captive Hammer the same question: "What is it that we seek?" It is quite clearly not really the narcotics (in the novel) or the box of radioactive material (in the film).

"Oh, My Mustache! My Father's Mustache!"

Nick and Mike Hammer share a love of fast cars. "Oh, my mustache! My father's mustache!" Nick yells in excitement when Hammer drives back to the garage in his new sportscar. How the car functions as a fetish is quite clear. But it is the cigarette that functions in both the film and the novel as the privileged fetish object. Hammer's relationship with Pat, who is his friend but also his link with the law, illustrates through the role of the cigarette the basic problem of the Mike Hammer relationship with a man. Their professional relationship, if it can be called that, is an uneasy one. There is a prohibition on their working together, and yet they quite obviously need each other and must work together if they are to discover the "great whatsit." In moments of doubt, when Hammer must concede to Pat's legal/moral authority, Hammer reaches into Pat's breast pocket for a cigarette—a phallic substitute for a surrender, in a context of affection/identification that cannot be expressed in any other way. By such means (which we see, for example, in the relationship between Neff [Fred MacMurray] and Keyes [Edward G. Robinson] in *Double Indemnity*), Mike Hammer can approach Pat while positing a distance between himself and the threat Pat potentially poses.[25] If they came too close to each other, their peculiar system of cooperation would break down. The threat of a collapse of the symbolic order, which the film hints would have homosexuality as either its cause or effect, can be heard in Pat's anxious words of advice to his friend: "Too many people like you have contempt for anything that has to do with the law. You'd like to take it into your own hands. But when you do that, you might as well be living in a jungle!"

On the first and last page of the book (and almost every page between) Hammer puts a cigarette in his mouth. He "fumbled out another cigarette" the moment Berga Torn [Christina Bailey] climbs into his car, and 175 pages later, when he is shot by Lily Carver, he tells us, "My mouth was dry. I wanted another cigarette. It was all I could think about. It was something a guy about to die always got. My fingers found the deck of Luckies, fumbled one loose and got one into my mouth. I could barely feel it laying there on my lips" (175).

One cannot give or receive a kiss when one has a cigarette in one's mouth. This is one of the reasons Hammer smokes. The implications of a kiss are too threatening, too deadly for him, and that is why in the film his kisses "lie." In the Aldrich film, the kiss lies because in Hollywood cinema the kiss often represents more than it usually does in actual life. In mainstream cinema (at least in the 1950s and before) the kiss was often the metonymy and metaphor of the sexual act itself, which we do not see on the screen. In Spillane, kisses do not lie in this way because Spillane's Mike Hammer is still safe at the level of the kiss, which is the only level of "normal" sexuality he can handle or is interested in. As John G. Cawelti has noted, Spillane's descriptions of sexual relations are not "the actual encounter of men and women but the conventionalized sexual ritual of the striptease."[26] They are foreplay. Sex as a conventional, followed-through encounter with an other is the bedrock obsession and problem in both the film and the book.[27] Mike Hammer in the film is invited by Lily to have this encounter, but he will not entrust his link to patriarchy to a woman (castrated, powerless, existing only in a shadowy relation to the phallic principle), and he seeks instead an unmediated approach to patriarchal power—hence the homosexual subtext of *Kiss Me Deadly*, and hence, finally, his impossible self-realization. The conventional means by which Lily as a woman might inscribe an identity for herself in a patriarchal setup is also perverted. When Mike Hammer rejects her, she conceives an aggressive will to self-realization. She becomes determined to break out of a patriarchal pattern in which she is merely an object trafficked between men.

THE "GREAT WHATSIT"

The contents of the box quite literally signify Mike Hammer's and Lily Carver's desire. Instead of entering desire's dialectic through the other, they try to reach it, to realize it directly, which is why they, (their) desire, representation

itself are all extinguished. Hammer had glimpsed the contents of the box before, and he was burned. The only way to see it (and this is precisely the
point, if we remember what it is that is ultimately desired) is in a reflection,
a shadow, or through a filter. Our whole system, the world as we know it, depends on the subject divided, split, in a process of constitution, and there is
no unifying it, except in suicide, in fantasy, and in fiction.

When Lily Carver is rebuffed by Hammer (and by Soberin), her conventional desire is displaced and, like Hammer, she burns to know what is inside
the box. Finally, when the box is within her reach at the beach house, she says
to Soberin, "I want half!" When he tells her the sobering truth that she cannot have half, she picks up the gun (what better signifier of what it is that she
wants) and says she will take all, which is a deadly impossibility when taken
to its logical conclusion. Like Hammer, she will not enter a partnership, a dialectic of active and passive that would make conventional hetero/sexuality
possible. (Some would argue that she and Hammer, in this sense, lack imagination.) But who wants conventional heterosexuality? In their search for the
"great whatsit," they demonstrate a remarkable and quite thrilling resistance
to normativity. They seek to evade symbolic mediations and to accede directly to the imaginary.

We recall the conversation Mike Hammer has with Christina Bailey at the
beginning of the film. At one point he says, "What I don't know can't hurt
me" (a dictum he applies only in the unknown territory represented by
women), and at another point Christina says, "You have only one real, lasting love—*you*." With an irony that we come to appreciate fully by film's
end—since Hammer needs to recognize and make a place for his feminine
and other selves—she muses facetiously: "Woman—the incomplete sex.
What does she need to complete her? Why, a man, of course!"

Not only does a woman need a man to make her complete, but, as we have
seen, so does this man . . . if he is not to be a fascist.[28] *Kiss Me Deadly* is invested with an excess of phallic sexuality that converts to homoerotic obsession. Unappeased, this obsession (produced and aggravated by repression)
drives Mike Hammer to fascistic behavior and gives the movie its themes and
visual style—its status, in short, as a landmark film noir.

The film opens on a blank, white screen, but on the sound track we hear, faintly at first, the unmistakable sounds of a movie western—horses galloping, guns firing, and cowboys and Indians whooping and yelling. The camera pulls back to reveal that the blank screen is literally that: a drive-in movie theater somewhere in Texas in the middle of the day. The sound of the western fades. A small boy, alone in the children's playground at the foot of the huge screen, is rocking back and forth on a squeaky toy horse, while some real horses graze nearby. We start to hear a man's voice on the sound track, exuberantly singing ("Whoopee yi yo! Git along, little dogie, for you know New York will be your new home . . ."), then the camera cuts to a shot of the naked feet of the man who is singing. He is taking a shower; and when he drops his bar of soap, the close-up of him reaching for it gives the shot a slight emphasis that hints at a hidden meaning. The camera then travels up the full length of his well-proportioned and muscular body. He is smiling, and his eyes are closed, as he soaps himself up and continues to sing.

Everything essential that *Midnight Cowboy* has to say about the hero's masculine identity, as an image constructed out of a series of identifications with (images of) other men comes out of this scene and is compressed in the shots that follow, of him getting dressed and looking at himself in the mirror. Joe Buck (Jon Voight) places a new cowboy hat delicately, but firmly, on his head, then dons the rest of his new cowboy outfit—a green, embroidered shirt; tight pants (the camera cuts briefly to a close-up of his crotch, as he pulls up the zipper); fancy, black boots; a fringed, suede jacket; a black bandana around his neck; and the final touch: an unlit cigarette clenched like a stalk of grass between his teeth. And then, in answer to the repeated question, "*Where's that Joe Buck?*" which he knows his coworkers are asking at the diner in town, he faces the camera/viewer and says with drawling contempt: "You know what you can do with *them dishes*! And if you ain't *man* enough

FIGURE 6.1 *Midnight Cowboy* (1969): "Whoopee yi yo! Git along, little dogie, for you know New York will be your new home . . ." Joe Buck (Jon Voight) takes a shower. (Courtesy Photofest)

to do it for yourself, I'd be happy to oblige! [*He strikes a match and lights his cigarette*] I really would!"[1] He then swings around, in a mock quick-draw, to face the mirror, and grins at himself.

The idea of a backstory is initiated here, as is the movie's central question of the hero's sexuality and sense of manliness. Although the blank screen in the film's first shot is meant to evoke the site of the film viewer's desire, the sound track gives a subjective dimension to the shot that suggests an origin of the hero's desire. That this screen will soon be filled by an image of his beautiful, naked body is very much to the point, as the viewer's desire is recognized by that of the hero, and vice versa. As Juliet Mitchell explains this dynamic, which is intrinsic to the processes of identification—as much in real life as in the cinema: "desire is the desire to have one's desire recognized—it is a yearning for recognition."[2] The sound of the western is part of an ancient memory. It begins to "fill in" the screen and start a story, which, we quickly infer, begins in the hero's childhood, and in movies about western heroes. The film's first flashback, then, is an aural one, merging the hero's subjectivity with the film's mode of narration, implying a psychoanalytic dimension of personality.

Strictly speaking, this chapter should not be titled "*Midnight Cowboy*'s Backstory" but rather "Joe Buck's Backstory," for *backstory* is a screenwriters' term referring to anything that occurred in the character's past that the writer can use to build the story's progressions. In other words, it is understood as a device, or function, of character exposition. Robert McKee, a well-known screenwriting teacher, observes that "powerful revelations come from the BACKSTORY—previous significant events in the lives of the characters that the writer can reveal at critical moments to reveal Turning Points."[3] It is worth quoting at length from McKee's influential screenwriting manual, *Story*, for he gets to the heart of the problem I wish to examine in *Midnight Cowboy*, namely Joe Buck's desire, and how the film attempts to offer an explanation from the past for the situation in the present:

> A character comes to life the moment we glimpse a clear understanding of his desire—not only the conscious, but in a complex role, the unconscious desire as well. Ask: What does this character want? . . . Behind desire is motivation. Why does your character want what he wants? You have your ideas about motive, but don't be surprised if others see it differently. A friend may feel that parental upbringing shaped your character's desires; someone else may think it's our materialist culture; another may blame the school system; yet another may claim it's in the genes; still another thinks he's possessed by the devil. Contemporary attitudes tend to favor mono-explanations for behavior, rather than the complexity of forces that's more likely the case. (376)

Indeed, through two distinctly different sets of flashbacks, the film will attempt to "explain" why Joe leaves his small Texas town to become a hustler in New York City (and why he fails as a hustler), and why he takes up with a ragged, small-time con man called "Ratso" Rizzo (Dustin Hoffman). As McKee observes about contemporary cinema in the passage above, and as Maureen Turim writes in *Flashbacks in Film* about the psychological melodramas that Hollywood produced in the 1940s, the hermeneutics of these narratives tend to "hold out a single key to psychic disorder. This single key to truth renders the narrative revelation orderly *and* psychoanalytically false."[4] But as Turim goes on to note—and it is the same point I wish to make about *Midnight Cowboy*—a "more deconstructive look" at the film's flashback form very often reveals that "there is more given than is being directly said" (149).

As a figure that makes specific use of the theory of associative memory, the flashback tells us a great deal about Joe Buck that he himself is not aware of. Turim points out at the beginning of her study that the etymology of the term "flashback" has expanded beyond its original reference to narrative technique to include the meaning given to it by psychology, in which it refers to the spontaneous recall of a memory image, especially in the context of a war trauma, in which former soldiers are said to have "battlefield flashbacks" (5). Although *Midnight Cowboy* deploys a range of flashback forms, it generally does so in the manner of film melodrama, which is to say, it "depicts emotional states of mind through the flashback representation of not only events in the past but also sites or images saturated with symbolic meanings within the structure and ideology of the narrative" (39). Like McKee's conception of the backstory, flashbacks in the kind of cinema to which *Midnight Cowboy* belongs "symbolize the conditions that inform a character's emotional trauma and initiate a shift of direction in the narrative. As such they activate conflicts and emphasize the symbolic thematization so central to melodrama."[5]

From a series of flashbacks to Joe's boyhood, we infer that he never knew his father, and we learn that he was abandoned by his mother, who one day left him in the care of his grandmother, Sally Buck (Ruth White). Little Joe obviously yearns for a father figure and adopts the film's ubiquitous sartorial symbols of Texan (western) masculinity, chief among which is the cowboy hat. In another flashback (more specifically, a nightmare), we see Joe being raped as a teenager by his male companions, just as he is about to have sex with a young woman one night in the back of a car.[6]

To use McKee's terms, these two sets of flashbacks constituting Joe's backstory suggest that his desires have been shaped by his "upbringing," on the one hand, and by a specific trauma on the other. The ways in which the film obfuscates and mystifies Joe's desire (and to a lesser extent, Ratso's desire) seem to belong to another era, one in which homophobia—in the name of the era's increased visibility and tolerance of homosexuality—could apparently function so insidiously as to escape the notice of most critics.[7]

In an essay titled, "Outlaw Sex and the 'Search for America'": Representing Male Prostitution and Perverse Desire in Sixties Film (*My Hustler* and *Midnight Cowboy*)," Michael Moon explores some of the political complexities of one of the most notable developments in American culture in the 1960s:

> the increasing visibility and audibility of gay men and lesbians and of the social institutions of same-sex desire, especially those of the urban underground, the neighborhoods, streets, parks, bars, and theaters where gay people mingled with each other and with other denizens of the underground: hustlers and their clients, female and drag prostitutes, drug users and dealers. (117)

Moon notes, however (not surprisingly), that these developments, as we see them represented in books, plays, and movies, are "by no means simple stories of 'progress' and 'increased understanding' on the parts of either producers or audiences" (118). This said, we might also remark that *Midnight Cowboy*'s filmmakers were perhaps only attempting to follow the kind of screenwriters' advice McKee offers as a piece of basic storytelling wisdom: "Think through to a solid understanding of motive, but at the same time leave some mystery around the whys, a touch of the irrational perhaps, room for the audience to use its own life experience to enhance your character in its imagination."[8]

Since its unique success more than thirty years ago as an X-rated film that went on to win Oscars for best picture, director, and screenplay, *Midnight Cowboy*'s narrative strategies—which attempt to preserve a bit of "mystery around the whys" of its characters' motives, while at the same time seeking to persuade the viewer that the filmmakers have "[thought] through to a solid understanding of motive"—have perhaps become a little clearer. For whatever reasons—and articles like Moon's are surely among them—Joe Buck's (unconscious) desire seems more legible now than it was in 1969. Although the emphasis of my own interpretation will be placed elsewhere, it might be useful to state here that I agree with Moon's witty description of the film's sexual politics:

> *Midnight Cowboy* is a film about how two men can have a meaningful S-M relationship without admitting to being homosexuals. Or perhaps it would be more accurate to say that the film is about the anguish of two men trying to establish a meaningful relationship despite their both being Ms in relation to each other, and finally having to settle for fiction's stock resolution to the M-M crisis: the death of one partner and the permanent bereavement of the other.[9]

But I am getting ahead of myself. The film's opening shots introduce almost everything the film knows about Joe's desire, as does the famous song that plays over the prologue/credit sequence.

"I'm Goin' Where the Sun Keeps Shining"

As Joe starts walking purposefully through the torpid streets of the small Texas town, to bid goodbye to a fellow dishwasher (Ralph, an old black man), before catching the bus to New York, the jaunty, optimistic song, "Everybody's Talkin'," begins on the sound track. Harry Nilsson sings: "I'm goin' where the sun keeps shining . . . through the pouring rain, goin' where the weather suits my clothes."

The film seems to be very clear at first about the performative nature of gender. Joe's purchase of a cowboy outfit in preparation for the career he hopes to have hustling rich women in New York City is an indication of this. But do clothes make the man? And how is the "weather" in New York? Will it suit him? New York is represented as a sexually charged place, a queer Mecca, where people live their lives as theater (or as a movie),[10] and when

FIGURE 6.2 Joe in Times Square, "where the weather suits [his] clothes." (Courtesy Photofest)

Ratso finally tells Joe—by way of partial explanation for Joe's failure as a hustler of women—that his cowboy outfit is "strictly for fags," we get a glimpse of Joe's unconscious desire. Bewildered, Joe stutters: "John Wayne! You're gonna tell me he's a fag?"

We have, in a way, been prepared for this exchange, for the prologue of the film includes an allusion to the great star. On his way to the bus stop, Joe walks past an abandoned movie theater, on the marquee of which we can just make out that the last film shown there was *The Alamo* (1960), starring John Wayne. Even more interesting is the fact that Wayne also directed that film. The highly contradictory suggestion is possibly this: the days when men "believed in" the image of themselves as "men," and when a man could direct what he believed (or at least what other men believed) was an innate, "natural" masculinity, are over. That paradoxical image of an authentically inhabited, traditional, "rugged" masculinity (paradoxical for being embodied/represented by an actor) is pretty much bankrupt by 1969, as the dilapidated state of the movie theater suggests. The causes of the progressive decay in the 1960s of what we might call "the idea of John Wayne" are of course numerous and complex, and are at least as complex as those contributing to the historical dismantling and collapse of Hollywood's "studio system," of which John Wayne, as a powerful icon of postwar masculinity, was a supreme product and symbol. Moreover, when we have an actor directing his own performance of manliness, as Wayne does in *The Alamo*, our attention is drawn to the performative nature of the whole enterprise, and the viewer may feel like Dorothy in *The Wizard of Oz* upon discovering that the awesome Wizard is merely a man behind a curtain manipulating a machine that produces wizard-effects.[11]

The usefulness of clothing as a signifier in the construction and representation of identities is exploited by the film in a highly self-reflexive way. As indexes of identity, appearances are vital in any society, but particularly so in those societies, like the United States, that are deeply marked by the features of modernity; and New York, as America's most "modern" city, offers the individual rich possibilities for self-representation.[12] The "languages" of clothing spoken in New York City are not going to be the same as those spoken in Joe's small town in Texas (which, in a different metaphor, the theme song acknowledges), and the film self-consciously offers a rich discourse on clothing as a means of developing its central theme of Joe's identity. The motif of the uniform, for example, appears frequently in the film.

Like the blank screen of the film's opening shot, Joe is first presented to us naked. And like the sounds of the movie western that start to cover this first shot, Joe's new cowboy outfit will clothe his body, to give us, in a step-by-step manner, the social constructionist thesis: the naked man starts becoming Joe, who, when he feels pressed to acknowledge, as he later will, that he is not "a 'for real' cowboy," is unconsciously revealing that he feels he is not a "for real" man, i.e., a heterosexual one. He will nevertheless always insist that his desire is real, and his yearning, despite his false advertisement of its nature, is undeniable to the end.

This being only the beginning of the film, however, and this being Texas, sometime around 1969, we may not be quite sure about how the cowboy look signifies in this time and place. But we start getting an idea very quickly. It begins with the surprised and irritated response of the manager at the diner where Joe works ("What the hell you doin' in that getup?") and will culminate in Ratso's outburst: "That great big dumb cowboy crap of yours don't appeal to nobody, except every Jackie on Forty-second Street! That's faggot stuff. You want to call it by its name, that's strictly for fags!"

Joe, of course, is no more a cowboy than he is a dishwasher (cf. Ralph's uniform). In the film's first few minutes, we not only see any number of Texas men wearing cowboy hats (and jeans and boots; but *not* embroidered shirts, nor bandannas worn around the neck, nor fringed jackets, and *not* walking with a pronounced swagger), but we also see, from the bus, two women trying on cowboy hats at a roadside curio shop. The cowboy hat, we are given to understand, has already become a bankrupt signifier—or rather, a sign emptied of its connotations of John Wayne-style masculinity. On his first day out in New York City, Joe will even see a fashionable woman wearing a "designer" cowboy hat made out of soft white felt, with a white strap tied artfully under her chin. Joe goes to New York, of course, because he (rightly, albeit unconsciously) believes the "weather" there will suit his clothes. But Ratso, out of personal frustration—because his own desire is so provoked by it—will eventually tell Joe what Joe on some level knows but does not want to know: that he is confusing the sign system to an intolerable degree; that in fact he is not dressing for the kind of weather he claims he wants. As Richard Dyer puts it, commenting on the rise of the macho style among gay men in the 1970s: "By taking the signs of masculinity and eroticizing them in a blatantly homosexual context, much mischief is done to the security with which 'men' are defined in society, and by which their power is secured. If that bearded, muscular beer drinker turns out to be a pansy, how ever are they going to know the 'real' men any more?"[13]

FIGURE 6.3 In one of the film's many scenes involving mirror-reflections, we understand that Joe is no more truly a cowboy-hustler than he was a dishwasher. (Courtesy Photofest)

When Joe as a boy is brought to live with his grandmother, we see that his mother has dressed him in a military-style uniform for the occasion. Not only is the cap too big for him, the uniform obviously makes the child feel uncomfortable. We are reminded of this scene later, when we see Joe on the bus to New York, holding his radio to his ear, trying not to hear the rowdy group of uniformed sailors singing noisily all around him. Other "uniforms" on the bus: a man in a business suit (he looks equally fed up with the sailors); and a nun, sitting next to Joe. If the uniform signals its wearer's membership in a group that shares a common identity, it also conveys, at least in this context (and according to the Hollywood use of stereotype), a particular approach to desire. The point of their appearance in the film is to tell us something about Joe's desire, and what it, or he, is not. The sailors represent a lower-middle/working-class sublimation of desire into homoerotic activities (some of them have their arms around each other as well). The man in the business suit: a conventional, somewhat inhibited, middle-class heterosexuality, the "excess" energies of which are channeled into "work." The nun: the renunciation of sex altogether.

At the end of the movie, when Joe arrives in Florida with Ratso, he will buy new clothes for himself and his friend (light, short-sleeved shirts, cotton pants) that are more suitable for Florida's weather, and we see him throwing away his cowboy outfit. When he gets back on the bus, he remarks to Ratso: "Hey, these shirts are comfortable, ain't they? Yours was the only one left with a palm tree on it. [*He lights himself a cigarette.*] Clothes are damned cheap here, too, you know that?"

Finally, Joe has bought clothes to suit the weather, instead of first buying the clothes and then looking for the weather that will suit them—which is a way of saying he is finally "comfortable" with who he is and has realized there is no need to resort to hustling to get what he needs emotionally from another man. Unlike his cowboy outfit, these Florida clothes are nonperformative, one could say. They do not advertise a role he is trying to play, but are meant to express, or signify, a more "natural" (less performative) sense of self. Moon quotes Dyer's observation that in the "novels of urban alienation" that appeared around the time of *Midnight Cowboy*, the hustler is motivated not so much by a desire to know his "true nature" as by an uncertainty about his masculinity and heterosexuality: when he "makes it" with a woman, he feels that he is proving his heterosexuality (i.e., that he is a man), and when he has sex with men for money, it is the *performance* that makes him manly—he is "acting like a man."[14] We see, then, that only when Joe stops conceiving of manliness as a performance (involving a costume, and some strain) does he find his true masculinity, which can admit to loving another man, and may even be homosexual, and which he discovers is both comfortable and less expensive—that is to say (continuing in the metaphors of capital), it is a masculinity that "works" for him, is less emotionally taxing. He decides to give up self-employment (as it were) because, "Hell, I ain't no kind of hustler! I mean, there must be an easier way of making a living than that! Some sort of outdoors work . . ."

Mirror/Screen

It is obvious that the Texas town he leaves at the beginning of the film does not work for Joe. "What have I got to stay around here for?" he asks Ralph rhetorically. If desire is the desire to have one's desire recognized, Joe is *dying* in Texas, where there is nobody and nothing to return his gaze, not even the cinema. The first shots of the film—the blank screen of the drive-in theater; the solitary boy on his toy horse; the pleasure Joe takes in soaping up his naked body; Joe talking to his reflection in the mirror—clearly signal that he yearns for recognition. He needs someone to love him.

The movie theater where *The Alamo* last played (the Rio) has been taken over by a shop selling secondhand furniture and assorted household junk. Significantly, we see a large mirror for sale, and a television set. Instead of John Wayne at the Rio, we see two old men wearing cowboy hats and sitting on a frayed couch in front of the theater, watching the world go by. It is an image of manhood emasculated by domesticity and enervated by consumerism. And like a "real" cowboy in a late western about the closing of the frontier, Joe is nearly run over by a truck as he attempts to cross the street (the theme of his loneliness is fleetingly referenced in the LONE STAR logo on the side of the vehicle). The frontier as a place of adventure and thrilling possibilities—as a site of *desire*—obviously closed a long time ago in this town. We see another truck, with "A & B Tree & Lawn Serv." painted on its side—an ironic reminder of the grand thematic tensions in the old western films between the Garden and the Desert, between Civilization and Wilderness. Now, instead of a romance between the cowboy and his western landscape, or between the viewer and a certain idea of the West, we see two women sitting on a bench, staring idly at Joe as he crosses the street. The one woman is old, the other young. The young woman, who has her hair in curlers, is drinking a Coca-Cola. We may ask: What does *she* have to "stay around here" for? She will eventually become the old woman sitting next to her. She may or may not get herself a "beau," as Sally Buck did—but we know he will not be Joe.

At the very end of the film, when Ratso has died, all the Florida-bound old ladies on the bus anxiously turn around in their seats, to stare at Joe and the dead man in his arms. The camera then cuts to a shot of one old lady looking into her compact mirror and powdering her face almost frantically. The question is the same for her as it might be for Joe, both at the beginning of the film and at the end: who will recognize their desire? The mirror here anticipates the look of the other. There must be a third term, we know, or there will be no desire. But if there is no real-person "other," that gaze into the mirror can become a regressive form of identification, because it creates a closed circuit of desire that must eventually lose its impetus. If that third term is always too firmly lodged in the imaginary, the subject may feel him- or herself caught in a lonely, narcissistic libidinal economy that wants something from the outside.

Near the beginning of the film, as Joe approaches New York on the bus, he picks up a New York station on his transistor radio. (Joe's radio, like his

cowboy costume, is one of his fantasy's crucial supports; the movie he in-
habits has color *and* sound.) He hears an interviewer asking a woman,
"What's your idea of a man?" and the woman's reply: "My idea is Gary
Cooper . . . he's dead."[15] Joe's face lights up: Gary Cooper! Another great
icon of the Hollywood western (and one who died, coincidentally, in the year
following *The Alamo*'s release). With mounting excitement, Joe starts imagining what the rich ladies of New York want in a man. He sees them all as
middle-aged, blonde, and pretty—not unlike his grandmother, Sally Buck:

> "A man who takes pride in his appearance."
> "[High in] consideration, first."
> "Tall. Definitely tall."
> "Someone I can talk to in bed."
> "A good sense of humor—not afraid of sex."
> "The Texas oilman."
> "Aggressiveness."
> "Outdoor type."
> "A rebel."
> "Young."
> [*Looking into the camera*] "*You!*"

Joe turns to the nun sitting next to him (the irony of this symbolism fore-
shadows his prospects in New York as a hustler of women), and he whoops
with delight. Joe's assessment of his own characteristics and charms is not
completely off the mark—but because his mirrors have perhaps too often
been screens, instead of real people, he will find himself duped, thwarted,
and overwhelmed by certain realities in New York City.

As soon as he checks into a hotel in Times Square, he unpacks his suitcase
and puts up on the wall, near the mirror, his poster of Paul Newman in *Hud*
(1963). Newman's exceptional beauty has been widely appreciated and exploited in almost every Hollywood genre during the actor's long and successful career, but it is this image of him as he appeared on the poster for *Hud*—
a "modern western" about father-son tensions and the adoration of Hud
(Newman) by his sixteen-year-old nephew (Brandon de Wilde)—that has
been, among the thousands of images of Newman in public circulation, the
one most often appropriated by gay men as an icon of homoerotic allure.[16]

First, Joe tries to get the TV to work. Failing that, he turns on his radio
and, bare-chested, walks over to the mirror. We see that he has also placed
in the upper-right-hand corner of the mirror—as an unconscious defense

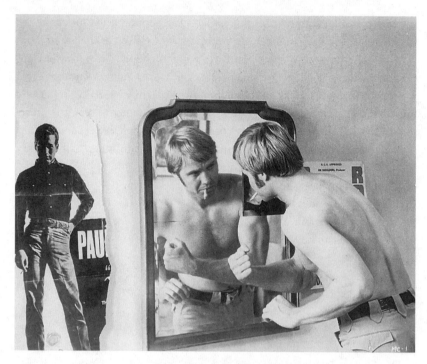

FIGURE 6.4 Joe in his hotel room in Times Square—a remarkable image that condenses the movie's discourse on Joe's desire. (Courtesy Photofest. Copyright © MGM/UA Entertainment Co. All rights reserved)

against the homoerotic implications of the large poster of Newman to the left—a small picture, perhaps torn from a magazine, of a bare-breasted, blonde woman in a seductive pose. On the wall to the right of the mirror is another poster, of a wrangler in cowboy hat and tight jeans, apparently advertising a rodeo in Texas. As a woman on the radio describes her remedy for insomnia (she moves all her furniture around—"So help me, everything but the sofa!"), Joe glances at the radio, then studies himself in the mirror and says: "My remedy is, ma'am, you just dial the hotel here—ask for Joe Buck!" While another woman on the radio tells the interviewer that her cure for insomnia is ironing her husband's shirts, Joe flexes his muscles and murmurs appreciatively to himself in the mirror, repeating his name: "Joe Buck!"

The scene is a remarkable hieroglyph condensing the movie's discourse on Joe's desire. According to the spatial and temporal logics of the scene, the evolution of Joe's desire begins in a maternal voice (the radio, usually with a male interviewer asking a woman what she wants, eliciting her desire; flashbacks initiated by Sally Buck's voice, the most poignant, which I discuss below, being her lullaby, "Hush, Little Baby"). Significantly, in this scene—the first moment of Joe's new life in New York City—Sally's voice has receded, or is inaccessible. And the television set, which flashbacks reveal was frequently Joe's only companion when Sally would go out, leaving him alone in the house, now has to be paid for through a slot machine.

The centrality and size of the mirror suggests that (for the time being) Joe has taken himself as his primary object of identification and desire. Paul Newman to the left of the mirror may be the ideal erotic image of masculinity, but the image *in* the mirror at least moves and talks and, in a manner of speaking, returns Joe's gaze.[17] Joe does not so much as glance at the small picture of the naked blonde woman tucked into the mirror frame on the right; she is, we realize, the repressed image of Sally Buck/his mother, feared and adored and resented and, more problematic still, his competition for the man he desires. The wrangler to the right of the mirror represents masculinity as performance—the man Joe is expected to be.

He starts to write a postcard to Ralph, then realizes it is pointless. He imagines Ralph reading it and being baffled. Joe tears the card up and flings the pieces out the window, into Times Square (an ironic allusion, perhaps, to the city's traditional ticker-tape parade for the homecoming welcome of national heroes).

In the film's discourse on the theme of Joe's sexual-emotional identity, there are several other important moments, or "Turning Points," as McKee might call them, involving mirrors as overdetermined sites of meaning, three of which are appropriate to mention here. When Joe's career in New York as a hustler quickly goes catastrophically wrong—Ratso hustles him by setting him up with a man who turns out to be a frightening, religious weirdo with a redemptive agenda—he retreats to his hotel room, takes a bath, and turns on the television set. He watches a program in which a childless old couple demonstrate, to grotesque effect, how they dress up their toy poodle in false eyelashes and wig. (There is a quick flashback to Joe as a boy, watching television alone, and Sally saying: "There's a TV-dinner in the fridge, loverboy! Expect me when you see me. I'll leave you movie money.")

A montage sequence follows, indicating that Joe wanders around Times Square for the next several days and nights, his sense of purpose dissipating. He sees a cowboy-hustler, much like himself. Then, he sees another. And another. And another. Always accompanied by his radio, Joe listens distractedly, as he watches and hears the ceaseless flow of human activity around him on the city's streets. "Why worry about your future?" a woman's voice is asking on the radio. "*What do you want, more than anything in the world?*" another asks. (And at this moment, Joe is passing a uniformed policeman, casually twirling his baton; the moving camera, presumably corresponding to Joe's gaze, focuses on the policeman's ass, and the baton, jerking at groin level. In less than two seconds, the image gives way to another, as a man's voice now on the radio is saying: "Take it easy . . . but *take it!*")

Joe's few belongings are seized by the hotel, in response to his failure to pay the rent on his room. A short time later, in an obscurely forceful image suggesting his "castration"/feminization—his sense of utter powerlessness—Joe spills some tomato sauce on his groin while sitting in a coffee shop. He descends into the subway station below Times Square—suggesting a descent not only into a demimonde but into his unconscious. He walks stiffly, as if in pain, as he tries to cover the stain with his hat, the once-proud symbol of his virility as a "cowboy" from Texas. He notices a mirror above a vending machine and, staring intently at his reflection, says rhetorically: "*You know what you gotta do, cowboy?*"

The camera cuts to a hustler on Forty-second Street, and then to Joe. Both perform the same gesture (taking a drag on their cigarette, and flicking the stub to the ground) in a precise and mannered movement that simultaneously expresses the "cool" and contempt in their pose of masculinity for sale. It is indeed interesting that Joe's first voluntary gay hustle should be initiated under the marquee of a movie theater (a poster of Steve McQueen is visible in the background), and that the boy who picks him up is about the same age Joe would have been when he was watching John Wayne movies at the Rio, back in Texas, and having sex with "crazy Annie." (The encounter is a failure, in that the boy has no money, and Joe experiences an obviously disturbing flashback/memory of taking his turn having sex with Annie at the back of a movie theater, while the other boys look on.)

After Joe moves in with Ratso, they briefly have a happy time together, surviving by petty-thievery, but as their economic situation worsens, they agree that Ratso should "manage" Joe's nonstarting career as a hustler. They get his clothes washed, his shoes polished, and his hat cleaned (by stealing all these services, of course). Back home, in their abandoned tenement building, Ratso gives him a haircut. When Ratso eagerly tells him to take a look at himself in the mirror, Joe reaches for his cowboy hat and carefully places it on his head, saying: "Don't rush me, boy! Got to take your time, here! Get myself *primed up!* Like I was turning on the charm for some pretty little blonde lady, you know? Then, when I'm feeling *cool*, and *good*, I spin around! [*Joe spins around and looks in the mirror*] There you are! You handsome devil, you!"

FIGURE 6.5 Joe's first gay hustle is a traumatic failure. The boy (Bob Balaban) begs Joe not to take his watch. (Copyright © MGM/UA Entertainment Co. All rights reserved)

Ratso watches him with a mixture of pride, love, thwarted desire, and sadness. "Not bad! Not bad," he repeats. "What a *cowboy!*" he adds, with a small, heartbroken smile. As the camera cuts back to Joe's reflection in the mirror (he is smiling at himself, rapt with wonder), Ratso repeats softly: "You're OK . . . you're OK."

Another especially striking moment in the film that shows Joe using the mirror image to fortify his ego precedes the film's most controversial scene, in which he gratuitously beats a man senseless in a hotel room for the money he needs to buy Ratso's bus ticket to Florida. While the man is concluding a brief conversation with his mother in the next room, Joe goes into the bathroom and faces himself in the mirror above the hand basin. "Look!" he says with determination, "I tell you, I got a sick kid on my hands. Well, he is, he's sick . . . and I got to get him South as quick as I can! [*The camera cuts to images of Joe struggling to get Ratso down some stairs*] I got a sick boy, and I'm gonna get him South! You understand me? [*He grits his teeth and shakes a fist at his reflection*] I'm gonna get him South!"

We realize, suddenly, that the "sick boy" is as much Joe himself as it is Ratso. Joe is desperate to save himself—to save his *amour-propre* from the abject fate which he now fears remaining in New York will bring about. While focusing extensively on the familial arrangements, psychological forces, and economic conditions that shape Joe, *Midnight Cowboy* cannot say whether, in the last analysis, it is always and only *environment* that determines everything, including sexual identity. If sexual identity is something that stabilizes after a long series of cause-and-effect experiences, when, more or less, does this stabilization occur? If the sexual constitution of human beings is made up of elements both innate and acquired, how much "choice" is ever involved in the outcome? In other words, if Ratso and Joe can get to Florida without further delay, can their lives be saved—saved for heterosexuality?

Moon remarks in "Outlaw Sex" that *Midnight Cowboy* plays on Middle American fears, exacerbated during the Vietnam War, that you can take the boy out of the country, but when it comes to New York (contrary to the adage), the city might succeed in taking the country out of the boy.[18] The movie's flashbacks to Joe's boyhood in rural and smalltown Texas fully prepare the viewer for this social constructionist debate about the extent to which the "country" has shaped, marked, or, in some fundamental sense,

FIGURE 6.6 As Joe and "Ratso" Rizzo (Dustin Hoffman) approach the nadir of their fortunes together in New York, Ratso yearns more desperately for them to move to Florida. (Copyright © MGM/UA Entertainment Co. All rights reserved)

constituted the adult Joe. The film's implicit question is whether Joe is a "faggot," as Ratso (perhaps only unconsciously) believes or hopes. And so the question becomes: Is one born a faggot? Or can one become a faggot? And if so, how does one become a faggot?

FLASHBACKS TO BOYHOOD

When we consider sexuality as the mainstay of identity, as the film does, we may think the terms *sex* and *sexual* are self-explanatory, but as Ethel Spector Person notes in a summary article about these terms, they are in fact difficult to define, "because sexual life in humans has so evolved that sex is not identical to the mechanism of reproduction."[19] Of the four separate, but related, physical-psychological sets of data comprehended by sex—biological sex, gender, sexual behavior, and reproduction—it is sexual behavior, covered by the term *sexual*, as used in everyday speech, that is "expressed by pleasurable genital activity and its associated fantasies, or by any sensual experience that has erotic meaning for the individual" (606). Theories about the nature of sexuality, Person observes, "are, in general, theories of sexual motivation, why people initiate or respond to erotic activity. They address the question of the source of sexual desire and arousal" (606).

The film's comprehensive paradigm of self-reflexivity is announced in its very first shots, as we have noted, and it does so in a way that quite spectacularly calls attention to the cinema as a regime of desire, and to the male body as the film's privileged object/site of fantasy. But we do not, at first, necessarily fully understand the meaning of the lyrics of the film's theme song: "Everybody's talkin' at me, I don't hear a word they're sayin'—only the echoes of my mind." It is soon revealed, however, that an important figure in the film's mode of narration is being alluded to: flashbacks originating in Joe's consciousness.[20]

The first flashback to Joe's childhood—aside from the film's opening shot, which exists in an unspecified time and undesignated consciousness, before Joe's character has been introduced—occurs when Joe passes Sally Buck's old beauty parlor, on his way to the bus that will take him to New York. He stares through the shop window, past the "For Rent" sign, to a memory of himself as a small boy giving his grandmother a neck-rub, after she has had a long day on her feet. "Ooh, that's nice, honey!" she repeats, in a moaning, gratified voice. She then turns in her chair and gives him an emphatic and affectionate kiss on the cheek.

As Jonathan Lear reminds us, there is a realm where the distinction be-tween whether something is fantasized or real is a false distinction: "What it is for parents to unknowingly act in seductive ways—ways that are experi-enced as seductive and thus *are* seductive—is a real problem of ordinary life."[21] Thus, at this early stage in the narrative, we must hold back on a "final" interpretation of the significance of this flashback (even as my own description of the scene begins that process of interpretation). Joe (that is, the movie) is telling me his "story," hoping that I (the viewer-analyst), might help him bring his "memories" to light. I thus play a part in the process by which Joe comes to accept—or evade—a particular identity which, presum-ably, will be established by the end of the film. From its very first shot, the film is discursive; it invites the perceptive viewer to ask "Who is speaking?" But the question is intractable; the status of the flashbacks in *Midnight Cow-boy* is difficult to decide, because the ways in which the concern for truth as it emerges in active viewing (analysis) can be used as a resistance. By follow-ing the filmmakers' lead in the attempt to discover psychological reality, I may very well be collaborating in the evasion of any encounter with it.

Most of the other flashbacks will be triggered by things Joe sees during his bus ride. Two teenage girls traveling on the bus giggle at Joe's cowboy getup and, interpreting their smiles as admiration, he gives his boots a quick polish with a handkerchief. His grandmother's voice-over then initiates a flashback: "You look real nice, loverboy, real nice. Make your old grandma proud! You're going to be the best-lookin' cowboy in the whole parade!" We see Joe as a boy, standing outside the western clothing store where his grandmother has just bought him the enormous cowboy hat he is wearing. Joe begins to smile uncertainly; but when the camera cuts to Sally, we realize he is watch-ing her playfully receive an ardent embrace from a tall man in a denim jacket and white cowboy hat (we guess he is, or soon will be, Sally's lover). Poignant-ly, neither of them is looking at Joe in his new hat; and it even occurs to the viewer that the visit to the shop was possibly first motivated by Sally's desire to see the man, who perhaps works there. We sense that Joe feels excluded, and that he wishes *he* were the one being embraced by the man and/or by Sally. A series of lap-dissolves and cuts follows. Joe stares out the bus window and sees an abandoned house in a field. The camera cuts to Sally on the front porch of the house. She is in her dressing gown, and waving at Joe: "Bye, honey! I'll leave a TV-dinner in the fridge—your old grandma got herself a new beau!" (In a later flashback, we will see Joe in his grandmother's bed with her and her lover, Woodsy Niles. She cuddles Joe, while Woodsy waves a beer bottle around and sings—a bit drunkenly, it seems.)

When a young woman on the bus asks Joe if he has a piece of gum he could give her daughter ("It's just 'til the Dramamine works—she gets carsick"), Joe is happy to oblige. As so often happens on journeys, it occurs to one that everybody has a "story," a fact that can be both reassuring and depressing—as in Lacan's mirror analogy about the formation of "the function of the I" as revealed in psychoanalytic experience, when the infant makes the thrilling discovery of its image in the mirror and almost simultaneously experiences a feeling of alienation and loss upon realizing that it is alone in the world. The little girl sitting next to her mother is about the same age Joe was in the previous scene, and she is equally shy. Joe cocks his hat at her playfully, and when she hides behind her comic book, smiling, we see she has been reading *Wonder Woman*. Not surprisingly, Joe suddenly feels lonely. It is entirely possible, moreover, that this little girl has no father, either. They are bound for Dallas, the woman tells him; but when Joe tells her he is going to New York City, she abruptly ends their conversation and turns away from him, using the pretext that the girl needs to sleep.

The film is unequivocal here about one of the discoveries of psychoanalysis, namely, how every child makes a primary identification with another being invested with omnipotence (usually the mother), which serves as the basis of what Daniel Lagache has called *heroic identification*, i.e., identification with outstanding and admirable personalities (John Wayne, for example, or Wonder Woman).[22] The ideal ego, as it may be called, is an essentially narcissistic formation, which comes into being in the same moment as desire. Later, when the force of the Oedipus complex is felt, the subject is inducted, as Kaja Silverman eloquently puts it, into "the speaking of his or her language of desire."[23] Silverman notes that our object-choices are always made from within specific geographical, social, economic, and historical circumstances and goes on to remark that, "although most of us make an initial libidinal investment in either our mother or our father, there is potentially nothing more individual and multifaceted, though less within conscious control, than the constellation of signifiers through which we signify those personages" (152).

The movie will appear to suggest that, in Joe's case, the boy's abandonment by his parents during a crucial early phase of his oedipal development had the consequence of fixating his desire at, or hampering its development much beyond, the mirror stage.[24] His desire is thus caught in a regressive kind of oscillation between his own image (rendered by the film literally, when he looks at himself in the mirror) and images of heroic, idealized men (John Wayne, Paul Newman) and women (the rich ladies of New York).

Despite the prominence given to Sally Buck in the narrative of Joe's boyhood, it is Joe's mother, we must infer, who was his first love. Although the film does not show him being forced by the Oedipus complex to give her up, it shows Joe quite literally being abandoned by her (as he was by his father), which will forever put him in doubt as to whether she loved him, and will overdetermine for him the question of his lovability. This question is further exacerbated by the fact that Sally will fondly cast Joe in the imaginary role of her "loverboy," but when she gets herself a "beau," will abandon Joe to evenings alone in front of the TV.

In a clearly associative train of thought, Joe recalls "crazy Annie," whom he repeatedly had sex with as a teenager. "*Do you love me, Joe? Do you love me? Do you love me?*" we hear her imploring in a small, plaintive voice. The camera remains for a moment on Joe's face, as he "remembers." We then see her running through a cornfield, toward an abandoned house, where Joe is waiting for her. The shots that follow are complex in their signification, cutting and dissolving between shots of Joe and Annie making love, a group of teenage boys (Joe is among them) cruising the streets of the town and leering at Annie, who appears to be soliciting and enjoying their attention. In one shot, Annie is being pursued by the boys across a sand dune. She stumbles and seems to be in a panic; but the shot gives way to one in which she throws herself joyfully into Joe's waiting arms (a return to the scene in which she is seen running through the cornfield to the house). Over the whole sequence, we hear her anxious, pleading voice: "*Do you love me? You're the only one. You're better, Joe. You're better than the rest of them! You're better than any of them, Joe!*"

The images of their lovemaking are more fraught than erotic, not least because of the girl's cries (again, we must bear in mind that this is Joe's "memory" of the event; the film clearly marks the point of view as his). The camera begins outside the room, a window framing the couple in a way that suggests Joe's self-consciousness. And as the camera dollies forward and comes to focus tightly on Annie's face, we realize that Joe's identification with her is acute, although shot through with ambivalence. *Does* he "love" her? Does *she* "love" him? *Is* he "the only one"? Is he "better than any of them"? These questions matter, because it is Joe who is replaying them now, as the bus carries him ever closer to New York, where he intends to reinvent himself as a hustler. The syntax of this multiple-shot flashback suggests that Joe has staged the memory as a rescue fantasy—the girl fleeing the gang of boys, but being "saved" by Joe—and as we know so well about rescue fantasies, they often mask the hero's desire to *be* rescued. And now, as he travels to New York, it is clear that he is attempting to save himself. (He looks out the window of the bus and sees an abandoned church, on the collapsing roof of which is written, in big white letters: JESUS SAVES.) Joe's decision to become a hustler, of course, is overdetermined, for—if hustlers usually like to present themselves as cynical or, at least, dispassionately professional, about sex—what are we meant to think about Joe's rationale for becoming a hustler: "Hell, the only thing I ever been good for is lovin'"? What he really means, surely, is that the only thing he has ever wanted is to be loved.

Still, as I see the film's "thesis" emerge, it occurs to me that the film invents its own seduction hypothesis. Since I cannot say what did or did not happen to Joe as a child or teenager (was Sally Buck too seductive? Was he raped by a gang of teenage boys?), I should be wary of any "explanation" offered by the film itself, especially one that encourages the idea that if only the historical truth could be discovered (itself an expression of a wish that something external be the cause of Joe's troubled sexuality), it would both legitimate and absolve Joe. But the film is all I have. And if, as Lear insists, "in psychoanalysis, truth emerges from the body,"[25] I must look to the body of the film/the film-as-body, for the truth.

In Lear's commentary on an analysis in which, throughout its early years, there recurred the theme that his analysand had possibly been abused by his father or uncle when he was a child, Lear articulates the same danger we see present in our analysis of *Midnight Cowboy*:

> At its deepest, the seduction hypothesis is not about seduction per se but about the role reality is to play in psychological explanation. The seduction hypothesis treats the intrusion of external reality as an Archimedian point, an end-of-the-line of psychological explanation. ("I'm gay because I was seduced as a child.") It tacitly assumes that historical truth is the one item within an analysis that is itself exempt from analysis. If the analyst were simply to go along with the search for historical reality or the attempt to recover a memory, he or she would in fact be collaborating with the analysand's defenses. For although the analysis would be proceeding in the name of coming to terms with one's homosexuality, in fact it would be acting out one more evasion of it.[26]

The question of what *Midnight Cowboy* is attempting to "come to terms with" might be recast ideologically. We might ask, what interests would be served by the suggestion that Joe becomes a hustler (read: screwed-up homosexual)[27] because of any or all of the following reasons: (1) he never had a father; (2) he was abandoned by his mother; (3) his grandmother treated him as her "loverboy"; (4) his first heterosexual experience was with a nymphomaniac; (5) the young men he used to hang out with gang-raped him one night.

And there is the question of Ratso's sexuality—more unambiguously homosexual—"caused" by (1) having an illiterate father who was even "dumber" than Joe, and who "spent fourteen hours a day down in that subway," shining shoes for a living—"stupid bastard coughed his lungs out from breathing in that wax all day—even a faggot undertaker couldn't get his fingernails clean"; (2) and/or his being born with a minor physical defect that causes him to limp; (3) and/or his being born in New York City in the first place.

There is no right, or final, answer to the question of Joe's sexual identity and its "causes," or to the question of the film's "intentions," but I see the film as a complicated moment in the history of the struggles for gay visibility in mainstream cinema. That the film can be accused of misfiring—of being homophobic—is a somewhat different discussion, having precisely to do with its historical moment. To quote J. L. Austin, by way of John Forrester: "All analytic statements are performative and thus are neither true nor false but, rather, either 'successfully perform' or *misfire*."[28]

Why, to repeat the question the film insistently, if implicitly, asks, does Joe become a hustler? Why does he choose *sex* as the medium in which to inscribe an identity for himself? In "Is the Rectum a Grave?" Leo Bersani announces his belief that, "There is a big secret about sex: most people don't like it"[29]—because, as he explains, sex is inimical to personhood, incompatible with the self/ego. Responding to this assertion, in an essay titled, "Straight with a Twist: Queer Theory and the Subject of Heterosexuality," Calvin Thomas makes a distinction between "heteronormative" and "queer" sex that is relevant to our understanding of Joe's sexuality: "Heteronormative sex is teleologically narrativized sex" that, in the language of Althusser, has as its purpose the reproduction of the conditions of production. Thomas thinks of heteronormativity as "antisexual in that it will only tolerate sex as a means toward the reproduction of 'the person'—both in terms of 'the child' and the ego."[30] But then he goes on to suggest that heteronormativity is abrogated whenever (straight) people actually like sex. He suggests that such people ("the childfree het couple, for example") are, in a sense, "queer."

Another question for us, then, is whether or not Joe and Annie "like" the sex they have together. This is a difficult, but not impossible, question to answer. Given that they are teenagers, however—which is also to say, still highly vulnerable to societal pressure to follow the hetero norm (the boys cruising the streets of the town together, with Joe in the very middle of the group; Annie's anxiety about whether Joe loves her, and her attempts to reassure him that he is "better than the rest of them")—it is probably not an appropriate question to ask, because teenagers are at that stage in life when they must find out, sometimes through radical experimentation, what they "like" or "don't like."

Nevertheless, this is a Hollywood movie, and every representation on the screen is supposed to "add up" to a thesis (or so we thought in 1969), and by the end of the film we feel that one thing is clear: while Joe has always wanted to be heterosexually normative, he will never succeed in being so. Thomas comments that "people who fuck in the name of identity, who make an identity out of whom they fuck, who fuck to reproduce 'the person,' are fucking heteronormatively" (33)—and we may remark that the hustler, particularly one who says, "I ain't a 'for real' cowboy, but I'm *one hell of a stud!*" is nothing if not a man who fucks in the name of identity.

TRAUMA, FANTASY, AND PERVERSION

As has been noted, *Midnight Cowboy* implicitly offers a theory about the nature of sexuality by emphasizing the way in which Joe's early object relations shape the experience of his desire. What the film renders ambiguous or undecidable, however, are the roles played by trauma and fantasy in his development.

By now, the reader may be wondering if there is a pun embedded in the title of this chapter. Certainly, the film wants the viewer to think that behind Joe's decision to become a hustler is a psychic event that may or may not have its origins in a structurally similar historical one: that whatever Joe's problem is, it has something to do with anal rape. When Ratso first invites Joe to come and stay with him, Joe's fortunes are at a new low point. Indeed, the twenty-four hours preceding the invitation have included his ejection from his hotel, and his disastrous homosexual encounter with the boy at the movie theater. In the manner of a "return of the repressed," the film's mise-en-scène becomes dense with signs of Joe's mounting distress. At the movie theater, while the boy masturbates Joe, the astronauts in the science fiction film on the screen are attempting to repair their spaceship. The images we see are rich with interpretive possibilities, as is the dialogue: "Spacecraft to Earth Control: Check trajectory—we have a malfunction of our instruments . . . orbiter module has failed to separate from upper-stage booster, as planned." The idea of where "home" might be—Earth, which we see a million miles away, silent and still; or the spaceship, to which the weightlessly floating Captain Grace is attached by a lifeline—is wittily evoked, and the truth of Silverman's analysis of the meaning of the Oedipus complex is illustrated:

> In eroticizing a particular familial axis or set of axes, the Oedipus complex awakens in us something that none of us can do without but that would otherwise be foreclosed to us: the capacity to be concerned with someone other than ourselves. And in obliging us to surrender the one we love for a series of substitute love objects, it makes room in our psyche for other people and things. . . . Only insofar as we are thrown into a kinship structure, for the effectuation of which the Oedipus complex is one possible vehicle, can there *be* a world.[31]

My preferred psychoanalytic reading, then, of the fragment of the science fiction film, is this: Joe will need Captain Grace, with his welding gun and umbilical link to the phallus-shaped "orbiter module," to get him back to Mother Earth—i.e., Captain Grace, the substitute love object, through the fantasies mobilized by sex (which the film alludes to in the close-ups of Captain Grace's crotch, his welding gun, and the latch on the spaceship that pops up when he begins welding it), will enable Joe to make the fantastic journey back to Earth, that orb symbolizing the subject's origins, maternal/pre-oedipal plenitude, unconditional love, and so on. The fact that Captain Grace's connection to the spaceship is severed when the latch (because maladroitly manipulated?) catapults him into space, could simply mean that Joe has yet to learn the language of his desire; and that until he does so, he will float in a zone of nonsubjectivity, between the inaccessible mother and the would-be vehicle of his desire.

Later, when Joe finally emerges from the movie theater, where he has spent the night dozing uncomfortably in front of the screen, we see on the marquee of one of the other Forty-second Street theaters the title of a pornographic film: *The Twisted Sex*. On Joe's transistor radio, a Wellesian, *War of the Worlds* voice is saying: "There's an invasion of America going on! You can spot the invaders easily, if they're by themselves. They're dark and heavy, and have noticeable accents. Every day, they're working themselves into more homes . . ."

As soon as Joe sees Ratso, sitting alone in a coffee shop (a return to "reality"), the voice on the radio reveals that it is nothing more than an advertisement for an invasion of "stylish furniture from Seaman's"—not an era-specific, paranoid rant about Mars-invaders, Communists, immigrants, or homosexuals.

When Ratso brings Joe home, they enter by a rear door: "I got my own private entrance, here—you're the only one who knows about it," he tells Joe complicitly, alluding unconsciously to the sodomitical theme. Upon entering the dingy apartment, Joe collapses on Ratso's bed and almost immediately falls asleep, his focus on Ratso's face dissolving and giving way to an image of Annie, whom Joe is holding in an embrace: "Joe?" she is asking him. "Do you love me, Joe?" Joe answers (or avoids answering) by kissing her ardently. When the camera cuts to an exterior shot of Sally Buck's house on a stormy night, and then to Sally entering the darkness of Joe's room, the images switch from color to black and white. As Sally turns on the light, the camera cuts to a shot of Joe and Annie in Sally's car. They stare in confusion and fright, as several young men shine flashlights into their faces and across their naked bodies. As Annie and Joe are dragged from the car by the men—Annie screaming, and Joe wide-eyed with terror—the camera intercuts the scene with shots of Sally administering an enema to Joe as a boy (she appears to be performing the task with a kind of sadistic resolve). Another shot shows her holding him across her knee and spanking his bare bottom. Annie manages to wrest herself free of the men and runs naked up to the house. Two of the men pursue her; and in the following shots, we see them raping her. Joe, meanwhile, is thrown violently across the hood of the car and sodomized by the other men in the group.

A close-up of Sally putting a chocolate in her mouth, and slowly chewing it with satisfaction, is followed by shots of uniformed policemen leading away the apprehended rapists (Ratso is among them; he is grinning into the camera), while Annie, wrapped in a blanket, points to Joe, and repeats, madly: "He's the one! He's the only one!"

The rest of Joe's brief nightmare combines elements from the day's residue (e.g., arriving at the back entrance to Ratso's building) with images of a condemned building collapsing under the impact of a wrecking ball; Joe being cornered in the alley behind Ratso's building, and being cornered in the same alley by his rapists from the scene before; Annie being taken away in an ambulance (a shot repeated with Eisensteinian obsessiveness, as Joe's nightmare reaches an intolerable pitch); Ratso provoking Joe with a broken bottle; and Annie's ambulance driving through Times Square, its siren blaring.

Joe wakes up in a violent, jerking movement, and stares wildly about the darkened room. In a panicky voice, he demands to know where his boots are. "The smart thing for me to do is haul my ass out of here," he says, thereby revealing the subtext of the scene—his "fear" of being raped by Ratso. "Well, you want me to stay here!" he blurts out, struggling to identify his fear. "You're after something! What are you after?" he says all in a rush. Ratso shrugs vaguely. Joe then says, half as a question: "You don't *look* like a fag . . ."

Ratso protests, "What's that supposed to mean?" and Joe replies, floundering: "Well, you want me to stay here tonight, that's the idea, ain't it?" Ratso answers him coolly: "Look, I'm not forcing you. Like, I mean, who's forcing you?"

The issue thus surfaces; but it is quickly suppressed. Joe suddenly announces, rather absurdly, that he has decided to "stay here a couple of days," adding: "I just thought you should know, that's all." As the scene ends, it is obvious that they both prefer not to acknowledge the unruly homosexual feeling at the root of Joe's anxiety, and that they will, in effect, pretend that the question has been settled: both men are straight, and their honor has been preserved against aspersions of homosexuality—Joe explaining that he hopes Ratso understands, "I'm a truly dangerous person" when someone "does me bad"; and Ratso telling Joe that, as long as Joe stays with him, in his apartment, he is to be called Rico, not Ratso. The scene ends on them getting ready to sleep. The camera catches Joe smiling to himself in the dark and hugging his radio close to his chest. And as a way of saying goodnight, he makes one, final (friendly) threat, signaling that the issue of their desire is still alive between them: "Keep your meat-hooks off my radio!"

In a short paper titled "Quandaries of the Incest Taboo," Judith Butler refers to the recent emergence of trauma studies, in which the point is made that trauma, by definition, is not "capturable" through representation or, indeed, recollection, because "it is precisely that which renders all memory false . . . and which is known through the gap that disrupts all efforts at narrative reconstruction."[32] In *Midnight Cowboy* we get a representation of an event (Joe being raped, etc.), but we cannot know if Joe actually was ever raped. The "scene" is clearly marked as a dream, but this does not necessarily simplify the problem of reading. The distortions specific to dreaming notwithstanding, the rape could be a wish transmuted into a false memory, or a representation of something unthinkable that actually did happen, or a traumatic fantasy produced by the incest taboo.

It is always possible, Butler remarks, to claim that from a clinical perspective it does not matter whether or not trauma happened, "since the point is

to interrogate the psychic meaning of a report without judging its reality"
(43). But, she asks:

> Can we really dissociate the question of psychic meaning from that of
> the "event" if a certain fuzziness about the event having taken place is
> precisely part of its traumatic effect? It may be that what is unthinkable
> is precisely a fantasy that is disavowed, or it may be that what is un-
> thinkable is the act that a parent performed (was willing to perform),
> or it may be that what is unthinkable is precisely their convergence in
> the event. (43)

The way in which *Midnight Cowboy* creates a certain fuzziness around the
links among Joe's recollection of Sally's (possibly) seductive manner toward
him (and, perhaps more importantly, her abandonment of him when she
finds herself a new "beau"); his yearning to be, or to have, her lover, Woodsy
Niles; Joe's competition with his cohort of teenage boys for Annie's sexual favors; and his rape by these same young men, suggests several interpretive
possibilities. But what concerns me most is the overarching connection the
film draws between the irregular familial arrangements of Joe's childhood,
coupled with his experience of an apparently specific trauma, on the one
hand, and Joe's manifestations of homosexual feeling (which may or may
not eventually consolidate in a homosexual identity) on the other. Although
the film's logic of sexual identity formation is in fact perfectly oedipal, it
means to show what can happen when the oedipal scenario goes *wrong*—
when the object of a boy's emotional-erotic yearning is for the "father"
rather than for the "mother."

Whereas Butler observes that "the very sign of trauma is the loss of access
to the terms that establish historical veracity—that is, where what is historical and what is true become unknowable or unthinkable" (42–43), she both
acknowledges that incestuous fantasy and its prohibition is the bedrock
mechanism of the Oedipus complex, and objects to the widespread notion
that the proper and normative solution to the incest prohibition is heterosexuality. *Midnight Cowboy*, in effect, illustrates her point: the movie would
seem to understand homosexuality only as a perversion (e.g., *The Twisted
Sex*) or as a disaster (a "falling away from the stars"—as we see it occur in the
science fiction film Joe watches). The oedipal scenario leaves no place for gay
people, except as aberrations from the norm. Homosexuality is conceived by
the ideology underpinning the film (or against which it is pitted) as "unthinkable," and must, therefore—like incest—be figured in terms of trauma,

which can only be mastered by a perverse strategy, such as dressing up in a cowboy outfit and exchanging sex for money.

"HUSH, LITTLE BABY . . ."

Like storytelling and dreams, perversions are a way of coping with events, giving order and shape to experiences that have to be mastered in some way, so that the subject can live. Louise Kaplan explains in *Female Perversions* that a perversion is a psychological strategy that differs from other mental strategies in that it demands a performance. The overall strategy operates in the same way for males and females, although "what makes all the difference between the male and female perversions is the social gender stereotype that is brought into the foreground of the enactment."[33] Joe Buck sees himself as a performer in a movie called "life" but, quite understandably, he wants his performance and his life to feel *real*. He needs, above all, to "connect" with another human being—to feel that he matters to someone who will not only appreciate the cowboy performance but see the Joe Buck in it and behind it. All the men and women who pick him up are, of course, playing out their own fantasies involving sex with a "cowboy," and so Joe, who has an insecure sense of a "self" apart from his cowboy persona, is alienated by these experiences. For example, at the Warholian party he and Ratso attend, a woman (Brenda Vaccaro) agrees to buy him for the night. When she learns his name, she squeals with delight: "Joe! Ooh, *fabulous!* Joe could be anyone—I like that!" Later, when he finds himself unable to "perform," she playfully reveals the funny image that has come into her mind: "I had this image of a policeman without his stick, and a bugler without his horn . . . *et cetera, et cetera, et cetera!*" Joe is mortified that he is unable to get an erection, because he has unwisely reduced his identity to that of a performing (heterosexual) penis. When she suggests they play "scribbage" (actually, Scrabble, though not named in the film) to ease his anxiety, Joe's problem—because repressed—returns in his inability to think of a word ending in "y" (i.e., *why*; the Scrabble game is emblematic of how the movie works—by connotation and association). She suggests: "Say, pay, lay. Hey . . . *gay* ends in 'y'! Do you like that? Gay, fey . . . is that your problem, baby?"

If we have to ask who the "real" Joe Buck is, we have only to remember the film's opening shots of him naked in the shower: as he himself knows, "reality," or "truth," is rooted in the body. He knows he "ain't a 'for real' cowboy," but his touchstone in a confusing world is his *desire* (symbolized by the film in those complexly signifying shots of him looking at himself in the mirror). One of the more intriguing things about *Midnight Cowboy* is its preoccupation with the question of whether Joe in this regard is really so very different from anybody else in late twentieth-century America. By the late 1960s, this postmodern conception of subjectivity, which sees gender as fundamentally performative, was beginning to be perceived as normal—not necessarily as perverse at all—just as homosexuality was beginning to find its place in the spectrum of normal (i.e., nonperverse) sexualities. The movie shows Joe struggling to find an appropriate language for his desire, to give a name to his feelings and still feel good about himself, which is why both Joe and the film are obsessed with "origins"—the origins of his desire, and whether they are related to his origins in a family without a father, and so on. Joe's orphan desire has no name, which is also why we are made to wonder if, or why, he was raped as a teenager—the logic being that this "event" might be the key to identifying his desire. The blank screen of the film's first shot is a reminder, however, that although the movie will explore Joe's origins in the oedipal terms of the nuclear family, the Oedipus complex is not about the nuclear family. It is, rather, as Juliet Mitchell insists, about the institution of culture—it "epitomizes man's entry into culture itself."[34] We recall that in the opening shots of the film we hear a movie western on the sound track and see the screen of a drive-in movie theater *before* Joe enters (the world of the film) and starts to tell us his story.

Whereas Butler focuses on the unrepresentable event-structure of incest and the way in which heterosexual kinship norms maintain a stake in the experiential unintelligibility of incest as an *event*, while successfully rendering it as a *taboo* with the power to organize culturally acceptable forms of love (i.e., to determine what is normal and what is pathological), Mitchell, in "The Vortex Beneath the Story," insists that "the trauma and its potential cure through the telling of it as a story are likely aspects of the human condition; they are not specifics of particular pathologies." She sees it as distinctly problematic that there has been a return in the last decade of the twentieth century of "the trauma and the story as cause and solution of psychic ill-being, rather than as aspects of the human condition."[35]

There is a sense in which Butler and Mitchell are in agreement. *Midnight Cowboy*, as a symptom of our culture, pathologizes Joe's desire, insisting that he should find his same-sex desires only a shade less unthinkable than incest, or that we should understand them as resulting from trauma. As I suggested much earlier in this essay, the film does what Turim observes is an abiding hermeneutic strategy of the psychological melodramas of the 1940s—it holds out a single key to psychic disorder, which renders the narrative revelation orderly yet psychoanalytically false.[36] But everyone, Mitchell points out, experiences many large and small traumas. These fall over the primary trauma—which she identifies as the helpless, newborn baby's first experience of anxiety "when its existence is threatened because of the failure of a provision of its needs."[37] Mitchell describes this in terms of an "effraction, or breaking in, of the neonate's protective shield," which becomes the condition of what is known as "primary repression." This effraction is "an energetic force that sets up a vortex within the individual and then draws chaotic and primitive representations to it" (48). This vortex, or gap, is "followed by a fantasmatic and an identificatory filling of that gap," which, she argues, we might call "a model of human or mammalian protodesire" (48).

Joe's grandmother—when she sings for Joe the lullaby, "Hush, Little Baby"—acknowledges in her commonsense way the many large and small traumas that everyone experiences. The song, in effect, offers a series of solutions—or rather, always the *same* solution—to life's long list of disappointed desires:

> Hush, little baby, don't say a word,
> Grandma's gonna buy you a mockin' bird.
> And if that mockin' bird don't sing,
> Grandma's gonna buy you a golden ring.
> And if that golden ring turns brass,
> Grandma's gonna buy you a looking glass.
> And if that looking glass gets broke,
> Grandma's gonna buy you a billy goat.
> Hush, little baby, don't say a word,
> Grandma's gonna buy you a mockin' bird.

I have always found *Midnight Cowboy* to be a depressing film—perhaps because the director cannot help making Joe Buck's story a melancholy one. Without the saving irony of a Sirk or a Fassbinder, John Schlesinger's melodrama suggests that perverse performances are always about desperate need. And Moon's insight that the film is about the anguish of two men trying to establish a meaningful relationship, despite their both being masochists in relation to each other, recalls Kaplan's observation that the extreme masochist's script (like that of Emma Bovary, whom Joe resembles in some striking particulars) is ultimately about "unbearable losses, profound depression, and death."[38] Like *Midnight Cowboy*'s later cousin, *My Own Private*

Idaho (1991), the movie suggests that for gay people (whom these films cannot distinguish from psychologically damaged people in general), the mocking bird will never sing, the golden ring will inevitably turn brass, and the looking glass will always break. The point, perhaps, is that Grandma—representing heterosexual kinship structures, shall we say—cannot buy Joe what he needs, cannot be his "looking glass," and so on. What he must do is to accept that he himself is the billy goat (as is Ratso) and to make his happiness with that. As a work of mourning, the film does try to suggest that, by the time Ratso dies, Joe's relationship with Ratso has sufficiently fortified his ego to enable him to carry on, indeed, to prevail, in a new life in Florida. The film wants us to feel that the image of Ratso (who *loved* him, *needed* him) has been internalized by Joe, where it will join the image of Sally Buck, to add social reality and meaning to that image of himself in the mirror.

But like the endings of most melodramas, the ending of *Midnight Cowboy* is not entirely persuasive. In the traditional form of the lullaby, there is theoretically no end to the stream of anticipated disappointments; it always recommences after the illogical stanza: "If that horse and cart fall down, then you'll be the sweetest little baby in town." In other words, *whatever* happens, know that you are *loved*. Only, in Joe's case, this crucial knowledge, or belief, is missing. Like every lullaby, the song is meant to soothe. It assures the child that whatever the disappointment, or even trauma, there is a solution, and there will be a way to cope. As a song about how to (in Joe's phrase) "git along, little dogie," it reveals that every object of desire is really, and always, a substitute object. In the successful formation of a sturdy ego, the subject's desire always returns to a fantasmatic origin—in the lullaby, as Joe recalls it being sung to him as a child, it is Sally Buck, his "grandma." But whether it is psychologically possible to replace even the "original" love object (grandma)—when it is discovered that she herself is a substitute love object for one that does not, for all practical purposes, exist (Joe not having internalized an image of his parents), and that her promises were in a sense hollow ("Grandma's gonna buy . . .")—is a question the film cannot really answer.

THE NOVEL

The film, while remarkably faithful to James Leo Herlihy's novel, flirts with the notion that Joe is a latent homosexual, whereas the novel is at once more knowing and less sure—both more troubled and pessimistic, and potentially more hopeful—about the whole question of Joe's sexual identity.[39]

Toward the end of part one, as Joe prepares to leave Texas, he starts to carry within him "a feeling, a belief, that everything would change for the better when he had created himself in a certain new image. He knew what the image was, that of a cowboy, but he never did press himself too far on the question of how that image would make his life different."[40] Then, echoing the description psychoanalysis gives of the formation of the ego through a series of identifications, and resonating with the truth of recent theory's insights into the performative nature of gender, the narrator comments:

> There is an Indian legend that at a certain time in the life of a young man he is given a dream in which he sees a mask, and when he awakens he must set to work carving a real mask in that dream image. This is the mask he must wear into battle in order to be victorious. It was as if Joe Buck had had such a dream, and his life was given over to the carving of the mask. (96)

Joe wanders the streets of the town at night, "like a warrior scout" searching for something. "Most of what passed his eye left no more of a mark on him than images leave on the face of a mirror." But there are three images that show themselves "in memory" to him over and over again:

> One was a cutout image of a young Hollywood actor floodlighted on top of a movie marquee. He stood there with his suntanned snarl in full color, two stories bigger than life, legs apart, pelvis thrust forward, and he was in the act of turning a big gun on you. The barrel of it was coming at you thick and gleaming, and it was about to go off.
>
> The second article in his nighttime collection of images was a brief scene on a street corner. A long white convertible was stopped for a red light. The woman in the driver's seat was looking at a tall, handsome young man in Western clothes standing at the curb. Her motor died under her. But she kept on looking at the young man. After a moment she said, "I can't get it started without help." And the young man said, "I'll *bet* you can't, honey."
>
> The third picture to remain in him from these walks was the only one he couldn't enjoy looking at later. But whether or not he liked it, it was one of the three and would not be discarded. This was a large poster depicting that bearded young man in whose eyes resides all the sorrow of history. Above his head was a message attributed to him in

large Gothic typeface, and on the bottom of the poster, scrawled there in raspberry-colored lipstick, were the words FUCK THEE.

And these were the things Joe Buck found as he was seeking to find his way. (97)

The novel thus streamlines Joe's backstory into three interlocking, overlapping themes, and like these same themes in the film, they are palpably charged by a libido seeking definition and a stable object. He feels himself to be potentially all of these "characters"—a movie cowboy; a lover of women; an abject figure of suffering—but does not know how to integrate his personality, to create a coherent identity. He does the best he can, but as he approaches New York City on the Greyhound bus, "It occurred to him that he might be embroiled in some colossal confidence game in which he was both victim and perpetrator" (102).

During his worst days in New York, he feels "an awareness entering him too momentous to acknowledge: he was a nothing person, a person of no time, and no place and no worth to anyone at all" (149). Homeless and destitute, and with his mind "fallen into that state of wondering in which all the usual kinds of sense are rendered hollow," the one thing that never fails to catch his interest is "the sight of other men at their labor" (152). He is fascinated by these men and their sense of purpose but feels excluded in some fundamental way. They are following a different script, one that was not written for him: "Why did a man work? For money. What did he spend it on? Rent, food, a family. It was as simple as could be. And therefore all the more baffling" (152).

Like his movie cowboy heroes, Joe does not have a family to support—although, at the very end of the novel, the collapse of Ratso's health will give him a keen sense of purpose, and he will tell "Townie," the man who picks him up the very night Joe resolves to get Ratso down to Florida: "I got family, goddammit, an' I got to get 'em down to Florida quick. Now you reach in there and peel me off fifty dollars" (232). (The movie, we remember, shows Joe rehearsing his speech in the mirror in the bathroom: "I got a sick boy, and I'm gonna get him South!" The change of inflection is very slight, but typical of the film's tendency to homoeroticize, or render ambiguous, what the novel more consistently suggests is a desperate yearning for a sense of familial connection.) Once they are on the bus to Florida, Joe realizes that he likes the feeling that this responsibility "for the care of another person" gives him: "He felt joined to everything that touched him, and pretty soon he fell asleep, dreaming his golden-people dream" (243).

Even (or especially) during the best days of his "alliance" (164) with Ratso, however, before the winter comes, and before Ratso's health starts to rapidly deteriorate, we realize that theirs is a perverse relationship. (But as Townie would say, "it works!") Herlihy describes how, "for the first time in his life [Joe] felt himself released from the necessity of grinning and posturing and yearning for the attention of others. Nowadays he had, in the person of Ratso Rizzo, someone who needed his presence in an urgent, almost frantic way that was a balm to something in him that had long been exposed and enflamed and itching to be soothed. God alone knew how or why, but he had somehow actually stumbled upon a creature who seemed to worship him" (165–66). Nevertheless, on the whole, Joe "remained cranky and disagreeable in his behavior toward the little blond runt. He realized it, too. Joe knew good and well he had become a pain in the neck, and what's more he was none too concerned about it. But there was a reason for his unconcern: He was happy" (165).

In Townie's theory of human happiness, Herlihy offers another caution to the reader who might be too quick to judge what is normal and what is

FIGURE 6.7 When Ratso's health collapses, his desire for Joe becomes a helpless need.

"sick."[41] The middle-aged bachelor from Chicago explains to Joe: "It's all very simple: The ideal of the infant is to maintain its mother's love—forever. I have done this. I have lived this ideal existence" (218). He admits he is passionate on the subject of his right to choose how he wishes to live, "and of course we live in an age in which all passion is suspect. All the old values have these ugly little clinical names now: Loyalty is fixation, duty is guilt, and all love is some sort of complex! . . . And you see, it's rarely the psychiatrist himself who talks such nonsense, it's your best friends! But don't you think it takes a *tiny* mind to hand down such judgments on the secret heart of another?" Townie's analyst assures him that his close attachment to his ninety-four-year-old mother is "an extremely successful relationship. And why? Because it works!" (218).

Townie's analyst may be right, but in Herlihy's novel there is always an-*other* side to every picture, an *under*side to every appearance—as we have it in the story about Tombaby Barefoot, the "big pale epicene Indian" (77) who lives with his mother, and who rapes Joe in a nightmarish scene which, like the scene of Joe's rape in the movie, resonates with incest dread.

When Herlihy recounts the Indian legend about how every young man, at a certain time in his life, is "given a dream" (by ideology?), which will tell him what mask to wear in battle, in order to be victorious, we recognize the process of identification at work in the performative function of masks (cf. *Batman*), but we may also wonder what is *behind* the mask. Herlihy's reference here to Native American culture, and to Joe's searching the streets of Houston "like a warrior scout," for something that will help him "find his way," is in a tradition that runs through American literature and art, and of course, the cinema, of the Native American as a noble embodiment of a certain idea of authenticity. As a policeman has his stick, and a bugler his horn, the cowboy, we could say, has his Indian.

Joe's "Indian" is an abstraction, a hazy idea having something to do with the qualities of a warrior (fiercely courageous, proud, *brave*) and a scout (active—the agent of his desire). Like Joe, he is a loner, and yet he belongs to a tribe, with its legends and its legacies that are passed down from one generation to the next. But the Indian Joe meets one night in a ramshackle town called Newville, Texas, is not this fantasy Indian invoked by the narrator. Tombaby Barefoot is an ugly, hermaphroditic creature, a "halfbreed," whose ghastly mother conspires with Joe's sinister, new "friend" Perry to ambush Joe in her whorehouse, so that her son may rape him there. ("You want it Tombaby, they's only one way you gonna have it," she tells her grotesque offspring.) What Joe "wants" is more difficult to say. Earlier in the evening,

Perry shares some marijuana with Joe in Joe's hotel room, saying: "[I am here] to help you find out what you want and show you how to take it" (63).

The first thing Joe wants, Perry correctly surmises, is to be "cool," like himself. Perry lies back on Joe's bed, and in his "friendly, deep, sweet and dark narcotic voice," instructs him: "You've got to get cool. Find out what you want and rule out everything else, and then you'll be as cool as can be" (64). Perry's aim, in this carefully controlled, perverse scenario, is to sexually humiliate Joe, whose naïveté and unconscious ambivalence (which he calls Joe's "virginity") excites him. "If we're going to be friends, Joe, there's just one rule [. . .] and the rule is, no crap. There is to be no crap. None. I am sick of people who know what they want and won't take it, won't even speak up and name it. When I say to you, 'What do you want, Joe,' you answer. You just say whatever that thing is you want. You understand me?" (65).

In response to Perry's pressure to name his desire, Joe has a dreadful vision in which he places a shovel in the hands of some shadowy creature, who then uses the shovel to dig a grave next to Sally's. There is an open coffin sitting next to the new grave, and the coffin has "a beautiful young person in it: himself." The vision is quickly extinguished, and Joe falls into a kind of delirium: "What's this sombitch want with me? his mind demanded over and over again. Don't he know I'm, I'm, I'm . . ." (68). As Joe returns to consciousness, Perry takes hold of his shoulders and pushes him onto his back with great force, and straddles him. These actions are "sudden enough to drive out the big, sharp-edged, heavy horror that was in him. . . . His face was wet. Apparently he'd been crying" (68). Joe decides that if Perry asks him once more what he wants—"just once more, I'll tell him, I'll tell him all right. Tell him I want a blonde lady to fuck, and have her take care of me all my life . . ." (67–68).

There is no doubt here—as there is some doubt in the movie—about what Joe wants, and there is no reason to think that his desire, as he identifies it, is really a substitute configuration for anything other than the entirely normal incestuous fantasy he has of himself in a coffin next to his grandmother's grave.

So dire is his need for that (mother)-son connection, which would validate him, that he is drawn, despite himself, into ever more desperate and perverse situations:

Joe knew good and well that the woman [Tombaby Barefoot's mother] . . . was a frightful person. She had said things appalling enough to shrivel the balls of Tombaby Barefoot a dozen times over, and she was clearly selfish and callous and disagreeable in all possible ways. He knew too that in Tombaby here, hands folded grandmotherlike across his stomach, was a cold skinny black tongue connected to a heart full of poison. And the house itself, with so many darknesses beyond the darknesses he could see, was fearsome as a nest of vipers. But still he would have moved into it with these persons on a second's notice. For they were not one, alone in the place, but two, sharing the horrors of it and of one another; and he saw clearly—without knowing what name to give it (love? hate?) or how it came to be or what it could lead to— some kind of priceless safety in their connection with one another. (84)

Among the other representations of desire offered by the novel, through which we, and Joe himself, may come to know Joe's "secret heart" (as Townie calls it), is the image of Hansel and Gretel MacAlbertson. Joe is fascinated by them: "They seemed to be brother and sister, perhaps even twins. There was no great difference in their apparent genders. Her hair was short for a girl and his long for a boy. Both were blond, gray-eyed, and gently pretty; neither wore any makeup. The girl was clearly the bolder of the two" (176). The contrast between what the MacAlbertsons represent and what is represented by the woman Joe meets at their strange, otherworldly party, and who takes him back to her apartment for a night of sex, could not be greater. At the point of bringing the woman to orgasm, when "it was clear to Joe Buck that the woman knew she was going to have her freedom":

[He] labored with greater and greater insistence to deliver it to her, not because he wanted her free but because he wanted to feel himself the deliverer, wanted to know that power again in himself, and then there was a long cry like a deliberate scream coming from her, and he kept on for a moment as if he wanted to sign his name in blood and with a flourish to what he had done; and in doing this, something unexpected happened: He himself was set free. (204)

Despite initial difficulties, this is the first (and last) time Joe is able to perform successfully *as a hustler*. It is a perverse performance that satisfies the woman—who has already admitted that "when the time comes [to discuss it with her analyst], naturally, I'll have to ask myself *why* do I choose a cowboy, and second, why a cowboy *whore*" (192)—and that satisfies Joe, for whom so much has been riding on his ability to perform on command. Joe wants to embody the image of masculinity he projects, and in a manner of speaking, he succeeds this once: When she first meets Joe, the woman says

FIGURE 6.8 The MacAlbertson "twins" (Gastone Rossilli and Viva), as they are called in Herlihy's novel, single out Joe for an invitation to their party. (Courtesy Photofest)

to him: "Tonight, when I came out of that bathroom and saw you, pure symbol—that's what you are, you know, symbol, oh yes, pure symbol, nothing more, nothing less. . . . Anyway, I *knew* I was going to make a *real* breakthrough" (192).

And yet, moments after he himself is "set free," he thinks of the MacAlbertsons, two young people in black, slender and blond and as plain as day:

He looked at these children in his mind and entered into their mystery. Saw them come into being full-grown before his eyes, saw them walking hand in hand against a backdrop of nothingness, together but unjoined, motherless and fatherless and without real gender, unconnected to the world or to who they themselves were, or where, or what, saw them wandering in search of others passing through the same empty regions, others born loose and alien and unconnected as they themselves were, and in this brief clarity Joe Buck had a sense of knowing just who the children were: his own. His own offspring, born full-grown from this very night's union. (205)

Herlihy successfully conveys the powerful dialectic in sex between ego and desire, self and the shattering of the self. The incestuous fantasy that the MacAlbertson "twins" unconsciously trigger in Joe when he first meets them is released into his consciousness because, despite everything—the woman's self-absorbed psychobabble; his own need to succeed as a "stud"; Ratso's contemptuous dismissal of the MacAlbertsons—he trusts his desire to set him free. Ratso has already declared his own desire, in effect, when he says to Joe: "If you want the word on that brother and sister act, *I'll* give you the word: Hansel's a fag, and Gretel's got the hots for herself. So who cares, right?" (188). But when Joe conjures the image of them, he answers for himself that question he heard on his radio, walking through Times Square one evening, *"What do you want, more than anything in the world?"*[42] He enters into their mystery: a realization of the self in the same moment of its dissolution, incest not as a trauma inscribed within the dire imperatives of the heterosexual kinship system's taboo, but as a fantasy of perfect union, together but unjoined, beyond gender, beyond time and space.

7

INNERSPACE
A Spectacular Voyage to the Heart of Identity

In a 1974 newspaper article entitled, "When Boy Meets Boy, What's a Girl to Do?" film critic Kathleen Carroll wondered, "Why, all of a sudden, does Hollywood seem so intensely interested in exploring man-to-man relationships? Not that movies haven't done it before. We have had Spencer Tracy and Clark Gable in *Boom Town*, Sydney Poitier and Tony Curtis in *The Defiant Ones*, and many more, but never so many movies on the subject at one time." Citing *Papillon*, *The Sting*, *Scarecrow*, and *Bang the Drum Slowly*, among others, Carroll observed that "Hollywood seems to be leaning towards the idea, first espoused by the ancient Greeks, that a friendship between two obviously virile males is the most desirable of all human relationships, and that it can be a far more fulfilling experience than the love relationship between a man and a woman."[1] Then, in a casually homophobic remark intended to be approving, Carroll told her readers that "men are learning what it means to care about another man, not in the homosexual sense (for none of the movies we are talking about have even the faintest suggestion of homosexuality), but in a very real sense."

Carroll's phrasing betrays a shallow understanding of homosocial desire (it is simply not true, for example, that the films she mentions haven't "the faintest suggestion of homosexuality"), but her glib observations signal a shift in popular perceptions of how the affective element in male homosocial relationships might be acceptably represented in mainstream cinema. If anything has changed since 1974, it is the presumptuous certainty that allowed Carroll, writing in the spirit of heterosexual entitlement that characterizes the mainstream press, to use the phrase "in a very real sense" (as opposed to "the homosexual sense") and assume her readers would know what she meant. Indeed, only two years later, writing in the *Village Voice*, Andrew Sarris declared that, "Above all, there is now a disturbing confusion about 'normality' where once there seemed to be blissful certitude. Or was there?"[2] He went on to observe that, "What is most fascinating about most movies is their virtually infinite capacity for reinterpretation. We think that we see everything at the time, but we never do."

A genre that has come in for complex rethinking is the buddy film, not because we can look back at old buddy films and reinterpret them as love stories between men, but because the genre itself is undergoing a crisis of self-consciousness.[3] Some recent developments in the evolution of the genre have been monitored by a number of critics. For example, Vincent Canby in 1979 sounded a defensive alarm in a *New York Times* article bearing the title, "Male-Bonding? Now Wait a Minute!" He argued that "it's men who are being condescended to and patronized by moviemakers, most of whom, it should be emphasized, are men. Brothers, it's brothers not sisters who are shattering our egos, making us uncertain about our identities and persuading us to question something called 'male-bonding,' which used to be known simply as friendship. Male bonding? Even the jargon is pejorative."[4]

In 1982, Molly Haskell noted irritably that "just when we thought the buddy-buddy film was finished—no more Paul Newman and Robert Redford riding off into the sunset—male bonding resurfaces in a new form. The latest twist is fathers and sons or, to use the currently fashionable term, "male parenting." *Kramer vs. Kramer. Ordinary People. Carbon Copy. Paternity. On Golden Pond.* The upcoming *Missing.* They all show busy or repressed fathers learning to love their offspring, usually male. The man-to-manness of the bond certifies the virility of the new parenting."[5]

Walter Goodman put in a good word for "boys" movies" in a 1987 *New York Times* article entitled, "Prankster Pals: the Appeal Never Ages." The pull-quote echoed his title: "From *Gunga Din* to *Stakeout*, buddies involved in good-natured mischief have proved an irresistible mix."[6]

In 1988, Haskell identified another variation of the buddy film in "The Odder Couples: Is Being a Misfit the New Precondition for Male Friendship?" Haskell obligingly pointed out that "male bonding is nothing new in the movies: Edward G. Robinson and Douglas Fairbanks, Jr. loved each other more than any woman in *Little Caesar* (1931), and Paul Newman and Robert Redford were boys together in *Butch Cassidy and the Sundance Kid* and *The Sting.* But men onscreen usually have shied away from displays of emotion that some of them associate with wimpishness. Taking their cue from women, men are starting to open up to one another, and going public in confessional forums like the 'About Men' column in the *New York Times Magazine.* Recent movies like *Dominick & Eugene, Patti Rocks,* and the classic *Birdy* reflect this new *glasnost,* but the tortured fraternal relationships in these films suggest that conditions still have to be very special for men to express their feelings of love for one another."[7]

Robin Wood takes the view that, within their social context, buddy movies of the 1970s are "more interesting than is generally recognized." He writes in *Hollywood from Vietnam to Reagan* that "the basic motivating premise of of the '70s buddy movie is not the presence of the male relationship but the absence of home."[8] He identifies *Butch Cassidy and the Sundance Kid, Easy Rider,* and *Midnight Cowboy* (all released in 1969) as the three films that effectively launched the cycle, and he makes a case for the later films, "of which *Thunderbolt and Lightfoot* [1974], *Scarecrow* [1973], and *California Split* [1974] are the most distinguished and idiosyncratic," as being variations on the principles established in 1969.

By 1987, the year *Innerspace* was released in the United States,[9] the American buddy film seemed to be on the verge of admitting that the homosocial desire which has always fueled the genre refers to a *continuum* of relations between men that includes mentorship, rivalry, "male bonding," and homosexuality. Whereas historically the collaborations of the male characters in the buddy film have been articulated in ways that "separate homoeroticism from the sanctioned male bonding that upholds patriarchy,"[10] *Innerspace* riskily invests the relationship of its two main characters with a degree of homoeroticism that deconstructs the genre.

Innerspace is an adventure-comedy about a man who is miniaturized in a scientific experiment to the size of a near-invisible speck. Instead of being injected into a rabbit, as planned by Ozzie the scientist, Tuck Pendleton (Dennis Quaid) and his diving pod are accidentally injected into a supermarket clerk, Jack Putter (Martin Short), when industrial spies raid the miniaturization laboratory. The villains make off with the reenlargement chip, which is useless without the miniaturization device now inside Jack, and of course Tuck cannot return to normal size unless Jack can retrieve the reenlargement chip from the villains.

But *Innerspace*'s unconscious is more interesting than its subtext. The film is driven by a pretended sexual anxiety that turns out to be real, and it attempts (impossibly) to regain confidence in some of the old certainties—epistemological certainties that governed the making of a film like *Fantastic Voyage* (Richard Fleischer, 1966), for example, and that have been eroded in what has come to be called postmodernity. The film in the end seeks to confirm the validity of "Hollywood" narrative; the space of Renaissance perspective; and the reassuring "rightness" of patriarchal culture's heterosexual paradigm. In so doing, the film's cocky confidence wavers, and it offers an overdetermined and contradictory discourse on the repression of homosexuality. The results are problematic for the spectator. One is presented with the postmodern difficulty of how to read a film that is so self-consciously ironic and knowing in its mode of address that it offers no stable position from which to properly gauge its ironies and transgressive effects.

Innerspace introduces Tuck and Jack as characters both with un-heterosexual tendencies, and the film's half-hearted ideological imperative is to make them into "normal," well-adjusted, heterosexual men. The film understands sexuality in Freudian terms of a narrative of successive phases moving toward sexual maturity, and it posits that Tuck is arrested in an autoerotic–latently homosexual phase, and that Jack is neurotically asexual. And yet there is an exuberant homoeroticism in the film's preoccupation with their relationship that exceeds the prohibitive function of dominant ideology.

A Repressed Desire

Tuck's "problem" is suggested in the film's opening scenes—even in the very first shot following the credit sequence, of an extreme close-up of some whiskey being poured into a glass filled with ice cubes. This unusual image not only spectacularly establishes the magnification/miniaturization theme but launches the ever-present themes in the film of repression and sublimation (Tuck drinks too much). While it is never explained explicitly why Tuck drinks too much, it becomes obvious soon enough, and when his girlfriend Lydia (Meg Ryan) tells him that their relationship is over, Tuck's pained response suggests the nature of the repressed desire that the film will treat more elaborately later on: "I don't get it. I get a little drunk; I make an ass out of myself. What's the big deal?"

The big deal, of course, is that "real" men do not make asses out of themselves. At the formal Air Force dinner at which Tuck causes an embarrassing scene, a fellow officer tells him to stop being ironic about the heroism of their public image as test pilots. Tuck's response refers in a very direct way to the film's core obsessions: "Oh, gosh, I'm sorry, Rusty. Really, you're right. But at least when *my* 'moment of truth' came, *I* didn't take a dump down the leg of *my* flightsuit!" While Tuck's remark may seem to be about human frailty, or a lack of courage, he means it to provoke specifically masculine anxieties

FIGURE 7.1 *Innerspace* (1987): Lydia (Meg Ryan) decides to leave Tuck (Dennis Quaid) because his alcoholic excesses are destroying their relationship.

about homosexuality (as sodomy)—the passivity it implies to these men, who can only understand passivity as a negative and feminine mode—and about the ancient memory of infantile dependency and helplessness that reference to a loss of control of the anal sphincter evokes. Since the masculine norm of society is committed to independence, and control, it is not surprising that sexual passivity (especially in relation to another man) and anal eroticism are disallowed.

When Tuck is later injected into Jack Putter's ass, however, his "cure" begins. Their incestuous adventure not only makes Jack into a "real" man, but it concludes with Tuck and Lydia's wedding, and we have to assume that Tuck's problem—signified by his drinking—has been resolved. This adventure, in psychoanalytic terms, is an elaborate *incorporation fantasy* in which the viewer can think of Tuck as one tiny spermatozoön, or as Jack's id and superego, or as a subject experiencing a fantastic leap from autoerotic narcissism to the field of the "other."

bing the Polaroid camera of another to snap a picture of himself and her, before climbing into the pod. These identity-affirming gestures are consistent with other evidence of an obsession with a masculinity guaranteed by the image.

RABBIT REDUX

After the scene in which he becomes maudlin drunk, we are made to share Lydia's impression that Tuck has been shifting his desire from her (i.e., the "normal" object) to gadgetry and rabbits. Some research on rabbits is presumably necessary for the miniaturization experiment he will undergo, since Ozzie intends to inject him into a rabbit, but he has taken it quite far (to a fetishistic degree—filling his apartment with robotic equipment, with stuffed rabbits, pictures of rabbits, toy rabbits), and when he is accidentally injected into Jack Putter, he says, "I think I blacked out! Am I in Bugs, or

FIGURE 7.2 Tuck takes a picture of himself with a coworker before submitting to the miniaturization experiment.

what?" Tuck's desire, repressed to the point of emerging only from a black-out of consciousness, can be heard in his own answer: "I'm in a man! I'm in a strange man! I'll be a son-of-a-bitch, I'm in a strange man!" The film's homoerotic undercurrents swerve up to the surface as Tuck's face suffuses with wonder at this crucial turn of events.

Rabbits come with an ancient, if illogical, heritage of associations with homosexuality,[17] although in *Innerspace* their function shifts according to the ideological and unconscious demands of the narrative. They are also sometimes (or simultaneously) associated with heterosexuality/reproduction—as they are, for example, when Tuck exclaims, "Ozzie, what they hell have you done to me? How the hell can I be inside a man? I studied up on rabbits!" (i.e., he has studied up on how to be heterosexual, and he doesn't know what to do inside a man).

There is a certain logic to Tuck's miniaturization as a trope expressing his repression. He must, on the one hand, drown his desire; he must make it *invisible*. On the other hand, his desire *is* to lose himself in a larger body, to experience a passivity that the mythic ideal of virility does not acknowledge for men.[18] It should be reiterated here that Tuck and Jack are aspects of the same subjective experience. While it may be the case that narratively Jack is penetrated and Tuck is incorporated, it is Tuck, after all, who drinks (incorporates) so much alcohol, to make good a sense of lack. Jack realizes his own *and* Tuck's desire—and the same is true conversely: Tuck's drama is a fantastic realization of Jack's desire, and his own.

What Jack Wants

Jack suffers from nausea, shortness of breath, headaches, and various other psychosomatic ailments. He even develops a rash from the hairspray he uses (the film's point, apart from the one that Jack is suffering the symptoms of conversion hysteria, is that no *real* man would be using hairspray in the first place). During one of his frequent trips to the doctor, we hear about a recurring nightmare Jack has, in which the cash register he is working goes haywire and rings up a total of over one hundred thousand dollars. The customer is a "horrible, obnoxious woman with bright orange hair" who says, "I don't carry that kind of cash around on me, sweetie." She asks Jack, "Will you take *this*, instead?" as she reaches into her purse and withdraws "this little pearl-handled pistol." As she pulls back on the trigger, Jack wakes up screaming.

Throughout this account the doctor is examining Jack. He almost chokes Jack with a tongue depressor as he performs a thorough inspection of his throat—unconsciously exacerbating precisely the sort of fears of vulnerability Jack suffers from. This oral "rape" suggests the enormity of the threat that Jack experiences from the "mother" of his nightmare, just as it inversely refers to Jack's unacknowledged desire for intimacy with another man. The doctor is a father figure to Jack, and the scene clarifies the way in which Jack's fears are related to his desires. Although we know nothing about Jack's relationship with his own father, his repeated visits to the doctor and the logic of the scene suggests that Jack is looking to make good some real or imagined difficulty in his relationship with his father. He does not, as his nightmare would seem to suggest, *simply* fear the opposite sex.

It is entirely usual to be attached to one's mother (Freud might have said that Jack is looking for a man whom he can love *as his mother loved him*),[19] but Jack's attachment to his mother is overdetermined, since she is the only one there is to love. The doctor can give Jack some of what he wants from a man, but it is obviously not enough. Jack's need is homosexual, although not necessarily sexual. His need is certainly psychological (homo-emotional). But we can include the possibility that Jack might find happiness in sexual relationships with men, and not merely use homosexuality as therapy (as it were) to resolve an abnormal detachment from his father, as part of his development toward a "correct" heterosexuality.[20]

In his recurring nightmare Jack has no control over the cash register, and he fears what the ugly woman will do when she discovers his failure. The scene demands a psychoanalytic interpretation. We read the dream's latent content, since the doctor, who offers no interpretation of it, suggests merely that Jack go on a cruise and avoid anything exciting. Clearly, this woman is a monstrous mother figure, and Jack's terror derives from the knowledge that he can never satisfy her, and he (unwillingly) overcharges her. The woman's monstrousness is signified by her unnaturally orange hair piled up on top of her head, her "castrating" gaze, her masculine jaw, the excessive makeup on her old face, her acid-green pantsuit, and her large size. Jack wants a man to love, to save him from this phallic mother.

Jack's nightmare is not just oedipal but also specifically the horror of finding that value and commodity (the price of Fancy Feast cat food) do not correspond with the reassurance of referential logic. Jack's nightmare is the feeling of being adrift in a nonreferential world, of finding that there's nothing safe about the Safeway supermarket where he works. The film conflates

Jack's fears because, as Baudrillard would say, "in a non-referential world even the confusion of the reality principle with the desire principle is less dangerous than contagious hyperreality. One remains among principles, and there power is always right."[21] Jack is describing a dream, and to our relief (the scene plays for laughs) it is familiarly Freudian. But later, Jack is thrown into the realm of the hyperreal when his dream in fact happens, exactly as he had described it. This time Jack screams desperately, "It's a dream! It's a dream!" We, however, have the ultimate reassurance: it *is* a dream; it is a movie, called *Innerspace*.

The Logic of Identification

Jack will only overcome his sexual insecurity through identification with Tuck, in a process of *introjection* (to use a term coined by Ferenczi), of which the film provides a corporeal/literal model. Perhaps some of the film's sodomitical logic becomes clearer when we see how Jack transposes some of Tuck's qualities to himself. When Tuck is injected into Jack, and he attaches himself to Jack's inner ear, he becomes Jack's role model, guide, and conscience. (Tuck could be said to function as Jack's *ideal ego*, since his identification with Tuck is *heroic*.) Since the distinction between an outside and an inside is confounded by the fact that Tuck is actually inside Jack's body, Jack achieves a literal kind of identification with Tuck.

Identification, according to psychoanalysis, is a "psychological process whereby the subject assimilates an aspect, property, or attribute of the other and is transformed, wholly or partially, after the model the other provides. It is by means of a series of identifications that the personality is constituted and specified."[22] The fact that by the end of the movie Jack feels "cured" of his hypochondria and "unmasculine" fears, even after Tuck has left his body and is reenlarged, attests to the psychological power (the *reality*) of these processes.

But until Jack feels he has achieved a decisive degree of masculinity "guaranteed" by a resolute heterosexuality, he is implicated in a discourse that betrays an anxiety about homosexuality. The anxiety is there because the desire is there. There are moments in the film when this desire breaks through and is confirmed—such as the moment when, at Tuck's urging, Jack bursts out of the truck where the villainous Scrimshaw (Kevin McCarthy) is holding him captive, and Tuck yells, "Jack, *I love you!*" At the end of the movie, too—at the moment when in classical Hollywood cinema the lovers embrace—Tuck kisses Jack. Ultimately, however, the film must (appear to) endorse the values of the dominant culture, if it is to succeed at the box-office. *Innerspace* must resolve the problem inherent in every buddy film, which is the same one Clarence Brown faced in 1927, when he made *Flesh and the Devil*, starring John Gilbert, Lars Hanson, and Greta Garbo. In an interview, Brown said: "You see my problem. How to have the two leading men wind up in each other's arms and not make them look like a couple of fairies?"[23] In *Innerspace* the two leading men do more than wind up in each other's arms—one is *inside* the other—and the filmmakers are caught between their conscious decision to have fun with the subtext (as Hitchcock does in *Rope*) and the discomfiting realization that their desire has reared its head too visibly for what it is. The homosexual desire that underpins the film's meanings exceeds the strategies that would contain it.

The film posits Tuck as being too masculine, and Jack as being not masculine enough, and we sense that the film will end when these imbalances

FIGURE 7.3 With Tuck inside him, Jack (Martin Short) becomes infatuated with Tuck's girlfriend, Lydia.

are rectified in the narrative. While Jack works at the local Safeway, he can be safely asexual. If nothing else, his nerdiness guarantees it. In response to society's demand for exclusive heterosexuality, he has disavowed his desire and sought a kind of nonsubjectivity. As a clerk ringing up the prices of goods at the supermarket (i.e., as neither buyer nor seller in the exchanges of consumer-capitalism), Jack is removed from the supermarket of life; he is not a desiring subject in the symbolic exchanges of love. Tuck's (homo-erotic) desire, on the other hand, has been charged by the excessively phal-lic ethos of his Air Force environment.

"A Cowboy Who's Never Seen a Cow"

Counterposed to Tuck's homoerotically inflected (but ostensibly hetero-sexual) masculinity is the queer parody of heterosexual masculinity as represented in the character of Cowboy. One of this character's functions is to show the inappropriateness of a heterosexual style of masculinity run rampant. As an element in the film's discourse on masculinity, Cowboy also reveals that there is a moral dimension to the film's implicit ideal of manliness.

Cowboy is not concerned with what is conventionally right or wrong. He swings both ways. He illegally sells technology to the highest bidder, whoev-er that may be, and his sartorial choices tell us that while appearances are im-portant in the construction of masculinity, striking the right balance—to ap-pear authentic—is everything. He wears snakeskin, steel-tipped boots, a Stetson, and claims (they are his first words in the film), "There's nothing like a good cigar!" In one scene we see him humming and singing to himself as he performs a mock shoot-out in front of his hotel room mirror, using an electric shoe-brush as a gun. He is in love with an image of masculinity taken from the movies, but his grasp of what it means to be masculine is arrested at the level of the image, and therefore incomplete.

At one point in the narrative, Jack even *becomes* Cowboy (in a computer-ized transfer/reconstruction of his face) as part of Jack's transition from nerdy asexual to heroic heterosexual. The scene functions as another sort of incorporation fantasy, and it contributes to the film's homoerotic theme. Cowboy traffics between terms, and while at first it may seem to be a mea-sure of the film's progressive effort that his masculine pose is parodied, the character does not, finally, subvert patriarchal culture's norms of sexual identity but confirms them.

Villainy and Perversion

The leader of the villains, Victor Scrimshaw, is meant to be read as homosexual. (Among other signs, he employs a Filipino valet/waiter called Murnau.)[24] His associate, Dr. Margaret Canker, is almost nymphomaniacally flirtatious; and Mr Igoe, their hit man, is the embodiment of cruel perversity, with an artificial hand that is more versatile, and lethal, than a Swiss penknife.

When Margaret first sees the miniaturization equipment at the laboratory, she remarks on the fastidious mechanical hand that inserts the microchip into the larger apparatus: "Look at this thing! Primitive! Definitely primitive." As with her appraisal of every man she meets, Margaret sees things in sexual terms, and with a lewd inflection in her voice sounds as though she is remarking here on a case of arrested sexual development, or referring to the fact that she finds conventional heterosexual sex unexciting. (We will see, later, a brief scene in which Margaret, in a bedroom, smiles seductively at Mr. Igoe as he attaches a vibrator to his electronic arm.) As for Victor, with whom she has a kind of sibling rivalry, there is a comic overparticularity about his sartorial style and personal manner that, in the language of movies, also hints at moral perversion.

What is at stake for Jack is that he be saved from such a perverse fate, and in order to ensure this the film rehearses a well-known story of subject-construction that starts with the mirror phase.[25]

The Mirror and Identity

When Tuck is injected into Jack, he has no idea where he is. He is like the pre-mirror phase child that has no sense yet of its body as an entity in the world. He can (like some unborn child with sight) see platelets and tubes, fat cells and viscera, and later—after he has penetrated Jack's retina with a video probe—he gets to see what Jack sees ("I can see! Oh, thank God! I can see!"). But until this vision is tied to an origin, an epistemology cannot form. It is disembodied vision—like, one could say, the vision of an infant before it recognizes itself in a mirror: only shapes, shadows, and movements. In psychoanalysis the bounds of the body provide the model of all separations between an inside and an outside, and until Tuck is able to gain a sense of the body he is inhabiting, he will not exist as a *subject*.

Similarly, as I have suggested, Jack needs a *sexual* identity. It is only after Jack and Tuck each knows what the other looks like that Tuck can acquire language (take some control over his own fate as he spurts around in Jack's body) and that Jack can begin his identification with Tuck that will gain for him a masculine identity. In the mirror phase described by Lacan, there must be another figure in the mirror that the child will recognize (usually the mother) if it is to "see" its own image there. In *Innerspace* this third term is provided in a rather peculiar way. Tuck, sitting on Jack's optic nerve, sees the world in framed black-and-white video images, but until he can get Jack to acknowledge his presence, he does not—for all intents and purposes—exist. So, after warning Jack that he will do so, he uses his "electromagnetic boost-er" (?) to blow up Jack's television set. "I am real, Jack! You do believe me now, don't you?" Jack believes him, and their new self—the "divided sub-ject" of psychoanalysis—enters history, as it were. "We're in this together," says Tuck, "and we're going to help each other out."

In the overdetermined manner of movies, elements of the mirror phase are repeated in variations. Tuck wants a drink, but can only have one if Jack has one, so he instructs Jack to gulp down mouthfuls of bourbon, some drops of which Tuck catches in his tiny flask. Tuck proposes a toast that oddly (ass-backwardly, one could say) refers to procreation: "To Ozzie: A good man who tried to save my ass by injecting me into yours." Jack's alco-holically inspired dance that follows is like the *jouissance* that the child expe-riences when it first recognizes itself in the mirror. It is *ecstatic*. When he col-lapses on the couch, spent and smiling, he gasps, "I didn't know dancing could be so much fun!" and Tuck immediately replies, "You ought to try it with a girl sometime!" thereby giving voice to the pressure of the film's ide-ological imperative: Jack must move from autoeroticism to identification with an other.

The reenacted mirror phase is concluded decisively when Jack sees a pho-tograph of Tuck and asks, "Is that you?" and when Tuck instructs Jack to stand in front of the mirror. The objectification of Jack's body that is now possible begins immediately. Since Jack is drunk, Tuck makes him perform the mirror-ritual we have already seen performed. He tells Jack to slap his own face, hard, and then asks him, "How does it feel?" "It feels good!" says Jack. "The Jack Putter Machine. Zero defects."

The film here and there claims some sort of homology between auto-eroticism and homosexuality, and it freely conflates the two discourses or switches from the one to the other (that in Freud's story of sexuality are dif-ferent stages). There is a scene in which Jack is standing at a urinal in a pub-lic lavatory, looking down, as he talks to Tuck. "I hate this!" he says. "Why can't we just tell [Lydia] the truth? She might even believe it." "No," says

Tuck. "Sorry. It's humiliating being this small." Jack's response—apart from being a funny double entendre—is what every child needs to believe: "You won't be small forever!" Not only is the phallic nature of masculine identity made quite clear here, but overlaying it are the discourses of autoeroticism and homosexuality. The public lavatory has had—in the movies, certainly— some semiotic status as a meeting place for homosexuals, and the pleasures of autoeroticism are acknowledged by the film when a man nearby says to Jack, "Play with it, pal, don't talk to it."

Earlier, Jack had remarked in wonder to Tuck, "You were seeing parts of my body that I will never get to see!" He is referring to his internal organs, but on another level is referring to the fact that nobody ever sees his or her own face, the privileged index of identity. The only way to see one's own face is in a mirror's reflection, in an *image*; one can only derive a sense of self from the reflections offered by others. Moreover, when Jack is standing at the urinal looking down, Tuck sees what he sees, and the autoerotic element of homosexuality (or the homosexual element of autoeroticism)—with its origins in the mirror phase (including the pre-mirror phase when the child sees its body only in parts)—is clearly suggested.

In this vein, of homosexuality as a desire and a logic to be repressed, certain dialogue takes on a peculiar resonance. For example, when Jack has sufficiently calmed down to consider the implications of the fact that Tuck is inside him, he says (tenderly, fearfully, as he is speeding down the highway in Tuck's red sports car), "No pain. That's the thing I want from you: no pain. I mean, just don't do anything weird in there, okay?" Tuck softly reassures him, "Okay, no pain." In the highly connotative register that makes *Innerspace* so giddy, this scene could represent Jack's first experience of anal intercourse. Their whole adventure began, as we know, with a syringe injected into Jack's ass. And later, when Jack is captured and held down by Scrimshaw's men, he is "raped" by them ("Igoe's in!" Margaret cries triumphantly) as Mr. Igoe, miniaturized in a germ-sized pod, enters Jack's bloodstream through a needle in his neck.

The only way for Jack to achieve a conventional heterosexuality, and for Tuck to confirm his, is to repress the homoerotic element in the origins of (their) desire. They will not succeed completely because *Innerspace* is in love with masculinity, not heterosexuality, and masculinity as the film seems to define it has a self-referential/narcissistic element that makes it a potentially homoerotic phenomenon. Heterosexuality, however, according to the logic of the film, requires for its dialectic a clear distinction between notions of masculinity and femininity—with masculinity (not surprisingly) as active

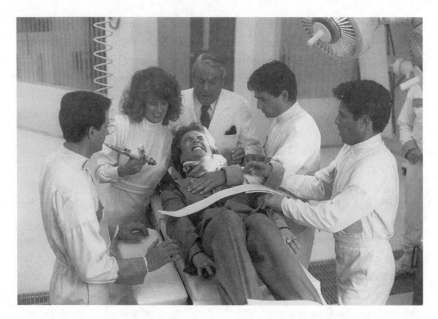

FIGURE 7.4 Jack is "raped" by the villains: Dr. Margaret Canker (Fiona Lewis),
Victor Scrimshaw (Kevin McCarthy), and the miniaturized Mr. Igoe (Vernon Wells).
(Courtesy Photofest. Copyright © 1987 Warner Bros. Inc. All rights reserved)

and aggressive, and femininity as passive. This distinction is maintained in
structures that repress the activity of women.

THE WOMAN

Lydia, who is a newspaper reporter, tells Jack: "Tuck used to say to me that
he actually did the things I only write about. Now *I* want to *do* the things I
only write about." But during Jack's first meeting with Lydia, Tuck advises
him: "Don't let her take control of the conversation! Be aggressive! Dominate her! Don't be a wuss-puss! *Be me!*" Lydia gasps when Jack violently
slams down his drink. "Look, Lydia," he says, "you're just going to have to
trust me, okay? Because there's not a lot of time for explanations." Tuck
crows with approval.

Every time Lydia picks up a gun or attempts to command a situation, she
is shown to be slightly ridiculous—even when she succeeds in some action,
as when she breaks into the enemy's laboratory to save Jack but betrays a

comic nervousness. In fact, the enemy is able to capture Jack in the first place because, when Lydia threatens the evil Mr. Igoe with a paralyzer-gun, she succeeds only in shooting Jack, who passes out immediately.

Tuck teaches Jack how to be aggressive, telling him where, when, and how to kick, punch, and knock out Scrimshaw's men. Masculinity, based on principles of violence and action, is shown to be partly a matter of bluff and belief, for Jack is able to knock out one of the enemy because he believes that Tuck has given him "the strength of ten men"—when in fact Tuck is now inside Lydia.

During a kiss between Jack and Lydia, when Tuck closes down all the electrical systems operating his remote-control senses, Tuck is transported into Lydia's body. The film creates this opportunity for unconscious reasons, since it plays no part in the plot. Tuck realizes he is in Lydia's body when he sees a foetus, thus grounding the film's obsession with sexual difference in the incontrovertible evidence of biology. The moment Lydia realizes that Tuck is inside her, she kisses Jack again to return him to Jack's body.

This encounter between masculine and feminine tests the relative incompatibilities of the two. The narrative does not know why it should be so, but this moment—one of the most significant in the film—clearly says that Tuck cannot "survive" in Lydia's body. The masculine cannot confirm itself without the mediation of the woman's body confirmed as female, and so the female body is represented as receptacle, not identity. The appearance of the foetus is not only a spectacular opportunity for masculinity to "see" its (reproduced) "self" but is a further means of separating the woman's body from her "self," thus making her distinct from the masculine, which defines itself here literally through its "own" body.

This can also be seen as the film's "sex scene," responding to a pressure to define sex—perhaps in unconscious response to the contemporary panic about AIDS—as an erotic exchange involving bodily fluids. There is no question that the kind of sexuality the film seeks to affirm is grounded in an ideology of vision, with vision marking the first distinction between an inside and an outside—and all difference(s) following from that first separation.[26] Following this logic, "sex" must be able to show for itself some physical, material, *visible* exchange.

In an earlier, highly revealing scene we hear Tuck reminisce to himself about his first meeting with Lydia: "Oh, Lydia! [*He sighs*] It was the night we first met. You were doing that article about me, and we had dinner, and talked 'til three in the morning, and then I got drunk, and threw up, and fell down a manhole walking you home." Clearly, from the start, Tuck has been inscribed in a narcissistic dialectic in his relation to his girlfriend. He fell in love with the fact that Lydia showed such an interest in *him*. If they talked until three in the morning, it was perhaps because Tuck was the topic of conversation (ostensibly, for the article), and because talking provided a form of evasion for Tuck, just as his drinking did. Finally, his falling down a "manhole" saved him from following through with this heterosexual encounter—it is where he would rather have been anyway. Interestingly enough, throughout this scene Tuck is nostalgically stroking Lydia's image as it appears on his television monitor. This is what she has always been: an image.

SAVING THE REALITY PRINCIPLE

As I have suggested, the film defamiliarizes spectacle in order to confirm it, and defamiliarizes the body in order to reexperience it. The crisis of vision (which is to say, of *knowing*) that the film treats in its science fiction narrative is inseparable from the crisis of desire that the film inscribes in a discourse on masculinity. *Innerspace* is self-reflexively a spectacular film about spectacle—a film that inscribes desire in/as images. The film's main effort is to save a conventionally *masculine* paradigm of desire's dialectic. The "contagious hyper-reality" of American culture described by Baudrillard requires us to pull back somehow from the limits of spectacle—of spectacle *as* desire; otherwise, like the villain, Victor Scrimshaw, we might wonder what it is all about:

> Nuclear weapons, Jack—they mean nothing. Everybody's got them, but nobody has the balls to use them. Am I right? "Space," you say. *Space is a flop!* Didn't you know that? An endless junkyard of orbiting debris. Ah, but, *miniaturization*, Jack, *that's the ticket!* That's the edge that everybody's been looking for. Who will have that edge, Jack? What country will control miniaturization? Frankly, I don't give a shit. I'm only in this for the money.

All of *Innerspace*'s main themes are condensed in this little speech. One might recall how the main characters of Robert Aldrich's *Kiss Me Deadly* (1955) (also) look for "the great whatsit," which, in light of the politics of the 1950s and the Cold War fears of the time, was—as much as anything else—the atomic bomb, or rather, the *meaning* of the bomb. In that film, the hero's search for "the great whatsit" becomes an excuse to pursue a homo-erotic obsession.

Scrimshaw, more than forty years after Hiroshima (and thirty years after *Kiss Me Deadly*), declares the bomb meaningless. Nuclear weapons "mean nothing" because "nobody has the balls to use them." And if "space" is a flop it is because, with the loss of the space program, we have lost the *narrative*. Since reaching the moon, NASA has had no story. Space ("outer" space) has the effect of making us lose our perspective; our earthly perspective is stretched to the point of incoherence and meaninglessness by space's infinity. The junkyard of debris is a fragmented, fallen-to-pieces narrative that cannot cohere: random bits of hardware whizzing about without purpose.

What is sought, to borrow Baudrillard's words, is the confirmation of "an order which can only exert itself on the real and the rational, on ends and means: a referential order which can only dominate referentials, a determinate power which can only dominate a determined world."[27] *Innerspace* responds to a nostalgia for conventional heterosexuality, and it seeks to confirm the "naturalness" of Renaissance perspective, since our way of knowing the world is grounded in this particular way of mapping space.[28] The way *Innerspace* maps its global anxieties onto bodies and in the terms of sexuality is clear: if we feel that we can never really *know* outer space, the ultimate Other (i.e., the real), then we should be able, at least, to know ourselves—our bodies. As Tuck takes his journey into the interior, we recognize the terrain: lung tissue, heart valves, blood cells. The whole film becomes, in effect, an answer to its opening shots (which are of an unreadable space): to confirm, precisely, that this is a body with organs,[29] to confirm the old distinctions between inside and outside, depth and surface, and so on.

In a parable suggested by Disneyland, Baudrillard has described how moribund principles are regenerated, how in America we "renew the cycle by the mirror of crisis." In Disneyland all of America's values "are exalted . . . in miniature and comic strip form."

> Disneyland is there to conceal the fact that it is the "real" country, all of "real" America, which *is* Disneyland. . . . Disneyland is presented as imaginary in order to make us believe that the rest is real, when in fact all of Los Angeles and the America surrounding it are no longer real, but of the order of the hyperreal and of simulation. It is no longer a question of a false representation of reality (ideology), but of concealing the fact that the real is no longer real, and thus of saving the reality principle.[30]

Saving the reality principle. Saving the principle of the principle. The characters of *Innerspace* do not ask themselves *why* they push themselves to

seek what the villain Scrimshaw calls, "the edge that everybody's been looking for." They only hurl themselves forward, in a search: the villains must get
the miniaturization chip, and Tuck/Jack must get the reenlargement chip.
Even when Scrimshaw gives utterance to the film's philosophical core, he
quickly looks past what he knows is always the real and only issue, *power*—
because he senses, with some sort of postmodern awareness, how strangely
abstract the workings of power are. He refers simply to a means of exchange:
money. ("Frankly," he says to Jack, "I don't give a shit. I'm only in this for the
money.") Even Scrimshaw's monologue that follows this drifts off into a
reverie about the years when he worked in "the great gold fields" of Alaska.
Gold. Again, it is a question of a standard, an ultimate principle, a transcen-
dent signifier that is sought which will marshal all signifiers into patterns,
into meaning, as metal filings are organized by the field of force of a magnet:
in Lacanian terms, the *phallus*.

Home Is Where the Heart Is

The film's formulaic features are deftly outlined by David Edelstein in his
Village Voice review, in which he suggests that "home" is "being full-size."[31]
The film's cheerfully paranoid discourse on homosexual desire (i.e., dominant culture's demand for its repression) suggests that full-size refers at the
very least to penis size, and home is all at once earth (as opposed to "outer"
space); being in/at-one-with a male body (since the movie's protagonists are
male); and—to get more metaphorical—home is "where the heart is." When
Tuck and Jack finally reach "home," they achieve a satisfactory identity in
dominant culture's terms. Or do they?

The film's various discourses and orders of metaphor converge on the
metaphor of the heart, which is literalized in the film at the same time as it
serves as a metaphor for heterosexual romantic love. From the first distinctions
between an outside and an inside (between outer space and innerspace, etc.)
comes the notion that things have a core, that inside the inside is a "heart."

The real "jeopardy" to which Edelstein refers in his structural summary of
the film is the threat of castration. While Jack's interior is lushly red and sexy,
with giant tubes and sphincters, swirling balls and platelets, the ultimate
danger to Tuck, as he careens about Jack's insides, is Jack's heart. (DO NOT
ENTER HEART! his computer tells him.) Tuck at one point comes per-
ilously close to it—and it looks like nothing so much as a giant, pulsating
vulva. The overdetermination of this narrative conceit is exceptional. At the

very least, the heart refers to Lydia/woman. We know that Tuck and Lydia separated because Lydia could no longer tolerate his excessive drinking, and that as Lydia was leaving, Tuck begged her to stay, saying, "I stubbed my toe on the cab when you opened the door. I think it's broken!" And later, as a form of proof to Lydia that he is inside Jack, Tuck has Jack say to her, "It was my *heart*, and not my toe, that was broken!"

Between his toe, which serves as bodily figuration of his psychic state, and his heart, which is what he shares with Lydia, Tuck is torn between a homoerotic approach to achieving a sense of phallic autonomy, and the desire, encouraged by dominant culture, of finding the phallus through/in the differently gendered other. As long as Lydia is the "other," however, he will live with a fear of being devoured by that heart. In its structure as a kind of dream wish-fulfillment, *Innerspace* dramatizes this very fear, which is both his and Jack's desire.

The narcissistic nature of Tuck's desire, or the extent of his fear, is evident even in this early scene, in his way of trying to persuade Lydia not to leave. He pleads, "Lydia, look, don't leave! You know you love me! Look, I know you're crazy about me!" But, we may ask, what about *his* desire? Is he crazy about Lydia? How does he love her? There are tears in his eyes as the taxi pulls away, and for a startling moment we have an affecting sense of the impossibility of his desire as the dominant heterosexual culture has determined it.

FIGURE 7.5 "DO NOT ENTER HEART!" On Tuck's journey through Jack's body, the villainous Mr. Igoe is not the only threat to his safety. (Courtesy Photofest. Copyright © 1987 Warner Bros. Inc. All rights reserved).

If Jack's incorporation of Tuck is a literalization of the psychological process of identification, then the incorporated body—the film suggests—must be male. If he wishes to assimilate "an aspect, property, or attribute of the other and [be] transformed, wholly or partially, after the model the other provides,"[32] this "other" must be a man. He will internalize this identification, but his object-choice, according to dominant ideology, must be a woman. Thus, in the melodramatic tradition of Hollywood cinema, *Innerspace* affirms dominant ideology in the conventional coda of a "happy ending": Tuck leaves Jack's body; Jack gives up his love for Lydia; Tuck and Lydia are married; and Jack now has the sexual confidence he formerly lacked.

Patriarchal culture's stake in preserving the power and authority of the phallus is decisively ensured by the wedding that concludes the film, and among the small reminders of what has been repressed in order to achieve Jack's "cure" and make possible Tuck and Lydia's marriage is the Cuban cigar that Jack offers Tuck. It refers nicely to the privileged signifier in patriarchal culture, the master symbol of an order in which—to have an identity—one must be inscribed, *identified* as having or not having the phallus (i.e., as being masculine or not-masculine).

For the patriarchal notion of masculinity to obtain, homosexual relations between men must be forbidden. They are forbidden because, as Irigaray observes, "*they openly interpret the law according to which society operates.*" That is, "once the penis itself becomes merely a means to pleasure, pleasure among men, *the phallus loses its power.*"[33] Male subjects, then, to be the agents of symbolic exchange, must give up the possibility of serving as commodities themselves. In patriarchal culture women serve as commodities, as fetish objects exchanged between men. This is why, regardless of the size of her role in *Innerspace*, Lydia is the heart of the film's symbolic system, and it is also why Jack offers Tuck a cigar. Jack now possesses the means to participate in the symbolic exchanges among men, and the cigar echoes the exchange of Lydia between them.[34]

We should not lose sight, then, of the fact that Jack, who started out neurotically asexual (profoundly repressed homosexual?—appearing to have no desire at all, until he adopts Tuck's), does in the course of the narrative evince desire. But it is for Tuck's girlfriend. While this is evidence that Jack has made the "correct" heterosexual object-choice, he must immediately repress that desire until he can find a girlfriend of his own. Clearly, heterosexuality and homosexuality work together (in a network of desires and symbolic exchanges that Irigaray calls "hom(m)o-sexuality") to serve the interests of masculinity. When Tuck gets married and Jack drives after them in Tuck's car, we can see how Jack and Tuck are still linked in a circuit of desire. On the narrative level, too, they will continue to work together, for Jack realizes that the chauffeur of the wedding car is Cowboy in disguise, and as we can confirm, Margaret and Scrimshaw—miniaturized to fifty percent of their normal size, and still hoping, therefore, to get hold of the reenlargement chip—are stowed away in the trunk.

Jack pulls off his bow tie (symbol of civilized repression) and looks at it for a moment. Then, with a smile on his face, he throws it away. As he tears after Tuck, speeding along the Pacific Coast Highway at Big Sur, the camera soars lyrically, transcendentally. It flies freely, without inhibition, as in a dream of sexual bliss.

A Problem of Reading

This attempt to show what is repressed in *Innerspace*—a text which on the one hand works classically to ensure a stable position of heterosexual masculinity and object-choice, and which on the other hand would appear to do the opposite—has obviously been a precarious project. This hermeneutic reading

FIGURE 7.6 Triangulated desire: the two men bond across the body of the woman. (Copyright © 1987 Warner Bros. Inc. All rights reserved)

demonstrates how *Innerspace* cannot be categorized simply as either a "progressive" or "reactionary" text. The film explicitly thematizes the narcissism and homoeroticism implicated in the normative heterosexual object-choice in a way that puts the viewer in some doubt as to the film's intentions. One cannot decide, in the way that viewers must, what is conscious and what is unconscious on the part of the filmmakers.

The injection of Tuck into Jack answers to Jack's desire (just as, it has been noted repeatedly, the reverse is true), and at the end of the film—with Jack at the wheel (figuratively of the narrative and literally of the car)—we are again made to share Jack's point of view. Is it Jack's story, after all? The film is post-classical in its inability to settle on a particular perspective, and it is clearly the issue of homosexuality that hystericizes the text. The comedy perhaps functions to inoculate against any genuinely subversive implications the film may have, and the sheer density of the film's allusions (to other films, other genres, other actors and performances) makes it impossible to establish a comprehensive point of view, to gauge the filmmakers' attitude to their material.

Men everywhere enjoy close relationships with other men, but among American heterosexual men generally there is, we know, an enormous fear of homosexuality. It could be said that *Innerspace* attempts to dodge this difficulty by treating homoeroticism explicitly, but in modes (comedy, irony, fantasy, parody) that simultaneously confirm and deny, acknowledge and disavow that homosexuality is the issue at the heart of the film's meanings. Joe Dante's remark that the filmmakers wanted "to make a picture about these two guys and their relationship"[35] actually supports the impression that the film's main effort is to show the intimacy of a homoerotically inflected relationship that has no taint of the "homosexual" on it. So, for the better part of the film, the relationship between Tuck and Jack is proposed as one between a mentor and protégé.

At the end of the film, when the camera returns repeatedly to Jack's face as Tuck and Lydia embrace, we are forced to consider where things now stand for Jack. What is the status of his desire? And for that matter, how are we to read the dynamics of desire among all the main characters? We could say that, in effect, Tuck has done for Jack what a father usually does for a son—teach him how to be a man. And like a traditional son, Jack must not identify erotically with the father (Tuck) or with his mother (Lydia). The son's desire has been shaped by his identification with his father, and his oedipal crisis resolved when he is able to fall in love with/marry a woman like his mother. The film retreats from some of its progressive and postmodern impulses, and we are encouraged, finally, to accept the implication that Jack will go off and fall in love with someone like Lydia, and in doing this he will confirm his identification with Tuck. To the extent that it functions classically, *Innerspace* encourages us to accept that Jack will forever carry within him the emotional representations and dictates of Tuck/the father (i.e., that he has internalized the logic of castration, that he has resolved his oedipal crisis).

Identification, however, does not identify object-choice. It might, therefore, be more accurate to describe Jack's identification as being *hysterical*—that is, characterized by an oscillating play of bisexuality both at the level of object-choice and at the level of identification. Jack's identification is hysterical because the filmmakers cannot accept the fact of primordial bisexuality. It has been pointed out that where the Oedipus complex consists of four trends—affection for and hostility to the mother, and affection for and hostility to the father—we should not, as Freud did, conflate "the story concerned with the Law and the phallus with the story about the oscillation of the drive."[36] Freud says that the identification with the mother results from the taking of the father as love object, and the identification with the father results from taking the mother as love object. But it should be stressed that while the two coexist, one does not imply the other.[37]

Understood in this light, *Innerspace* is a hysterical text structured in accordance with the heroes' oscillating identifications and object-choices. This hysteria gives the film its "off-the-wall sensibility,"[38] and it turns on the fact that Jack and Tuck have made their spectacular voyage to the heart of identity uniquely *together*. We have two characters, but they are a corporate body, and on the psychoanalytic plane they function as a single, complex desiring experience. As in the science fictional narrative itself, this produces a blurring of boundaries, a collapse of terms and certainties, and to the extent that it is a buddy film, *Innerspace* reveals a new level of "confusion about 'normality' where once there seemed blissful certitude."[39] Whether mainstream critics like it or not, the film—as an index of shifts in contemporary American attitudes toward male homosocial desire—calls into question "something called 'male-bonding,' which used to be known simply as friendship,"[40] and reveals that the line separating homoeroticism from the sanctioned male bonding that upholds patriarchy is a fine one. Where *Innerspace* seeks both to confirm homosexual desire as a perversion and "true" masculinity as heterosexual, it also denies this. The film cannot, in effect, say—as *Fantastic Voyage* could twenty years before—that "*man is the center of the universe*," because contemporary notions of what it means to be a man are in crisis around the issue of how the affective element of male homosocial desire might be expressed. For it cannot be any longer denied that what we call male homosocial desire is a continuum that includes homosexuality.

BATMAN AND ROBIN
A Family Romance

Every hero has his "origins" story, and in Batman's case the story of how Bruce Wayne was orphaned as a boy and how later he took up the secret identity of a masked crusader against crime is crucial in defining the hero. Since the Batman character's first appearance in 1939, his writers have returned again and again, obsessively, to the shocking scene of the murder of Bruce Wayne's parents.[1] Young Bruce and his parents had just seen a movie, and as they were walking home through the dark streets of Gotham City, they were attacked and shot. Bruce Wayne's childhood trauma runs like a thread through the hundreds of adventures that have put Batman in an astonishing variety of situations, and it resonates powerfully as the defining moment in Batman's increasingly complex personal mythology.

Bruce vows that he will avenge the senseless deaths of Thomas and Martha Wayne. At their grave he swears, "I'll dedicate my life and inheritance to bringing your killer to justice . . . and fighting all criminals! I swear it!" (*Batman #47*, 1948). He then spends several years preparing for his destiny: "He mastered scientific criminal investigation! He trained his body to such physical and athletic perfection that he could perform any daredevil feat . . . Then, one day he was ready for his new role." Sitting alone in one of Wayne Manor's cavernous rooms, he says to himself, "Criminals are a superstitious, cowardly lot, so I must wear a disguise that will strike terror into their hearts! I must be a creature of the night, like a . . . a . . . ." ("*And, as if in answer, a winged creature flew in through the open window!*") "A bat! That's it! It's like an omen! I shall become a bat!" ("*Thus was born this weird figure of the shadows . . . this avenger of evil—THE BATMAN!*") (*Batman #47*, 1948).

In one story, Bruce Wayne has a nightmare in which the entire drama of Batman's origins is replayed, and as the bat enters the window of his study at Wayne Manor it speaks: "You are *mine*, and you will *become* me . . . I am your *true* father . . . and you are my son."[2] And in *Batman: Year One*, in a strange, internal dialogue with his dead father, Bruce Wayne recalls how the bat came "crashing through the window of your study . . . and mine." The bat merged with a bust of Thomas Wayne mounted on a pedestal near the window; and, looking up at it as he had eighteen years before, Bruce says: "It frightened me . . . as a boy . . . frightened me . . . yes. Father. I shall become a bat."[3]

There is a sense in which Batman becomes the father to young Bruce, who persists in Batman's psyche as a remembered image of happy innocence.[4] While Batman is self-invented, his identity does not come out of nowhere. He was *inspired*. Bruce's creation of Batman illustrates Freud's notion of the "family romance." Freud coined the term "family romance" to describe the neurotic's fantasy of "getting free from the parents of whom he now has a low opinion and of replacing them by others, who, as a rule, are of higher social standing."[5]

If Thomas and Martha Wayne are not really Batman's parents, who, in terms of Freud's family romance, is generating the fantasy? Some writers, such as Danny Peary, insist that "Batman is not Bruce Wayne's alter ego. . . . Put Batman and Bruce Wayne together and you still don't come up with a full person. . . . Bruce Wayne ceased to exist once Joe Chill killed his parents and has been in the comic book, as Dennis O'Neil believes, 'only Batman's tool, his fictional creation.'"[6] But it does not matter much in the end whether we say that Batman spends very little time as Bruce Wayne, or that Bruce Wayne spends a great deal of time as Batman.

A useful way to make sense of this complex matter of point of view, identification, and parentage—since it is pointless to look for "a full person"—is to read the *Batman* stories as elaborate forms of the family romance. When it is said that in comic books "you can deal with terrible problems and have spectacular resolutions. [They] are made for 12-year-old adolescent male minds,"[7] we know what is meant—for the family romance is a kind of daydream, and Bruce Wayne and Batman are Fathers. They express the contradictory feelings a boy has for his father—feelings that the epilogue of "To Kill a Legend" identifies as "grief, guilt, vengeance," and "awe, mystery, gratitude" (*Detective Comics #500*, 1981). To read *Batman* is to put oneself in the place of a child, and to understand, in Freud's words, that "the whole effort at replacing the real father by a superior one is only an expression of the child's longing for the happy, vanished days when his father seemed to him the noblest and strongest of men and his mother the dearest and loveliest of women."[8]

FATHERS

There are different versions of the fateful night when Bruce Wayne was orphaned in Crime Alley, but they vary only slightly. The story is always, of
course, a flashback, a childhood trauma, and what is invariably recalled—
with rather odd specificity—is that the film the Wayne family had just seen
before Thomas and Martha were murdered was *The Mark of Zorro* (directed
by Rouben Mamoulian 1940). The film is perhaps the single most important
intertext offered by *Batman*'s writers as a clue to the hero's origins and psychological makeup, and as such it warrants at least a brief examination.

Diego (Tyrone Power) returns to California after years in a military academy in Spain to find that his father is no longer the alcalde there, having been
deposed by a cruel buffoon. Like young Bruce Wayne, Diego vows to avenge
his father's humiliating defeat, becoming Zorro, a masked hero, who succeeds in restoring the masculine/paternal principle. By the end of the movie,
Diego's father is the alcalde again, and Diego's mother is restored to her
proper position of social eminence.

In the fantasies of boys in patriarchal societies, this motif of avenging a
humiliated father is a common form of resolution of oedipal conflicts. Initially, as Freud observed, little boys find fathers glamorous: "A little boy will
exhibit a special interest in his father; he would like to grow like him and be
like him, and take his place everywhere. We may say simply that he takes his
father as his ideal."[9] The father is "aligned with reality and the growing toddler's exuberant would-be conquest of it."[10] Only later does the boy see his
father as an envied and feared rival, when he "notices that his father stands
in his way with his mother."[11]

As Freud later wrote in *Moses and Monotheism*, "A hero is someone who
has had the courage to rebel against his father and has in the end victorious-
ly overcome him."[12] We see that Diego's heroic actions in *The Mark of Zorro*
are motivated by conflicting desires—on the one hand to win his father's
love, and on the other hand to prove, by putting his father in his debt, that
he is more powerful than his father. It is an effort on Diego's part to make
his mark on the world—and this is literalized in the "Z" he carves at the site
of every daring deed performed as Zorro. Just as he graduates from the military academy in Spain (a training ground for masculinity), he must graduate as a son, and this can only be done by superseding the father in some way.

In "A Special Type of Choice of Object Made by Men," Freud discusses
the idea of *rescue* in the family romance, and he describes the kind of boy
who "forms the phantasy of *rescuing his father from danger and saving his life;*

in this way he puts his account square with him."[13] This fantasy is produced when the child has learned that he owes his life to his parents and consequently wishes to repay them for this gift. In this "saving" fantasy there is an attitude of defiance as it applies to the father: "It is as though the boy's defiance were to make him say: 'I want nothing from my father; I will give him back all I have cost him'" (172). What tender feeling there is in the saving fantasy is usually directed toward the mother, for "the mother gave the child life, and it is not easy to find a substitute of equal value for this unique gift." The child is able, by "a slight change of meaning, such as is easily effected in the unconscious," to make the rescue of his mother acquire the significance "of giving her a child or making a child for her—needless to say, one like himself" (173). Freud explains further:

> His mother gave him a life—his own life—and in exchange he gives her another life, that of a child which has the greatest resemblance to himself. The son shows his gratitude by wishing to have by his mother a son who is like himself: in other words, in the rescue-phantasy he is completely identifying himself with his father. All his instincts, those of tenderness, gratitude, lustfulness, defiance and independence, find satisfaction in the single wish *to be his own father*. (173; emphasis in original)

Convoluted as this sounds, it is made clear again and again in the repeated scene of the murder of Bruce Wayne's parents and the boy's vow to avenge their deaths. As Batman, Bruce becomes "the father of himself," and this is rather literalized in his role as benefactor to Dick Grayson/Robin—with whom he spends the rest of his life as a knight, saving people in danger.

Not only can *Batman*'s defining story and *The Mark of Zorro* each be read as a fantasy in which the son removes his father who stands as a competitor for the mother's affections, or seeks to repay his father and become quits with him—but it can be understood that these sons feel rage at the absent father, the father who was *not* there. Certainly, a boy needs a father's protection in the world, and both Diego and young Bruce Wayne feel vulnerable in a decisive moment of trauma. The identity each conceives for himself is founded on an insecurity, and it includes a component of eroticized yearning for an all-powerful father.

As the immediate inspiration for the young Bruce Wayne, *The Mark of Zorro* provides Bruce with the father of his dreams, who contrasts vividly with the ordinariness of his real father. The boy resolves, in effect, to grow up to be like such a man (Tyrone Power/Zorro), and he will spend years

FIGURE 8.1 The story of how all selves are formed in a matrix of filial fear and desire. ("Rite of Passage: Trial by Fire," *Detective Comics #621*, 1990. Copyright © 1990, 1993 DC Comics. All rights reserved)

working on his body—phallicizing it, making it strong and powerful—to help achieve this. He is fascinated by the image on the screen, in a moment analogous to the mirror stage described by Lacan. As Batman, he becomes the ideal that substitutes for the narcissistic fantasy of his childhood in which he was his own ideal.

But Batman is always in a state of imminent disintegration, and Lacan's mirror stage inadequately describes his formation as a desiring subject. Batman's problem is precisely one of identification, and it is an impossible one because Bruce Wayne lost not only his father but also his mother. In a "normal" wish-fulfillment the mother survives, but as Bruce Wayne's loss is doubled his identification is doubly difficult, and while his wish at first appears to be "to out-herod Herod,"[14] it becomes clear that the bedrock issue for Batman is sexual difference (castration), not overcoming the father. The family romance is not a solution to the Oedipus complex but a supplement to it, for Bruce's real trauma is the loss of his mother. The family romance, in other words, does not compensate him for her loss. The child's disillusionment is shattering, and the family romance temporarily provides a means of forging an identity from the disorder of his warring emotions. Denial and displacement work to produce a fiction that simultaneously destroys and idealizes the parents.

Batman stories represent the fantasy of a storyteller (a family romancer) who does not distinguish between an identification with the father and the choice of the father as object. As Freud makes the distinction, "In the first case one's father is what one would like to *be*, and in the second he is what one would like to *have*."[15] Indeed, the whole point of the family romance (from the point of view of the romancer) is that one can *be* and *have* it all.[16] But in this sense, the drama of Batman's identity is not really a matter of object relations at all. Rather, it refers always to his original loss—which is to say, to castration.

The murder of Bruce's parents dramatizes the son's psyche not only by playing out an oedipal, patricidal fantasy in which the Father that replaces Thomas Wayne is both noble and benign (Bruce Wayne of Wayne Manor) and terrifying and erotic (Batman), but also by replaying what Jennifer Stone calls the "pipistrello principle"—an eroticized irruption from the real which resists symbolization and (re)appears elsewhere.[17] When Bruce Wayne decides to become Batman, the bat so very clearly is a reminder of his primordial loss. It figures in a deferred action of remembering (after the event, *après coup*). The bat's unforgettable screeching, and the way in which its flight through the window of Bruce Wayne's study is depicted in the comics in panels of splintered frames and text and shattering fragments of glass, is a *primal scene*—a retroactive fantasy. The bat is phallic. (Its connotations of castration are even stronger in French: *chauve-souris*—bald mouse.) Its screech evokes the child's imaginary memory of an orgasmic scream as primal scene. The comic strip itself, moreover, functions as a fantasy of ideal speech—as in watching silent movies. The foundations of the Batman myth indulge not only the rage and desire of oedipal emotions and the consequential guilt; they allow readers to remain in thrall to an immaturity that we do not really want to escape.[18] This primal scene is depicted again and again, in the *jouissance* of repetition.

In *Batman* we have a family romance which, as a fantasy (a fiction, precisely), keeps the hero in a perpetually unresolved oedipal crisis. Freud wrote that "every new arrival on this planet is faced by the task of mastering the Oedipus complex; anyone who fails to do so falls a victim to neurosis,"[19] and Batman is nothing if not deeply neurotic. When Freud speaks of resolving or surmounting the Oedipus complex, he is referring to the way in which an organized body of loving and hostile wishes which the child experiences toward his parents orients his desire and results in a particular sort of object-choice. But Bruce Wayne and Batman do not make a "full person"—because they are components of a myth, or family romance—and only to the extent that we may speak of Batman as if he were a person, could we say that he loves (as Freud would describe it) "according to the narcissistic type." That is, he loves an image of what he once was (the young Bruce/Robin), and what he would like to be—an embodiment of the all-powerful father.

The "scene" in Crime Alley makes Batman permanently lonely, and many stories have his loneliness as their major theme. This feature of his character speaks of his narcissism. He wants, more than anything, to be loved. To the extent that Batman has an object-choice in the narratives, there is (as has been noted) the Boy Wonder, whose place in the family romance mirrors our own, just as—in the words of "Dr. Socrates S. Rodor, Professor Emeritus of Twentieth Century History, Gotham University"—it is "easy, and perhaps unavoidable, to speculate that The Batman identified with the orphan child, seeing in the Grayson tragedy a reflection of his own."[20]

ROBIN, THE BOY WONDER

As the introduction to "Robin Dies at Dawn" puts it, "The friendship of Batman and Robin is one that has stood steadfast as a rock! To Batman, Robin is like his own son—and Robin would brave any danger to keep Batman from harm!" (*Batman #156*, 1963). This "friendship" between father and son, however, hardly resembles the kind of relationship most boys have with their fathers, which in reality is fraught with difficulties.

Danny Peary offers a straightforward explanation for the addition of Robin as a *Batman* character in April 1940 ("Robin, the Boy Wonder," *Detective Comics #38*): "To win over youngsters who dreamed of fighting alongside a superhero, Kane introduced Robin as teenage sidekick. It was a masterstroke that increased the popularity of the comic, but it resulted in a much more restrained and respectable Batman. He didn't seem so fearsome and his world didn't appear so evil and mysterious with a cheery, brightly dressed boy sharing the frame."[21]

And yet, in his "Introduction" to *Batman from the 30's to the 70's*, E. Nelson Bridwell writes that, "A certain psychiatrist decided that a man and a boy living together spelled homosexuality. Unfortunately, many people eagerly seized on this view—especially the gay set themselves. Today, when a comedian calls someone Bruce, you can almost bet he means the guy is a swishy character. Yet nothing could be further from the truth."[22]

Bridwell finds it "puzzling" that the comic book convention of a boy as his partner's ward was so widely copied after Batman and Robin—with the Shield and Dusty, Captain America and Bucky, the Green Arrow and Speedy, the Wizard and Roy, T.N.T and Dan the Dyna-Mite, the Sandman and Sandy, and so on—and he is at pains to explain that in the case of Batman and Robin the idea was necessary "because Bruce's life had been pretty well sketched out, and he had no son or kid brother." The point, which Bridwell seems unwilling to see, is that in making Dick Grayson Bruce Wayne's ward, the writers of Batman have a structure that is enormously flexible. It provides a great many possibilities for the fantasies of writers and readers alike. As Dick Giordano recognizes, "Various and radically different interpretations of The Batman can coexist."[23] Two examples will suffice, to illustrate how different writers and artists can inflect our interpretation of the relationship between Batman and Robin.

In "Robin Dies at Dawn," Batman submits to a series of tests that are designed to "determine how long, and what kinds of strains an astronaut can endure in loneliness, before his mind starts imagining things." As the doctor explains to Batman after the experiment, "One of man's most primitive fears is loneliness! When a man is isolated too long, the mind plays strange tricks . . . In your case, you imagined that you were indirectly guilty of Robin's death . . . Your constant concern about the boy's safety came to the surface in your hallucinations!"

First, Batman observes that he is on an alien planet that has twin moons; then he notices that his utility belt is gone. He is "touched by a tiny fear—the instinctive fear of any man who is isolated and weaponless—and confronted by the *unknown!*" He says to himself, "It's *not knowing* that's so disquieting! And somehow I sense terrible danger—waiting! I—I've never felt so *alone* in all my life—" Then, while trudging through this alien landscape, he is suddenly seized by a huge and bizarre plant. "*Great Scott!*" he exclaims. "That plant's tendril has elongated and wrapped itself around me!" The plant, per-haps significantly, has a small, red protuberance at the center of its strange arrangement of feathery leaves, prehensile tendrils, and reptiliform scales. "If only Robin were here to help me!" he cries. "*Robin! Where are you, Robin? Robin!*" Then, "suddenly, a familiar, sturdy figure races forward . . ." Of course, it is Robin, with his little yellow cape streaming behind him, yelling, "I'll get you free!"

There are more threats to Batman, including a group of mobile, octopus-like plants, a giant, stone figure (that "suddenly rears erect!"), a deep chasm that nearly prevents their escape from the stone colossus, and a dinosaur with huge, glaring eyes. Like Ann Darrow and Jack Driscoll in King Kong's jungle, Batman and Robin are in a situation that dramatizes the stakes of love in an unconsciously sexualized mise-en-scène. Heroism and helplessness are mixed in an intense fantasy of need. The narrator describes the "blind, un-reasoning fury" of the stone giant as it "seizes a great boulder and strides across toward his puny foe!" But he could be describing the absolute nature of the love between Batman and Robin. It is his love for Batman that makes Robin go too far; and when Robin is killed by the giant, Batman grieves: "Robin sacrificed himself for me! He died so I could live! Oh, Robin . . . Robin . . ." When the purple dinosaur with the glowing eyes attacks Batman, he says, "Let it come! I don't want to live! It's my fault Robin died! I don't want to live . . ."

Chapter 1 ends on a poignant image of Batman leaving the doctor's labo-ratory with his arm around Robin's shoulders in a fatherly gesture of pro-tection from which Batman also draws comfort. In the foreground of the image, watching them go, is the doctor. He, in turn, feels protective toward Batman. As they go "home," a white-haired, mustachioed man in a uniform (he is the government representative of the Space Program that is sponsor-ing these experiments) says, "Doctor, you look worried . . ." The doctor functions as the reader's delegate figure in this image, which says, in effect, that both Batman and Robin need our love. "I am [worried]!" says the doc-tor. "Batman's a hardy specimen, with an above-average mind—but even a Batman can succumb to stress and shock! I just hope there won't be any after-effects . . ."

In chapter 2 of "Robin Dies at Dawn," Batman does suffer some aftaref-fects of the experiment. When he dreams that he is being strangled by the (*vagina dentata*) tentacle-plant, Robin and Alfred rush into his bedroom in their pajamas and wake him up. Robin suggests that Ace (their dog) sleep with Batman so that he won't "feel so alone."

Throughout this story Robin is a capable, "sturdy figure," and the adventure resonates with the logic of a boy's fantasy. The mise-en-scène is science fictional, not gothic, and there are almost no close-ups or canted images. The story is unself-conscious in its presentation of a "friendship . . . that has stood steadfast as a rock!" And when the narrator tells us that, "To Batman, Robin is like his own son," we are to understand that this is the very proof of the innocent nature of their relationship.

In "The Deadshot Ricochet," however, written fifteen years later, we see that Batman as a "father" to Robin has tried to teach his ward how to become like the best version of himself, and the story introduces the theme of mentorship when Robin—apparently now a student at Hudson University—says, "I'll sure be glad when I graduate—get back on the streets!" (*Detective Comics #474*, 1978).

Batman in a flash grabs Robin in a wrestler's grip: "Forgotten all I taught you, huh? Let's see!" Their capes swirl, as Robin yells, "Hey!" In close-up, we see their faces, only a few inches apart, the great pointed ears of Batman's cowl dominating the image in an almost sexually aggressive way. "You're on!" Robin says. And as he hurls Batman across the floor of the Batcave, he shouts good-humoredly, "I can match you *any* time I *want* to, old-timer!"

"'Old-timer'!?" In the next three frames they pit their strength and fighting skills against each other. Batman is all sharp fins and a grim smile: "Doubled—and redoubled—'*small-fry*'!" Robin's upraised thigh and buttocks dominate the last frame of this panel in which, with a thump, Batman flings Robin onto his back as Robin pulls him forward.

When their tumble is over, Batman, now on his back on the floor, says, "You look pretty fit to me, kid! Just a little wet behind the ears, still!" The narrator observes, "It's not often that laughter echoes in the Batcave—not true breathless laughter, shared by two old friends!" In the background of this frame we see, as if looking down on the two panting figures on the floor, Batman's father's cape and cowl in a glass case.[24] The narrative, now at a standstill, is rescued by a buzzing signal. In close-up we see Robin look down at his crotch: "Nuts! My belt-radio!"

The signal is from Wonder Girl, who, in the next frame, is sitting in an unconsciously seductive pose at her control panel. Her voluptuous breasts and sleek thighs are encased in a scarlet, skin-tight body suit. "Come to Gabriel's horn at once!" she tells Robin, who replies, "Well—heck, Donna, I'm tied up with Batman now—!" Overhearing this, Batman says, "Nonsense! If the Titans need you, go to it!" As Robin prepares to follow up on Wonder Girl's call, Batman kids, "You're seeing a lot of Wonder Girl and

The Harlequin these days, I hear!" Portrayals of the two women fill the upper half of the frame as Robin replies, "Like you said, Bruce—I learned a lot from you—about both *gunmen* and *girls*! You just look after Silver St. Cloud, and leave the heavy stuff to the experts!" Batman smiles, and says with mock sternness, "All right! That does it! Out!" With a wave, Robin speeds off on his motorcycle: "Catch ya later, Bruce!" Batman's response—"Good luck, Dick—and *thanks!*"—is followed by a thought bubble: "It was good to see you . . . *pal.*"

The "innocence" of Batman and Robin's father-son relationship in "Robin Dies at Dawn" gives way in this story to an uneasy rivalry and attraction between the two, which recalls Freud's remark that, "It is well known how easily erotic wishes develop out of emotional relations of a friendly character, based upon appreciation and admiration, (compare Molière's "Kiss me for the love of Greek"), between a master and a pupil."[25] When Wonder Girl calls, there is a sense in which a homoerotic element in Batman and Robin's roughhousing has been safely deflected in the nick of time toward heterosexual and group imperatives, and there is a slight mournfulness in Batman's parting thought—as if he were struggling with the power of his love for Robin, and the constraints on its expression in "friendship." Their calling each other "Bruce" and "Dick," although dressed in their "Batman" and "Robin" outfits, is a final, small indication of the depth of their intimacy, which this entire opening scene exists exclusively to represent.

Dick Grayson/Robin eventually leaves Batman and, as Nightwing, becomes the leader of the Teen Titans;[26] and the next Robin (Jason Todd) is killed by the Joker while he is trying to discover the true identity of his mother.[27] A third, computer-literate Robin (Tim Drake) appeared in late 1989. In Frank Miller's earlier, four-issue miniseries, *Batman: The Dark Knight Returns* (1986), "everything is exactly the same," observes Alan Moore in his introduction to the collection, "except for the fact that it's all totally different"[28]— including the incarnation of Robin as an androgynous thirteen-year-old girl, Carrie Kelley, which is almost proof, at last, of the homoeroticism inherent in the relationship between Batman and the Boy Wonder.

By 1998, in the animated television series *Batman Beyond*, Robin ceases to exist altogether—"The unthinkable has happened: the aging Bruce Wayne has hung up the cape of the once invincible BATMAN! But when a brave, young high school kid named Terry McGinnis stumbles onto the secret of Batman's true identity, a new alliance is forged. And an awesome new hero is born!"[29] In the series' 41-minute "origins" story, *Batman Beyond: The Movie*, Terry literally dons Bruce Wayne's Batman suit and becomes "the

Batman," while Bruce Wayne, leaning on his walking stick, shuffles around alone in the vast, gothic gloom of Wayne Manor. After Terry's father is killed by a villainous "corporate kingpin" called Derek Powers, Terry becomes Bruce Wayne's employee (Bruce looks him in the eye and, offering his hand, says: "Welcome to my world!"), although Terry continues to live at home with his mother and younger brother, while attending high school.

This reconfiguration of the Batman/Robin family romance is momentous and appears to be a further attempt to heterosexualize Bruce/Batman and "Robin." In a sense, *Batman Beyond*'s creators have made the relationship between the two (men) more realistic, although hardly any less homoerotic. The atmosphere of homoeroticism is everywhere—for example, the first time we see Terry at his high school, he is on his hands and knees, locked in a wrestler's embrace with a Bruce Wayne look-alike called Nelson; and when Bruce Wayne pays Terry a visit at home, to offer him a job, the young man is shown asleep in his underwear on the top of his bed—for the series' creators seem to understand that *Batman* would not be *Batman* without the erotic "bond" between the two men: "Powered by the bond between legendary master and youthful crusader, *Batman Beyond* introduces a new hero, for a new era!"[30]

BATMAN AND WOMEN

Bridwell's defense of Bruce Wayne's heterosexuality conveniently summarizes thirty years of the Caped Crusader's relationships with women:

> Other heroes have a girlfriend. Not so with Bruce Wayne. When I say he's a playboy, I mean it. There was Julie Madison, who was his fiancée for a time before and after Robin came on the scene. She was succeeded by Linda Page, a society girl who turned to nursing to be of some service to the world. Then came Vicki Vale, news photographer, in the late forties (a too-obvious copy of Lois Lane), who was continually trying to ferret out The Batman's secret identity. Next, The Batwoman appeared—like Robin an ex-circus star. . . . Vicki and The Batwoman were rivals for The Batman for a time. When they faded, anything like a permanent romance faded too. There have been plenty of girls, but obviously, Bruce doesn't hanker to be tied down to any *one* female.[31]

Though Bruce Wayne has girlfriends, Batman hardly ever does. Nowhere is the theme of the dichotomous personality that is so central to the Batman mythos more crucially defined than in Bruce Wayne's relationships with women. Bruce Wayne's guise as Batman is an attempt to disavow the polymorphism in which human beings are grounded. A coherent self-image is achieved by pressing the world into binary terms and insisting on man's double nature. All *Batman* stories are dedicated to this vision of a binary universe, and many will sustain it as a motif in a web of suballusions.[32]

Batman's sexuality—which his writers feel compelled every so often to treat explicitly in a story involving one of Bruce Wayne's girlfriends—is obscure at the best of times, for Batman/Bruce's sexual instincts are inhibited in their aims. In "The Deadshot Ricochet," after Bruce Wayne has an argument with Silver St. Cloud, Bruce is pictured in shadows as he thinks to himself: "A lovers' spat! Our first! This is getting serious! It's beginning to really matter what she thinks of me! And yet—she doesn't really know me—not *inside*! There's a part of me she can't *ever* know! Always the same problem—ever since the first girl I loved, Julie Madison! They love Bruce Wayne—but Bruce Wayne has become a daytime mask for The Batman! The problem is—would I have it any other way?"

Indeed, would he have it any other way? As Jonathan Rutherford has written, male heroes are in flight from women:

> The appeal of the hero is his freedom from women: the snares and entrapments of dependency and vulnerability. . . . He presents us with a sexual identity free of doubt while he masters and controls his surroundings. Yet somewhere in the story there will be the nostalgic memory of a previous life of domestic happiness: a woman in his past. It's as though his masculinity can only function with an idealized version of a lost woman's love. Its reality in the here and now would end the image and reality of a self-contained and independent man.[33]

Later, Bruce and Silver have lunch together, and Silver brings up the topic of Batman. In a series of anxious thought bubbles, Bruce says to himself, "She's watching me so intently! This isn't just a casual question! Does she *suspect*?" He tries to get off the subject, but Silver persists for a moment longer. "She *does* suspect!" he says to himself. "I *thought* she did the night I first met her! I've chided Alfred for playing his role too broadly, but it may be myself I have to watch! It won't do to get careless with a lady this sharp!"

In a manner of speaking, the first and only woman in Bruce Wayne/Batman's life is Martha Wayne, whose memory evokes not only an image of plenitude but of dependence also. Bruce/Batman's masculine identity is founded in his separation from his mother; and all women, as Rutherford suggests, are an uncomfortable reminder to the hero of his vulnerability as a child. The hero's response, like Rick's in *Casablanca*, is to harden himself against needing anyone, or at least to *appear* autonomous. We see this response in "To Kill a Legend," which begins in a nightmare Bruce is having about how his parents died. When they are shot, the narrator observes, "They will never move again. They will never *hold* him . . . never *comfort* him after a bad dream . . . never know how much he really *loved* them." Bruce wakes up, and we see that he sleeps in the nude (like a child, who has no need of fetishes, disguises, armor). He gets out of bed and immediately puts on his Batman costume, saying, "I guess I'm lucky, in a way. Whenever it gets too painful being Bruce Wayne—I can always become The Batman! I wonder how normal people manage to cope?" He then swoops down into Gotham City on his Batrope—an image of freedom, strength, autonomy.

FIGURE 8.2 "Whenever it gets too painful being Bruce Wayne . . ." ("To Kill a Legend," *Detective Comics #500*, 1981. Copyright © 1981, 1988 DC Comics Inc. All rights reserved)

If Silver St. Cloud must never learn of Bruce Wayne's identity as Batman, Selina Kyle (Catwoman) can come closer to the truth—because, in some way, she is like Batman. She is his mirror image. Catwoman is Batman's enemy, but, as Batman notes, "there had always been an attraction between us" (*The Brave and the Bold #197*, 1983). Catwoman's origins are similar to Batman's, and when she explains to him why she abandoned her identity as Selina Kyle, all the pain of Batman's own tortured psyche is thrown into sharp relief: "I hate feeling so—so *helpless!*" she says (in reference to the husband who used to beat her). "I became the Catwoman so I'd never have to be at anyone's mercy ever again."

In "The Autobiography of Bruce Wayne," the painfully divided nature of Batman's identity, as it can be articulated in terms of heterosexual desire, is revealed in a narrative that is poignantly explicit. Batman recognizes himself in Selina Kyle's confession of how she became the Catwoman, and it moves him: "Funny, we both chose our paths out of anger . . . and we both found ourselves *trapped*. You lost Selina Kyle, and I lost . . . someone else. But you found a way *out*, and I don't know *how* to get out." They embrace, and as Batman recalls, "I never wanted to hold on to someone as much in my life . . . but . . ."

But Batman pulls away, saying, "This isn't right. Not while Robin and the others are still missing. We have to find them!" Batman, as the boy Bruce Wayne, lost what everyone loses on the level of the unconscious—an imaginary, perfect unity with his mother/(father?), who offered total love and trust—and in a powerfully reflexive drama of identification, he can only love Robin, his younger self. Selina implores, "Don't you see? All your life you've been terrified of losing anyone else the way you lost your parents! So you created a world for yourself—a world of conflict and confrontation—a world where no one could ever get that close again!"

But his world, as we know, is divided into two spheres: Wayne Manor and Gotham City. Wayne Manor, although it does not feature much in the comic books, is an absolutely necessary corner of Batman's world. Precisely because it must stand as the very rock of stability in Batman's life, it is not very often the site of an escapade involving Gotham City criminals. The baronial Englishness of Wayne Manor, its Victorian stolidness, and above all Alfred, the English butler, stand for the kind of continuity with the past, and a sense of all things fixed and certain, that Batman and the small boy inside Bruce Wayne need. The touching preposterousness of Wayne Manor speaks of an attempt to regain the sense of security that Bruce Wayne took for granted as a child before his parents were killed. The house itself, we could say, stands for the impressive, protecting, glamorous father, and the Batcave beneath it

FIGURE 8.3 *Batman* (1989): Bruce Wayne (Michael Keaton) standing in front of the gothic and gloomy Wayne Manor.

represents the security of the child's attachment to his adored mother, a bond both libidinal and nurturing, archaic and always present. The cave, at the heart of the outward form, is a secret, primal, empty space from which all desire springs.

Wayne Manor is an entirely masculine domain in which the antique and courtly Alfred, at the risk of being a camp figure, serves as Bruce Wayne's mother, father, servant, and "oldest friend." Batman/Bruce will often consult Alfred on important matters, for he is almost the only character in Batman's world who is not neurotic, and his answers are usually taken by the reader to represent the wisest counsel or most moral truth that one is ever likely to find in a *Batman* story.

After a hard night of crimefighting, Batman will come home to find Alfred waiting up for him, as a mother might wait up for a child. When Batman is hurt, Alfred is there to tend to his wounds. We may observe that he is in some ways *better* than a mother, because he makes no claims on Batman/Bruce that the hero has any difficulty in honoring. There is no desire or guilt in his love for Alfred because Alfred's status as his manservant/butler is straightforward—unlike Robin's status (as his ward), which is complicated by a familial dimension.

In "A Caper a Day Keeps Batman at Bay" (*Batman #312*, 1979), Bruce is confined to bed by the effects of some ultrasonic waves used on him by the Calendar Man during a confrontation in Gotham City. When he tries to get out of bed, Alfred will not allow it ("You'll do nothing of the kind, sir! You are staying in bed, Master Bruce—if I'm forced to sit on you to keep you there!), and Bruce retorts with wry affection, "Alfred, has anyone ever told you you'd make a great mother?" No one, of course, can ever replace Bruce's mother. But Alfred, at least, provides Bruce with some of the function of protective plenitude. He performs a role that very slightly resembles (in the child's view) the mother's role before she is discovered in a "primal scene," which alters fundamentally and permanently the child's feelings toward her.

A PRIMAL SCENE

In "The Origin of Batman," the narrator asks, "Have you ever wondered why Bruce Wayne, a society blueblood, chose the dangerous career of Batman? What made him become a relentless, hard-hitting crime-fighter? How did he

FIGURE 8.4 *Batman* (1989): Bruce Wayne and Alfred (Michael Gough), his major-domo. (Copyright © 1989 DC Comics Inc. All rights reserved)

train himself in athletic and scientific skill until he became the nemesis of the Joker, the Penguin, Catwoman and other nefarious criminals of our time? What inspired the Batmobile and the Batplane? Here is the answer . . . the inside story of a boy who made a grim vow . . ." In this (the first) version, the street criminal wants Martha Wayne's necklace, and it is because Thomas Wayne protests—"You hoodlum! Don't you dare put a hand on my wife!"— that he is shot. The narrator observes, "That single bullet really killed two people, for Martha Wayne's weak heart stopped from the sudden shock!"

As a family romance, the scene of the murder(s) not only represents a child's wish to see his parents dead, in order that he may invent himself and create superior parents, it is also, in some sense, a primal scene. It corresponds to the moment of disgust and horror in a child when he understands that his parents are sexual beings. The father's sexual embrace is seen as a violent act that defiles the child's mother—that "dearest and loveliest of women." The moment is profoundly alienating, and in young Bruce Wayne's case he will forever afterwards see Gotham City, where this happened, as a filthy, disgusting place. The imagined perfection of a pre-oedipal harmony is shattered, and the swarming, writhing reality of the city becomes associated with the frightening claims of a nascent and confusing adult sexuality. Young Bruce's response will be to seek the reassuring unity of a binary identity in Batman/Bruce Wayne (lord of Wayne Manor). Bruce's invention of the Batman persona, and his metamorphosis into a handsome, wealthy man who is a pillar of the Establishment, provides a coherent identity that is as neat as the two halves of Dr. Jekyll and Mr. Hyde.

In Batman's story as family romance, the child displaces his patricidal impulse into a representative of evil—a villain. The Joker becomes the Batman's "number one nemesis," who, in an overdetermined twist of logic, has his own origins in an emasculating inability to protect and support his pregnant wife.[34] He is "a figure suggesting a ghastly, deliberate mockery, like death taunting life,"[35] and the logic, finally, of his place in Batman's world is made very clear in the 1989 *Batman* movie, which suggests that it was the Joker who, all those years before, killed Bruce Wayne's parents. While this offers an "explanation" of why they are enemies, it reduces the complexity of their relationship. It also departs from forty-one years of stories that say a small-time criminal named Joe Chill killed Wayne's parents.

The Joker figures largely in Batman's world because he evokes the "ghastly, deliberate mockery" of the child's helplessness—in the narrative and also metaphorically in the scenario as primal scene: the child's retroactive fantasy of finding his parents in a sexual act. To put it less literally: the child comprehends his father's claim on his mother, and he suffers an acute sense of loss, exclusion, humiliation, anger, and disgust. The scene marks the child's first realization that the world is full of lies and deceit. Things are not always what they seem; and the Joker, whose androgyny is opposed to Batman's masculinity, is the most emblematic figure of this awareness that all signs are partial, contradictory, provisional, contested: "A man smiles a smile without mirth . . . rather a smile of death! The awesome, ghastly grin of . . . The Joker!"[36] The Batman's battle becomes one against chaos—the chaos of an endlessly protracted oedipal moment, of the world represented by the labyrinthine streets of Gotham City.

In "To Kill a Legend," the narrator writes that young Bruce "learned what death was" that night in Crime Alley. This is another way of saying he discovers the meaning of the phallus and castration. Gotham City comes to represent the impossibility of human communication. Its streets echo with the truth of Lacan's remark that *there is no sexual relation*. Batman will spend a lifetime penetrating its darkest corners.[37] He will try, hopelessly, to clean it up—to make it the safe place he remembers it was before Park Row became Crime Alley.[38] He will even return to Crime Alley every year, as one might visit a grave, to see Miss Thompkins (who, significantly, never married). When Bruce's parents were killed, "nobody noticed the boy wracked with endless sobs . . . nobody except a woman, who knelt by him and said, 'I'm Leslie Thompkins. Come with me. I'll do what I can.' And in all the world, there was nothing . . . nothing except the warmth of her arms and the comfort of her soothing words . . ." (*Detective Comics #457*, 1976). This is what the boy will spend a lifetime wanting, but will never entrust himself to seek in another person: the unconditional embrace of the pre-oedipal mother.

Martha Wayne is robbed. Her pearl necklace is seized. We might consider the significance of the fact that the Joker in most stories is a jewel thief (and that most of the criminals in Gotham City are thieves). Of course, the robbing of jewels functions in the stories as a Macguffin, a convenient plot device, but for Batman (and subtextually for the reader), every robbery evokes the humiliation of that original surrender, that kind of rape in which Bruce lost his mother.

"A SKIN-TIGHT COSTUME OF BLACK, GRAY AND BLUE . . ."

Batman's monicker, the Dark Knight, expresses perfectly the duality of his image. He is both a caped crusader, a chivalrous knight, like Superman; and he is a masked avenger—a mysterious, brooding figure with a "relentlessly trained body, powered by unquenchable will" (*Detective Comics #404*, 1970). As Dennis O'Neil observes, Batman is "not an optimistic character. Trauma colors everything he does." O'Neil believes that "Batman, like the Shadow, is essentially a transformed villain."[39] The contradictions of Batman's character are figured, primarily, in a style of masculinity that always returns to the body.

At Wayne Manor, Bruce Wayne collects medieval suits of armor. They suggest his efforts to protect himself, and they refer to the frailty of the human body, of the man inside who is vulnerable. The medieval/gothic inspiration of Bruce Wayne/Batman's world has an adolescent appeal, for it gives the moral stakes a clarity and makes the struggle Manichaean. In *The Mark of Zorro*, Diego, disguising his other identity as Zorro, says dismissively to the beautiful, young Lolita: "Dashing about with a cutlass is quite out of fashion. Hasn't been done since the Middle Ages!" Lolita replies with unassailable logic: "It seems to be quite effective! He's like a lion among a lot of frightened sheep." In his costume, Batman means to be terrifying, just as he was terrorized by his parents' murder (although, in "The Batman Nobody Knows!" Batman observes, "Hmm, whatever else it proves—The Batman's frightening image scares the guilty . . . not the innocent!") (*Batman #250*, 1973). Robert Greenberger, in his "Endnotes" to *The Greatest Batman Stories Ever Told*, is right to observe that "the gadgets and hardware aided The Batman, but his most useful tool was his very image."[40] This image, grounded in costume, is indeed very effective.

In "Death Strikes at Midnight and Three," the narrator writes: "A careful observer would have noticed that the clothes had been cunningly tailored to disguise Wayne's lithe, athletic musculature. He was now clad in a skin-tight costume of black, gray, and blue synthetic fabric which reflected no light. His upper face was concealed by a cowl that subtly altered the contours of his head and a voluminous cape billowed behind him. Against the gloom of the alleyway, he was nearly invisible" (*DC Special Series #15*, 1978). This disguise, like Robin's, always refers us to the notion that Batman has something to hide. It implies that he possesses a "true" identity, which is always hidden, the main index of which is his face. What, then, lies behind his mask? What would we read there?

Susan Sontag (writing about Ingmar Bergman's *Persona*) suggests that, "If the maintenance of personality requires safeguarding the integrity of masks, and the truth about a person always means his unmasking, cracking the mask, then the truth about life as a whole is a shattering of the whole façade—behind which lies an absolute cruelty."[41] There is, I propose, no "absolute cruelty" behind Batman's mask. There is nothing. To borrow Jennifer Stone's words on Pirandello's *As You Desire Me*, "Behind the naked mask . . . there is nothing but a blank space, a wilderness of undifferentiated meaninglessness—any frightful content only being a retroactive effect of the mask itself."[42] We have in Batman's mask, rather, the very condition of desire, a sense in which masculinity itself (identity) is an assumed disguise—a disguise, precisely (mask and costume), that produces the mystique. As Sontag notes, "the Latin word *persona*, from which the English 'person' derives, means the mask worn by an actor. To be a person, then, is to possess a mask." Batman and Robin's identities are grounded in fetishism. They draw courage from the fetish; without their masks and costumes Batman and Robin are unable to perform.[43]

Batman's cape, in its billowing, baffling fluidity, serves to emphasize the phallic nature of his hard body at the center of the whole effect. His cowl and Robin's mask are also erotic in that a mask voyeurizes the world for the wearer. There is a sexual terror associated with its removal, as an early scene in the 1966 *Batman* movie suggests. Catwoman, disguised as a Soviet news-

FIGURE 8.5 Michael Keaton in *Batman* (1989): Batman's mask as the very condition of desire, a sense in which masculinity itself is an assumed disguise. (Copyright © 1989 DC Comics Inc. All rights reserved)

reporter, boldly asks Batman to remove his mask, and all the men gasp in shock at the suggestion. "Great Scott! Batman take off his mask?!" blurts Commissioner Gordon. "She must be mad!" another man says.[44] In "The Jungle Cat-Queen" (*Detective Comics #211*, 1954), the story is pervaded by an atavistic eroticism when Batman and Robin are captured by the Catwoman's men and stripped almost naked. "I'll give you both ten minutes' start before I begin trailing you with my cats!" she exults. "And taking off your masks will be the climax of my chase!"

Batman and Robin's masks are also, finally, a sign to each other, and to us (*to me*), of their special bond. In Batman's case, the cowl masks his suffering and his passion. Or, to be more precise, the mask simultaneously hides and declares what Roland Barthes would call "the turbulences of his passion: his desires, his distresses; in short, his excesses (in Racinian language: his *fureur*)."[45] Barthes observes that, while it is "a strictly heroic value" to impose the mask of discretion upon one's passion, "passion is in essence made to be seen" (42). And so it is with Batman and Robin: masked, they reveal their passion to us. (The only ones for whom they will remove their masks are each other, and us.)

One of the most intensely emotional moments in all of *Batman* occurs in "White Gold and Truth" (*Batman: The New Adventures #416*, 1988)[46], when Dick Grayson (now as Nightwing)—in a gesture that is given four frames in a single panel of close-ups—takes off his mask and says to Batman, "I want to talk." He wants Batman to tell him why he has taken on a new Robin. "I think you owe me an explanation or two, Bruce," he says. Batman swings around: "What makes you think I owe you anything?" Dick is deeply hurt: "The years . . . the years we spent together as Batman and Robin. We were the Dynamic Duo . . . Don't you remember?" Dick recounts the painful story of how they broke up, and how he went on, eventually, to lead the Teen Titans as Nightwing—and then how his "whole world came crashing down" when he learned in the newspapers about Batman's new sidekick. "I think I have the right to know why," he demands. Batman is at first silent, and then he says: "That's not an easy question to answer." Trembling with hurt and rage, Dick shakes his fist: "*Well, why don't you take off that damn mask and give it a try!*" Batman takes off his cowl, but cannot at first bring himself to reveal his true feelings, and the various reasons he gives for having taken on a new Robin are dismissed by Dick, who insistently demands the truth. "*All right!*" Batman screams. "I admit it. I was lonely. I missed you."

Batman and Robin's skin-tight outfits of course reveal their bodies (just as Bruce Wayne's suits are designed to conceal his body). The terror that

Batman hopes to inspire in Gotham City's criminals has a sadistic element that suggests it is grounded in young Bruce Wayne's fear of and desire for his father's body. In *The Mark of Zorro* all the men are costumed in skin-tight pants, and Tyrone Power in particular is photographed to reveal the contours of his legs and the bulge of his crotch. Here, as in Superman (invented two years before), is a major inspiration for Batman's costume.[47] The fact that the Batman first appears in a vampire story suggests that the bat element of his image has its origins in the darkly erotic associations of bats with vampires.[48] This image, with its myriad meanings, resonates powerfully because it is inseparable from Batman's "story."

An Old Story

Whether we agree that the family romance has its origins in the boy child's wish to remove his father in the "competition for the tender love and devotion of the mother,"[49] or in the child's "feeling of being neglected" (76), or in a retroactive resentment over the trauma of the primal scene (over the fact that his origins are grounded in loss, and that his origins cannot be known)[50]—we recognize that the fantasy is an expression of the child's efforts, by a form of denial, to come to terms with the fact of castration.

Castration, as the founding trope of psychoanalytic discourse, describes a traumatic experience characterized by an element of separation from or loss of an object—and in *Batman*, separation and loss are the main recurring themes. Batman's "story" begins in Bruce Wayne's traumatic loss of his parents, and this experience is one that all *Batman* readers have had on an unconscious level.

The apparently immutable fact that every human subject experiences oedipal conflict is suggested explicitly in several stories. In "To Kill a Legend," for example, Batman meets a tall, mysterious man called Phantom Stranger, who says to him:

> There are worlds beyond worlds . . . hundreds of earths like your own, existing in as many different dimensions. On one such earth, Batman, forty years ago, another Bruce Wayne saw his parents murdered . . . and vowed to avenge their deaths. Twenty years later, on this earth, you watched your parents die . . . and became, like your predecessor, The Batman. Now—on still another earth—the cycle is about to repeat itself.[51]

It is the story of how all selves are formed in a matrix of filial fear and desire. It is a story that is told again and again, a cycle, endlessly repeated. As a family romance, Batman and Robin's story refers to Freud's master narrative—the Oedipus complex—which explains, in part, why these comic book characters have endured for more than half a century.

BATMAN FOREVER AND BATMAN AND ROBIN

Of the four live-action *Batman* films made by Warner Bros. since the comic book character's fiftieth anniversary in 1989—*Batman* (1989), *Batman Returns* (1992), *Batman Forever* (1995), and *Batman and Robin* (1997)—only the latter two, written by Akiva Goldsman and directed by Joel Schumacher, include Robin's character.[52] The filmmakers seem to have wanted to delay confronting as long as possible the controversial and increasingly plausible rumors that Batman and Robin (and even more problematically, Bruce Wayne and Dick Grayson) might be gay. It is obvious that they wished to bring out the homoerotic resonances of the relationship between the two (or four) characters—yet they appear to insist that, in the final analysis, Batman/Bruce Wayne is straight, and that, as the Riddler (Jim Carrey) says in *Batman Forever*, Robin secretly "dreams of one day being bare-naked with a *girl!*"

The filmmakers' attempts to simplify and render the sexuality of the two characters in pop-psychological terms are problematic, but they are interesting nonetheless and deserve a more detailed analysis than my own attempt permits here. Both films have occasional problems of tone, which perhaps originate in Schumacher's stated desire to create "a living comic book, and I think the word *comic* is important."[53] The opening shots of *Batman Forever*, for example, have a dignified and courtly Alfred (Michael Gough) asking a dark and menacing-looking Batman (Val Kilmer): "Can I persuade you to take a sandwich with you, sir?" and Batman replying solemnly: "I'll get drive-through."

It is by now a commonplace observation that all the villains in *Batman*'s world are projections of aspects of Batman's own psyche, but precisely why they and Bruce Wayne figure so largely in the movies is not immediately obvious. Goldsman notes that the requirements of the comic-book form are different from those of the movie screen, and "although you add motion and sound in the movies, the rendition of Batman himself is more limited. In the comics, the cowled face takes on a variety of expressions that the movie cowl can't. As a result, much of the work you do as a movie writer is with Bruce

Wayne."[54] He speculates that the villains dominate the screen more than they do the comic-book page because, essentially, viewers want Batman to be predictable, whereas they want and expect the villains to be unpredictable. He goes on to make an interesting analogy, which draws attention to the erotic component of viewer identification:

> Our requirements of Batman are more stringent than our expectations of the villains. Think of it as the difference between dating and marriage. From the villains we want to be wowed, charmed, excited. Since we know our relationships with these wrongdoers are short-term, we want the flash and sizzle of a hot first date. What we expect of Batman is something more. We want something both familiar and, at the same time, novel, the unique combination of consistency and freshness we expect of a partner with whom we anticipate spending the rest of our lives. (8)

It is for this reason precisely that viewers might feel ambivalent about the endings of both films: In *Batman Forever*, Dr. Chase Meridian (Nicole Kidman) has discovered Batman/Bruce Wayne's dual identity, and she appears thereby (in a form of emotional blackmail) to have secured her place as his long-term girlfriend. "Your secret is safe," she assures Bruce. And then, like a wife to a husband who has just told her he will not be home for dinner (echoing the film's opening exchange between Alfred and Batman), she turns to enter the car in which Alfred will chauffeur her back to Wayne Manor, as she says to Bruce, with a smile: "Don't work too late!"

Batman and Robin ends on a pact between Alfred's niece, Barbara Wilson (Alicia Silverstone), and Dick Grayson (Chris O'Donnell) to be partners as Batgirl and Robin. Their handshake is sealed by Bruce (George Clooney), who confirms his inclusion in the partnership—and the final, iconic shot of the film is of the three of them in costume, silhouetted, running in slow motion toward the camera. As Les Daniels dryly observes in *Batman: The Complete History*, "Batgirl's appearance suggested a degree of desperation."[55] Certainly, whatever attempts the movie makes to celebrate what psychoanalyst Jessica Benjamin calls the "father-son love affair" (referring to the identificatory homoerotic bond between toddler son and father, which is the prototype of ideal love—"a love in which the person seeks to find in the other an ideal image of himself"),[56] are betrayed by Batgirl's inclusion in the story, and particularly by her place in the film's final shots.

Batman Forever contains several sexually charged exchanges of dialogue between Batman/Bruce Wayne and Chase Meridian, in the Hollywood style of 1940s' film noir, which reveal some of the film's core concerns. For example:

Batman: What's wrong?

Chase: Last night, at the bank, I noticed something about Two-Face [Tommy Lee Jones]. His coin—it's his "Achilles' heel." It can be exploited.

Batman: I know. You called me here for this? The Bat-Signal is not a beeper!

Chase: Well, I wish I could say my interest in you was purely professional.

Batman: Are you trying to get under my cape, Doctor?

Chase: A girl can't live by psychoses alone.

Batman: It's the car, right? Chicks love the car.

Chase [She laughs]: What is it about the wrong kind of man? In grade school, it was guys with earrings. College—motorcycles, leather jackets. Now [*she fondles his breastplate*], black rubber!

Batman: Try firemen—less to take off.

Chase: I don't mind the work. Pity I can't see behind the mask.

Batman: We all wear masks.

Chase: My life's an open book: you read it.

Batman: I don't blend in at a family picnic.

Chase: We could give it a try! I'll bring the wine [*she slips back her coat to reveal her bare shoulders and décolletage*], you bring your scarred psyche.

Batman: Direct, aren't you?

Chase: You like strong women—I've done my homework. Or, do I need skin-tight vinyl and a whip?

Batman: I haven't had much luck with women.

Chase: Maybe you just haven't met the right woman.

Several of the film's major themes are launched in this exchange. First of all, the Bat Signal summons is a false alarm (the sexual symbolism of which is quite suggestive—this being the first time Batman has responded, albeit unwittingly, to a woman's call). It was not Commissioner Gordon who beamed the signal in the night sky, but a bold and beautiful young woman whose professional area of expertise is abnormal psychology, specializing in multiple-personality disorders. According to the idea of "rescue" in the family romance discussed by Freud, we may see Commissioner Gordon as standing for the father whom the son wishes to repay by saving his life on some dangerous occasion.[57] But here the fantasy is disrupted by a woman who, in her own rescue fantasy, hopes to save Batman from his "abnormal" sexuality.

Ironically, Chase's description of "the wrong kind of man" that she has always been attracted to fits Dick Grayson/Robin exactly—who is the man Bruce/Batman will choose to live with and take as his partner. Dick wears an earring and, like Bruce/Batman, has a fetish for motorcycles, leather jackets, and black rubber. Chase's glib reference to Batman's "scarred psyche" in this context reveals the fundamental flaw in the theory of sexual identity underpinning the film. To the extent that the movie invites the viewer to "read" Bruce Wayne/Batman as an uneasy/unhappy bisexual or latent homosexual, it identifies Bruce's childhood trauma of witnessing his parents' murder as the cause of his sexual ambivalence.

During Bruce's first visit to Chase's office, to consult with her about the Riddler's motives ("He's obsessed with you," is her diagnosis), he picks up a Malaysian fetish-doll he sees lying on the window sill, a "dream warden,"

FIGURE 8.6 Val Kilmer and Chris O'Donnell in *Batman Forever* (1995): Batman/Bruce Wayne and Robin/Dick Grayson share a love of motorcycles and black leather.

one side of which is painted white, the other black. "Some cultures believe she protects you from bad dreams," Chase informs him. "You look so sad," she adds. "Do *you* need one?" Later in the movie, she gives it to him as a gift. In the last shots of the film, Bruce returns the doll to her, saying: "I won't be needing this anymore. Thank you for giving me a new dream." They kiss, as Alfred looks on approvingly.

The film thus proposes conventional heterosexuality as the desirable norm for Bruce, and suggests that the sexuality of "guys with earrings," or of guys who ride motorcycles and wear leather jackets, or black rubber, is the result of a singularly damaging trauma. In any allusion to Bruce Wayne/Batman's sexuality, trauma is privileged over fantasy—because, as Françoise Vergès has noted in another context:

> With fantasy one admits that there is a psychic reality; there is a domain which resists total mastery and control, is heterogeneous and speaks in many voices. It is the construction of a narrative in which one's own desire is expressed. This domain cannot be assimilated to reality. With traumatism you are a victim: there is no conscious desire. One can attempt to find the source of the trauma which has wounded one's psyche and then find a cure.[58]

Chase Meridian offers herself as a form of therapy to Batman; heterosexuality is proposed as the cure for his sadness—and there lies the peculiar failure of this kind of Hollywood film (that cannot transcend its own homophobia, despite the best intentions of its gay director)—for to suggest that Bruce Wayne/Batman has a fear of heterosexual intimacy because of an unusual childhood trauma is to disown responsibility for the complexity of sexuality.[59]

As I have suggested, however, we may see the murder of Bruce's parents as a function of the proto-queer boy's family romance, in which he rewrites his circumstances so that he might live with a rich and handsome man in a vast house, with an English butler to take care of them—or he might cast himself in the role of the enviably dashing bachelor (cf. Edward Nygma's desperate attempts in *Batman Forever* to be as much like Bruce Wayne as possible, right down to the mole on [Val Kilmer's] cheek). And in this fantasy, they go out at night, disguised as Batman and Robin, and have thrilling, dangerous, *sexy* adventures in Gotham City.[60]

Indeed, in the scene that follows the death of Dick Grayson's parents,[61] Bruce cannot help but recall the death of his own parents and the wake that was held for them at Wayne Manor. In the half-light of his vast living room, he closes his eyes and sees himself as a boy in the same room. He walks past his parents' coffins, and past the priest reading the Twenty-third Psalm to the gathered mourners. Young Bruce approaches a red, leather-bound journal lying on his father's desk, as a wind blows open its pages to the last, hand-written entry, which he starts to read.

Adult Bruce is jolted out of this reverie by Alfred, who enters the room and turns on a light:

Alfred: Master Bruce . . . Master Bruce!
Bruce: Just like my parents . . . it's happening again . . . monster comes
   out of the night . . . a scream . . . two shots. *I killed them.*
Alfred: What did you say?
Bruce: He killed them—Two-Face. He slaughtered that boy's parents.
Alfred: No! No, you said: "*I* killed them."

The film could not be more clear about its own status as a family romance, and the viewer who "writes" the fantasy with Bruce.[62]

Later in the film, when Bruce remarks on Chase's obsession with Batman, she admits to being fascinated by him: "What makes a man do this?" she asks, referring to the photographs and newspaper stories on her desk reporting Batman's various exploits in Gotham City. "It's as if he's cursed to pay some penance. Now, what crime could he have committed, to deserve a life of nightly torture?" This is a curious reversal of the notion that Batman/Bruce Wayne is a victim. The "crime," of course, is the one committed by every reader and viewer in his or her unconscious—the murder of (Bruce Wayne's) parents, in order to clear the way for our entry into the world of *Batman.* "I guess we're all two people," Bruce replies—referring, in effect, to me in the audience and himself/Batman on the screen.

In the final confrontation between Batman and his two adversaries, set up by the Riddler like a super-television game show as it might be staged in Las Vegas, the Riddler has Chase trapped in one glass capsule (concealed under a curtain), and Robin in another:

Riddler: Can Bruce Wayne and Batman ever truly coexist? We'll find out
   today! But first, let's meet our contestants! Behind Curtain Number
   One . . . [*he lets the curtain drop, as if stripping her naked*] the absolutely fabulous Dr. Chase Meridian! She enjoys hiking, getting her
   nails done, and foolishly hopes to be the love of Bruce's life. Hah!
   And behind Curtain Number Two . . . [*again to oddly pornographic*

effect, he drops the curtain concealing Robin], Batman's one and only partner.[63] This acrobat-turned-orphan likes Saturday morning cartoons, and dreams of one day being . . . bare-naked with a *girl*!

The scene perfectly poses the riddle of Batman/Bruce Wayne's sexual identity: "Not enough time to save them *both*! Which one will it be, Batman?"

Of course, Batman is able to save them both, because—contrary to Danny Peary's assessment of his character—when you put Batman and Bruce Wayne together you do, in a manner of speaking, "come up with a full person" (the reader/viewer). Batman is able to save Chase and Robin by outwitting the Riddler with a riddle: "I see without seeing. To me, darkness is as clear as daylight. What am I?" The Riddler thinks the answer is easy (*"Please!* You're as blind as a bat!"), but in fact the moment has nothing to do with riddles and their answers—or is perhaps a meta-riddle—for, as Batman is posing his riddle, he is unhooking a tiny Baterang from his utility belt, which he hurls at the interactive-holographic-fantasy mind-control machine above their heads, which causes the Riddler to lose control of the situation. Batman has the last word: "Poor Edward. I *had* to save them *both*. You see, I'm both Bruce Wayne *and* Batman—not because I have to be, no. Because I *choose* to be."

Batman and Robin generally retreats from the kind of story elements of *Batman Forever* that very nearly demonstrated how Bruce Wayne and Batman *can* "truly coexist." For example, in *Batman Forever*, Chase Meridian figures out Bruce Wayne/Batman's dual identity because it is almost inevitable that a doctor specializing in multiple-personality disorders will do so. But in *Batman and Robin*, Bruce's vapid but beautiful girlfriend, Julie Madison (played by supermodel Elle MacPherson), is in no way essential to the plot (indeed, she does not even appear in the comic-book adaptation of the movie).

If Julie is meant to give Bruce Wayne some sort of "normal" identity, she succeeds only in seeming to serve as his "beard." Any real threats posed by female sexuality are instead embodied in one of the villains, Dr. Pamela Isley/Poison Ivy (Uma Thurman), whose heated pursuit of the two heroes has deadly implications. "Batman isn't gay," one of his most famous writers, Frank Miller, assures us. "His sexual urges are so drastically sublimated into crime-fighting that there's no *room* for any other emotional activity. Notice how insipid are the stories where Batman has a girlfriend or some sort of romance. It's not because he's gay, but because he's obsessive. He'd be *much* healthier if he were gay."[64] But the extratextual assertions of *Batman*'s writers are, finally, in a sense, irrelevant. As Andy Medhurst (who is not one of *Batman*'s writers) says: "If I want Batman to be gay, then, for me, he is. After all, outside of the minds of his writers and readers, he doesn't really exist."[65]

We are given choices of interpretation, for Batman himself is always being caught on the horns of a dilemma. Whereas the villains in *Batman Forever* are the Riddler and Two-Face—expressing Bruce/Batman's sexual confusion and ambivalence—the villains in *Batman and Robin* are Mr. Freeze (Arnold Schwarzenegger) and Poison Ivy—expressing, in the metaphors of cold and heat, either Bruce's low (hetero)sex-drive, as a function of his passionate emotional attachment to Dick/Robin; or more simply, the film's rather muddled encoding of his homosexuality. "Can you be *cold*, Batman?" asks Mr. Freeze. "You have eleven minutes to thaw the bird! What will you do—chase the villain, or save the boy? *Ha, ha*! Your emotions make you *weak*! That's why this day is *mine*!"

The film proposes that biology also makes us "weak," when it gives Poison Ivy the ability to blow "pheromone dust" at Batman and Robin, which activates a hormonal response in them and dissolves their reason. The emotional attachment between Bruce Wayne/Batman and Dick Grayson/Robin may be a powerful one forged in a matrix of psychological imperatives, but both men's sexual desires (and their objects) are apparently dictated by biological factors. The unsurprising message is that sexual desire cannot be trusted and should be monitored by the superego; but to the extent that we may think of Bruce/Batman and Dick/Robin as three-dimensional characters from whom we can learn something about our own sexuality, what are we to make of Poison Ivy's complaint that the two men prove to be "much more resistant to my love dust than expected"? Is a general point about (hetero)sexuality being made? Poison Ivy resolves to "give them a stronger dose" next time—as if sexuality were not a matter of orientation but of biochemistry.

The film articulates principles of masculinity and femininity in the cartoon terms Schumacher intended. Mr. Freeze, a camp parody of the supremely masculine man, is physically strong and emotionally cold; and as Dr. Victor Vries, he is (or was) a spectacularly accomplished scientist, and a loving husband. He still loves his beautiful wife—who awaits his next attempt to bring her out of the cryogenic suspension that keeps her alive but inert—and therein lies the hope for his moral redemption (and the plot twist that ends the movie on a happy note). The dominant psychoanalytic trope in Batman's world—castration—defines Mr. Freeze as much as it does Batman, in the sense that both men have been profoundly marked by loss. But Freeze's dreams of bringing his wife back to warm life are, we realize,

FIGURE 8.7   George Clooney and Chris O'Donnell in *Batman and Robin* (1997): The "Dynamic Duo" confront Mr. Freeze (Arnold Schwarzenegger, out of frame). (Copyright © 1997 DC Comics Inc. All rights reserved. *Photo:* Christine Loss)

doomed. The (original) lost object is irretrievably lost, and his desire, like that of most *Batman* characters, is firmly lodged under the sign of fetishism, with his wife—and the diamonds with which she is associated—standing as the ultimate fetish.

The dowdy, bespectacled Pamela Isley's metamorphosis into the gorgeously seductive Poison Ivy represents female sexual liberation as a male nightmare of women's devouring appetites and excessive fecundity. Bruce senses the danger she represents, even the first time she introduces herself to him as Pamela Isley, on the occasion of Wayne Enterprises' donation to Gotham Observatory of the world's most advanced telescope. As several security guards try to prevent her from approaching him, Bruce says: "You're not going to hurt me, are you, Miss . . . ?" To which she replies firmly: "*Doctor* . . . Pamela Isley." We are meant to see her not only as a woman who might seek revenge for being neglected by men who think her plain (the lovely Julie's demure presence at Bruce's side confirms this interpretation), but as a specifically feminine threat to men in the public sphere, whose command of capital will not necessarily protect them from the challenge of a woman's intelligence.

Poison Ivy, as the other face of Pamela Isley, will be accused by Batgirl later in the film of using her "feminine wiles" to get what she wants: "Trading on your looks? Read a book, sister! That passive-aggressive number went out long ago. Chicks like you give women a bad name!" Poison Ivy, we note, focuses her libidinal energies primarily on Robin. Or rather, it is he, more than Batman—in keeping with biology's imperative that younger men be more driven by sexual desire than older men—who finds himself responding helplessly to her toxic allure. "Youth does have its advantages: endurance, stamina," she flatters Robin. She exhorts him to "*forget* the geriatric bat! Come join *me*—my garden needs tending"—as if the sexual interest she is inviting Robin to take in her were simply the flip side of his interest in Batman.

The tone of *Batman and Robin* is almost consistently camp, as a defense against the homoerotic premises of the film, or as an attempt to have it both ways, simultaneously confirming and denying the homosexual motif. Before the movie begins, Batman's logo on the screen is joined by that of Robin— the one shield swooping in and settling on top of the other and creating a warm glow at their point of contact—like two winged creatures in a carnal embrace. It is the bond between Bruce/Batman and Dick/Robin that provides the film with its inexhaustible core of meanings, so that even when Dr. Isley, at the beginning of the film, is seen muttering into her tape-recorder— "My work would proceed faster if Dr. Woodrue weren't always whisking my venom samples back to his mysterious Gilgamesh Wing. Why won't he let me into his lab? What *is* he doing in there?"—we understand her to be articulating the film's main theme, of a contest between male friendship and heterosexual romantic love.

Pamela Isley's reference to Gilgamesh is an allusion to an ancient literary tradition dramatizing male friendship. The Gilgamesh epic, dating from approximately 1600 B.C., is the earliest recorded version of a myth that developed in pre-Babylonian times and persisted in variations among ancient Semites, pagan Greeks, medieval Christians, and the modern secular West.[66] The early part of the Gilgamesh epic contains an episode which relates how the gods, seeing that Gilgamesh, King of Uruk, was lonely, created Enkidu to be his friend. In their article, "Gilgamesh and the Sundance Kid: The Myth of Male Friendship," Dorothy Hammond and Alta Jablow comment that "the gods, interestingly enough, chose to provide a friend rather than a wife and family to assuage loneliness. Enkidu, an artifact of the gods, was a total isolate. Without kin or community, he could be absolutely committed to his friend and concomitantly became the instrument that prevented Gilgamesh's marriage."[67] Enkidu had barred Gilgamesh's access to the bride's house, and in the fight that followed, Enkidu defeated Gilgamesh and thereby won Gilgamesh's heart, causing him to forget about the marriage and embrace Enkidu as his true friend. As Marina Warner puts it, Gilgamesh and Enkidu recognize that they are "a true match for each other." They "feel a twinship, and become boon companions, beloved friends, the first buddies of literature."[68]

Hammond and Jablow note that the story of Gilgamesh and Enkidu is exceptional only in the divine creation of a special friend; otherwise it conforms to all the narratives of heroic friendship that follow:

> All make high drama of the relationship, endowing it with glamour and beauty. The friends are heroes: aristocratic, young, brave, and beautiful. In their free and wholehearted response to one another, they openly declare their affection and admiration. They engage in many adventures and battles, sharing danger, loyal to the death. Throughout life, they remain devoted and generous to each other.[69]

Contemporary homophobia prevents Batman and Robin from openly declaring their affection and admiration for each other. Just as warfare provides the agonistic setting for ancient tales of devotion between male friends—giving the heroes opportunities to express their love for each other, as they seek personal honor and fame—Gotham City, with its crime-ridden back alleys and larger-than-life villains, gives purpose to Batman and Robin's lives as crime-fighting "partners," allowing them to demonstrate in action (rather than words) their mutual trust and high regard for each other. The peculiarly erotic charge of their friendship is fueled by a more-or-less consciously deployed homophobia. The filmmakers are required to respect the essentials of the *Batman* legend, and they are constrained by the commercial imperatives of blockbuster filmmaking, both of which factors rest on heterocentrist assumptions; and so the agonistic setting in which the heroes forge their bond is not only Gotham City but includes the force-field of homophobia in which the viewer and the film are inscribed. It is understood that the power of the bond between the two heroes, which is inseparable from the bonds of identification between the viewer and the characters on the screen, would be diminished if it were revealed that Bruce and Dick were/are, merely, latent homosexuals, or even lovers (!).

The filmmakers, then, plant clues throughout the film that serve no purpose other than to sustain the guessing game, or to make the text more richly capable of a number of different, sometimes contradictory, interpretations.

For example, Poison Ivy sets up her headquarters in a former Turkish bath-house. We may interpret this small detail either as a logical choice on Poison Ivy's part, since her diabolical plan to grow an array of lethal tropical plants will be more efficiently realized in a building that was designed to accommodate profuse quantities of water and steam; or we may see it as an allusion to the homoerotic atmosphere which can often be found in Turkish bath-houses, connoting homosociality in general, which she is bent on destroying for her own demented, eco-feminist, antimale reasons.[70]

Bruce tells Julie, "I'm not the marrying kind. There are . . . things about me you wouldn't understand." This could be code-language of the same sort Pee-wee uses in *Pee-wee's Big Adventure* (1985, directed by Tim Burton, the director of both *Batman* and *Batman Returns*), when he tells Dottie, his would-be girlfriend: "There's things about me you don't know, Dottie—things you wouldn't understand. Things you *couldn't* understand. Things you *shouldn't* understand. . . . You don't want to get mixed up with a guy like me. I'm a loner, Dottie, a *rebel*." Or Bruce could simply be trying to prevent Julie from discovering that he is Batman (i.e., that he goes out at night dressed in black rubber). Clearly, the filmmakers want to offer subtexts. But the overriding theme of the movie, about which they are never ambivalent, ironic, or camp, is that of Batman and Robin (and Alfred) as a family. In both the Freudian and ordinary senses of the phrase, theirs is a family romance.

All of Bruce/Batman's "issues" (to use Dick's phrase, as in: "You've got some real issues with women, you know that?") have to do with *trust*. "How are we supposed to work together, if you won't trust me?" Dick asks Bruce. "How, indeed?" Alfred presses him—to which Bruce replies: "I can't trust him not to get hurt." Alfred then gives a little speech, using diction that signals this is the film's main message: "Despite all your talents, you're still just a novice in the ways of family. Master Dick follows the same star as you, but gets there by his own course. You must learn to trust him, for that is the nature of family."

Of course, the filmmakers are being disingenuous in attempting to link the idea of trust with that of family, when all they are really trying to do is articulate an idea of intimacy—of *love*—that is free of the taint of sexuality. If they can establish that Bruce and Dick are *family* (a gerundive condition; not quite the same thing as being *a* family), they might be able to remove any suspicion that the two men are, or will soon be, lovers.

Dick is also made to promote the theme of trust as a familial commodity: "You know, in the circus, the Flying Graysons were a team," he lectures

Bruce. "We had to trust each person to do his job—that's what being partners is all about. Sometimes counting on someone else is the only way you
win." He emphasizes the usefulness—the necessity—of trust in a working relationship, when, really, what he is asking for is some proof of Bruce's love:
"This is no partnership! You're never going to *trust* me!"

As always in *Batman*, the narrative is constructed out of symmetries, parallels, and binary terms; and there follows a scene in which Robin, under the
influence of Poison Ivy's pheromone dust, decides to go to the deadly
temptress. Batman, like Enkidu barring Gilgamesh's access to his bride's
house, now realizes he must demonstrate his love for the young man or lose
him forever. It is that moment which eventually arrives in every *Batman* narrative, when Bruce/Batman will allow himself to be vulnerable and trusting—but only for a moment: "You once said to me that being part of a team
means trusting your partner, and sometimes counting on someone *else* is the
only way to win. Do you remember that? You weren't talking about being
partners, you were talking about being a family. So, I'm asking you . . . friend
. . . partner . . . brother. Will *you* trust *me* now?"

Dick, who has loved Bruce from the beginning, now knows that he has
won Bruce's heart; and he is able to go to Poison Ivy without mortal risk of
succumbing to one of her poisonous kisses. The scene in which Robin tests
Poison Ivy's sincerity becomes a conspiracy between the two men to defeat
the woman:

> *Robin:* I want us to be together, but I want to make sure you're serious
> about turning over a new leaf. I need a sign . . .
> *Poison Ivy:* How about "slippery when wet"?
> *Robin:* . . . of trust. Tell me your plan.

Robin confirms that Batman was right—Poison Ivy's kisses cannot be trusted. Despite Alfred's dictum to his niece that "only family can be trusted," the
motif of trust is revealed in this scene to be a floating signifier, a term that
defines more than one kind of relation, that comprehends more than one
kind of love. Dick *was* "talking about being partners," even if Bruce would
rather call it "talking about being a family." It comes to the same thing: their
relationship, the dyad that Bruce/Batman has such difficulty defining.

Alfred has no difficulty calling Bruce his "son," but Bruce—because he is a
sexually viable figure of identification for the viewer—is made by the filmmakers to pull back from any completely candid declaration of love for another man. His emotional diffidence, after all, is fundamental to his character

and is a key element of his charm. Even when Alfred and Bruce have a conversation in which they both acknowledge that Alfred is dying, Bruce qualifies his sentiment. With tears in his eyes, he says: "I love you . . . old man." And Alfred replies: "I love you, too." The scene is very affecting, but Bruce's endearment—"old man"—added after a slight pause, seems to betray a hint of anxiety, as if Bruce needs to establish that his love for Alfred is familial and safely circumscribed by the generational difference between them.

The film ends, as pointed out, on the "correct" ideological note. The heroes, of course, defeat the villains; but more importantly, an idea of family is consolidated, with Batgirl/Barbara and Robin/Dick as siblings, or cousins; Batman/Bruce as a paternal figure; and Alfred as both mother and grandparent. They "win" according to their philosophy that "sometimes counting on someone else is the only way to win," although exactly what has been won is up for interpretation. At the very least, the forces of chaos have been subdued, and even death itself has been held at bay (a cure for the early stages of the "MacGregor's Syndrome" afflicting Alfred having been produced by Mr. Freeze, in a bargain to bring his own wife back to life). In the Manichaean struggles between the forces of light and the forces of darkness, the forces of light are represented by the characters' working together in the name of "trust" to preserve their "family." The love that sustains this family is homoerotic, ideal love—the love young Bruce felt for the hero on the screen one afternoon at the movies, all those years ago.

9

MY OWN PRIVATE IDAHO AND THE NEW QUEER ROAD MOVIES

In 1990, writing in the *New York Times*, Caryn James announced unequivocally that, "Today's Yellow Brick Road Leads Straight to Hell." The film that prompted her to lament "how far film makers have come from the road to Oz," and that made her realize there was something that should be identified as "the new, subversive road movie," was David Lynch's *Wild at Heart* (1990). Unlike most film critics before her, James has a very definite notion of what the (classic) road movie is:

> Films like *The Wizard of Oz* [1939] and Preston Sturges' *Sullivan's Travels* [1941] defined the standard pattern for road movies: whether the hero was a scarecrow or a rich film director bumming cross-country during the Depression, characters traveled through danger and disillusionment to healthy self-knowledge and back to the safety of home. They followed an optimistic course as old as the American West and as deeply entrenched in our culture as Whitman's "Song of the Open Road."[1]

James believes that *The Wizard of Oz* has profoundly influenced the contemporary road movie, but that "the creators of today's road movies recognize that the road leads to the nightmarish wilds of society and of their characters' own hearts" (25). Using *Wild at Heart* and *Something Wild* (1986) as her primary examples, James noted that in the happy endings of such films, however, contemporary filmmakers "fight for the persistent hope that the road still leads to a place where dreams come true" (25).

The road movie genre took yet another turn in the 1990s with the appearance of a veritable wave of independently produced queer films—some of the more successful or critically interesting ones being Gus Van Sant's *My Own Private Idaho* (1991), Gregg Araki's *The Living End* (1992), and Steve McLean's *Postcards from America* (1994, adapted primarily from two of

David Wojnarowicz's semiautobiographical books, *Close to the Knives: A Memoir of Disintegration* and *Memories That Smell Like Gasoline*). In the mainstream, too, gay-themed or queerly inflected road movies appeared in the 1990s: *The Adventures of Priscilla, Queen of the Desert* (1994), *Boys on the Side* (1995), *To Wong Foo, Thanks For Everything, Julie Newmar* (1995), and *Total Eclipse* (1995). But it can hardly be said that the independently produced queer road movies end happily, even if there is a sense—implicit in the films' struggle against homophobia—that the road may yet lead to a place where dreams come true. For whatever reasons, the queer cinema of the 1990s has emerged as a distinct phenomenon and has drawn considerable attention in the mainstream press; and it is one of the aims of this essay to examine why this should be so.[2]

Thomas Waugh has observed that the "same-sex imaginary" of the gay-authored narrative cinema from 1916 to 1990 has remained remarkably constant in its preservation, and even heightening, of "the structures of sexual difference inherent in Western (hetero)patriarchal culture," but that it "usually stops short of those structures' customary dissolution in narrative closure."[3] Since the 1980s, however, we have seen a new breed of young gay directors who are "very much plugged into their gay constituency." Moreover, as Waugh notes, "the international circuit of gay festivals has begun to consolidate something like real gay genres, gay audiences, and gay authors, arguably for the first time in our history" (154).

And yet what do we make of films—like *My Own Private Idaho* and *Postcards from America*—that could be interpreted as suggesting that homosexuality is caused by unhappy childhoods, or worse? When *Postcards from America* was screened at the 1994 New York Film Festival, Stephen Holden, blaming the filmmaker, wrote in the *New York Times*: "Mr. McLean's film adaptation . . . makes a heavy-handed Freudian equation between the vicious beatings Wojnarowicz endured at the hands of his father and his cruising for rough trade at truck stops and on the road."[4] And of *My Own Private Idaho*, one critic observed that, "Inevitably . . . *Idaho* says many things about homosexuality, and the indirect message is troublesome in how it eerily recalls films from the 50s and 60s, when homosexuality tentatively emerged from the cinematic closet only to be embraced by (presumably straight) directors eager to reduce it to Freudian pathology."[5]

But the new queer filmmakers have not felt under pressure to make propaganda films for the gay movement, especially as, with hindsight, some of them believe the "gay liberation criticism" of the post-Stonewall decade—with its simplistic eagerness to endorse "positive images" and condemn negative stereotypes—has largely failed us.[6] Gregg Araki, for example, subtitles *The Living End* "An Irresponsible Movie," which says, in effect: "Take it or leave it." Araki hopes his movies will also be seen by nongay viewers, but he speaks and works as a gay filmmaker with little interest in second-guessing the hypothetical nongay audience.[7] On the eve of *My Own Private Idaho*'s release, Araki expressed some curiosity about what sort of impact Van Sant's film would have on mainstream attitudes and markets. "I think [*My Own Private Idaho*] will be important as a test of Hollywood's acceptance of the concept of a young *auteur* who makes films with quasi-gay themes and big stars," he told the interviewer. But Araki made it clear that there is a price to pay for "Hollywood's acceptance," and it is not one he is willing to pay:

> There's a real danger in following the Hollywood "carrot": the worst thing in the world to me would be becoming one of those filmmakers who is perpetually "in development." I would rather make a cheap movie than talk to "D-girls" and lawyers for three years. But I guess that's just my bad attitude. . . . The freedom of [independent filmmaking] is that you can do whatever you want.[8]

Van Sant told *Elle* magazine the same thing: "If I'm going to do something without the muscle and money of Hollywood, I should be able to do something that they wouldn't do."[9] Clearly, if the road movie as a genre has developed a new, queer variant, it is because of what the independent film in the 1990s made possible. But what are the likes of Araki, Van Sant, and McLean saying in their films? How are those of us who are traditionally unrepresented, or underrepresented, or misrepresented by Hollywood in fact being represented in the new queer road movies?

There appear to be a number of affinities between the road movie genre and the contemporary homosexual imaginary. The symbolism of "the road" as freedom from constraints (the freedom to travel, discover, forget, experiment, escape, *move*) has a correspondence, first of all, in the gay affirmation of sexuality: of sexuality as a celebration of the body and the senses. Gay men now generally acknowledge the centrality of the erotic impulse in the gay imaginary, and the dominant patterns of gay male sex—accurately described by Lynne Segal, echoing Richard Dyer, as "a basic romanticism combined with an easy acceptance of promiscuity"[10]—appear in the narratives of the new queer road movies, just as they do in some of the narratives of male gay pornographic film. It is easy to see the attraction of gay filmmakers to the road movie genre, with all the possibilities it provides characters who choose to live and love outside the institution of the monogamous heterosexual partnership and the conventional nuclear family. In the 1970s, gay cinema—when it mirrored the master narrative of the hetero-patriarchal cinema built on the conjugal drive—would usually not show its gay protagonists coming together at the end. The reason "gay closures are seldom happy endings," Waugh writes of the cinema in the seventies, is that, "We don't establish families—we just wander off looking horny, solitary, sad, or dead."[11] Waugh's half-ironic remark, "We don't establish families," is also a gesture toward the liberating notion that as gay men and women we are free to invent our own narratives, take a different road, form new definitions of family, and make new rules for the partnerships we might wish to enter. The queer road movies of the 1990s, more often than not, don't have conventionally happy endings, but something has certainly changed, for they cannot be called *un*-happy endings, either.

THE HUSTLER

In what follows, I wish to examine in particular the figure of the hustler, who has been prominent in the cinematic and literary gay imaginary for quite some time, and who can be seen as emblematic of the queer road movie protagonist. Like his female counterpart a century ago, the male prostitute is a subversive figure. Mary Ann Doane notes the increased fascination in the literature and art of the late nineteenth century with the figure of the prostitute as emblematic of the new woman's relation to urban space—the prostitute as the epitome of the female *flâneur*. Doane also suggests that "the prostitute represents the collapse of sublimation as a concept and hence the downfall of the 'sublime'—the 'end of the aura and the decline of love.'"[12] The concept of the sublime (the sublime as "the locus of non-exchangeability," in accordance with Kant's understanding of it as indissociable from an individual subjective experience) is "seriously threatened" when "the body becomes a form of property which is exchangeable, when subjectivity and sexuality themselves are perceived as being on the market."[13]

The figure of the contemporary hustler, thus, not only comprehends this scandal, he also threatens the very underpinnings of the patriarchy, in which men can never themselves serve as commodities on the market. (As Luce Irigaray observes, the patriarchal order—as an economy of desire—is a man's game, in which *women* are circulated among men.)[14] Indeed, the frequent insistence on the element of exchange in so many homosexual encounters, or the clear articulation of dominant and submissive roles (among Arabs in North Africa, for example) can be seen as an attempt to imaginatively save the structural underpinnings of the patriarchy, as the very condition of desire.[15] The hustler and his john play roles, which may or may not correspond to the real reasons that bring them together.

The complexities of hustler-john dynamics have been perceptively analyzed by Michael Moon, and they suggest the extent to which the erotic undercurrents of the road movie—whether or not a hustler figures in the plot; and always in buddy movies—are inscribed within a force-field of homophobia:

> The supposedly spoiled and stigmatized role of john may be recuperated for some johns by making a kind of imaginary straightness of his own depend on the performed straightness of the hustler: a john's not descending to (in his mind) the depths of being queer while continuing to have sex with young men may depend on his success at maintaining the pretense that he does not have sex with queer men or boys and is consequently "not really queer."[16]

Almost every mainstream road movie in which two men travel together—whether it be *Road to Morocco* (1942) with Bing Crosby and Bob Hope, *Scarecrow* (1973) with Gene Hackman and Al Pacino, *Thunderbolt and Lightfoot* (1974) with Clint Eastwood and Jeff Bridges, *Les Valseuses/Going Places* (1974) with Gérard Depardieu and Patrick Dawaere, *Planes, Trains, and Automobiles* (1987) with Steve Martin and John Candy, *Innerspace* (1987) with Dennis Quaid and Martin Short, or *Dumb and Dumber* (1994) with Jim Carrey and Jeff Daniels—contains at least one scene that turns on homosexual anxiety and the taboo of same-sex attraction. In *Road to Morocco*, for example, Bing Crosby and Bob Hope are shipwrecked and washed up onto a Moroccan beach. They make their way to a city and find a restaurant, where they eat an enormous meal for which, of course, they haven't the money to pay. As they're discussing their dilemma, a local man comes in and gestures to Hope. Hope is afraid to talk to the man, so Crosby goes over to him. The man offers to buy Hope (for the Princess Shalamar/Dorothy Lamour) and gives Crosby some money. When Hope realizes he has been bought, he panics, and in a very funny exchange of dialogue, asks his friend: "Why would a guy buy a guy?"[17] The pornographic basis of the fantasy (of the man who manages to capture another man for use as an unwilling sexual object) is thus explicitly acknowledged, and Hope's anxiety about it is the reason the scene plays for laughs.[18] In a sense, too, the scene is made possible because it occurs in a road movie, which puts the characters in a strange land where—we're told—the people are "peculiar" and will "buy anything."

A similar moment occurs in *My Own Private Idaho*, during a conversation in a coffee shop between the two hustler friends, Mike (River Phoenix) and Scott (Keanu Reeves). Mike falls into a narcoleptic fit while trying to evade a man he thinks is "a pervert" (Hans, played by Udo Kier). When Mike returns to consciousness, he finds himself with Scott, whom he now asks sarcastically, "So, how much do you make off me when I'm asleep?" Scott replies gravely: "What! You think I'd sell your body while you're asleep? No, Mike . . . I'm on your side." The scene does not play for laughs, not only because the film is not a comedy but because it acknowledges the reality of male hustling and pimping in the lives of its characters; and the two men will acknowledge, later in the film, that their friendship is virtually indistinguishable from love (but defined, ultimately, by its nongenitality). Although Mike is saying, in effect (just as Bob Hope's character protests to his friend), "You can't sell me! You don't own me!" he does not ask why a guy would buy a guy. Fifty years after *Road to Morocco*, the road movie can explore some of the erotic complexity of male-male friendships, without prohibitive cultural anxieties and Production Code pressure making comedy the only genre in which such questions can be honestly addressed.

One of the reasons the hustler can be proposed as an emblematic road movie figure is that, like the nineteenth-century *flâneur*, every hustler can be seen as living his own daily road movie, whether on the open road or on the streets of the city. But if the *flâneur* is a man of pleasure, the hustler is a worker—he is on the job. One must therefore make the crucial distinction between real hustlers and hustlers on the screen.

Cinematic hustlers are overdetermined figures, with a complicated relation to "reality," because, among other reasons, filmmakers often seek to make even more ambiguous the already ambiguous question of the extent to which the hustler is hustling for money or hustling for sex (under the guise of hustling for money). Where the reasons a young man will become a prostitute are sometimes—perhaps often—confused and obscure to him, the subjectivity of his cinematic representation is a rather different matter. The hustler on the screen is a figure of identification for a viewer, and need not be identified with literally. In other words, a hustler on the job more often than not just looks like a (gay) man cruising for sex. In movies, he is a hustler for narrative reasons: to give him an identity, to give him something to do, to make possible the sexual encounters that are part of the plot.

It was only a matter of time before the queer road movie proper would emerge as its own genre, and not surprising that so many of them should include scenes of male hustling. Whether in *Midnight Cowboy* (1969), or *Pee-wee's Big Adventure* (1985), a man on the road is a man looking for something, and who sooner or later finds himself pretending to be something he isn't, or thinks he isn't, or wishes he were, or doesn't realize he wishes he were. It is in the nature of movies as dream-texts to speak the characters' unconscious desires, or those of a narrator. Thus, we have the hustler—who may only be a hitchhiker, like Sissy Hankshaw in Van Sant's *Even Cowgirls Get the Blues* (1994), who hustles rides. Regardless of the kind of ride the hustler is looking for, the road, as Pee-wee can attest, is a big adventure, where almost anything is possible.

"Quasi-Gay Themes and Big Stars": *My Own Private Idaho*

There is no question that the new queer movies under discussion in this essay deal with the affective bonds between men in a way that is unprecedented in the (quasi-mainstream) American cinema. But as discourses on masculinity in contemporary American culture, these films demonstrate that the progression toward a more frank treatment of homosexuality—of homosexual *desire*—does not necessarily clarify the issues involved. Thus we're given to understand in *My Own Private Idaho* that Mike is hopelessly in love with Scott, and that Scott (the "prince" in the story) is going through a conventionally rebellious, experimental phase—on his way, we might say, to resolving his Oedipus complex. But the film does not identify Mike unambiguously, or unproblematically, as gay. And Scott's willingness to have sex with men (albeit as a hustler) is offered simply as his chosen method of upsetting his father. On the one hand, the film implies that Mike's desire—which comes into focus as an unrequited love for Scott—has something to do with his tragic yearning for his lost mother, and is a function of his incestuous family history; and on the other hand, the film leaves Scott's desire relatively unexamined, as if heterosexuality needed no analysis, and homosexuality were just a phase in a Freudian sequence leading to proper object-choice (autoeroticism → narcissism → homosexual object-choice → heterosexual object-choice).

Most reviews of the film imply that the bond between Mike and Scott can be explained in fairly simple terms (i.e., they both just happen to be hustlers,

FIGURE 9.1 *My Own Private Idaho* (1991): The desire for flight without a name: Scott Favor (Keanu Reeves) and Mike Waters (River Phoenix) on the road.

but the one is gay, the other not), and that they take to the road because Mike is looking for his mother and Scott wants to get away from his father. Interviewers, too, felt safe at this level of analysis, and the actors themselves responded accordingly. When, for example, Keanu Reeves and River Phoenix were asked by *Interview* magazine if, "in deciding to do this film," the theme of the search for home and family in *Idaho* was important to them, Reeves immediately replied: "Oh, not for me." Phoenix, on the other hand, said: "I have really strong feelings about the search for home and mother. I thought it was very, very touching."[19] The overtly homoerotic aspects of the movie are scarcely mentioned in the interview.[20] *Interview*'s readership would include members of that "heterosexual, alternative audience" that Araki believes his films are "in sync with,"[21] but such readers and their magazine are too "cool" to consider whether some young men who trade sex for money might do it not only for economic reasons but for their own compelling psychological reasons as well.

Van Sant, at least, is honest and direct about why Mike is a hustler. He told Gary Indiana, in an interview for the *Village Voice*:

You only get to see Mike having pleasure when he hugs the guy at the end . . . in that scene where he watches *The Simpsons*. He was supposed to hug the guy like it was something he lost that he needed very badly. He did only have it once, it's true, but it was one of the main ideas behind his hustling, that he needed to be held, and touched. He didn't necessarily need to have sex. But he needed to be close. It was one of the reasons he liked being a hustler. . . . [He needed] to be wanted, and he could be wanted by men who wanted him for slightly different reasons than he wanted them to want him. He was really after attention and affection. But still what he missed was basically from a man, and not from a woman. He didn't have a father.[22]

Keanu Reeves, rather less articulate than his director, told *US* magazine: "I don't think [my] part is risky; there's not a lot in the film about sucking dick and getting fucked. I think it's more about family and the lives out there. I mean, it's *more*."[23] There seems to be no holding back in his remark. Reeves seems to want to be candid. But there is a note of defensiveness in what he says; and he would appear to be trying to separate the film's subject matter from its meanings. If, as he implies, "family and the lives out there" have little or nothing to do with "sucking dick and getting fucked," then why, we may ask, have the main characters—who *are* searching for home and family, it is true—both chosen to be hustlers? We might ask what kind of "home" and "family" the characters are searching for; and how the film articulates the theme of their search. It is the *"more"*—whatever it is—that an analysis of the figure of the hustler ought to reveal.

Clearly—but no doubt for different reasons—Van Sant and his actors (and *Interview*) have a stake in a certain kind of mystification of the subjectivity of the hustlers in the film. Indeed, Van Sant told Lance Loud in *American Film* magazine that he didn't think that the characters are really gay: "They're . . . whatever street hustlers are."[24] He complained to Gary Indiana that

One thing I figure, a person's sexual identity is so much different than just one word, "gay." You never hear anyone referred to as just "hetero." If you're "hetero" that doesn't really say anything, and that's why people don't say it. If you're gay, that also isn't saying anything. You'd have to qualify it more. It's too broad a thing. There's something more to sexual identity than just a label like that.[25]

Film critic Amy Taubin would seem to be correct, then, in observing that, while Van Sant is "one of the few openly gay directors in Hollywood, [he]

bridles at turning sexuality into a soundbite. He's attracted to the liminal, to barely perceptible thresholds between identification and desire."[26]

There has always been a certain ambiguity and "mystique" surrounding the figure of the hustler in gay cinema, which was given its most extended treatment in Warhol's *My Hustler* (1966), and in *Flesh* (1968), the Warhol-produced/Morrissey-directed feature-length movie starring Joe Dallesandro.[27] *Flesh* and *Idaho* differ, however, in the way they evoke this mystique: which perhaps tells us something about what has changed in the gay political climate in the twenty-three years between the two films. The question remains, however: How do these films speak to *my* (or your) desire? How am I interpellated or identified by these films? What fantasies do they mobilize? There is also the profound issue of empowerment, both individual and collective. Do the films ultimately, and by whatever means, "translate into a fantasy of general sexual empowerment in a hostile social setting"?[28]

For Van Sant, there is purportedly a political stake in maintaining the aura of ambiguity surrounding the hustler, which he suggests by letting us know that his actors are straight: "It's a political act to do a film like this.

FIGURE 9.2 Mike with a client (Grace Zabriskie), moments before falling into a narcoleptic sleep.

They're handling it very well for being obviously straight."[29] But audiences never really know about an actor's real-life sexuality. We may sometimes think we know the "real" story, but the discourses that produce that (image of) sexuality are complex, ever-shifting, and contradictory—resulting in a perception or, more properly, a *fantasy*, that rarely has much to do with anything we could call the "truth." What does it mean to say that River Phoenix and Keanu Reeves are straight? Why are we even told this? Because, as Van Sant would like us to believe, it is politically more effective in the struggle against homophobia if the actors can be seen as endorsing tolerance toward homosexuals without being accused of having a personal reason for doing so. It may also sharpen the sexual edge of the film to have two well-known, ostensibly straight actors play gay. Still, there is the possibility—and it is disturbing to consider—that Van Sant's remarks are a 1990s variation on the closet: he is an openly gay director reassuring the public that his actors aren't "Other." There is, too, the complex matter of Van Sant's own erotic imaginary, which viewers perforce are asked to assimilate—an imaginary that is obviously engaged and even aroused by trade: the straight hustler who has sex with other men.

THE ROAD FROM OZ

The hustling theme is announced early (and with great wit) in *My Own Private Idaho*. Not since *Flesh* has a feature-length film confronted the subject so directly. We see a man entering a porn shop, and as he passes a rack of magazines, the cover boys come to life and speak directly into the camera. Scott, bare-chested and wearing a cowboy hat, his magazine coverlines announcing that he is "Ready to Ride," or is a "Homo on the Range," speaks:

> *Scott:* I never thought I could make it as a real model. . . . It's all right so long as the photographer doesn't come on to you, and expect something for nothing. I'm trying to make a living. I like to have a professional attitude. Of course, if the guy can pay me—hell, yeah!—here I am for him. I sell my ass. Do it on the street occasionally for cash. Or I'll be on the cover of a book. It's when you start doing things for free, that you start to grow wings. Isn't that right, Mike?
>
> *Mike:* What? [*Mike, on the cover of his magazine, appears in a loincloth, trussed up against a pillar, like Saint Sebastian.*]

Scott: Wings, Michael. You grow wings and become a fairy.

Mike: What do you care about money? Shit, you got plenty of money. Why don't you just go ahead and just do whatever it is that you do—I can only imagine what that is—and do it for free?

FIGURE 9.3   Mike as Saint Sebastian: How does such a film speak to my (or your) desire? How does it interpret or identify me? What fantasies does it mobilize?

All the boys on the covers of the other five magazines start talking at once. One of them looks over to where Scott is and says, "So, what are you doing on the cover of that magazine, slumming?" Scott ignores all their comments and questions. He simply looks into the camera, and says: "Actually, Mike is right. I am going to inherit money, a lot of money."

A danger in commercial narrative films is that the significance of such dialogue can often be overlooked in the hungry demand for action and the unfolding of a plot. When Scott says he never thought he could make it as a real model, he could, paradoxically, be saying that he never thought he'd make it as a real man. But he then discovered that manliness is largely a matter of posing—an image. The irony, of course, is that models are not quite the thing itself. A model provides an image (a model) of the thing. And so, what is it for which Scott proposes himself as the model? The cowboy as gay icon? Do we have, in this world, only models of men? What, then, does Scott mean when he talks about hoping to (appear to) be a *real model*? Like Joe in *Flesh*, getting paid for what he does makes all the difference to Scott (he likes to have "a professional attitude"). It gives him an *identity*. In our culture, it is traditionally masculine to conceive of identity as deriving from one's work. The center of the film's meanings, however, is condensed in Mike's mumbled, almost inaudible question: "*Why don't you just go ahead and just do whatever it is that you do—I can only imagine what that is—and do it for free?*"

As in most classical Hollywood movies, the first five minutes of *My Own Private Idaho* announce several of the film's main themes, inscribed in the oneiric logic of metaphor and hallucination. After a dictionary definition of narcolepsy—"a condition characterized by brief attacks of deep sleep"—a title card tells us we're in Idaho. Then: a shot of the road. Mike enters the frame, and in voice-over says: "I've always known where I am by the way the road looks. Like, I just know that I've been here before."[30] In road movies, of course, the road is never less than a hieroglyph containing many meanings, and Mike continues: "There's not another road anywhere that looks like this road, I mean, *exactly* like this road. . . . Like someone's face . . . like a fucked-up face." As Mike stares intently at the road—which leads straight from the camera to the distant horizon of snowy mountains—he falls in a narcoleptic seizure.

The camera cuts to a strange, telephoto-close shot of the snow-capped mountain peak at the horizon, half obscured by swirling white clouds, and then cuts to a shot of Mike with his head resting in his long-lost mother's lap. In this shot, like a representation of the Virgin Mary mourning over the dead body of Christ, she is dressed in white, and saying softly, as she runs her hand through his hair: "Don't worry, everything's going to be all right. I know, it's okay . . . I know." Then, as one critic describes it, the screen fills with a supremely ambiguous image: "an unpainted wood farmhouse, isolated against a hillside of empty fields—at once pure and bleak, alluring and abandoned-looking, home or a hollow shell."[31] The music on the sound track rises lyrically into song: ". . . the cowboy is singin' this lonesome cattle call." A star shoots across an evening sky; more shots of the road are intercut with a shot of a giant, roadside effigy of a square-jawed cowboy, and shots of Mike getting a blow job from a john in a room in Seattle. Eddy Arnold continues to sing: "He rides in the sun, 'til his day's work is done, and he rounds up the cattle each fall." As Mike starts to come, we see an extraordinary, metallic-glittering shot of salmon leaping upriver at sunset. The song on the sound track ends; we get a shot of the lake where the salmon were spawned and where they have returned to propagate and die. Then, as Mike reaches orgasm—in a witty and shocking allusion to the tornado-borne vehicle in *The Wizard of Oz* that takes Dorothy from Kansas and lands her in Oz—the farmhouse falls from the sky and crashes noisily into a million splinters on the Idaho road. The john, whose name turns out to be Walt, drops twenty dollars on Mike's belly and walks out of the room. Mike asks him for two more dollars, and Walt says (in a line that actually explains why Mike is a hustler): "What's the matter, you can't get it from your dad?" Mike pleads: "My dad and I don't get along too well, you know that, Walt." Walt, who is fat, middle-aged, and ugly, replies teasingly: "I know, we don't get along too well now either, do we!" Mike continues to plead, and Walt gives him another ten.

My Own Private Idaho is essentially Mike's story, and as such it would seem at first to offer the viewer a depressing thesis about homosexuality. It is the viewer who gains some insight into the subjectivity of the main characters, but by the end of the film the main character is on the same road where he began, appearing to have gained no liberating insight into his desire and who he is. The lesson he learns—if that it be—is that the oedipal scenario is immutable, damaging, and tragic; but, for all that, and for those forged under the pressure of its dire imperatives, it is perhaps better than nothing. The viewer, on the other hand, may learn a slightly different lesson: that if the oedipal scenario is damaging, it might be rejected altogether. While the ending of the movie is ambiguous—we do not know who it is that picks up Mike on the road after he has fallen into a narcoleptic sleep—the published screenplay indicates that it was Van Sant's original intention to have Scott pick up his friend.[32]

The most liberating thing about *My Own Private Idaho* is that it resists the notion that the oedipal scenario, which is resolved in an image of home and family, is the inevitable, and only, happy one. The film ends on an image of the car disappearing down the road, followed by a shot of the deserted farm house, and finally a title card that reads: have a nice day. The film implies that the ego is the enemy of desire: though Scott settles on an identity—he internalizes the image of his father—Mike is still "on the road" at the end of the film. He is still desiring. While many gay viewers may see Mike as a sad, down-and-out gay man who just can't find his way home to gay happiness, I prefer to read the endings of both the published screenplay and the film itself as being radical, in that they refuse to offer an identity politics. This is what makes the film *queer* (as opposed to gay).[33]

Idaho's homages to *The Wizard of Oz* are very telling of the distance between the two films and of how utterly different the destinies of Mike and Dorothy must be in a hetero-patriarchal world. Van Sant makes full use of the irony that *The Wizard of Oz* is sometimes described as an allegory for gay men fleeing the drab (i.e., black-and-white) world to a Technicolor fantasyland over the rainbow. The camp response to a hostile world, it would seem, is a difficult one to support in the 1990s (the success of the 1995 gay comedy *Jeffrey* notwithstanding), and one not much favored by gay independent

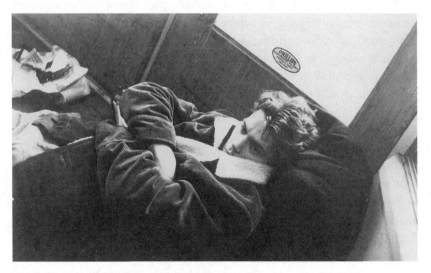

FIGURE 9.4 Even hustlers need someone to love: Mike, after Scott has abandoned him to marry Carmella. (Copyright © 1991 New Line Cinema Corp. All rights reserved. *Photo:* Abigayle Tarsches)

filmmakers (Araki "despises" *Torch Song Trilogy*, which, only a little less so than *The Birdcage* [1996], appears to have been made by and for straight people). When Dorothy begs the good witch Glinda, "Oh, will you help me? Can you help me?" Glinda replies: "You don't need to be helped any longer. You've always had the power to go back to Kansas." The Scarecrow asks Glinda why she never told Dorothy this before, and Glinda tells him: "Because she wouldn't have believed me. She had to learn it for herself." Dorothy is instructed to tap her heels together three times and think to herself: "There's no place like home!" After she does so, we get a shot of the farmhouse flying through the sky and coming down to land in Kansas. The lesson Dorothy has learned is that, "If I ever go looking for my heart's desire again, I won't look any further than my own back yard, because if it isn't there, I never really lost it to begin with."

As a mainstream Hollywood movie made in 1939, *The Wizard of Oz* tries to end on an ideologically "correct" note ("There's no place like home"). But as Salman Rushdie rightly protests, "The movie's Kansas is informed not only by the sadness of dirt-poverty, but also by the badness of would-be dog-murderers. And *this* is the home that "there's no place like"? *This* is the lost Eden that we are asked to prefer (as Dorothy does) to Oz?"[34] The queer difference between a studio-era road movie like *The Wizard of Oz* and an independent one like *My Own Private Idaho*, obviously, is that the narratives of Hollywood, as they do to this day, can only achieve closure if they end on a hetero-patriarchal principle (family and home or heterosexual coming-together as telos of Hollywood narrative epistemology).[35] While it may be true that many gay men and women see Dorothy's escape from Kansas as a potent fantasy that speaks to their own sense of entrapment in a homophobic society, the film, ultimately, is made for that mythically homogeneous heterosexual mainstream audience, the members of which may feel excluded or "different" in some way, but who want ultimately to belong to that mainstream, to take their rightful place in its familial ordering of affective ties and identities.

The new queer road movie may not take its protagonists to the Emerald City and leave them there, but it does not sell out in this way either. It refuses categorically to endorse the "family values" that have done so much to make gay men and women miserable. Back home in black-and-white Kansas, Dorothy "begins her second revolt, fighting not only against the patronizing dismissals of her own folk but also against the scriptwriters, and the sentimental moralizing of the entire Hollywood studio system. *It wasn't a dream, it was a place*, she cries piteously. *A real, truly live place! Doesn't anyone believe me?*"[36] The new queer road movie believes in the dream—in the sense that queer happiness is understood to be possible—which is why the new queer road movie eschews the "happy ending" of Hollywood cinema, a tacked-on coda that at best is ironic and at worst a reinstatement of the repressive structures the protagonist(s) sought to escape.

For Mike, there is no "home" to go to. There is no Uncle Henry and Auntie Em waiting anxiously for him to open his eyes when he returns from his dream or nightmare; and when his farmhouse crash-lands, it is destroyed. If Mike has recognized anything new by the end of the film, it is that he is doomed—always to be alone and lonely; not even to have a dog to comfort him, as Toto is always there to comfort Dorothy. He will, in a sense, never find his mother, as Scott has done. And he does not have a father. He can never "come home," as Scott does. He can never take his place in a familial order, which is the *only* order understood by society. Mike's homosexuality is figured as an impossible identity. The fantasies in which love and identity are grounded are short-circuited by incest (Mike's father is his brother); and Mike cannot be inscribed within the oedipal structure that makes it possible for others to live—makes it possible for them to sustain fantasies, or believe in illusions (which are perfectly real), of connection, arriving, and recognition. Mike's seizures are a metonymy and metaphor for this short-circuit of meaning. The oedipal scenario, which Scott's story represents, does not comprehend Mike. Only in the fantasies made possible by hustling—as one of the gaps, or contradictions, in society's sexual system—can Mike have any identity at all. The only hope, perhaps, is that a good fairy will pick him up one day. This is the underlying fantasy of most road movies that are on some level about cruising, hustling, or hitchhiking: that the next encounter will be the one that will take the protagonist "home."

THE SEARCH FOR AN OBSCURE OBJECT OF DESIRE

While it has been noted frequently that the special resonance of the American road movie derives from "the ways freedom and social mobility have been linked to physical mobility as themes in North American culture, or at least that part of it which Hollywood has attempted to represent,"[37] we might say that the *queer* road movie has emerged as a development in the cultural and psychoanalytic crisis of gender (and genre) described by Timothy Corrigan in *A Cinema Without Walls*. Corrigan historicizes the road movie as a postwar phenomenon in which, "more and more, the family unit, that oedipal centerpiece of classical narrative, begins to break apart, preserved only as a memory or desire with less and less substance."[38] He suggests that the car "becomes the only promise of self in a culture of mechanical reproduction. As in the economic politics of most postwar societies, boundaries and borders disappear (at least temporarily) in a car and with them the sanctions, securities, and structures of a family tradition" (146). With the disruption and dismantling by the Second World War of the ideal represented by the family, "the most secure and likely replacement for that heterosexual unit is the male buddy-group left over from that war" (147). Not surprisingly, Corrigan insists that most road questers invariably want "an authentic home, a lost origin where what you see is what you are" (154).

The queer variant of the road movie is only that—a variant—but it is nevertheless interesting for its radical rejection of what we can call, with some irony, "family values." What distinguishes the queer road movie from all other Hollywood genres is the centrality of homosexual desire. But, considering that we live in a patriarchy, this is not, and cannot be, merely a matter of changing the gender of the protagonists in a hetero-patriarchal narrative driven by the conjugal imperative. It is therefore worth quoting from an interview between Félix Guattari and George Stambolian, for the light it sheds on the radical potential of the queer road movie's conception of desire:

> F.G.: For me desire is always "outside"; it always belongs to a minority. For me there is no heterosexual sexuality. Once there's heterosexuality, in fact, once there's marriage, there's no more desire, no more sexuality. In all my twenty-five years of work in this field I've never seen a heterosexual married couple that functioned along a line of desire. Never. They don't exist. So don't say that I'm marginalizing sexuality with homosexuals, etc., because for me there is no heterosexuality possible.
>
> G.S.: Following the same logic there is no homosexuality possible.
>
> F.S.: In a sense yes, because in a sense homosexuality is counterdependent on heterosexuality. Part of the problem is the reduction of the body. It's the impossibility of becoming a totally sexed body. The sexed body is something that includes all perceptions, everything that occurs in the mind. The problem is how to sexualize the body, how to make bodies desire, vibrate—all aspects of the body.[39]

Guattari's remarks about the problem of how to "sexualize the body" are crucial to the implicit project of the queer road movie. The road movie protagonist, after all, is a body moving through space—functioning "along a

FIGURE 9.5   Scott en route to his father's funeral. The film leaves Scott's desire and class origins relatively unexamined, as if heterosexuality needed no analysis and paternity determined destiny. (Copyright © 1991 New Line Cinema Corp. All rights reserved. *Photo:* Abigayle Tarsches)

line of desire"—and although (Deleuze and) Guattari's concepts are not at all Freudian (indeed, they are specifically anti-Freudian), we might consider Freud's comment on "the dissatisfaction with home and family" that so often motivates the traveler. The queer road movie protagonist's specific dissatisfaction with home and family invariably has to do with the fact that the traditional family is a hetero-patriarchal structure which does not acknowledge (his) desire.[40] If to become a subject (to become a person) is to "learn one's place," the queer subject learns early that—with subjectivity necessarily and fundamentally a spatial achievement[41]—he has no place in the traditional family. If he is to be a desiring subject, a sexed body, he must leave the spaces of home and family. The true queer road movie narrative thus never ends but remains conscious of and committed to what Guattari is attempting to articulate when he talks about sexualizing the body. As narratives without conventional closure, functioning along lines of desire, not moving toward marriage and the containment of sexuality, queer road movies are quintessentially postmodern, with implications that are liberating for some, and perhaps disorienting and disturbing for others. As Paul Schmidt very perceptively argues, "Homosexuality is an alienation introduced into the very root of the social order, into sex as procreation. We say

FIGURE 9.6 *My Own Private Idaho*'s heartrending campfire scene.

usually that the opposite of homosexuality is heterosexuality, but that's not quite it. The opposite of homosexuality is marriage."[42] In this sense, we can see how the queer road movie is fundamentally opposed to marriage. Instead, as Schmidt puts it, the genre examines "the problem of trying to establish a relationship beyond the patterns of kinship, and within a state that is defined precisely by the denial of bonds and ties: by separateness, apartness, in-betweenness, individualization, and reflexivity. And by vision, ultimately: the vision of Otherness" (242).

If the average queer road movie is not quite so ambitious in its vision, nor its protagonists so extreme in their attempts to establish a relationship "beyond the patterns of kinship," it shares at least some of this questing belief in happiness, in a liberation of desire, in the totally sexed body, in the powerful reality of queer love. As Mike says to his friend, in *My Own Private Idaho*'s heartrending campfire scene: "I could love someone even if I . . . you know, wasn't paid for it. I love you, and . . . you don't pay me. I really want to kiss you, man. Good night, man. I love you a lot. You know that. I do love you."

10

"THE THINGS WE THINK AND DO NOT SAY"
JERRY MAGUIRE AND THE BUSINESS OF PERSONAL RELATIONSHIPS

Jerry Maguire (1996) opens on an image of the world, as seen from outer space. We hear the voice of Jerry Maguire. It's as if he's talking just to us: "So, this is the world, and there are almost six billion people on it. When I was a kid, there were three. It's hard to keep up." The title of the film, superimposed on this image, grows rapidly smaller and dissolves into the earth, as if to draw the viewer from the global scale to the personal—to the very center of the universe we are entering, namely, the world of a young man called Jerry Maguire (Tom Cruise). And the film ends on a shot of Jerry's favorite old sports agent and mentor, Dicky Fox, who looks into the camera and says: "Hey, I don't have all the answers. In life, to be honest, I've failed as much as I've succeeded. But I love my wife. I love my life. And I wish you *my* kind of success."

There, we have the question posed by the film, and we are given an answer. Finding it "hard to keep up"—which refers not to his professional life but rather to the more serious matter of his subjectivity, to his faltering ability to "see" himself and know who he is in this big world—Jerry will eventually take a wife, and become a father. The film implies that he thereby (re)discovers how to love his life, the way he believes he did when he was a kid, when there were only three billion people on the planet (or only three: "daddy-mommy-me").[1] At the same time, the film wrestles with one of modernity's paradoxes, which is that, as Krin and Glen Gabbard observe: "Today our heroes are no longer warriors, conquerors, or generals . . . . The criteria for success have been re-defined with the advent of the pervasive influence of the media."[2] What Dicky Fox has to teach the likes of Jerry Maguire about success is only half the recipe. Like several of Tom Cruise's other films (*Top Gun* [1986], *Born on the Fourth of July* [1989], and *A Few Good Men* [1992] being the most obvious examples), *Jerry Maguire* demonstrates that "hero status has been replaced by celebrity status as the ultimate narcissistic goal";[3] and, to use a metaphor that is especially apt for the film, it suggests that ordinary fathers leave sons feeling shortchanged.

Jerry Maguire is what Daniel Dervin calls a "guy film." Guys "operate in intermediate spaces between boys and men, partaking of both while constrained by neither. . . . While guys are not gay, their libidos lack determinacy, and they often find their comfort zone in a homosocial matrix."[4] Dervin situates guy films on a regressive/progressive developmental axis, which implies that sooner or later the guy(s) in question settle on an identity. But as I shall try to reveal in the following analysis of *Jerry Maguire*, only the guy himself (i.e., the viewer) can name his desire. The film—*viz.* ideology—may decide that "guys are not gay," but the viewer may decide something else. The viewer knows that identity is an ideologically determined construct, and regardless of how the film ends, it is only from the film's discourse, in an act of reading, that he will learn anything at all about desire, and love, and identity.

As an agent with Sports Management International (SMI), Jerry Maguire is not happy with his life. "Who had I become? Just another shark in a suit?" he asks rhetorically. "I hated myself . . . I hated my place in the world. I had so much to say, and no one to listen." What Jerry must do, of course, is change his place in the world, and the general movement of the narrative's ideological pressure is toward his commitment to a wife, who (according to conventional oedipal logic) will love him unconditionally, as a mother loves her son; and his commitment to a male friend (who will listen to him, and whom he can love like a father, or like the viewer who is interpellated by Dicky Fox talking into the camera). So, one night, alone in a hotel room, Jerry decides to write a "Mission Statement," and what starts out as one page soon becomes twenty-five. He gives it the title, "The Things We Think and Do Not Say: The Future of Our Business." His "Mission Statement" indicts the greed that permeates professional sports; and, not surprisingly, shortly after he has it photocopied and distributed to his colleagues at SMI, he is unceremoniously informed by a smarmy and competitive fellow agent (Bob Sugar, played by Jay Mohr) that he has been fired. "Somewhat regretting his momentary twinge of honor," as one popular film dictionary puts it, Jerry desperately tries to salvage his career by allying himself with his "obnoxious and least important client" Rod Tidwell (Cuba Gooding, Jr.), as well as Dorothy Boyd (Renée Zellweger), "an adoring young accountant with a lovable young son" (Jonathan Lipnicki).[5] Rod and Dorothy will not only play crucial roles in getting Jerry back on his feet professionally; they offer him a means to forge a new and satisfactory self-identity.

Following the sociological analysis offered by Anthony Giddens in *Modernity and Self-Identity*, and drawing on psychoanalytic insights discussed by

Stephen Frosh in *Identity Crisis*, this chapter examines *Jerry Maguire* as a particularly clear-cut example of some of the difficulties involved in the project of forging a (masculine) self in late twentieth-century America, and of the truth of Danish sociologist Henning Bech's observation that "friendship between men is a social impossibility in modern societies, at least for most males."[6] The world of high modernity, alluded to in the film's opening shots, "intrudes deeply into the heart of self-identity and personal feelings," writes Giddens; and the process of "finding oneself" is one that the social conditions of modernity enforce on all of us.[7] Frosh writes about the "identity crisis" of individuals in contemporary society, explaining how the self is never secure: it "requires unremitting protection and nurture, is always in danger of being undermined, of withering away or exploding into nothingness."[8] Modernity is a post-traditional order in which, Giddens concurs, "the question, 'How shall I live?' has to be answered in day-to-day decisions about how to behave, what to wear and what to eat—and many other things—as well as interpreted within the temporal unfolding of self-identity."[9] And the question, "What do men want?" (which is, in effect, the question posed by *Jerry Maguire*), is one for which, Giddens writes, there has been a clear answer, understood by both sexes, from the nineteenth century onward: "Men want status among other men, conferred by material rewards and conjoined to rituals of male solidarity."[10]

But the male sex, Giddens contends, has here "misread a key trend in the trajectory of development of modernity. For men self-identity was sought after in work, and they failed—we always have to add, by and large—to understand that the reflexive project of self involves an emotional reconstruction of the past in order to project a coherent narrative towards the future."[11] Jerry, having tried (and failed) to forge a satisfactory sense of self-identity through his work as a sports agent, senses that he must "go back" to his emotional roots if he is to become the man he wants to be. Indeed, it is the passion and energy with which he pursues his goal that attracts Dorothy, who will leave with him when he is fired from SMI, and who will later confide to her sister Laurel that she loves Jerry "for the man he wants to be, and . . . for the man he almost is."

GETTING INTO THE PICTURE

The film is proposed as Jerry's reflexive project of building/rebuilding a coherent and rewarding sense of identity; and it suggests that to be truly successful and happy in this world, a man not only needs the love of a good woman but must secure the confidence and love—the *recognition*—of a man as well. And for the cycle to repeat itself (the cycle in which, to use Aristotle's phrase, "it is man who engenders man"), he should, in his turn, become a father. As a mainstream movie with blockbuster aspirations, *Jerry Maguire* understands that its characters embody culturewide disturbances about how to be a self (or how to "be true to yourself") in contemporary society; and it concludes, in the contradictory way of melodrama, that successful subjectivity has to be forged the old-fashioned way—in the smithy of oedipal conflict and desire—despite modernity's promise of an unlimited choice of possibilities. Like most individuals living in the developed countries of the world, Jerry is eager to believe that we are, not what we are, but what we make of ourselves. He launches a trajectory of the self. He embarks on a course of self-therapy, as it were, to try and find out more about who he is—in order to find his version of what Rod Tidwell calls "the kwan," which, Rod explains, means "love, respect, community, and the dollars, too, the entire package."

The globalization of culture and capitalism that is so threatening to Jerry's sense of self, and upon which Rod is dependent for his professional identity as an athlete earning "the dollars" (that crucial element of "the kwan"), is broadly acknowledged in the first five minutes of the film. And the notion that the global culture of high modernity is really American culture—a kind of imperialism of American capitalism—is specifically acknowledged in the second shot of the film: a medium close-up of the earth, with the North American continent now identifiable through swirling skies, as satellites and other pieces of skycasting equipment float by, and as Jerry informs us: "That's better. That's America. See, America still sets the tone for the world." Modernity, Giddens advises, can be understood as roughly equivalent to "the industrialized world," so long as it be recognized that industrialism is not its only institutional dimension.[12] A second dimension of modernity is capitalism, where this term means "a system of commodity production involving both competitive product markets and the commodification of labor power."[13]

The significance of understanding the basic features of modernity becomes obvious in our analysis of *Jerry Maguire* when we see how both Jerry and Rod, for example, feel that their labor has been commodified. Jerry experiences this commodification as a profound alienation from his primary sources of affect (i.e., the love of men); and Rod, while ambivalently accepting that his labor power is a commodity to be bought and sold, is embittered by his perception that it/he is undervalued ("Show me the money!" he demands, repeatedly). Moreover, and crucially for the film's main theme, the friendship that develops between the two men is itself commodified, causing them both some confusion and pain.

But all of Jerry's relationships with men are commodified, despite his desperate need for a "pure relationship" with a man. As an agent with too many clients, he is everybody's friend and nobody's friend. His profession gives him the illusion that he matters to his clients *personally*, at least as much as he wants to believe they matter to him, i.e., as a son matters to a father, or a father to a son.

In the highly charged, televised interview during which Rod learns that he has won the yearned-for contract with the Arizona Cardinals, Rod ends the interview by looking into the television camera and saying: "I love everybody! I love my wife, Marcee! I love my kids. . . . I love my teammates . . . I'm leaving somebody out here. I want to send out some beautiful love to my offensive line. . . . Wait! I'm forgetting somebody . . . [*he looks into the camera, his face contorted with emotion, as he finally remembers*]: Jerry Maguire, my agent! You are my Ambassador of Kwan, man!"

Coming, as it does, so close to the end of the film, it is obviously meant to convey one of the movie's most important messages: a business relationship,

FIGURE 10.1 Jerry Maguire (Tom Cruise) and his sole remaining client, Rod Tidwell (Cuba Gooding, Jr.), after Jerry loses his job at Sports Management International. (Copyright © 1996 TriStar Pictures. All rights reserved. *Photo:* Andrew Cooper)

no matter how inflected by feelings resembling love, is not, cannot be, a pure relationship. It cannot compete with romantic love, nor with love of kin. Indeed, as Rod is acknowledging that he's finally got "the kwan," Jerry is already being introduced to his next client, Troy, who murmurs, "I enjoyed your memo." And yet, for what it is worth, Rod's reference to Jerry on national television as his "Ambassador of Kwan" is a sign to Jerry (despite their promiscuous deployment of the vocabularies of love and friendship throughout the movie) that he considers them to be friends. Only Jerry, presumably, knows what Rod means by the "kwan." In their world, which is so deeply marked—indeed it is *structured*—by the alienating features of modernity, Jerry and Rod have a special stake in trying to forge a friendship that is somehow free of the taint of money. Knowing that this is impossible, however, they seek to demonstrate to themselves and to others that they have a personal relationship *as well*, apart from their business relationship—by acknowledging (on camera) that they "did it" together.

Leo Charney and Vanessa R. Schwartz have identified six elements that are central to "both the cultural history of modernity and modernity's relation to cinema,"[14] elements that go a long way toward explaining what kind of world Jerry and Rod live in, what they want, and how their desires are dialectically linked:

> The rise of a metropolitan urban culture leading to new forms of entertainment and leisure activity; the corresponding centrality of the body as the site of vision, attention, and stimulation; the recognition of a mass public, crowd, or audience that subordinated individual response to collectivity; the impulse to define, fix, and represent isolated moments in the face of modernity's distractions and sensations, an urge that led through Impressionism and photography to cinema; the increased blurring of the line between reality and its representations; and the surge in commercial culture and consumer desire that both fueled and followed new forms of diversion. (3)

Jerry and Rod are two sides of the same coin. Both crave to be *seen*, recognized, acknowledged: *loved*. And both are highly narcissistic, emblematic figures of our time. A crucial aspect of modernity, as Charney and Schwartz note, is "the increasing tendency to understand the 'real' only as its representations" (7). As photography began in the late nineteenth century to capture the real, "the 'real' became inconceivable and unimaginable without the photograph's verifying presence" (7). Thus, near the beginning of *Jerry*

Maguire, as Jerry is introducing himself to us, a newspaper photograph fills the screen, and he says in voice-over: "You know those photos where the new player holds up the team jersey and poses with the owner?" (The picture is of precisely that: an athlete holding up a jersey and standing next to a team owner.) "That's me on the left," he says. The camera lingers for an instant on the picture, to reveal that there is indeed someone standing to the left of the athlete; but the figure has been almost entirely cropped, and no more than his ear is visible. Similarly, after we see a shot of SMI, the anonymous skyscraper in the nameless city where Jerry works, Jerry informs us ironically that he is one of "thirty-three out-of-shape agents guiding the careers of 1,685 of the most finely tuned athletes alive." Jerry's predicament is poignant. When he says he hates his place in the world, he means that he would like to be fully in the picture. He has clients all over the country, but he spends most of his time on the telephone (i.e., in a virtual reality), and in transitional spaces such as airports, airplanes, and hotel rooms. By the end of the film, we are left with no strong impression of where it is that Jerry lives, or of the place he would call "home." Agents like Jerry focus their considerable energies on putting their clients' interests first. But the unhappy consequence of this extreme identification with his clients is that Jerry's sense of his own identity—apart from his athletes—is destabilized and felt to be uncertain.

When Rod is knocked unconscious while catching a game-winning pass during his career-making game against the Dallas Cowboys in Tempe, Arizona, and he returns to consciousness, he cannot disguise his joy when he realizes that all eyes are on him: "Just let me enjoy this for a minute," he says. It is as close as a subject in modern life can come to "the sensation of being present inside the present."[15] This moment, represented as one of bliss, can of course only be confirmed as such by the presence of the television camera. Rod appears to be "'carried away' in the transporting moment,"[16] but he also seems to be calculating that his performance of experiencing this moment will win him a place in the celebrity-saturated imaginations of America's football fans. Flat on his back, with the entire stadium hushed and waiting for some move that will reassure them that he has not been paralyzed, or worse, Rod slowly breaks into a grin—knowing that his family is watching his image on a TV screen, and tens of thousands of television viewers in living rooms, bars, and airports all over the country are doing the same. He then gets up onto his feet and in a showboating display of enthusiasm demonstrates to the wildly cheering crowd that he has not been hurt. Rod gets the public to *see* him, finally, by inviting viewers to identify with his joy at being alive, in the present.

Television, certainly, as one of modernity's "new forms of entertainment and leisure activity"; Rod's body, as "the site of vision, attention, and stimulation"; his "recognition" by a mass public; and the "meaning" of Rod's play to the crowd, "defined and fixed" in a televised performance of exuberance and "heart"; the "blurring of the line between reality and its representations," as Tyson kisses the TV image of his father, or as Marcee Tidwell follows the drama taking place in the stadium by watching her TV screen at home, while talking on a telephone to Jerry—this all comes together successfully to get Rod his $11.2 million contract, "commercial culture's" big prize, as a reward for the "consumer desire" his performance has "fueled and followed."

But how does this kind of publicity coup get Jerry or Rod what they really want? Common sense suggests that it cannot offer more than a *temporary* sense of the recognition that is so crucial to the project of forging and maintaining a secure sense of self. Rod will get his contract (and Jerry will get his 4 percent of the $11.2 million) because of this fleeting, television moment—

FIGURE 10.2 "I'm an athlete . . . not an entertainer" Rod tells Jerry. (Courtesy Photofest)

but it will not, for example, help Jerry achieve the intimacy he craves, and it cannot, logically, save his marriage. In the frenzied excitement of the moment, we are meant to overlook the fact that the contradictions that set the narrative in motion have not been resolved. It is a postmodern moment, in the sense that "postmodernism emphasizes the fragmented nature of contemporary experience—fragments which are exciting but also meaningless in their interchangeability and lack of significant relationships. From this perspective, it is the *image* which is the most vibrant metaphor for modern reality: the image as on a television screen, with no substance behind it, creating, playing, disappearing, all in an instant gone."[17] But the image also helps "to define, fix, and represent isolated moments in the face of modernity's distractions and sensations"[18]—for "the instabilities of society are internalized as instabilities of the self."[19]

If one of the characteristics of modern life is a frequent sense of "falling into lostness," as Heidegger called the fundamental alienation inscribed into the structure of daily life, the present's lostness, Charney observes, "could be partly redeemed by valorizing the sensual, bodily, prerational responses that retain the prerogative to occupy a present moment."[20] This explains what is happening when Rod jumps about with joy, playing to the crowd, celebrating and demonstrating that he is *alive*. But he obviously cannot forget for a moment that he is performing for an audience.

"The 'Me' I'd Always Wanted to Be"

After the game, while Jerry waits with the crowd of reporters and photographers outside the locker room, the manager of the team gives Jerry the "thumbs up" sign, to which Jerry mouths: "*The money!*" When Rod emerges from the locker room, the media people mob him. Rod, affecting not to notice them, walks over to Jerry and embraces him, as the journalists become even more excited. "We did it!" he chokes. "*You* did it," Jerry replies, as tears run down their cheeks. The camera cuts to Bob Sugar with a client, his soon-to-be-superathlete Troy, who asks him: "Why don't *we* have that kind of relationship?" When Sugar tries to embrace Troy, in imitation of the one between Jerry and Rod, the athlete pushes him away in disgust and returns his gaze to Rod and Jerry, a look of wonder and yearning in his eyes. With hindsight, we recognize that the kind of relationship implied by this embrace is what Jerry has wanted from the start, just as Ray (Jerry's inner child, as it were) wants and needs a man's embrace.

As we see him writing his "Mission Statement" at the beginning of the film, Jerry tells us in voice-over:

> Suddenly, I was my father's son again. I was remembering the simple pleasures of this job. . . . With so many clients, we had forgotten what was important. . . . Suddenly, it was all pretty clear: the answer was fewer clients. Less money. More attention. Caring for them. Caring for ourselves, and the games, too. Just starting our lives *really*.

His voice changes to a brisk, self-conscious register: "Hey, I'll be the first to admit, what I was writing was somewhat touchy-feely. I didn't care; I'd lost the ability to bullshit. It was the 'me' I'd always wanted to be."

The implication that Jerry has been misrepresenting himself, to himself and to others, recalls English child analyst D. W. Winnicott's true-self/false-self distinction, the former, in Frosh's words, being "the spontaneous representation of the individual's actual needs and desires, whilst the latter is a conforming, protective shell taken on as a protection against loss of love."[21] The false self is an expression of "an attempt to fit in, to anticipate the other's demands in order to maintain some kind of object relationship" (111). Obviously, Jerry succeeds brilliantly in anticipating the demands of others. As he says: "It's what I do best."

We hear that Jerry even went so far as to ask his girlfriend Avery (Kelly Preston) to marry him, not because he loved her (or she him), but because he felt pressured to do so by convention and circumstance, and because, as several ex-girlfriends attest, "he cannot be alone." (He will later marry Dorothy for essentially the same, problematic reasons.) The movie will diagnose Jerry's problem in unequivocal terms: he is incapable of an intimate relationship. It is the theme of the "tribute film" that has been made for Jerry's bachelor party, at which one of his friends hands him a cigar and says, "This is what it's all about, man: Everybody loves you!" The cruel irony is that the kind of love the friend is referring to is not the kind of love Jerry really needs and desires; he needs more than the empty symbol of a cigar, or the kind of love that "everybody" (i.e., anybody) can give. The ex-girlfriends who have been interviewed for the tribute film all say essentially the same thing:

"He cannot be alone."

"I mean, Jerry is great at friendship, he's just really *bad* at intimacy."

"He can't say, 'I love you.'"

"He's an agent: he lies."

Jerry looks a little confused or embarrassed during the screening of the tribute film—as if he were learning something about himself for the first time or is surprised that his friends have so effectively identified a "problem" in his character that had been obscure to him. The tribute film functions like the "News on the March" newsreel in *Citizen Kane*: it offers some kind of objective truth about the eponymous character whose mystery the movie seeks to explore, if not penetrate. The "Rosebud" of *Jerry Maguire* will be the answer to their implicit question: Why can't Jerry say, "I love you" (to a woman)? The simple answer is that, whether he comprehends it or not, Jerry wants male intimacy in a culture that is uneasy about intimacy between men. The more complicated answer has to do with his narcissism.

If "intimacy, or the quest for it, is at the heart of modern forms of friendship and established sexual relationships,"[22] it is also true that intimacy is "only possible between individuals who are secure in their own self-identities" (95). The film draws the same link Joseph Bensman and Robert Lilienfeld do in their book *Between Public and Private*, between the growing concern to achieve intimacy in modern societies ("the demand for intimacy persists to the point where it is virtually compulsive")[23] and "the alienating effects of the development of large, impersonal organizations in the modern world."[24] Jerry confesses to feeling alienated by his work at SMI, and it is implied that in his relationship with Avery he has confused intimacy with sex (and she has confused intimacy with what Jerry calls "the thing where we tell each other everything"):

> *Avery:* Open your eyes . . . [*she makes him look at her*]. If you ever want me to be with another woman for you, I would do it! I'm not interested in it—there was a time, yes, when it felt normal for me—but it was a phase, a college thing, like torn Levis, or law school for you. Want anything from the kitchen? I'm going to get some fruit . . .
> *Jerry:* You know, I don't think we need to do the thing where we tell each other *everything*.
> *Avery:* Jerry, *this is what intimacy is!*

Jerry may or may not be disturbed by Avery's revelation that there was a time in her life when having sex with a woman "felt normal," but it is surely disturbing for him to consider that she would do it again (and would do it *for him*). In his own struggle to master the terms of identity, anxiety, and desire, Jerry needs sexual relations with a woman to confirm his heteronormativity.

"Heteronormative sex," Calvin Thomas explains, is "teleologically narra-tivized sex—sex with a goal, a purpose, and a product. The ends—children—justify the means, which are otherwise unjustifiable."[25] It is queer enough that he and Avery like sex but are not inscribed in a hetero-patriarchal, conjugal narrative, but it is apparently *too queer* for Jerry to entertain the idea of sex that does not confirm his identity as heteronormative.

"I'm Trying to Raise a Man"

In certain respects, *Jerry Maguire* is like a number of Clift, Dean, or Brando films of the 1950s, in which the rebel hero is tested for his suitability as a com-panion, rather than provider, for the woman. In *Creating the Couple*, Vir-ginia Wright Wexman explains how "traditionally [before the 1950s], Holly-wood love stories had focused on *courtship*, which must declare its romantic ideals in the face of *external* obstacles. In the films of these new stars, how-ever, love came to be seen as a *relationship* in which the woman ministered to the *internal* conflicts of a neurotic male who was unsure of his masculine identity. Women who had formerly thought of romance as a means by which they could be taken care of by a competent and chivalrous provider now began to see it as a way to participate in the drama of the male personality."[26] Interestingly, Wexman notes that in the three films of the 1950s most often cited in connection with the Method acting techniques identified with the new rebel heroes—*On the Waterfront* (1954), *East of Eden* (1955), and *Rebel Without a Cause* (1955)—"the central conflict concerns the rebel hero's diffi-culty defining himself in relation to a father figure" (170). This is true also in *Jerry Maguire* and, as in the fifties films Wexman cites (in which the love story might seem peripheral to its central concerns), the love story here is in fact essential to its articulation of the male hero.[27] Dorothy finds that Jerry is not suitable as a companion, but may be suitable as a role model for her son Ray. She appears to resign herself to the likelihood that Jerry's most passion-ate attachments will always be to men, not women; but she recognizes he has potential use-value as a father.

From the start, Dorothy is presented as a mother in search of a father for her son. Indeed, the film overdetermines the notion that, if only Jerry would marry her, everything would be wonderful because traditional familial iden-tities are the key to happiness—*and* (to echo Dicky Fox again) they help en-sure the smooth workings of capitalism. The film insists that heterosexual marriage, as a kind of business contract and as the cornerstone of patriarchal society, provides not only the best economic basis for the raising of children but also the proper matrix in which patriarchy's masculine and feminine identities are forged. In an ideal world, little boys admire their fathers, see them as heroes, and want to grow up to be like them. Supportive, nurturing mothers are models for the kind of woman the little boy wants to marry when he grows up, and so on. Thus, while *Jerry Maguire* is ostensibly about Jerry's subjectivity (his search for the Father/his becoming a father to himself when he becomes a father to Ray), it is also about Ray (a son in need of a father), and about Rod (who never had a father), and Tyson (who already has a narcissistic disorder, caused by problematic parenting).[28] Dorothy, as one critic put it, is "borderline pathetic"[29] as a character, because—more than any other in the film—her character's subjectivity (the question of what she wants) is subordinated to Jerry's quest.

Indeed, the film's unrelenting focus on Jerry's search for (him)self has caused a number of critics to remark on his narcissism or "to wonder whether the film itself isn't somehow enabling Jerry's pathological self-absorption."[30] Despite Avery's complaint to Jerry ("It's all about *you*, isn't it? Soothe *me*! Save *me*! Love *me*!"), the film does little to critique the notion that what matters most is always a *male* subjectivity and the construction—or maintenance—of a *masculine* identity. The film has its doubts about whether a woman can have an intimate friendship with a man (Marcee's relationship with Rod notwithstanding), but it is clear about the usefulness of marriage for the raising of a (male) child. As Dorothy explains to Laurel while she is preparing to go out with Jerry on their first date: "Do you know what other women my age are doing right now? They're out partying in clubs, and they're trying to get a man, trying to keep a man. Not me, Laurel. *I'm trying to raise a man.*" Her responsibility now, she feels, is not to herself but to her son.

The film makes it clear that Dorothy and Ray are working together to find a father for Ray. Indeed, the film could not be more blatant about the boy's need/wish for a father, and about his judgment that Jerry is the man for the job. With his oversized spectacles giving him a "little professor" look, Ray is presented as a child trying to be "grown up" (for his mother).

To set about snagging Jerry for herself, Dorothy shows him that she possesses the kind of integrity he admires. Her opportunity presents itself when he is fired from SMI, and she loyally follows him into a very uncertain future. As they leave, a young couple, obviously in love, step into the elevator with them. It appears that one of them is (or perhaps both are) deaf, for the man tells the woman in sign language: "You complete me." The phrase will eventually become Jerry and Dorothy's motto, just as "Show me the money!"

(which Rod calls "a very personal, very important thing") becomes the motto that seals the bond between the two men.

Despite its thesis about what Jerry needs and wants, the film's discourse on masculinity attempts to deny that a man embodied by the likes of Tom Cruise could lack something crucial in his sense of himself as masculine. It is curious, but not surprising, that the motto Jerry and Dorothy choose for themselves—"You complete me"—should be offered by the film as "proof" of the authenticity and exclusivity of their love for each other. But Jerry can say these words to Dorothy only *after* Rod has won his $11.2 million contract. Dorothy (and Ray) and Jerry "complete" a circuit of desire that absolutely must include Rod. The ideal relation is familial, as it is expressed in *The Lion King*'s theme song about "the circle of life" or, as a terrified Marcee explains to Jerry, when Rod is knocked out during the big game with the Dallas Cowboys: "My whole life is this family—*and it does not work without him!*"

When Jerry calls Dorothy in a state of high excitement to tell her that he has resigned Frank Cushman (Jerry O'Connell), she says: "I'm so happy for you." He corrects her: "Happy for *us*!" (as Rod corrected him earlier, when teaching him their motto: "No, not show you, show *me* the money!"). At that moment, the camera cuts from Dorothy repeating, "Happy for *us*," to a shot of Ray, who is smiling at his mother. Thus are the complex circuits and dialectically linked discourses of love and money, affect and commerce, romance and family figured in a few seconds of film.

Dorothy (and of course the film itself) believes that Ray needs a father, or a certain kind of male role model, if he is to construct a successful masculine identity for himself. (Chad, the gay baby-sitter who calls himself a "child technician," is understood to be ineligible.) The one thing that is crucial for the construction of an authentic masculine identity—the thing that Jerry can give—is *a father's love*.

The film is rather insistent on this point. When Dorothy drives Jerry to the airport, Ray (in the backseat) tries to impress Jerry with some facts he has recently learned, such as: "Jerry, do you know the human head weighs 8 pounds?" and "Did you know bees and dogs can smell fear?" Jerry tries unsuccessfully to "compete" with Ray by offering some sports statistics. Dorothy, meanwhile, smiles to herself, as if she knows Jerry will get the hang of it sooner or later—how to be a father to a five-year-old. The film leaves no doubt in the viewer's mind that Jerry would, in their opinion, be an ideal father to Ray and a good husband for Dorothy.

Such is the ideological power of romantic love—as the driving force of nearly all Hollywood narrative—that it comes as a surprise to the viewer to discover that *Jerry Maguire* is in fact not about how the good-looking young man inevitably ends up marrying the young and attractive woman because of something irrational and inexplicable called "love." The element of heterosexual romance turns out, rather, to resemble a law of anthropology or animal behavior: the young woman, in need of a mate, persuades the young man that she understands him and can provide the key to his happiness. She initiates him into a familial discourse that will change his "place" within that discourse. She teaches him how to realize the "self" through the "other," by presenting her son as a small boy who desperately needs, specifically, *him*. The morning after they have spent their first night together making love, Jerry overhears Dorothy joyfully tell her sister: "Why should I let this guy go, why? When everything in my body says that *this one is the one!* . . . I love him, Laurel. I love him. I love him."

The evidence that these are the words Jerry needs to hear is given in the next scene, in which Jerry bonds with young Ray at the breakfast table while Dorothy and Laurel look on approvingly. As a loving father to a son, Jerry can find the love he needs for himself as a son. The very words Dorothy uses—"I love him for the man he wants to be, and I love him for the man he almost is"—reveal the logic of what draws the couple to each other: Jerry's narcissism responds to Dorothy's desire to participate in the drama of his growth into (male) selfhood, exactly as she is trying to raise a son.

Before asking Dorothy to marry him, however, Jerry experiences doubts about the nature of his feelings for her, just as he did before proposing marriage to Avery. He is not sure how to classify his relationship with Dorothy and thinks perhaps he is "dating" her. In an unconscious attempt to draw himself closer to Rod, he asks the married athlete what he knows about "dating a single mother." Rod's answer provides a key to understanding why he is attracted to Jerry: "Plenty. I was raised by a single mother." In his role as Rod's agent, Jerry fulfills some of the function of the father that Rod never had. Which explains why Rod has to suppress his anger at Jerry's question. "First of all," he lectures Jerry, "single mothers don't 'date.' They don't date. They've been to the circus, you know what I mean? They've been to the puppet show, and they've seen the strings. Do you love her?"

This apparently simple question goes straight to the heart of the matter:

Jerry: How do I know?
Rod: What do you mean, "How do I know?" You know when you know.

FIGURE 10.3 "You complete me." Jerry thinks—but is not sure—that he is "dating" Dorothy (Renée Zellweger). (Copyright © 1996 TriStar Pictures. All rights reserved. *Photo:* Andrew Cooper)

Jerry: When I'm feeling a little, you know . . . I mean, I don't want her to go. I've been hanging out at her place a lot.

Rod: Oh, wait a minute, that's it right there! That's bullshit! You've got to be fair to her. A single mother, man, that's a sacred thing. You've got to have the talk. She loves you. If you don't love her, you've got to tell her.

In the scene that follows, Dorothy is preparing to leave for a job in San Diego. Jerry has obviously let the matter drift. He has neither had "the talk" with Dorothy nor asked her to marry him:

Dorothy: I'll see you in a couple of days, and, uh . . . I love you.

Jerry: I love you, too, you know. [*He leans forward and gives her a brisk kiss*]

The camera cuts to Ray, who looks on with interest. Then Dorothy makes the speech that, together with what we might call the "Ray factor," convinces Jerry to ask her to marry him:

> *Dorothy:* Look, if this weekend should turn into next month, and next month should turn into . . . whenever, don't make a joke of your life. Go back and read what you wrote. You're better than the rest of them. You're better than the Bob Sugars. Don't forget that. [*She kisses him tenderly*]

Perversely, the film appears to be celebrating the popular notion that if men have difficulty expressing their true feelings, then an inability to say "I love you" (for example) actually confirms a man's manliness and enhances his appeal, because it reveals his vulnerability, which, for being so rarely admitted, is flattering to the woman who is the cause of it. As Dorothy turns to leave, Jerry calls out:

> *Jerry:* Wait! Wait a second. I know of a way we can save on medical, and rent . . . What if we stayed together? What if we got married? What if I said that? Would you stay?
> *Dorothy:* No, no, don't do that. Don't say that, unless . . . Well, say it if you want to.

Jerry looks at Ray, and the camera cuts again to the boy. That decides it. "Will you marry me?" he asks. Behind her dark glasses, Dorothy's response is inscrutable to Jerry. "What are you thinking?" he asks her, momentarily doubting that they are even remotely on the same wavelength—which reveals the extent to which Jerry relies on appearances to "know" what Rod tells him there should be no doubt about how to know. When he sees that she is crying (with happiness, or gratitude), they embrace. *Again*, the camera cuts to Ray. What is so shocking about this scene in which Jerry asks Dorothy to marry him is that his question appears to have been inspired by a glance over at Ray, who has been trying to look as "cute" and forlorn as possible. Jerry's marriage proposal, in other words, is a rescue fantasy.[31] Moreover, Laurel, who is watching the scene from the living room, is muttering to herself, as if to Dorothy: "Get in the car. Get in the car, Dorothy! No, no. Oh, God, no, don't listen to him, Dorothy!" The effect of this telepathic interdiction—the ideological intention of it—is not what it appears to be; Laurel anxiously biting her lip and silently urging Dorothy to leave before Jerry can ask her to marry him, works precisely to challenge fate to do the opposite. Laurel (unconsciously) wants Jerry to marry Dorothy. Ray wants Jerry to marry Dorothy. The editing of the scene (i.e., the narrative itself or the ideological imperative motivating the filmmakers) wants Jerry to marry Dorothy. Dorothy wants Jerry to marry Dorothy. And so, finally, Jerry is persuaded that Jerry wants to marry Dorothy. The semiotics are clear: it is this little man who has brought Jerry and Dorothy together as "husband and wife."

After the wedding, alone in the kitchen with the groom, Laurel holds up her beer bottle to Jerry's in a toast: "You fuck this up, I'll kill you," she says with a deadly smile. And Jerry suddenly realizes what he has done. Although spoken by a woman, Laurel's threat speaks with the full force of patriarchal law. Here, only moments after Dorothy has said to Jerry, "We did it!" and Jerry has replied, "We sure did!" the meaning of patriarchy as a system of benefits and responsibilities, with the threat of castration to back it up, becomes frighteningly clear to Jerry. Having pushed him to take this decisive step toward heterosexual maturity (in its ideological project of affirming heterosexual, monogamous, married sex as the ideal and the norm for men and women), the film now makes it perfectly clear that Jerry has made a mistake (or is simply not ready yet).

In Russell Gough's memorable critique, "*Jerry Maguire*'s ending inspires with neither true happiness nor idealism. Instead of offering a refreshing and sobering resolution to Maguire's personal and moral struggles, the film ends up merely perpetuating one of Hollywood's most beguiling and destructive myths: that the road to happiness and personal fulfillment is paved with money."[32] Short of making Jerry gay, the film cannot do much more than it already does to say that heterosexual romance ending in marriage isn't for everybody. The question implicit in Dorothy's assertion, "I'm trying to raise a man," is nothing less than the one informing the entire film: *What does it mean to be a man* (in contemporary America)?

Jerry Maguire's crisis is a generalized representation of a perceived crisis of the middle-class, white American male, caught at this moment in history between his old role as breadwinner for a family[33] and his new role as a self with an identity politics. Jerry's problem is that he does not have an identity politics, which the film highlights by making the narrative turn on his relationship with an African-American. Jerry's identity is not one that is inscribed in the familial terms which, for better or worse, are the ideological underpinnings of mainstream American film—which is why his identity is announced and marked from the beginning as unstable. But if Dorothy can get Jerry to marry her, Ray would get a father, which would be extremely helpful in her mission "to raise a man"; and Jerry would become a husband and father, which would foreclose on the ambiguities of his sexuality, resolve his oedipal difficulties, and be a solution to his fear of "being alone." The question of what Dorothy would get from the marriage is seen by the film (and by her) more in terms of what she wants for her son and what she can do for Jerry, than in terms of what she might want for herself (a companion and lover). If identity is the product of an interaction between self and society, the question of a stable identity for Jerry, the film insists (while offering ample evidence to the contrary), would be neatly settled by his integration into society's most important institution: a family.

"What Do You Stand For?"

Later, in response to Rod's jeering comments about Jerry's failing marriage, Jerry defends himself by saying, simply: "Not everyone has what you have."

> *Rod:* Then why did you get married? I'm just asking, as a friend.
> *Jerry:* You want an answer? *Loyalty.* She was loyal. You know, I mean, everything grew from there. Just . . . grew from there.
> *Rod [shakes his head in baffled concession]:* That's an answer! [*He bursts out laughing*]
> *Jerry:* That's the answer!
> *Rod [incredulous]:* It's not sexy! Shit! That's an answer! "Tell him what he won, Bob: 'a beautiful marriage!'" [*He whoops with laughter*]

The film in a sense acknowledges that the heart of its concerns is the friendship between the two men, not the romance between Jerry and Dorothy; and the peculiar honesty of this insight—that what many American men need is not so much a romantic relationship with a woman as a pure relationship with another man—possibly accounts for some of the film's success at the box office (although the film, of course, does not show a pure relationship between the two men).

To the extent that the film proposes anything as an alternative to sexual attraction and unanalyzed "love" as the basis for marriage, it proposes "loyalty"—which, by definition, is durable, and therefore as good a reason as any to get married. Rod thinks Jerry's reason for marrying Dorothy is not "sexy," but he acknowledges that it is a reason. The theme of loyalty is very attractive in a world that, in Frosh's formulation, is "characterized by rootlessness, instability, rapid transition from one state to the next, one fetish to another."[34] And at the intertextual, or meta-cinematic, level, there is also the ultimate reassurance provided by the fact that Jerry Maguire is played by Tom Cruise. The film shows Jerry enduring a long series of humiliations and setbacks, which are surely meant to evoke the average man's (or woman's) experience of daily frustration and thwarted desire, the pinch of financial need, the frightening capriciousness of the marketplace, and the ever-present threat to one's livelihood. Jerry has to endure insults from everyone—Rod, Marcee, Bob Sugar, Avery, Matt Cushman (Frank's father)—and his betrayal by colleagues and friends is a constant possibility. Jerry's humiliations are perhaps only endurable because he is played by Tom Cruise, one of the most charismatic and successful movie stars of his generation. We know Cruise is making more money than Rod Tidwell ever dreamed of. And so—conflating the star and the character he plays—we can almost believe, as the film's advertising catchphrase has it, that "Jerry Maguire learns that loving well is the best revenge." This is the message for viewers who are not, and never will be, Hollywood superstars or charismatic athletes: love (or loyalty)—something *everybody* can practice—has a redeeming power that no $11.2 million contract can match (although, just in case we don't quite believe that "loving well is the best revenge," Rod and Jerry get their "love" *and* "the money").

Loyalty is one of the film's major preoccupations, and it is one of the film's aims to give loyalty a face because, as Henry Louis Gates Jr. has observed, we live in a time when "casual and fleeting associations have become central to our careers, displacing the deeper and longer-term relations of old. (Such strong ties—and the paradigmatic strong tie is loyalty—require a degree of personal commitment to which contemporary life gives little support.)"[35]

At the height of American public interest in the Monica Lewinsky affair in the spring of 1998, Gates published an article in *The New Yorker* entitled "The End of Loyalty: Why Has Betraying Clinton—and Everyone Else—Become a National Pastime?" In it he notes that the trait of loyalty is an endangered one in modern American politics because "loyalty is, in essence, a premodern virtue" (36). He writes that the Enlightenment's gift to us, and its curse, has been to replace "the old codes of duty and honor" with "the cool calculus of moral rationalism" (36). Loyalty's natural context is "a social world of reciprocal dependencies: lords and vassals, lieges and subjects" (36); and in post-Watergate America, loyalty is a quality that appears to be "suspiciously integral to the world of gangs and gangsterism" (41).

Among Gates's remarks on loyalty, the ones that are especially apt for the theme in *Jerry Maguire* are those in which the costs of loyalty are measured against its benefits (one of the first lines of dialogue in the film is a question put to Jerry: "How much is this going to cost me?"). "It's easy to say you're for loyalty until loyalty conflicts with another value," Gates quotes a Clinton aide as saying, which is precisely the issue at stake when Marcee—not happy with the Arizona Cardinals' proffer that comes through by fax—wonders if she and her husband might not be better off with Bob Sugar:

> *Jerry:* It's OK, it's OK, this is how the game is played. Now I'm going to go back to them.
> *Marcee:* And say what? "Please remove your dick from my ass"?
> *Jerry:* Let's not take this emotionally. We're going to roll with this problem, OK?
> *Marcee:* What are you so calm about? What do you mean, "roll with this problem"? "Don't take it emotionally"? You ask me, you haven't gotten emotional enough over this man! You know what— somebody give me Bob Sugar on the phone!
> *Rod:* Marcee . . .
> *Jerry [incredulously]:* You want to leave me?
> *Marcee:* Well, you know what? A lot of agents say a lot of shit! So, what do *you* stand for?
> *Jerry:* You want to leave me?
> *Marcee: What do you stand for?*
> *Dorothy:* How about a little piece of integrity in this world that is so full of greed and a lack of honorability [*sic*] that I don't know what to tell my son, except: "Here, have a look at a guy who isn't yelling, 'Show me the money!'" Do you know he's broke? He is broke—and working for *you* for *free*!

The scene has its symmetries: Each woman supports her man, and the men are both made proud (and embarrassed) by this fierce show of female loyalty. When Rod implores Jerry to tell him what to do, Marcee explodes. Rod tries to calm her, by making that crucial distinction (that is frequently confused by the characters throughout the film) between personal loyalty and contractual loyalty: "Marcee, please, I'm talking to my agent."

> *Marcee:* No, no, no. No, listen! This is what you're going to do. [*She forces him to look into her eyes*] You're going to reject that shitty contract. You're going to play out your existing shitty contract. And you are going to be a free agent next year. Baby, this is *us*. You and

me, *we* determine our worth. You are a strong, proud, surviving, splendid black man!

Rod breaks into a grin and falls into Marcee's arms, kissing her. They murmur and kiss, oblivious of Jerry and Dorothy. Jerry watches them for a moment, and then reminds Rod with cold logic: "If you get injured, you get zero."

> *Rod:* Whatever happens, I'm strong in mind!
> *Marcee:* That's right!
> *Jerry:* It's a risk.
> *Rod:* You bet on me, like I bet on you. Huh? You know? [*He offers his hand to Jerry, and when Jerry takes it, pulls him forward in an embrace*]

Marcee, *as a wife*, will only tolerate the bond between the two men if it will "show [her] the money." She has a stake in believing that Jerry and Rod have contracted to have a relationship *only* for the material rewards it might bring them. She distrusts the affective element of their bond. She is threatened by the possibility that her husband derives some of his sense of self-worth from Jerry. This is why she blatantly invokes the image of Jerry with a "dick up [his] ass." She wants it understood that she thinks Jerry is being ineffectual, and that, by his association with Jerry, her husband's integrity (figuratively, in the image of anal penetration) is also being compromised. Marcee reveals the parallels that exist between what an agent can do for a man's self-esteem and what a wife can do. Rod tries to keep their emotions in check by referring to Jerry in this scene as "my agent," but this only proves (to the viewer, at least) that Jerry is *more* than an agent to Rod. To perform his best as an athlete, and to believe in the image of himself that the agent promotes, Rod has to believe in Jerry's love. If love does not seem to be the right term to describe the transference that has occurred—or must occur—between Rod and Jerry, it is because there is a vast discourse on love that exists in Western culture for heterosexual couples, but only a very restricted discourse on the love between heterosexual men.

That love between men, whether or not it is safely inscribed within the interstices of a legally binding contract, can be every bit as powerful as heterosexual love. And Marcee knows this. She wants Rod to believe that, "Baby, this is *us*. You and me, *we* determine our worth." But Rod knows that this is not quite so. When she screams at Jerry, "*What do you stand for?*" she is re-

FIGURE 10.4 "Baby, this is *us*. You and me, *we* determine our worth," Marcee (Regina King) tells her husband Rod. (Copyright © 1996 TriStar Pictures. All rights reserved. *Photo:* Andrew Cooper)

ally saying at least two things. She is brazenly asking Jerry what he can offer Rod that she does not already give him; and, with fraudulent logic, she is implying that Bob Sugar can offer Rod something Jerry cannot.

Jerry wants a strong emotional bond with Rod, but how is he to go about securing it? And on what basis? (We strongly suspect that after Rod gets his $11.2 million contract, their relationship will wither.) That question we hear early in the film—"How much is this going to cost me?"—resonates with added significance when we realize it is the same one Jerry in effect asks when he begins his search for an intimate friendship with a man. When he says in his "Mission Statement" that he feels that the company (he) should have fewer clients, we know that what he is really looking for is *one* male friend. But he fears what this will cost him, and his fear is bound up with his homophobia. Jerry fears what he knows about homosocial bonding—that it depends on keeping its distance from homosexuality. In the film, the historically constructed link between male homosocial bonding and homophobia is certainly present in Jerry's relationship with Rod, but it is mostly reconfigured so that their relationship is not one of passionate attachment accompanied by intense dislike, but rather split into two characters and two relationships: Bob Sugar becomes the despised enemy—the man you cannot trust, the man who will betray you—and Rod (safely married to Marcee and contractually bound to Jerry) becomes the friend. Still, Jerry's friendship with Rod has an erotic undertow. For example, moments before the big game against the Dallas Cowboys, Bob Sugar sidles up to Rod and tries to persuade him to drop Jerry and sign up with him. Just at that moment, Jerry appears, violently pulls Sugar away from Rod, and growls aggressively, like a possessive lover: "*Hey! Get away from my guy!*" Rod smiles with relief, and thanks Jerry for coming. "I missed you," Jerry replies by way of explanation, "What can I say? You're all I've got." This dialogue is spoken tongue-in-cheek, but with absolute and affecting sincerity. Under the cover of their professional relationship, Jerry is trying to acknowledge the part Rod plays in the satisfaction of his emotional needs.

If we accept that Jerry's homosociality is grounded in sublimation—as surely the film is saying—then there is a significant stake in keeping things that way. If Jerry were to unravel and act on the hidden meanings of his earlier declaration to Rod, yelled over the telephone during their first bonding ritual—"You my motherfucker!"—the logic of desublimation suggests he would lose at least some of his effectiveness as an agent.

"Talking Is Only a Primitive Form of Communication"

In a chapter of *Modernity and Self-Identity* entitled, "The Trajectory of the Self," Giddens observes that self-identity, as a coherent phenomenon, presumes a narrative: "Autobiography—particularly in the broad sense of an interpretive self-history produced by the individual concerned, whether written down or not—is actually at the core of self-identity in modern social life" (76). Jerry not only writes his "Mission Statement" (a kind of autobiography), he narrates the film. His commentary about how he came to write his "Mission Statement" clarifies (for the viewer, if not for himself) what the stakes are in his quest for subjectivity. To echo his old mentor's dictum: the key to Jerry's happiness—which is the real "business" of the movie—is personal relationships. What he misses is the feeling of being his father's son. Or, to put it another way, Jerry needs emotional intimacy with a man, as he imagines he once had, or wishes he had, with his father. "The 'father hunger' shown by the sons of absent fathers is primarily a reaction to lack of homoerotic love," Jessica Benjamin has observed: "In heterosexual men it becomes an impediment to loving women not because the role model is remote, but because the real erotic energy is tied to the frustrated wish for recognition from the father."[36]

But the problem, as Phyllis Chesler remarks in *About Men*, is that "most men expect only competition and betrayal from other men."[37] (Indeed, we see Jerry betrayed by men throughout the movie, the most duplicitous of these being Bob Sugar and the father/son team of Matt and Frank Cushman.) American men may need male sympathy, but "only Hollywood movies," Chesler writes, "present male friendship as the mythic ideal—precisely because it doesn't exist in reality; because it is yearned for as ardently as men yearn for their fathers to love them, protect them, and name them heir to some legacy" (239).

The only direct reference Jerry makes to his father in the film clearly signals that at the origin of his unhappiness is a sense of paternal failure. One evening, at the nadir of his fortunes, Jerry pays Dorothy a visit at the house where she lives with Laurel. While the sisters are in the kitchen preparing a sandwich for Jerry, Ray comes through the living room in his pajamas. The telephone rings, and the child picks it up. The call is from Rod, who is in the middle of taking a bath with his son. When Rod realizes he is not talking to Jerry, he demands: "I need to speak with my agent! I need to *be* my agent! My agent and I should be *one!*" Urged on by Jerry, Ray teases the football player: "You talk too much!" Now mock-desperate to connect, Rod yells into the phone: "No, no, no! *Talking is only a primitive form of communication!*" The camera cuts to Dorothy and Laurel in the kitchen, as Dorothy is saying: "I just want to say one thing: you *do* listen to me," to which Laurel replies: "Well, I love you." As they continue preparing the sandwich, the camera (outside the house) pans from the kitchen window to the living room window. Ray, now sitting on the couch next to his hero, is watching, bleary-eyed, as Jerry talks to himself: ". . . repression as a religion. My daddy worked for United Way for thirty-eight years. You know what he said when he retired? 'I wish they'd given me a more comfortable chair.' For thirty-eight years he sat there . . . !"

Ray interjects: "When my dad died, my mom took me to the zoo, and I *loved* the zoo."

"No, no, wait," Jerry persists, "because I want to tell you more about *my* dad."

"No, let's go to the zoo."

"Okay, okay . . . you're right. I don't know, it's just . . . my whole life I've been trying to talk, I mean *really talk*. But no one wants to listen to me. You know the feeling?"

Ray nods vigorously. "Let's go right now! Let's go to the zoo!"

The film thus draws the link between Jerry's narcissism (about which all his ex-girlfriends complain in the tribute film) and the early formation of his subjectivity within the family. Like Ray, Jerry was once a little boy in need of a father who would listen to him (or take a bath with him), a father he could look up to, and who would show his love by putting the child's interests first ("Let's go right *now!*"). Jerry reveals in this scene that he is still the father-wounded son, and that he has never gotten over his disappointment in his father. The scene reveals in an economical way not only the origins of Jerry's psychic pain but how he might begin to dissolve that knot of oedipal conflict. Jerry's narcissism prevents him from *listening*, and from understanding how listening (a form of loving) is a form of being heard (i.e., of being loved). The paradox is this: if Jerry starts to listen, to *really listen*, he might begin to be heard—just as Dorothy loves Laurel, who listens to her because she loves her. By identifying with Ray, Jerry can become a father to himself. In becoming the kind of father to Ray that he wanted for himself (a father who listens), Jerry might finally overcome the image of paternal failure that colors his sense of himself (as a son).

A scene that illustrates well the truth of Rod's insight that "talking is only a primitive form of communication" takes place at a major turning point in

FIGURE 10.5 Jerry asks Ray (Jonathan Lipnicki): "My whole life I've been trying to talk, I mean *really talk*. But no one wants to listen to me. You know the feeling?"

the relationship between Rod and Jerry—when Jerry has terminated his relationship with Avery, lost Frank Cushman to Bob Sugar, and failed miserably
to renegotiate Rod's contract. After a practice game, Jerry waits for Rod just
outside the locker room, to have a frank talk with his client about why "the
big, sweet dollar" is eluding him. Their conversation begins while Rod is still
wet from the shower ("I air-dry" he explains). Jerry advises Rod to "bury the
attitude a little bit" and show (them) "the pure joy of the game." Rod flies into
a rage, calling himself "an athlete . . . not an entertainer!" Jerry asks him if,
way back when he (Rod) was a kid and he first started playing the game, "it
wasn't just about the money, was it? Was it? *Was it?*" Jerry pleads with Rod,
trying to make him understand that they will only succeed if they work together: "*Help me help you,*" he implores. Rod suddenly bursts out laughing,
and says: "You are hanging by a very thin thread, and I dig that about you!"
Jerry believes now that he has failed utterly to make his point. But as he turns
to leave, Rod steps forward (the camera cutting to a long shot of him), and we
are suddenly reminded that he has been stark naked throughout the scene. He
follows Jerry out the door: "Jerry, come on, man! Hey! So, that's the difference between us: You think we're fighting, and I think we're finally talking!"

They are "finally talking" because finally they are both naked, as it were.
It is interesting, however, that this breakthrough in communication between
them should be marked by a display of the black man's naked body. Rod's
body, as the "site of vision, attention, and stimulation"[38] is not only the central commodity of their business, it refers to the origins of Jerry's desire: the
father's body—the *lost* body of the father. But this "father" of "primary identification"—which is what we are really talking about, and as Freud made
clear—is a "father in individual prehistory." It is an Imaginary Father (which
Jerry seeks). Such a "father," as Kristeva clarifies in *Tales of Love*, is the same
as "both parents":[39]

> The problem is not to find an answer to the enigma: who might be the
> object of primary identification, daddy or mummy? Such an attempt
> would only open up the impossible quest for the absolute origin of the
> capacity for love as a psychic and symbolic capacity. The question is
> rather: of what value would the question be when it actually bears on
> states existing on the border between the psychic and the somatic, ide-
> alization and eroticism, within analytic treatment itself? (28)

The relationship between Jerry and Rod (narrated in more or less autobi-
ographical terms by Jerry) functions not unlike an "analytic treatment."

Kristeva notes that "the analyst's couch is the only place where the social contract explicitly authorizes a search for love—albeit a private one" (6). Thus, the agent-client contract between Jerry and Rod authorizes an ambiguously close friendship, which the film knows (as the characters seem to know) covertly authorizes a search for love.[40]

Jerry as an agent is only doing what he wishes a man would do for him. Jerry needs to keep alive that relation, to inscribe himself in that male-male love, even if he has to give it and not receive it. If Rod wants him to see that they are "finally talking," when Jerry thinks they are "fighting," he remains naked throughout the scene because, as Chesler observes, "Among men, the presence of a penis is still the proof of a shared and common humanity; still the proof of a truce between father and son, however uneasy a truce it is. It is still the trigger for male-male empathic identification."[41] Throughout the scene in the locker room, Rod draws attention to his body by generally preening and strutting in front of Jerry. The way in which his vulnerability and his strength are inseparable is communicated in this way. If they can bond, admit their vulnerability, help each other and agree not to hurt each other, then they might be a good team—work together to realize the "kwan."

But Rod, standing naked before Jerry—showing Jerry the money, as it were, and telling him: "These are the A-B-Cs of me, baby"—uneasily recalls the historical American memory of Africans as commodities on the slave market. Rod's body is the commodity with use-value against which the exchange-value of all goods is ultimately measured in his and Jerry's world. We know that it is in *money*, which has no use-value, that the exchange-value of all commodities is expressed, which is why he demands: "Show me the money!" Rod wants to convert the use-value of his body into an exchange value—to make the transition from real terms (the quantum of his human labor) to the phenomenal terms of money. What this will do, we know (because Jerry has already had to reproach Rod for it), is conceal the value-creating character of his human activity, the social character of individual labor. Rod thinks he can almost afford to take this gamble—because he has Marcee's love—but Jerry explains that if the football fans sense Rod's alienation from the game, the illusion at the heart of spectator sports will be broken, and his value in the game will be compromised. What Rod does *is* show business, and he knows it. And within any given stage of productive methods, exchange value is variable, whereas the use-value is constant.

Moreover, he knows he is running out of time ("I've got a shelf life of ten years, tops. . . . I'm out of this sport in five years"). He knows he must show the football fans what they have come to the stadium to see: the male body in

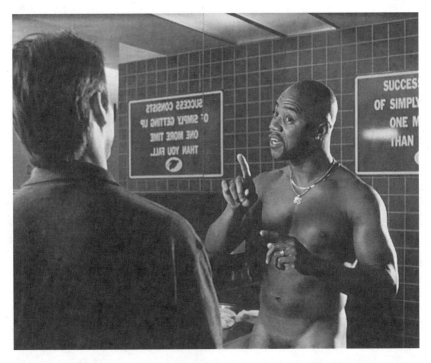

FIGURE 10.6   "You think we're fighting, and I think we're finally talking!" Rod tells Jerry. (Courtesy Photofest)

motion; a body at its best, capable of wondrous feats of prowess and endurance—the antithesis of the spectator's body, or the body of the "out-of-shape" agent—before he loses this body, his capital. On the ideological plane, there is a reason for making this body a black one. The filmmakers show us—white viewers—what we want to see (whether or not we understand what that is): "At the level of representation, whites remain, for all their transcending superiority, dependent on non-whites for their sense of self," Richard Dyer observes.[42] And so *Jerry Maguire* does what many Hollywood movies do: it shows us a character traversing an oedipal period "in which complementarity is accomplished by insisting on polarity, mutual exclusivity, black and white, male and female, can and cannot."[43] If the issue in *White Men Can't Jump* (1992) is whether a black basketball hustler and a white basketball hustler can trust each other and work together (a question framed by the film, as the title suggests, in terms of racial difference), in *Jerry Maguire* the intertwined issues are primarily about the status of heterosexuality (hegemonic masculinity vs. queer masculinity), affect (friendship vs. intimacy/love), and authenticity (stable vs. fluid identities). If Rod were not cast as black, there would be no corporeal specificity to identify Jerry and Rod as *different*. The corporeal logic that attends race and gender significations is very necessary to this story, otherwise the homoerotic implications of their relationship would be unbearably obvious for the dominantly heterosexual audiences for whom the film was ostensibly made. This is also why Rod must be shown as married, and as a father to boot (an attempt to signify unequivocally what can never be unequivocal: that he is "heterosexual"). In our culture, and overwhelmingly so in the cinema, the body is cast as the definitive "sight" of difference, but there is no corporealizing specificity for gay identity, and the fear of the possibility of a queer reading of the relationship between Jerry and Rod motivates at least in part the decision to cast the one character as a black man and the other as a white man.

Most of the film, unusually for a mainstream movie, questions heterosexual complementarity as the goal of development, and privileges identificatory love over object-love. It tries on the one hand to show the "naturalness" of heterosexual love and family values (Rod and Marcee), while also showing that the Tidwells are neurotic and greedy; and it implies that, being black, they are enviably closer to the body (Rod dancing around his kitchen with his shirt off while talking on the telephone with Jerry, who looks harried and desperate in white shirt and tie; Rod taking a bath with his son Tyson; Marcee, accurately described by the screenplay as "African-American, gorgeous, a heat-seeking smartbomb. She is also five months pregnant," and so on). On the other hand, the film appears to be trying to find ways to assert the superiority of Jerry's values and to justify his inhibitions. Consider, for example (as we consider Tom Cruise's body), Dyer's observation that "many of the formal properties of the built body carry connotations of whiteness: it is ideal, hard, achieved, wealthy, hairless and tanned."[44] Jerry is supposedly an "out-of-shape" agent—which means, in effect, that his body is not his only capital, as it is for Rod—and yet Tom Cruise's body is no less "in shape" than Cuba Gooding Jr.'s body. What this not so subtly suggests is that Jerry/the white man basically has more going for him than Rod/the black man. He won't be out of a job in five years, as Rod will. In this partnership of equals, Jerry emerges as the superior man. It is *his* story, *his* movie. Tom Cruise's body is a constant visible reminder on the screen that

> The built white body is not the body that white men are born with; it is the body made possible by their natural mental superiority. The point after all is that it is built, a product of the application of thought

and planning, an achievement. It is the sense of the mind at work behind the production of this body that most defines its whiteness.
(Dyer, *White*, 164)

If Tom Cruise is not a bodybuilder, exactly, he is a *star*. He has built a career, as Jerry is building a self. His star body is like that of the hero of a colo-
nial adventure in which "the built body . . . is a formula that speaks to the
need for an affirmation of the white male body without the loss of legitima-
cy that is always risked by its exposure, while also replaying the notion that
white men are distinguished above all by their spirit and enterprise."[45] Jerry,
in other words, is the real entrepreneur, the one whose brains, drive, and ambition will make the money that the film worships. And there is nothing,
Jerry Maguire finally tells us, that is more sexy and *masculine* than money.
Globalization is understood as a Darwinian struggle (as we see it in the relationship between Jerry and Rod) in which competition and cooperation are
dialectically linked; and the white man's concern is that ultimately *he* be the
real winner, the businessman with a commodity to trade.

Like the sexuality of the rich industrialist Mr. Burns in the TV cartoon series, *The Simpsons*, Jerry's sexuality—and Tom Cruise's sexuality, for that
matter—is ambiguous ("sexuality" being the defining measure of the authentic self in contemporary American culture). Except for Smithers, his
loyal factotum, Mr. Burns is friendless. But Mr. Burns is feared and admired
for his intelligence and enterprise—of which his money is the final and most
convincing proof; and even if he is not "normal," with a wife and children
and friends, he is some kind of evidence that in our culture money is more
phallic than muscle, or a heterosexual identity.

"I Love You . . ."

On their way to an athletic draft, Jerry greets Rod in the airport and then immediately abandons him to be part of the clamor surrounding Frank Cushman. This is inevitably hurtful and embarrassing to Rod, but when Jerry finally catches up with him at the hotel where the draft is being held, he
succeeds in boosting Rod's morale by calling him "the best-kept secret in the
NFL, the most commanding wide-receiver in the game. You are *fast, fierce,
wildly charismatic!* You are the man! You are the man! Are you ready? Let's
go!" Then they "walk the lobby," meeting and greeting media people and
representatives of companies seeking to have their products endorsed by the

athletes. The moment Rod and Jerry pause on the mezzanine, to gauge the success of Rod's impact, they glance down at the activity below. Rod notices that "[they are] shooting the Reebok ad down there," and turns to his agent: "Hey, Jerry, where are *my* endorsements? You know what I'm saying? You know, I ain't gettin' no love from Chevy. I ain't gettin' no love from Pepsi. I even ain't gettin' no love from that little Energizer bunny!" As Rod is ranting, Jerry sees that the agent representing the athlete who has won the Reebok contract is Bob Sugar, who now looks up at Jerry and slowly mouths the words, "I-love-you!" as he makes a gesture that unintentionally parodies the (deaf man's) declaration of love ("You complete me") that Jerry and Dorothy witnessed a few days before.

It is a moment that condenses some of the film's (and the characters') confusions and uneasiness about the meanings of "love." Love, as one of the master-narratives of legitimation, has been severely shaken by postmodernity, and this crisis of the meaning of love is perhaps the central theme of the film—which is why the film attempts to settle the question, or provide some closure for the theme, when Jerry can say to Dorothy at the end not "I love you," as in countless movies of old Hollywood, but: "You complete me"—a new way of saying what we used to mean (or think we meant) when we said "I love you." If, as Roland Barthes writes, "Once the first avowal has been made, *'I love you'* has no meaning whatever; it merely repeats in an enigmatic mode—so blank does it appear—the old message (which may not have been transmitted in these words),"[46] then it must be acknowledged at the very least that love is a *discourse*. It is spoken/written/represented in a number of ways. It can mean many things, including its ironic and hateful "opposite." Bob Sugar telling Jerry "I-love-you" is a formula uttered with the intention of humiliating Jerry.[47]

The tragedy that the film is attempting to come to terms with is the way in which (in Jerry's world) commerce and love have become confused. In Jerry's own—exemplary—case, the problem is exacerbated by Dicky Fox's advice that "the key to this business is personal relationships." That key, of course, is an oxymoron, or at the very least is an insight with dangerous implications. The subject has to *know* that what he is involved in is "show business," and yet *believe* that what he has is a "personal relationship." Dicky Fox further mystifies the meaning of "love" when he looks into the camera and tells us, as he once told Jerry: "Unless you love everybody, you can't sell anybody."

Jerry of course knows that Dicky Fox was not his father, but he loved his late mentor. And a grain of doubt and confusion appears to be lodged in Jerry's unconscious about how the old man loved him. Did he love Jerry as a father loves his son? Or did he love him as the coach "loves" his athletes, or the agent his clients?

Jerry interrupts Rod's rant about not getting any "love" in the form of those "jewels of the celebrity endorsement dollar" by reassuring him that, "Down there, for about five minutes, you unloaded that rather large chip that resides right there on your shoulder. And you know what? You let people in, and you were *brilliant!*" As Jerry is walking away (to talk to Frank Cushman), Rod shouts after him: "You lovin' me now, aren't you!" Jerry replies: "I'm not about 'love.' I'm about 'showing you the money!'" Rod's reply reveals that he knows Jerry is motivated, in the final analysis, by love, not money, and he understands that heterosexual men in this culture can only declare their love for each other indirectly—through irony ("love" in quotation marks, for example), or in metaphors like *money*: "I was just testing you, Jerry! But to hear you say that makes me love you, baby!"

When Jerry confronts Matt Cushman and forces him to admit that, behind Jerry's back, he struck a deal with Bob Sugar, Matt Cushman's only defense is: "I'm sorry, I . . . love my son." The lesson Matt seems to be teaching Jerry is that a child can have only one real father—and Jerry is not Frank's father. Jerry is really saying to Matt: "Love me!" For Matt has just said, in effect: "I don't love you, Jerry, I love my son. If it's a father's love you want, go to your own father." We saw earlier how Jerry embraces Matt when Matt says: "We decided to stay with you . . . I told myself: 'He shows up, we stick with him.'" Jerry throws his arms around the older man and finds that he "can't let go." Only when Matt's two sons walk into the room, looking indignant, jealous, and embarrassed, does Jerry let go of their father. The homosocial logic of the scene becomes even clearer when Matt says: "Now, you know I don't do contracts. But what you do have is my word, and it's stronger than oak." Like the father who gives his daughter's hand to a suitor in marriage, Matt is promising his son to Jerry in a partnership. When Avery hears that the Cushmans have reneged on this promise, she blames Jerry: "Jerry, you and I are salespeople. We sell. It's not: 'Love me.' It's not: 'Trust my handshake.' It's: 'Make the sale! Get it signed!' There shouldn't be any confusion about that." She reminds him that *their* "deal" when they first got together was "brutal truth"— and then, with violent gestures and in a raised voice, she delivers the speech that, for Jerry, will precipitate an epiphany about "love":

> *Avery:* Jerry, there's a "sensitivity" thing that some people have. I don't
> have it. I don't cry at movies, I don't gush over babies, I don't start
> celebrating Christmas five months early, and I *don't* tell the man

who just screwed up both our lives: "Oh, poor baby!" That's me, for better or worse. [*She pauses, puts her hands on his shoulders, looks him in the eyes, and says*] *But I do love you.*

In the stunned silence that follows, Jerry realizes that if this is love, he wants no part of it. He returns Avery's gaze and announces: "Avery, it's over."

At the restaurant where Jerry and Dorothy go to celebrate their belated acknowledgment that they have a romantic interest in each other, Jerry tries to explain to Dorothy that his breaking up with Avery was his fault, caused by his "laziness": "*Somebody* is always to blame. You go for it . . . like you do a job . . . work at it." To which, wisely, gently, she says: "But maybe . . . love shouldn't be such hard work." It is a crucial moment in the movie, because it reveals that all the energy Jerry puts into his job is a quest for love; and the proof that his love for Avery was inauthentic—as he should be able to see now—is that it was such hard work (like rock climbing). Authentic, reciprocated love, Dorothy is trying to tell him, has its own energy. The heartbreaking revelation for the viewer is that Jerry has clearly never known this kind of love.

DAVID GEFFEN's "RELATIONSHIP ECONOMY"

In Hollywood mogul David Geffen, as he is portrayed in a February 1998 *New Yorker* profile of him written by John Seabrook,[48] there would appear to be a contemporary, real-life example of the Jerry Maguire personality, which is revealing of the film's attempt to say that "personal relationships" are more important than material success, and its contradictory demonstration of the opposite.[49] Seabrook suggests that a man like Geffen cannot have a personal relationship with another man outside the context of a business relationship, and vice versa.

Geffen represents the kind of Hollywood that *Jerry Maguire* comes out of, and indeed, he produced *Risky Business* (1983), the film that made Tom Cruise famous and consolidated elements of his emerging star persona that are strongly present in *Jerry Maguire*. Seabrook in effect explains the pathology that drives the narcissist to succeed at business and yet fail to find personal happiness. The first section of his article is given the subheading, "The Relationship Economy," and in it he establishes that Geffen ("the only man in the history of American cultural capitalism who has succeeded in three

different industries—popular music, Broadway, and Hollywood")[50] is bored
and unhappy, despite his phenomenal success in the entertainment business—which is reminiscent of Jerry's stated desire at the beginning of *Jerry
Maguire* to change his place in the world; and of his mentor's dictum that
"the key to this business is personal relationships"; and of the implication
that Jerry will only succeed in forging a stable self-identity if he puts "personal relationships" first. "With a personal fortune of more than two billion
dollars, much of which came from the sale of Geffen Records to MCA, and
the subsequent sale of MCA to Matsushita, Geffen is perhaps the most powerful man in Hollywood, both widely admired for his guile and his anger"
writes Seabrook (110). The key to the mogul's success, he thinks, is that "in
the increasingly corporate world of global entertainment, Geffen is a throwback to a more individualistic era" (110). He explains:

> If Geffen may be said to have invented anything, it is an economy
> based on the rapid exchange of information across a network small
> enough to fit on a speed dial—a network in which you have a market
> interest in the information but are also motivated by a genuine per-
> sonal connection. "David would never say, 'I'm in business with you,'"
> says Tom Freston, the chairman of MTV Networks. "He would say,
> 'We've got a relationship.'" (110)

Like Jerry Maguire, David Geffen admires loyalty ("I'm a stand-up guy. I can
be counted on by my friends"),[51] and Freston considers it one of Geffen's
strengths that he is "a very personable guy. As the world has conglomerated,
David has carried on making personal relationships. And it works."[52] The
"it" that Freston is referring to, of course, is the business of dollar profit. And
yet Geffen himself seems to acknowledge that all is not well: "My life can't be
a failure, right? My life is a success: I'm a happy guy."[53]

There is "boredom in [Geffen's] eyes," writes Seabrook (108), and clearly
he is disappointed and angry about something ("At the end of the day, no
one's powerful. You know? If you work for Rupert Murdoch, you can say
he's powerful, but he's not powerful to me. I don't give a shit about Rupert
Murdoch,"[54] which is reminiscent of Jerry's disappointment in his father).
Seabrook describes Geffen as "easily bored, petulant, insecure, unburdened
by history, and blessed with the plastic enthusiasms of the fifteen-year-old
impulse buyer" (117). And like Jerry Maguire, Geffen is a (self-described)
"searcher" (111) whose "only long-term project through the years has been

himself" (108). He has spent years pursuing New Age experiments in consciousness-raising and is trying to "temper the god of vengeance and anger with forgiveness and mercy."[55]

Guy Oseary, a twenty-five-year-old partner in Maverick Records (Madonna's company), analyzes Geffen's relationship economy thus: "I'd say it's 30 percent about the business and 70 percent personal. Advice on personal relationships, seeing a movie, having dinner—it's not, like, just about work."[56] While no doubt there has always been an element of the "personal" in the most successful "work" relationships (those relationships in which "the money" is held clearly in view as the object of the relationship, and in which material profit ultimately defines their "success"), it becomes a risky business when the balance between the "personal" and "work" is weighted in favor of the personal. Geffen's example, like Jerry Maguire's, suggests that a law of capitalism is involved: the risks in blurring the line between the personal relationship and the business relationship are great, but so are the possibilities for spectacular profit. Howard Rosenman, a Hollywood producer who is a former Geffen friend, reveals in Seabrook's article what is at stake when, for whatever reason, the relationship fails. As it is for Jerry and Rod in *Jerry Maguire*, the loss is experienced as *personal*: "David hates me, but I love him. He was good to me, but I didn't appreciate it at the time. David felt that I betrayed him, and he was right. I let my own anger and resentment stand in the way of all he had done for me."[57]

Seabrook suggests that *Risky Business* is perhaps Geffen's "most self-revealing project": Geffen "insisted on changing the screenwriters' ending for the movie, in which Tom Cruise was punished for his misdeeds by not getting into Princeton. In the version that the world now knows, Cruise gets the good life *and* Princeton" (118). As in *Jerry Maguire*—which questions the "integrity" of its greedy characters and then goes on to demonstrate that in the end money is the most important thing, after all, and selling out is okay if the price is right—Geffen's Tom Cruise character in *Risky Business* wants to believe in the values of the Father (represented by Princeton-integrity; a legacy; values transmitted from one generation to the next), but (Geffen) has an ambivalent relation to the paternal signifier. He wants the validation of the Father but doubts its worth. The laws of capitalism appear to be more reliable (less likely to disappoint, easier to manipulate) than the Law of the Father, and they appear, moreover—all disclaimers of patriarchal ideology to the contrary—to be valued by society *above* the Law of the Father. But sooner or later, it is felt, their benefits cannot compensate for, or replace, that original loss or lack (of the father's love). If a positive image of the father is not internalized in childhood, the boy may spend his lifetime searching for replacement images to "believe in." Seabrook writes:

> Geffen's mother, who ran a corset-and-brassiere-making business out of the family's home, in Borough Park, Brooklyn (where young David slept on a couch in the living room), was his hero and role model. Geffen's father, on the other hand, was a scholar, who could not support the family and disappointed David. "After I realized my father didn't take care of the family, he sank somewhat in my eyes," Geffen told me. Some believe this to be the original wound that has driven Geffen in a series of complicated relationships with powerful men throughout his career, from Ahmet Ertegun to Steve Ross and on to Lew Wasserman. (113)

Jerry Maguire's mentor, we know, was Dicky Fox. But Jerry and Dicky Fox are from two different eras (suggested in many ways, but most obviously in the way Dicky talks directly into the camera, and always from the same space; whereas Jerry is more often *in transit* and on a cellular phone), just as there is a significant difference between Ahmet Ertegun and David Geffen—a difference, Seabrook observes, that "offers an interesting lesson in the history of cultural capitalism" (117). In the 1970s, when Geffen's star in the music business was on the rise, "Geffen was bright and brash, but he didn't have any of the connoisseurship, the cultivation, or the style that Ahmet Ertegun had. Ertegun was hip. He was an adept" (117). But all has changed:

> Intimate knowledge of black-roots music, such as Ertegun possessed, made it hard for him to grasp the fundamental change in the meaning of rock and roll, in the seventies, from something that was primarily about music and history to something that was primarily about image and style. (117)

As much as Jerry wants to believe he is in sports management for "the way a stadium sounds when one of my players performs well on the field," and Rod wants to believe he's "an athlete . . . not an entertainer," they both know that what they do professionally is primarily about image and style and earning "the big, sweet dollar." They are both businessmen, trying to use their business relationship to realize personal goals of self-identity; and both are seeking to tap the potent wellsprings of a personal relationship to succeed in business. As Dicky Fox says (assuming we know how to maintain proper boundaries between the public and private spheres): "If *this* is empty [he points to his heart], *this* doesn't matter [he slaps the side of his head]."

The nostalgia for "the game" in *Jerry Maguire* is like all nostalgia, a yearning for something lost, and here it refers, ultimately, to the lost father. Nostalgia for the father also explains why Jerry marries Dorothy (even though he does not love her); just as it appears to explain why David Geffen wanted to marry Cher (even though he is gay). Seabrook writes: "[Joni] Mitchell shared a house with Geffen, in accordance with a characteristic of his early career: total absorption in the client's life. (Later, when Geffen moved to L.A., he had a sexual relationship with Cher. 'David wanted to marry me,' she told me. 'He proposed to me in Hawaii—he had a ring, and everything')" (113). Geffen's example forces us to consider fully the implications of the question Dorothy asks Jerry one night, when they are in bed together: "*Why do you love me?*" Before Jerry can reply, the real answer—Ray—bursts into the room: "Jerry, can I come in and watch TV?" As the child leaps onto the bed, and Jerry cuddles him affectionately, Dorothy looks at her husband in baffled sadness mixed with gratitude. She realizes that he does not love her, after all. Blaming herself, she confronts him shortly afterwards with the proposition that they separate: "I took advantage of you, and worst of it is I'm not alone, I did this with a kid. I was just on some wild ride, where I thought I was in love enough for both of us . . ." Jerry then asks her what she wants—his "soul"? She answers: "Why not? I deserve that." Jerry's reply is crucial, for it is as close as the film can come to giving him real insight into his own desire: "*What if I'm not built that way?* No, listen, what if it's true? 'Great at friendship, bad at intimacy'? Oh, come on! It's the theme of my bachelor film, for God's sake . . ."

He knows he has been found out; but when he asks, "What about Ray?" she sums up the situation perceptively: "On the surface, everything looks fine. I've got this great guy, and he loves my kid. And *he sure does like me a lot*. And I can't live like that. [She's crying now.] It's not how I'm built."

"SHELTER FROM THE STORM"

The film contradictorily asserts that we are all born (or in the social constructionist argument, are hard-wired very early) with an identity that names our desire and dictates for life who and how we will love. In the face of modernity's exhilarating, scary promise of infinite possibilities, it is paradoxically reassuring to believe that we are all "built" a certain way. And yet we see how the film puts Jerry and Dorothy together again as husband and wife (the "happy ending"), only moments—in film time, that is—after they have more or less agreed that their marriage is a failure.

The ending of the film suggests that the mythology of "heterosexual attraction/true love" is an ideal, but for most people (which, as nice, average, middle-class, white Americans, is what Jerry and Dorothy represent) it is an ideal which may have to be tempered by compromise. The "adult" message is that behind or above every puppet show are the strings, and if you can accept this reality, you will have a chance at (ordinary) happiness. It is a way of saying that the Oedipus complex—the "storm" in the song Bob Dylan sings over the film's closing credits—will toss you this way and that; and instead of riding it out (because you never know where it will take you!), you should seek shelter. Jerry's "shelter" of course is Dorothy ("'Come in,' she said, 'I'll give you shelter from the storm'" is the song's refrain), and the "storm" is the complex of feelings aroused in him by men.

The lesson the film offers the male viewer is that the key to success—the "kwan," measured largely in terms of money—is *sublimation.* And the only truly reliable affective tie is "the husband and wife thing," as Rod calls it. When Jerry rushes back to Laurel's house after Rod's big game, he bursts in on the divorced women's support group that regularly meets there, and says: "I'm looking for *my wife.*" The Christmas tree in the corner of the living room affirms the notion that in the end the only enduring values are family values. They are the values upon which we should stake our happiness in this world which, Jerry informs Dorothy and the women in the room, is "a cynical world . . . a cynical world." Christmas, the holiday that the tree symbolizes, is the day on which our culture celebrates the completion of its mythic first family, and it reaffirms the family as the central and natural form of human relations. In the tradition of melodrama, *Jerry Maguire* cannot really imagine any form of human relations other than the familial one. Homoerotic identificatory love cannot be acknowledged in the world Jerry lives in, except between father and son.

In its conservative function to remind female viewers of their role, or place (in Jerry's world—cf. the film's opening shots)—when guys like Jerry are struggling to consolidate their masculinity—the film shows that professional ambition in a woman (as we see it in Avery) is unattractive; and while sisterhood is all fine and good (the women's support group that Dorothy is contemptuous of), it won't get you a man like Tom Cruise. In their crucial role as mothers, women above all must assist in the project of turning boys into men like "the man [Jerry] wants to be and . . . almost is."

When Jerry discovers, in the final moments of the film, that Ray knows how to throw a ball, he finds his ultimate client and truly becomes a father, at last. "We'll develop his talent!" he enthuses to his wife. He will dedicate himself to making Ray over in his own image. And as a father to this little boy, he may legitimately enjoy the only socially sanctioned homoerotic bond available in his society. There is, as I have repeatedly tried to make clear, a sense in which Jerry and Ray have identical needs. When Ray demands a hug from Jerry, Dorothy takes her sister aside and observes excitedly: "That is the first time I have ever seen him kiss a man, just like a dad! Wasn't that just thrilling? He must really have been needing that, you know?" Jerry, we know, also yearns for a man's embrace. But he will never get to kiss a man, or receive a kiss from a man. That's all behind him now; he has changed his "place in the world." He has become that man—the man he wanted to be, or to have.

CONCERNING HAPPINESS: AN AFTERWORD*

I began this study by quoting from Gore Vidal's memoir, *Screening History*, in which it occurs to Vidal that the only thing he ever really liked to do was go to the movies. It is of course in part my narcissism that makes me choose Vidal as a figure of identification, but for me the essay behind his memoir— which in a general way informs my assumptions and intentions, and which attempts to address more comprehensively the question Vidal broaches (and shortly answers, by adding: "Naturally, Sex and Art always took precedence over the cinema")[1]—is Freud's *Civilization and Its Discontents*. In this small book, which he published late in his life, Freud observes that "happiness, in the reduced sense in which we recognize it as possible, is a problem of the economics of the individual's libido. There is no golden rule which applies to everyone: every man must find out for himself in what particular fashion he can be saved."[2]

The main theme of Freud's essay—the irremediable antagonism between the demands of "instinct" and the restrictions of civilization—is one that Lacan reformulates in terms of desire, which, as has been noted, springs from the relation between one's own body and language. And my own theme, in this exploration of the ways in which some Hollywood films negotiate the eroticism intrinsic to identification as it occurs between one male and an- other, has followed certain strands of Freud's argument, with its emphasis on ways of seeking happiness and averting suffering.

Although Freud concluded that the progress of civilization is dialectically linked to repression, we are alert to Foucault's argument that sexuality is not so much repressed as socially constructed and controlled. The "repressive

---

*This book is dedicated to my brother Gordon, who died in 2000 at the age of forty-one. This chapter was written during the last month of his illness.

hypothesis," as Foucault dubbed it, supposes that society sets barriers to instinctual gratification, when, in fact, as Michael Warner puts it in his wonderfully sane book, *The Trouble with Normal* (1999), "civilization doesn't just repress our original sexuality; it makes new kinds of sexuality. And new sexualities, including learned ones, might have as much validity as ancient ones, if not more."[3] Warner's argument is Foucauldian in its insistence that the social control of sexuality does not simply bar unwanted sexual practices or desires; it produces "normal" and "aberrant" sexualities alike. The cinema, I have been arguing—if we are imaginative and cineliterate viewers—offers us access to sexualities of every type and vintage. It provides, in Ethel Person's apt phrase describing fantasy, "a theater in which we preview the possible scenarios of our life to come."[4]

Freud wrote that men strive after happiness (and aim at an absence of pain and unpleasure) by a variety of means, including voluntary isolation (in which we might find the "happiness of quietness"); or (in his opinion, the "better path"), that of "becoming a member of the human community."[5] The most interesting methods of fending off suffering, however, are those that seek to influence our own organism: intoxication (including the effects of substances in the chemistry of our own bodies, which perform like an intoxicating drug); "the employment of the displacements of libido which our mental apparatus permits of and through which its function gains so much in flexibility" (79) (such as the activities of artists and scientists); and illusions, "which are recognized as such without the discrepancy between them and reality being allowed to interfere with enjoyment" (80) (i.e., "the life of the imagination," as in the enjoyment that may be derived from beauty).

Freud went on to observe that "the man who is predominantly erotic will give first preference to his emotional relationships to other people; the narcissistic man, who inclines to be self-sufficient, will seek his main satisfaction in his mental processes; the man of action will never give up the external world on which he can try out his strength" (83–84).[6] Although, among Freud's "techniques of living," I may appear in this book to have privileged what he calls "illusions," I do so because the movies, through their unique deployment of the processes of identification, comprehend *all* types of men and women, and because, as Person puts it: "Fantasies, by definition, subvert the status quo and therefore always have a potential impact on the future, sometimes in the direction of radical change."[7]

For so long, dreams have been a favorite analogy for films and how they work, but, like Christian Metz, I think the *day*dream serves us better—the daydream, or conscious fantasy, as an imaginative engagement with alternative possibilities.[8] The films I have chosen to analyze inspire resistance to culturally ingrained notions of romance, marriage, and family, but the responsibility for the potential for change that they implicitly offer will always remain with the viewer. Such is the lesson of *Being John Malkovich* (Spike Jonze, 1999), as the most remarkably sustained and self-reflexive example in mainstream cinema to date of a narrative that seeks to illustrate the truth about the variety of paths identification can take (and, for our purposes, some of the specific meanings and functions of same-sex/identificatory desire). Person's working definition of a conscious fantasy is worth quoting here, since it serves nicely as a preface to the few remarks I shall make, by way of conclusion, about Jonze's film:

> [Conscious fantasy] is a daydream that surfaces in the stream of consciousness, a narrative compounded of emotion, thought, internal dialogue, and (predominantly visual) sensory impressions. Sometimes highly schematic and abbreviated, sometimes minutely articulated and detailed, it is shaped by the imagination to coalesce ultimately around wish-fulfillment, emotional regulation, assurance of safety, containment of unpleasant emotions, working through of trauma, crystallization of perception, or aspirations for the future. The goal of fantasy is to achieve an overall change of state—a change in how one feels. . . . Whatever the fantasy's form, the effect is beneficent and protective.[9]

A major reference point for some of the most interesting work by psychoanalysts and film theorists on fantasy is the essay by Laplanche and Pontalis, "Fantasy and the Origins of Sexuality," in which the authors argue that fantasies constitute scenarios with multiple points of entry and are marked by multiple and fluid identifications on the part of the subject.[10] Person's *By Force of Fantasy* is indebted to their now classic psychoanalytic account, as are considerations of fantasy in notable essays on the issue of cinema and sexual difference by Elisabeth Lyon, Elizabeth Cowie, Constance Penley, and Steve Neale, who have described and defined fantasy as the setting and articulation of desire, as a scenario in which the subject's desire is staged, imaged, and narrated.[11] Penley, for example, observes that in fantasy,

> All the possible roles in the narrative are available to the subject: he can be either subject or object and can even occupy a position "outside" the scene, looking on from the spectator's point of view . . . it is only the formal positions themselves that are fixed (there are "masculine"

and "feminine" positions of desire); the subject can and does adopt these positions in relation to a variety of complex scenarios, and in accordance with the mobile patterns of his or her own desire.[12]

This is what happens in *Being John Malkovich*, when Craig Schwartz (John Cusack), the film's erstwhile protagonist, discovers a "portal" offering access to the actor John Malkovich's subjectivity—a conceit we may take as representing what happens every time we enter a movie theater and watch a film. Craig falls in love with Maxine (Catherine Keener), but she does not, at first, return his love. She admires his persistence but is simply not attracted to him. She believes that "the world is divided into those who go after what they want, and those who don't." She explains her credo to Craig and his wife Lotte (Cameron Diaz): "The passionate ones—the ones who go after what they want—well, they may not get what they want. But at least they remain *vital*, you know? So, when they lie on their deathbeds, they have few regrets. And the ones who don't go after what they want . . . well, who gives a shit about them, anyway!"

The interest Maxine finally takes in Craig will be commercial ("I need you, Craig—you're my man on the inside"). She decides that they should exploit the discovery of the portal for profit—charge people $200 for fifteen minutes inside John Malkovich. JM, Inc., as they call their new business, "provides a service" in essentially the same way that psychoanalysis or the cinema does. *Being John Malkovich* thus renders explicit Hollywood cinema's status (or function) as fantasy and the spectator's role (or responsibility) in creating new realities with it.[13]

Freud holds that "a closer investigation of a man's day-dreams generally shows that all his heroic exploits are carried out and all his successes achieved only in order to please a woman and to be preferred by her to other men"[14]—and this would certainly appear to be true in Craig's case. But the viewer who is interested in what men can do with one another may inscribe him(or her)self in this story differently, may experience what Craig calls "making friends with the Malkovich body" (the process whereby he "becomes" Malkovich) as a liberating act of masculine identification offering a degree of sexual and subjective freedom. Whether or not we agree with Freud that "the programme of becoming happy, which the pleasure principle imposes on us, cannot be fulfilled," we recognize, as Freud did, that "we must not—indeed, we cannot—give up our efforts to bring it nearer to fulfillment by some means or other." At a minimum, as Maxine suggests, it takes a bit of passion, will, and imagination.

NOTES

PREFACE

1. Following Ellis Hanson in his edited anthology, *Out Takes: Essays on Queer Theory and Film,* I use the term *queer* in the sense in which it refers to "a rejection of the compulsory heterosexual code of masculine men desiring feminine women, and it declares that the vast range of stigmatized sexualities and gender identifications, far from being marginal, are central to the construction of modern subjectivity" (4). Queer theory's aims "are at once philosophical, political, and erotic—an effort . . . not only to analyze but also to resist, dismantle, or circumnavigate hegemonic systems of sexual oppression and normalization by revealing the theoretical presumptions and rhetorical sleights of hand by which they establish, justify, and reinforce their considerable power" (ibid.).

See also Alexander Doty's delightfully straightforward and persuasively argued book, *Making Things Perfectly Queer: Interpreting Mass Culture,* in which he attempts to account for the existence and expression of a wide range of positions within culture that are "non-, anti-, or contra-straight."

1. MASCULINE INTERESTS

1. *The Prince and the Pauper* (William Keighley, 1937). Based on the historical romance by Mark Twain; produced by Warner Bros.

2. Gore Vidal, *Screening History,* 24. Subsequent page numbers will be cited in the text.

3. Vidal, Ibid., 12; see also caption under photograph facing page 52.

4. Chuck Norris with Joe Hyams, *The Secret of Inner Strength*: "John Wayne and Gary Cooper . . . were my role models during childhood, when I grew up essentially without a father. There weren't many heroes of that type on the screen in the

1970s, and I felt that kids needed this kind of positive image. Perhaps I could become a role model for today's youth" (118).

5. As this book is about movies, I rely on the sense (and metaphors) of sight in my formulation of what I mean by "masculine interests." Of course, the media and mechanisms of identification are rarely limited to just "looking." As Jacques Lacan has pointed out, "All sorts of things in the world behave like mirrors" (*The Seminar, Book II*, 49).

6. Tim Dean, "On the Eve of a Queer Future," *Raritan* 15.1 (Summer 1995): 133. I borrow some other phrases from Dean's brisk article: the ego, or self, "formed mimetically, via models"; developing the ego "through a series of imaginary identifications or 'role models'"; the oppressive implications of "adaptation, maturity, and cure."

7. Needless to say, Vidal's hyperbole ("I wanted no company at all") is a form of literary license.

8. This inspired representation of fantasy as "the mise-en-scène of desire" is by Elizabeth Cowie, by way of Jean Laplanche and Jean-Bertrand Pontalis. See Cowie, "Fantasia," *m/f* 9 (1984): 71–104; and Laplanche and Pontalis, "Fantasy and the Origins of Sexuality," *International Journal of Psycho-Analysis* 49, part 1 (1968) (reprinted in Burgin, Donald, and Kaplan, eds., *Formations of Fantasy*, 5–34). Obviously, I do not mean that we should start behaving as though life were a movie, as the Renée Zellweger character does in *Nurse Betty* (Neil LaBute, 2000). Rather—as in the conclusion of *Nurse Betty*—we might allow films to be a vehicle *through which* we *realize* our desire.

9. As some readers will recognize, I have been influenced by Gilles Deleuze and Félix Guattari's *Anti-Oedipus: Capitalism and Schizophrenia* (English-language translation, 1983) and *A Thousand Plateaus: Capitalism and Schizophrenia* (translated in 1987). For reasons primarily of focus, however, and to avoid the explanatory and polemical digressions that an overt engagement with their work would entail, I regrettably leave that influence for the most part implicit. I see no real contradictions between Vidal's rather old-fashioned notion of desire as a pursuit of the whole (which comes from Plato), Freud and Lacan's dialectics of lack and plenitude, and the avowedly anti-Freudian/Lacanian theories of Deleuze and Guattari. I am not interested in "being" a Lacanian, a Deleuzo-Guattarian, or anything else (at least, never for very long) but rather hope that the intellectual nomadism of this book will help me and the reader each find our own language of desire.

10. Dean, "On the Eve of a Queer Future," 128.

11. Henning Bech, *When Men Meet: Homosexuality and Modernity*, 47 passim (emphasis in original; subsequent page numbers will be cited in the text). Although Bech's book helped to crystallize my own theme, my title *Masculine Interests* was in fact proposed to me by my friend and colleague Candace Clements, to whom I am

very grateful, not only for this inspired contribution but for her generous intellectual and moral support throughout the writing of this book.

12. Stephen Neale, *Genre*, 19.

13. Frank Krutnik, *In a Lonely Street: Film Noir, Genre, Masculinity*, 9.

14. The reader may wonder to whom I am referring when I say "we." In his fascinating and highly readable study *Film/Genre*, Rick Altman considers several important questions like the one implicit in my remark above (i.e., where is the genre primarily located: in the author, the text, or the audience?), which I generally embed in my discussions of individual films. (The answer to the question of generic location, as Altman reasonably concludes, is that "genre is not permanently located in any single place, but may depend at different times on radically differing criteria. Like the notion of nation, the very idea of genre exists in the singular only as a matter of convenience—or ideology" [86].)

15. Judith Butler, *Gender Trouble: Feminism and the Subversion of Identity*, 140.

16. Ibid (emphasis in original). Performativity should not be misread as performance in a commonsense way, as a simple matter of choosing how to behave or present a "self." Despite Butler's choice of drag as her main example of parodic gender performativity, and the apparent implication in the quotation above that the gender effect is produced through manipulations of "style" as easy as changing clothes, Butler is at pains to make clear (in her later book, *Bodies That Matter: On the Discursive Limits of "Sex"*) that performativity is not a "willful appropriation" but the condition for the emergence of gendering: "The 'activity' of this gendering cannot, strictly speaking, be a human act or expression, a willful appropriation, and it is certainly *not* a question of taking on a mask; it is the matrix through which all willing first becomes possible, its enabling cultural condition. In this sense, the matrix of gender relations is prior to the emergence of the 'human'" (7). Nevertheless, there is an ordinary sense in which—within the constraints imposed by the requirement of intelligibility in terms of the current gender system—filmmakers do make choices and have some control over how they represent their characters and tell their stories.

17. Butler, *Gender Trouble*, 141.

18. Robert Warshow, "Movie Chronicle: *The Westerner*" (1954), in *The Immediate Experience*, 153.

19. To the extent that the cowboy learning how to dance is encoded in the western as his learning the techniques of loveplay or sex, there is a sense in which, reversing the code, we can say Rio teaches Billy (Jack Beutel) how to dance, by initiating him into the pleasures of heterosexuality (which, like dancing, is only a very occasional activity for the cowboy).

20. Eve Sedgwick, *Epistemology of the Closet*, 93.

21. Ed Sikov, *Laughing Hysterically: American Screen Comedy of the 1950s*, 186.

22. Luce Irigaray, *This Sex Which Is Not One*, 193.

23. It is very interesting to see the attempt in *The Hi-Lo Country* (1998) to erase this recent history of the buddy film—to return, as it were, to a state of innocence or ignorance regarding homoerotic/homosexual (under)currents in close friendships between men. The movie is an intensely homoerotic tale about two handsome young cowboy friends in post-World War II New Mexico who fall in love with the same woman. The director, Stephen Frears, remains scrupulously careful throughout the film not to seem "knowing" in any way about *why* the two men "happen" to fall in love with the same woman. (Frears, it cannot be forgotten, is the man who in 1985 directed *My Beautiful Laundrette*, a landmark of the New British Cinema, about two young men in Thatcher's London from markedly different social and ethnic backgrounds, who become friends, then business partners, and then—seemingly as a logical development of their friendship—lovers.)

24. Cf. Susan Jeffords, *The Remasculinization of America: Gender and the Vietnam War*, Yvonne Tasker, *Spectacular Bodies: Gender, Genre, and the Action Cinema*, and Susan Jeffords, *Hard Bodies: Hollywood Masculinity in the Reagan Era*.

25. Cf. Eileen R. Meehan, "'Holy Commodity Fetish, Batman!'": The Political Economy of a Commercial Intertext," in Pearson and Uricchio, eds., *The Many Lives of Batman*, 47–65.

26. Amy Taubin, "Trials and Tribulations," *Village Voice*, May 24, 1994, 28

27. *Midnight Cowboy* can be read as a proto-queer road movie: although Ratso dies at the end, the narrative logic of their fantasy of moving to Florida would have the two men living happily ever after as a "married" couple.

28. Roland Barthes, *The Pleasure of the Text*, 47.

29. Stephen Frosh, *Identity Crisis: Modernity, Psychoanalysis, and the Self* (New York: Routledge, 1991), 118. Subsequent page numbers will be cited in the text.

30. Kaja Silverman, "The Language of Care," in Brooks and Woloch, eds., *Whose Freud? The Place of Psychoanalysis in Contemporary Culture*, 151. Subsequent page numbers will be cited in the text.

31. Vidal, *Screening History*, 28.

2. Oedipus in Africa: *The Lion King*

1. Michael D. Eisner, with Tony Schwartz, *Work in Progress*, 341. Subsequent page numbers will be cited in the text.

2. If I focus on the male subject's psychic development, to the relative neglect of the dynamics involved in that of the female subject, I do so not in order to sideline questions of femininity or female oppression under patriarchy but to streamline my discussion about Simba's classically oedipal trajectory, to discover how boys

become heterosexual men in patriarchal societies. The asymmetry between male and female development, which Freud acknowledged and which is centrally relevant to my argument, has its origins in the fact that all human beings, both male and female, have a unique attachment to the mother, the parent with whom the child has been physically intimate from the outset, and who dominates the private sphere of childhood.

3. Sigmund Freud, *Three Essays on the Theory of Sexuality*, vol. 7 of the *Standard Edition of the Complete Psychological Works* (hereafter, *SE*), 226n.

4. Mark Poster, *Critical Theory of the Family*, 26.

5. Peter Brooks, "Freud's Masterplot: A Model for Narrative," in *Reading for the Plot*, 90–112. Brooks emerges from reading Freud's "Beyond the Pleasure Principle" (1920; in vol. 18, *SE*) with a dynamic-energetic model of narrative plot that "proposes that we live in order to die, hence that the intentionality of plot lies in its orientation toward the end even while the end must be achieved only through detour" (108).

6. Katha Pollitt, "Subject to Debate," *The Nation*, July 3, 1995, 9.

7. In *Iron John: A Book About Men*, Bly laments that "the United States has undergone an unmistakable decline since 1950" (35). Subsequent page numbers will be cited in the text.

8. As we shall see, Simba's Uncle Scar is languid and witty (not "harsh" or "silence-loving"), and one can certainly imagine him being seductive and charming. This is precisely why Bly would not think him properly masculine, and partly how the film suggests his villainy.

9. Jessica Benjamin, *The Bonds of Love: Psychoanalysis, Feminism, and the Problem of Domination*, 107.

10. Lynn Hunt, *The Family Romance of the French Revolution*, 3. Subsequent page numbers will be cited in the text.

11. John MacInnes, *The End of Masculinity*, 10.

12. Cf. Victor Burgin's comment ("does *choice* ever really come into it?—'coup de foudre'"), which will be noted again later. Burgin, "Man–Desire–Image," in Appignanesi, ed., *Desire*, 32.

13. Juliet Mitchell, *Psychoanalysis and Feminism*, 377.

14. *Generation* is defined by most dictionaries as the "1. Act or process of producing offspring; procreation. 2. (a) A single stage in the succession of natural descent; hence the body of men, animals, or plants of the same genealogical rank or remove from an ancestor. (b) The ordinary period of time at which one rank follows another, or father is succeeded by child" (*Webster's New Collegiate Dictionary*).

15. MacInnes, *End of Masculinity*, 64.

16. For an extended account of the interrelationship between capitalist society and the individual, and its inscription in private life, see Eli Zaretzky, *Capitalism,*

the Family, and Personal Life. For an interesting analysis applied to film, see Chuck Kleinhans, "Notes on Melodrama and the Family Under Capitalism," *Film Reader* 3 (February 1978): 40–47.

17. Dinnerstein, *The Mermaid and the Minotaur: Sexual Arrangements and Human Malaise*, 50n.

18. Ibid., 111. In light of our observation that Simba to an extent resembles Shakespeare's Prince Hamlet, a comment by Janet Adelman in her essay, "'Man and Wife Is One Flesh': *Hamlet* and the Confrontation with the Maternal Body," is worth quoting here, for the way in which she draws attention to a fantasy of female sexuality as maternal and engulfing (with its potential for incestuous nightmare): "What the idealized father ultimately protects against is the dangerous female powers of the night. The boy-child masters his fear of these powers partly through identification with his father, the paternal presence who has initially helped him to achieve separation from his mother" (274).

19. Freud, *Analysis Terminable and Interminable*, SE 23:251.

20. Nala's compensation later for being excluded from the public sphere will be to have a baby. (Cf. Freud, ibid.: "the appeased wish for a penis is destined to be converted into a wish for a baby and for a husband, who possesses a penis.")

21. Freud, "Creative Writers and Day-Dreaming," SE 9:150.

22. It should be clear by now that my analysis of the film is focused on the repressed unconscious ideas that surround the events of Simba's life. As Mitchell puts it, "The Oedipus complex is the *repressed* ideas that appertain to the family drama of any primary constellation of figures within which the child must find its place. It is not the *actual* family situation or the conscious desire it evokes" (Mitchell, *Psychoanalysis and Feminism*, 63).

23. Freud, *New Introductory Lectures on Psycho-Analysis*, SE 22:67.

24. In "Looking at Obstacles" (*On Kissing, Tickling, and Being Bored: Psychoanalytic Essays on the Unexamined Life*), Adam Phillips observes that "it is impossible to imagine desire without obstacles, and wherever we find something to be an obstacle we are at the same time desiring" (83). It becomes clear very quickly in *Tarzan, the Ape Man* that the Mutea Escarpment—this obstacle—is "a way of not letting something else happen, a necessary blind spot" (ibid.). Phillips goes on to comment that "it is part of the fascination of the Oedipus story in particular, and perhaps of narrative in general, that we never know whether obstacles create desire, or desire creates obstacles. We are never quite sure which it is we are seeking" (ibid.). The escarpment, like the "northern border" of the Pride Lands in *The Lion King*, means different things depending on whose desire we are talking about. If, as Phillips remarks, "desire without obstacles is merging or incest, and so the death of desire" (ibid.), we can see how the escarpment and the elephant graveyard that lies beyond it are available to a number of readings that overlap in their application to both Jane and her father.

25. Krzysztof Wodiczko evokes this dialectic in an essay on memorial architecture, in which "the ultimate social definition of the form of the father's body" is an "imperturbable, unshaken, inflexible, sober-minded, sexless and lifeless, silent, cold, odorous with death, ghastly pale (all blood transfused to the state's disposal), tired but powerful and self-disciplined, disciplining structure. The body of an unmoving father, barricading vast social territory, creates heavy traffic, the traffic which the father will then regulate himself. His lifelessness will regulate life; his sexlessness wants to castrate." Wodiczko, "Public Projections," *October* 38 (Fall 1986): 6.

26. Burgin, "Man–Desire–Image," 32.

27. As Benjamin reminds us, "The figures of mother and father are cultural ideals, but they need not be played by 'biological' mothers and fathers, or even by women and men" (*Bonds of Love*, 105). So too are the "maternal function" and "maternal body" not necessarily found in, or offered by, a biological mother—as *Tarzan, the Ape Man* famously demonstrates. *Tarzan* tells us nothing about Jane's biological mother; but this, as we have said, is not really the point, since we are talking about object relations, and anything we may wish to say about Jane's flesh-and-blood mother will have to be drawn from inference.

28. Rutherford, *Men's Silences: Predicaments in Masculinity*, 146.

29. Freud, "Creative Writers and Day-Dreaming," *SE* 9:147.

30. As an "original fantasy" (Freud), the graveyard provides a representation of, and solution to, one of the major enigmas that confront the child—the origin of the difference between the sexes. We also note that in this scene Simba does save Nala from capture and death. Falling behind, Nala calls to Simba for help, and he turns just in time to swipe one of the hyenas across the face with his claws, drawing blood, and momentarily arresting her predator's deadly pursuit. Nala is hanging by her front paws over the edge of a bone-strewn cliff, with Simba above her. This particular representation of mortal danger—of being at the limit, on an edge, a border—is one that will be repeated twice more in the film (it occurs in *Tarzan* also, when Jane falls off the Mutea Escarpment, on their way to the elephant graveyard): when Mufasa is threatened by the stampeding wildebeests and implores his brother for help; and later when Simba finds himself in the same position, and discovers that it was really Scar who killed his father. As an important moment in the long process of the resolution of Simba's oedipal struggles, this one articulates the way in which Simba will learn to make Nala represent his "lack."

31. Dinnerstein, *The Mermaid and the Minotaur*, 121.

32. The last shot of *Tarzan* is not unlike that of *The Lion King*, but much stranger: Jane and Tarzan standing together on a rocky rise, with a chimpanzee in Jane's arms.

33. Paternal recognition has a defensive aspect, Benjamin notes. With it the child denies dependency and dissociates himself from his previous maternal tie (as we see when Sarabi tries to bathe Simba, and he protests: "Mom! You're messing

up my mane!"). "Recognition of himself in the father is what enables the boy to deny helplessness, to feel he is powerful, to protect himself from the loss of the grandiosity he enjoyed in the practicing phase. When the boy is not actively playing daddy, he flies about, announcing his new name—Superman" (Benjamin, *Bonds of Love*, 104).

34. Andrew Britton, "Blissing Out: The Politics of Reaganite Entertainment," 24.

35. Pollitt, "Subject to Debate," 9.

36. Dinnerstein, *The Mermaid and the Minotaur*, 87.

37. In a manner that blurs questions of emphasis, Bettelheim wrote that when a man "tries to find greater fulfillment of his fatherhood by doing more for the child along the lines only mothers used to follow, the result is that he finds less rather than more fulfillment, not only for his fatherhood, but also for his manhood. . . . The relationship between father and child never was and cannot now be built principally around child-caring experiences. It is built around a man's function in society: moral, economic, political." Bettelheim quoted by Larry May and Robert A. Strikwerda in "Fatherhood and Nurturance," in May and Strikwerda, eds., *Rethinking Masculinity: Philosophical Explorations in Light of Feminism*, 85.

38. These allusions are, of course, to the famous presidential slogans by George Bush and Theodore Roosevelt, respectively. The real issue, as in Freud's essay "A Child Is Being Beaten" (1919; in *SE* 17), is who does the beating and who gets beaten with this big stick.

39. Bly, *Iron John*, 121.

40. Burgin, "Man–Desire–Image," 34.

41. Dinnerstein, *The Mermaid and the Minotaur*, 49.

42. Benjamin, *Bonds of Love*, 106.

43. There is also the sense in which the cub's ambivalent feelings toward his father are divided and displaced into two characters—Mufasa and Scar—a not uncommon narrative/psychological strategy which I discuss below.

44. Freud, *The Interpretation of Dreams* (1908 Preface), *SE* 4:xxvi.

45. Laplanche and Pontalis, *The Language of Psycho-Analysis*, 234.

46. Pumbaa's use of the phrase "passing craze" is an allusion to popular psychology's description—employed usually by anxious parents—of a period in adolescence marked by sexual experimentation (homosexuality, in particular) as a "passing phase."

47. "Parrish's creatures live in a pre-sexual wonderland," writes Maurice Sendak in his introduction to *The Maxfield Parrish Poster Book* (Project Planning by Woody Gelman and Len Brown). "Robust sexuality was the dark cloud that never tainted the heavenly blue of a Parrish sky" (5). At ground level, in medium shot, Pumbaa and Timon's "humble home" looks more like the jungle paintings of Henri Rousseau, but without the sinister presence of other creatures lurking in the shadows.

48. As Barbara Ehrenreich notes in *The Hearts of Men: American Dreams and the Flight from Commitment,* "The ultimate reason why a man would not just 'walk out the door'" in the 1950s and early 1960s "was the taint of homosexuality which was likely to follow him. Homosexuality, as the psychiatrists saw it, was the ultimate escapism" (24). Echoes of this peculiar understanding of homosexuality (and of heterosexuality) persist to the present day, often in an accusatory tone that reveals how deeply entrenched is the notion that the truly masculine man is a breadwinner, or at the very least, heterosexual. Consider Molly Haskell's famous remarks in her landmark study, *From Reverence to Rape: The Treatment of Women in the Movies* (2d ed., 1987), on the subject of "love in which men understand and support each other, speak the same language, and risk their lives to gain each other's respect": "But this is also a delusion . . . this is the easiest of loves: a love that is adolescent, presexual, tacit, the love of one's *semblable,* one's mirror reflection" (24).

Among psychoanalysts who have criticized phallocentrism as precisely a homosexual enterprise, Julia Kristeva is perhaps the most antagonistic: "And we know the role that the pervert—invincibly believing in the maternal phallus, obstinately refusing the existence of the other sex—has been able to play in antisemitism and the totalitarian movements that embrace it. Let us remember the fascist or socialist homosexual community (and all homosexual communities for whom there is no 'other race'), inevitably flanked by a community of Amazons who have forgotten the war of the sexes and identify with the paternal word and its serpent" (*About Chinese Women,* 23).

49. As Pumbaa and Timon start singing their "Hakuna Matata" song, Timon takes one of Simba's paws and files off a claw. Just as "Oedipus" means "swollen foot," which may be interpreted as an allusion to an erect penis—such as Sándor Ferenczi notes when he posits that "the myth completely identifies with a phallus the man who achieved the monstrous feat of sexual intercourse with the mother" (quoted in Peter L. Rudnytsky, *Freud and Oedipus,* 261)—the extension and retraction of lions' claws in this film constitute a fairly consistent semiotic referring to the activity of the libido. That Scar's claws are invariably extended is an unambiguous sign of the aggressiveness of his desire ("My teeth and ambitions are bared," he sings). Simba, during this period of his life, will not be needing his claws.

50. Phillips, "Worrying and Its Discontents" (in *On Kissing, Tickling, and Being Bored*), 51. Subsequent page numbers will be cited in the text.

51. Poster, *Critical Theory of the Family,* 25–26.

52. Hocquenghem, *Homosexual Desire,* 98. Subsequent page numbers will be cited in the text.

53. Moreover, when Pumbaa and Timon first take Simba in, comfort him, and try to distract him from his misery, they prop him on his back on a bed of leaves.

The image recalls an early moment in the film when, just prior to Simba's "baptism," Rafiki rattles his gourds above the infant cub in his mother's arms, and the cub looks up in distracted wonder. The reader's attention is drawn to an observation Freud makes regarding the sexual object during early infancy: "All through the period of latency children learn to feel for other people who help them in their helplessness and satisfy their needs a love which is on the model of, and a continuation of, their relation as sucklings to their nursing mother" (*Three Essays on the Theory of Sexuality*, SE 7:222–23).

54. Ibid., *SE* 7:222.

55. Timon's choice of the word "disaster" is ironically appropriate in this context (of the sung assessment that "the world, for once, [is] in perfect harmony"), considering that the etymology of *disaster* is: a falling away from the stars.

56. Adelman, "'Man and Wife Is One Flesh,'" 275.

57. Ibid., 263.

58. A case can be made for Scar as a Freudian homosexual, or at least a lion with what Freud would call "disturbances of the sexual instinct." Consider the following remarks by Freud in "Some Neurotic Mechanisms in Jealousy, Paranoia, and Homosexuality": "Observation has directed my attention to several cases in which during early childhood impulses of jealousy, derived from the mother-complex and of very great intensity, arose [in a boy] against rivals, usually older brothers. This jealousy led to an exceedingly hostile and aggressive attitude towards these brothers which might sometimes reach the pitch of actual death-wishes, but which could not maintain themselves in the face of the subject's further development. Under the influences of upbringing—and certainly not uninfluenced also by their own continuing powerlessness—these impulses yielded to repression and underwent a transformation, so that the rivals of the earlier period became the first homosexual love-objects" (*SE* 18:231).

59. David Gutmann, "Male Envy Across the Life-Span," in Burke, ed., *Gender and Envy*, 269.

60. Benjamin, *Bonds of Love*, 111. It is interesting to note that the film does not show female envy of male prerogatives. Instead—among the lions, at least—Scar becomes the repository of all envious feelings. Female submission to male authority is understood therefore to be normal and desirable, while male envy is conflated with homosexuality and a variety of evils (to the extent that Scar, as Pumbaa and Timon's corrupt opposite, is a signifier of "bad" homosexuality).

61. Stimpson, "Foreword," in Brod, ed., *The Making of Masculinities*, xii.

62. Cf. "Ideology and Ideological State Apparatuses," where Louis Althusser reminds us that in Marxist theory, "the State Apparatus contains: the Government, the Administration, the Army, the Police, the Courts, the Prisons, etc."—almost all of which, in *The Lion King*, are combined in the institution of the monarchy and

embodied in the king—which "'functions by violence'—at least ultimately (since repression, e.g., administrative repression, may take non-physical forms)" (142–43). Althusser further clarifies: "All the State Apparatuses function both by repression and by ideology, with the difference that the (Repressive) State Apparatus functions massively and predominantly by repression, whereas the Ideological State Apparatuses function massively and predominantly by ideology" (149).

63. Upon this remark, the viewer cannot help wondering if Zazu himself is a gay uncle. In any case, it should be noted that Zazu, like Scar, is English. There is a tradition of the English majordomo in American popular narratives involving a hero team (we may include Batman and his majordomo Alfred as a "hero team"); and in a discussion about the ideological construction of masculinity in television, John Fiske makes some observations that are applicable to the relationship between Mufasa and Zazu: "Higgins in *Magnum, P.I.* is English, embodying variously the meanings of tradition, of the old-fashioned, of weakness, of excessive submission to authority and convention. These traits can be used for comic effect, but can just as frequently be used as ideological underwriters of the more aggressive, pragmatic, even amoral American values embodied in Magnum himself" (Fiske, "British Cultural Studies and Television," 264).

64. In another (the ideological) sense, of course, Scar does have a function in the maintenance of the hetero-familial order—as Judith Roof observes: "Both male and female homosexual, according to Freud, reinforce and sustain the centrality of the father, which is the covert function of familial narratives anyway" (*Come As You Are*, 100). Or as Richard Dyer puts it: "Where gayness occurs in films it does so as *part of* dominant ideology. It is not there to express itself, but rather to express something about sexuality in general *as understood by heterosexuals*. Gayness is used to define normality, to suggest the thrill and/or terror of decadence, to embody neurotic sexuality, or to perform various artistic-ideological functions that in the end assert the superiority of heterosexuality" ("Rejecting Straight Ideals: Gays in Film," in Steven, ed., *Jump Cut: Hollywood, Politics, and Counter-Cinema*, 294).

65. This is an allusion to the line spoken by Jeremy Irons in *Reversal of Fortune* (Barbet Schroeder, 1990), in his Oscar-winning performance as the enigmatic and sinister Claus von Bülow, who was accused of attempting to murder his wealthy socialite wife Sunny.

66. Garber, *Vested Interests: Cross-Dressing and Cultural Anxiety*, 121.

67. Lacan, quoted in ibid., 121.

68. Cf. Freud's comments in *Three Essays on the Theory of Sexuality* about the "unmistakable feeling of *disgust*" which protects the individual from accepting perverse sexual aims (notwithstanding the fact that the limits of such disgust are "often purely conventional") (*SE* 7:151); and his observation that, while "visual impressions remain the most frequent pathway along which libidinal excitation is

aroused," it remains a fact that "we never regard the genitals themselves, which produce the strongest sexual excitation, as really 'beautiful'" (156n2).

69. Like Pumbaa's flatulence, these roiling liquids and gases that explode and hiss from fissures and holes in the ground express the idea of desires that cannot be contained, that exceed the boundaries of society's norms, that transgress.

70. The protagonist, Pink, has nightmarish visions/memories of his lonely childhood; he desperately misses his dead father, and remembers his mother as an overbearing figure; and he fantasizes about being a fascist, skinhead leader.

71. Mitchell, *Psychoanalysis and Feminism*, 210.

72. Cf. Susan Sontag's "Fascinating Fascism" in *Under the Sign of Saturn* (also reprinted in vol. 2 of Nichols, ed., *Movies and Methods*). Much of what Sontag has to say about fascist ideals and aesthetics applies to Mufasa's command over the creatures of the Pride Lands. For example: "A utopian aesthetics (identity as a biological given) implies an ideal eroticism (sexuality converted into the magnetism of leaders and the joy of followers)" (41). Elsewhere in her essay, Sontag identifies fascism as standing for an ideal in which intellect is repudiated and "the family of man (under the parenthood of leaders)" is celebrated (43). See also Matt Roth, "A Short History of Disney-Fascism," *Jump Cut* 40 (March 1996): 15–20.

73. Burgess, "If Oedipus Had Read His Lévi-Strauss," 259 (quoted in Rudnytsky, *Freud and Oedipus*, 246).

74. Quoted by Claire Johnston, "Towards a Feminist Film Practice: Some Theses," in Nichols, *Movies and Methods* 2:320.

75. On Rafiki's function as a kind of priest, cf. Phyllis Chesler's insight into why it is so important for kings and contemporary political leaders to show or claim obedience to higher heavenly authority: "The sight of a king, dictator, or oligarch kneeling before a male God, a male paternal authority, somehow obscures the inequality between male leaders and male followers. The ruler's obeisance before 'higher authority' is meant to appease any chaos or insurrection born of humiliation and inequality among the ranks of male followers. Even the king, even the president, accepts the will, the authority, of a 'higher' male figure. Thus are all men really equal." Chesler, *About Men*, 208.

76. Sophocles does not actually cite the Sphinx's riddle in the text of *Oedipus the King*, yet as Peter Rudnytsky points out in *Freud and Oedipus* (265), there can be no doubt that Sophocles assumed the riddle to be familiar to his audience and that it is deeply embedded in the dramatic action. In its simplest formulation, the riddle asks: What creature has four feet in the morning, two at midday, and three in the evening? To which Oedipus replies: Man, who in infancy crawls on all fours, who walks upright on two feet in maturity, and in his old age supports himself with a stick.

77. Rudnytsky, *Freud and Oedipus*, 246–47.

78. Ehrenreich, *The Hearts of Men*, 11–12.

79. In *Holy Smoke*, Kate Winslet plays a young woman from suburban Sydney, Australia, who joins an ashram in India. Her family, fearing that she has joined a "cult," get her back to Sydney on a false pretense and then hold her under a form of house arrest, while a hired "cult exiter" (Harvey Keitel) tries to persuade her, in effect, that Australia is "home" (and that he, a white American in his fifties, is more desirable than her Indian guru), and that she should not return to India.

80. Again, I am indebted to Peter Brooks's chapter, "Freud's Masterplot: A Model for Narrative," which uses Todorov's well-known essay in structural narratology, "Narrative Transformations," as a springboard for a discussion of Freud's "Beyond the Pleasure Principle," which Brooks suggests is a model that might "provide a synthetic and comprehensive grasp of the workings of plot, in the most general sense, and of the uses for plot" (90).

81. The viewer will recall the opening shots of the film, in which, as the song begins ("From the day we arrive on the planet"), we see a mother giraffe crest a hill (as if emerging from the earth itself), followed by her baby, blinking in the sun— an image that launches the autochthonous motif.

82. Henry Krips, *Fetish: An Erotics of Culture*, 68. Subsequent page numbers will be cited in the text.

83. "*The Lion King*: Fact Sheet." Clippings Archive, Museum of Modern Art Film Study Center, New York City.

84. Ibid.

3. To "Have Known Ecstasy":
Hunting Men in *The Most Dangerous Game*

1. Virginia Wright Wexman, *Creating the Couple: Love, Marriage, and Hollywood Performance*, ix.

2. Freud, "Hysterical Phantasies and Their Relation to Bisexuality," *SE* 9:159.

3. Richard Connell, "The Most Dangerous Game," in *O. Henry Memorial Award Prize Stories of 1924*, 71–92. Subsequent page numbers will be cited in the text.

4. Connell, "The Most Dangerous Game," 92.

5. John G. Cawelti, *Adventure, Mystery, and Romance: Formula Stories as Art and Popular Culture*, 39–40.

6. Indeed, Connell's story is described in the introduction to the *O. Henry Memorial Award* volume as being "distinctive among the year's horror stories. One judge wrote of it: 'Impossible situation, of course, but most interesting to the last word.' Another recalled that it absorbed 100 per cent of his attention, provoked him to sit erect and hold his breath while awaiting the outcome of the struggle to

the death between the champion hunters, Rainsford and General Zaroff. In its final phases the struggle is over-condensed, but the ultimate thrill more than compensates. Poe would have envied the author this tale" (xi).

7. Robin Wood, *Hollywood from Vietnam to Reagan*, 82.

8. Bruce Kawin, "Children of the Light." In Grant, ed., *Film Genre Reader*, 237–38.

9. Thierry Kuntzel, "The Film-Work, 2," *Camera Obscura* 5 (Spring 1980): 35.

10. Cf. Orville Goldner and George E. Turner, *The Making of King Kong: The Story Behind a Film Classic*, in which the authors discuss the fact that *The Most Dangerous Game* was made at the same time as *King Kong*, and that *The Most Dangerous Game* is based on an "ingenious adaptation" of Richard Connell's award-winning short story of 1924.

11. Marty Roth, "Homosexual Expression and Homophobic Censorship," in Bergman, ed., *Camp Grounds: Style and Homosexuality*, 272.

12. Chesler, *About Men*, 155.

13. Kawin, "Children of the Light," 241.

14. Kuntzel, "The Film-Work, 2," 9.

15. Deleuze and Guattari, *Anti-Oedipus*, 78.

16. Adrienne Rich, "Compulsory Heterosexuality and Lesbian Existence," *Signs* 5.4 (1980): 631–60.

17. Chesler, *About Men*, 239.

18. Freud, "Some Neurotic Mechanisms in Jealousy, Paranoia, and Homosexuality," *SE* 18:232.

19. Rhona J. Berenstein, "Attack of the Leading Ladies: The Masks of Gender, Sexuality, and Race in Classic Horror Cinema" (Ph.D. diss., University of California, 1992), 292. Berenstein's book, *Attack of the Leading Ladies: Gender, Sexuality, and Spectatorship in Classic Horror Cinema*, based on her dissertation, does not contain this passage.

20. David Leverenz, *Manhood and the American Renaissance*, 73. Subsequent page numbers will be cited in the text.

21. It is not surprising that the evil Dr. Moreau in *The Island of Lost Souls* (1933) is a soft and corpulent man (played by Charles Laughton), while the man whom he perceives as a sexual challenge is young and handsome (played by Richard Arlen). Like Count Zaroff in *The Most Dangerous Game*, Laughton's Dr. Moreau is portrayed as a man who cannot compete with good looks and youth, and so resorts to cruelty and cunning (to seduce/impress the younger man).

22. Constance Penley, "Time Travel, Primal Scene, and the Critical Dystopia," *Camera Obscura* 15 (Fall 1986): 75.

23. Kuntzel, "The Film-Work, 2."

24. Freud, "The Economic Problem of Masochism," *SE* 19:169.

25. Kuntzel, "The Film-Work, 2," 55–56.

26. The repetition of the word "dread" is striking in view of its resonances in psychoanalytic writing. Consider the following preamble to Kristeva's analysis of Freud's thesis that the morality of man starts with the two taboos of totemism, *murder* and *incest*: "*Totem and Taboo* begins with an evocation of the 'dread of incest,' and Freud discusses it at length in connection with food and sex prohibitions. The woman- or mother-image haunts a large part of that book and keeps shaping its background even when, relying on the testimony of obsessional neurotics, Freud slips from dread (p. 23: 'His incest dread'; p. 24: 'the incest dread of savages'; p. 161: 'The interpretation of incest dread,' 'This dread of incest') to the inclusion of dread symptom in obsessional neurosis. At the same time he leaves off speculating on incest ('we do not know the origin of incest dread and do not even know how to guess at it,' p. 162) in order to center his conclusion in the second taboo, the one against murder, which he reveals to be the murder of the father" (Kristeva, *The Powers of Horror: An Essay on Abjection*, 57). It is worth noting, also, that Barry Keith Grant has edited an excellent anthology bearing the title, *The Dread of Difference: Gender and the Horror Film* (Austin: University of Texas Press, 1996).

27. Freud described the fetishist as someone who both believes in the "reality" of castration and refuses to believe it. As the little boy in Octave Mannoni's example says, "I know very well, but all the same . . . " (O. Mannoni, "'Je sais bien . . . mais quand même': La Croyance," *Les Temps Modernes* 212 [1964]: 1262–86).

28. General Zaroff, who becomes Count Zaroff in the film, bears more than a passing resemblance to that famous vampire of legend, literature, and film: Count Dracula. Consider the following description of the Dracula figure in Alain Silver and James Ursini's *The Vampire Film*: "The dark clothes and full-flowing red-lined cape, the hair brushed back straight and flat from the forehead, the lips extraordinarily crimson and distended in an eerie smile which reveals abnormally long canines" (61). In "Dark Desires: Male Masochism in the Horror Film" (in Cohan and Hark, eds., *Screening the Male: Exploring Masculinities in Hollywood Cinema*, 118–133), Barbara Creed describes Count Dracula as being depicted usually "as a sinister but seductive heterosexual male who dwells in a Gothic castle characterized by long winding stairs, dark corridors, cobwebs, and a crypt or cellar containing his coffin. . . . [In John Badham's *Dracula* (1979)] Dracula is a sleek, elegant, aristocratic figure who wears a flowing black cloak, with red lining, speaks in softly modulated tones and glides silently through the dark on his nocturnal journeys. He is linked with images of bats, spiders, rats, and the deadly *vagina dentata*" (122).

29. Cf. Freud, "A Special Type of Choice of Object Made by Men," *SE* 11:165–75.

30. Kuntzel, "The Film-Work, 2," 17.

31. Kristeva, *Powers of Horror*, 58.

32. Ibid. There is a chance relevance of this allusion to Louis-Ferdinand Céline's *Journey to the End of the Night* in that the hunt takes place at night, with the dawn signaling the survivor's victory.

33. Louise J. Kaplan, *Female Perversions: The Temptations of Emma Bovary*, 9.

34. Kristeva, *Powers of Horror*, 35 (emphasis in original).

35. Mark Simpson, *Male Impersonators: Men Performing Masculinity*, 73 (emphasis in original).

36. Jacques Lacan, "The Mirror Stage as Formative of the Function of the I as Revealed in Psychoanalytic Experience," *Écrits: A Selection*, 1–7.

37. Cf. ch. 5, this volume ("Looking for the 'Great Whatsit': *Kiss Me Deadly* and Film Noir").

38. Because of the radical absence of the woman in Zaroff's narrative, I am inclined to agree here with Susan Lurie's argument in "Pornography and the Dread of Women: The Male Sexual Dilemma" (in Laura Lederer, ed., *Take Back the Night*, 159–73), that castration fear is first generated by the mother and not the father.

39. The intertext of the gruesome, real-life story of how Tsar Nicholas II and his family were trapped and shot like animals by the Bolsheviks in July 1918 at Ekaterinburg gives another troubling dimension to Zaroff's mania for hunting. Although he is a character invented by a journalist born in Poughkeepsie, New York, Zaroff can be seen as a man who is trying to exorcise, in his own dire game of mastery, this humiliation and death of parental figures; or, he can be read as the projection of an author of a particularly sadistic family romance, in which the parents are punished in a manner that is indistinguishable from impulses that produce pornography.

40. Kaplan, *Female Perversions*, 10.

41. In the movie, Zaroff describes how he built his fortress on the ruins of an old Spanish fortress that was on the island when he bought it.

42. Janine Chasseguet-Smirgel, *Creativity and Perversion*, 12.

43. As a response to "the blows dealt to his narcissistic dreams and fantasies of omnipotence," and to the disillusionment of discovering the ordinariness of his parents, a child will attempt to "compensate for these assaults upon his self-esteem by imagining himself to be an adopted foundling. Although tied to the ordinary life of his ordinary 'foster parents,' he imagines that in reality he is the unique offspring of exceptional (usually royal) parents." Vlada Petric, "Psychological Evolution of the Pop Film Hero: From Tarzan to Superman," *Film/Psychology Review* 4.2 (Summer-Fall 1980): 222.

44. This last remark situates the story historically and is a clue to the possible model for Zaroff. In *Côte d'Azur: Inventing the French Riviera*, Mary Blume writes: "With the outbreak of war in 1914, the world changed even, to a degree, on the . . . Côte d'Azur. In Monte Carlo, the SBM [Société des Bains de Mer] lost, *morts pour*

la patrie, 87 French employees, 93 Italians, 9 Belgians, and no Monagasques. Sir Basil Zaharoff, the detested and widely honored arms merchant, further enriched by supplying arms to both sides, had already bought heavily into the SBM in preparation for taking over the throne with his Spanish mistress, later wife. When she died he lost interest but he gave Monaco a lasting legacy, its first proper constitution, drawn up for Zaharoff by his friend, the French Prime Minister Georges Clemenceau, in 1918" (69). Elsewhere in the book, Blume writes of the Russians who opened tea shops.

45. The parallels between Zaroff and Bruce Wayne/Batman will be obvious to the reader.

46. Leverenz, *Manhood*, 306.

47. Thomas Strychacz, "Trophy-Hunting as a Trope of Manhood in Ernest Hemingway's *Green Hills of Africa,*" *Hemingway Review* 13.1 (Fall 1993): 37.

48. Leverenz, *Manhood*, 73.

49. Ibid. Certainly, Rainsford's conscious self is "sensible." At the beginning of the film, when the men on the ship discuss the fact that "the channel lights aren't just in the position given on the chart," the doctor says, "I think we should turn back and take the outside course." Rainsford appears inclined to agree with the doctor, saying, "Now, wait a minute, fellahs, let's talk this over! There's no use taking any chances!"

50. Gore Vidal, "Notes on Pornography," in Buchen, ed., *The Perverse Imagination: Sexuality and Literary Culture*, 132. The theme, of course, is not peculiar to pornography, nor does it define as pornographic a work in which it appears—as Vidal's own *Myra Breckinridge* attests.

51. The rather camp quality of the film, typical of jungle pictures of the 1930s as we view them now, is conveyed in the following description, in which the significance of Zaroff's scar is explained with charming simplicity: "Standing among the exaggerated shadows of his big-game trophies as he chats with his guests, he absently runs his fingers over the scar that symbolises his madness. His eyes glisten with tears when he realizes that the only man in the world he dared to hope would share his mania considers him insane, and he seems genuinely hurt when the woman he admires upbraids him for murdering her brother. In the jungle, garbed in black hunting togs, he becomes an unfettered savage as he races through the fog, gleefully sounding the horn to summon the hounds to the kill." Goldner and Turner, *The Making of King Kong*, 73.

52. Strychacz, "Trophy-Hunting," 36.

53. Neal King, *Heroes in Hard Times: Cop Action Movies in the U.S.*, 175.

54. Freud, *Civilization and Its Discontents*, SE 21:111.

55. Kristeva, *Powers of Horror*, 88.

56. Lacan, *The Seminar, Book I*, 221–23

4. Friendship and Its Discontents: *The Outlaw*

1. Leonard Maltin, ed., *Leonard Maltin's Movie and Video Guide, 2000 Edition.*

2. Edward Buscombe, ed., *The BFI Companion to the Western*, 43. In Tom Ryall's description of the film in part 3 of *The BFI Companion*, he acknowledges that "it is usually Howard Hughes' calculated exploitation of Jane Russell's celebrated physique that dominates discussion of the picture," but observes that "its centre of interest seems often to lie elsewhere," and that the narrative "focuses on the jealousies of a small male group."

3. Parker Tyler, "The Horse: Totem Animal of Male Power—An Essay in the Straight-camp Style," in *Sex Psyche Etcetera in the Film*, 29–38.

4. David Thomson, *A Biographical Dictionary of Film*, 356.

5. For a brief account of *The Outlaw*'s unusual production history and publicity campaign, see Tony Thomas, *Howard Hughes in Hollywood.*

6. George N. Fenin and William K. Everson, *The Western: From Silents to the Seventies*, 266–67 (emphasis in original).

7. Ibid., 266. For an account of *The Outlaw*'s censorship problems, see chapter 6 of *The Dame in the Kimono: Hollywood, Censorship, and the Production Code from the 1920s to the 1960s* by Leonard J. Leff and Jerold L. Simmons.

8. J. Hoberman, "On How the Western Was Lost," *Village Voice*, August 27, 1991; reprinted in Jameson, ed., *They Went Thataway: Redefining Film Genres*, 51.

9. Vidal wrote another version of the same story as a TV film called *Gore Vidal's Billy the Kid* (1989), directed by William A. Graham and starring Val Kilmer. The tag line for the film is: "He Was a Cold-Blooded Killer and the All-American Boy."

10. Jane Tompkins, *West of Everything: The Inner Life of Westerns*, 45.

11. Douglas Pye, "Introduction: Criticism and the Western," in Cameron and Pye, eds., *The Book of Westerns*, 12.

12. Both the 1923 and 1929 films were adapted from *The Virginian; a Play in Four Acts* (1923) by Owen Wister and Kirk La Shelle. The most recent adaptation of *The Virginian*, directed by and starring Bill Pullman, was made in 2000 by TNT for television.

13. Tompkins, *West of Everything*, 151.

14. Leslie A. Fiedler, *Love and Death in the American Novel*, 209.

15. Pam Cook, "Women and the Western," in Kitses and Rickman, eds., *The Western Reader*, 296.

16. Martin Pumphrey, quoted in Buscombe, ed., *BFI Companion to the Western*, 182.

17. Dana Polan questions whether the oedipal trajectory that Raymond Bellour sees as central to American film narrative ("a logic that endlessly retells a story in which two people, man and woman, become a single unit, a marital couple") has

ideological relevance in the new space of late capitalism. Polan observes that in "films of the forties—a period that many sociologists take to be pivotal for the development of a society focused on modes of production—we can see a certain disavowal of Oedipus, of the formation of a domestic unit as the psychoanalytically necessary answer to initial narrative problems." Dana Polan, "Brief Encounters: Mass Culture and the Evacuation of Sense," in Modleski, ed., *Studies in Entertainment*, 179.

18. Peter Murphy, "Friendship's Eu-topia," *South Atlantic Quarterly* 97.1 (Winter 1998): 180–81.

19. Murphy, "Friendship's Eu-topia," 175.

20. Emphasis added.

21. Thomas, *Howard Hughes in Hollywood*, 84. See also Nick Barbaro, "*The Outlaw* (1943)," *CinemaTexas Program Notes* 13.3 (November 15, 1977): 61–66. (The other half of the story, according to a Jane Russell interview that appears in a TCM documentary about Hughes, is that as a director Hughes often had difficulty explaining what he wanted in a scene, and during shooting would waste a great deal of time on details that prolonged production of the film. Hughes was almost obsessively preoccupied with the making of the movie, she suggests, but did not follow industry practice when it came to budgets and schedules.)

22. Murphy, "Friendship's Eu-topia," 172.

23. Philip French, *Westerns*, 16–17.

24. Thomson, *Biographical Dictionary of Film*, 362.

25. Eisenschitz, quoted by Buscombe, ed., *BFI Companion to the Western*, 126.

26. Thomson, *Biographical Dictionary of Film*, 362.

27. Lee Clark Mitchell, *Westerns: Making the Man in Fiction and Film*, 167.

28. Martin Pumphrey, "Why Do Cowboys Wear Hats in the Bath? Style Politics for the Older Man," in Cameron and Pye, eds., *The Book of Westerns*, 56.

29. Buscombe, ed., *BFI Companion to the Western*, 127.

30. Warshow, "Movie Chronicle," 153.

31. Paul Willemen, "Voyeurism" (1976), cited in Neale, *Genre*, 57.

32. Willemen, "Anthony Mann: Looking at the Male" (1981), in Kitses and Rickman, eds., *The Western Reader*, 211.

33. Neale, *Genre*, 57.

34. Pye, "Introduction," 18.

35. Jane Marie Gaines and Charlotte Cornelia Herzog, "The Fantasy of Authenticity in Western Costume," in Buscombe and Pearson, eds., *Back in the Saddle Again*, 179.

36. To be more precise, both men are bathed in the strong light of late afternoon. Doc looks *up* at Billy (the young man at the dawn of his adult life), and Billy looks down at Doc (the older man in the late afternoon of his life).

37. Louis A. Ruprecht, Jr., "Homeric Wisdom and Heroic Friendship," *South Atlantic Quarterly* 97.1 (Winter 1998): 40.

38. Cf. Jim Kitses, *Horizons West*, 11.

39. I do not mean to be confusing: the film leaves the question open as to whether Pat and Doc are (former) lovers; or whether Pat is a repressed homosexual; and whether Doc was always gay, or is only now "coming out" in middle age.

40. Murphy, "Friendship's Eu-topia," 170.

41. Ruprecht, "Homeric Wisdom and Heroic Friendship," 47–48.

42. Tompkins, *West of Everything*, 39.

43. Eve Kosofsky Sedgwick, *Between Men: English Literature and Male Homosocial Desire*, 15.

44. Sedgwick, *Between Men*, 6.

45. Agnes Heller, "The Beauty of Friendship," *South Atlantic Quarterly* 97.1 (Winter 1998): 16–17.

46. Murphy, "Friendship's Eu-topia," 174.

47. Pye, "Introduction," 18.

48. James L. Smith, *Melodrama*, 21. The point I am trying to make here is that the drama revolves around Billy not because of anything he *does* (his theft of Doc's horse notwithstanding), but because of what he *is* (the object of somebody else's fascinated interest).

49. Laura Mulvey, "Afterthoughts on 'Visual Pleasure and Narrative Cinema' Inspired by *Duel in the Sun* (King Vidor, 1946)," *Framework* 15–16–17 (1981): 12–15.

50. Vladimir Propp, *Morphology of the Folktale*, trans. Laurence Scott (1968).

51. Mulvey, "Afterthoughts," 14.

52. Of course, one is uneasy about the Freudian notion that such a choice as Doc and Billy make should be described as "narcissistic," or as a "phase of play and fantasy"—but only because the normative heterosexual object-choice of the Freudian paradigm of "mature" sexuality is homophobic in its characterization of homosexuality as narcissistic, or as an arrested stage of development.

53. Mann quoted in Cook, "Women and the Western," 293.

54. Boetticher, quoted in ibid., 293.

55. See Bellour's remarks in an interview with Janet Bergstrom, "Alternation, Segmentation, Hypnosis" (*Camera Obscura* 3–4 [Summer 1979]: 71–103): "On the one hand, the function of the woman in the organization and the motivations of the narrative is far more determining than is often thought. . . . . On the other hand, the western is subtended from one end to the other by what one can call the problematic of marriage" (88). Bellour goes on to discuss the example of William Wyler's *The Westerner* (1940): "At the end, the hero must accept as his own a positive relationship between desire and the law" (90), which means "accepting the place of the subject in the Western family as it massively constituted

itself during the 19th century. And what strikes me as absolutely fundamental in this perspective is that the American cinema is entirely dependent, as is psycho-analysis, on a system of representations in which the woman occupies a central place only to the extent that it's a place assigned to her by the logic of masculine desire" (93).

56. Tompkins, *West of Everything*, 40.

57. My thanks to Jean-Pierre Bertin-Maghit for this observation. In the interests of accuracy and of the symbolism through which we see Rio attempting to elimi-nate her (male) rivals for Billy's love, we note that a narrative digression prevents Rio from actually eating the chicken herself. Aunt Guadalupe alone will eat the bird, while Rio climbs naked into bed with Billy—ostensibly to keep him warm during a life-threatening bout of fever.

58. These two lines of dialogue must be the strangest in the film. We don't know what "it" is, but have been prepared by at least two rape scenes (Billy's rape of Rio in the barn, and Rio's "rape" of Billy during his fever) and various scenes of hu-miliation, to read these lines as evidence of a perverse subtext.

59. Peter Brooks, *The Melodramatic Imagination: Balzac, Henry James, Melodra-ma, and the Mode of Excess*, 4.

60. I do not wish to labor the obvious point that, in addition to any other reg-isters in which they may function, western rituals such as this work in a register of sexual connotation. Gaines and Herzog say it best: "The gunfight itself is a master-ful example of the ritualization of sexual tension and release, the elongation of an-ticipation in the cross-cutting between two men faced off against one another, ex-posing their weapons, cupping trigger-ready hands, opening the coat, readying for what viewers and diegetic onlookers know will be short ejaculations of fire. It often seems in the heat of the gunfight that the two figures 'come' together. At the same time, it is clear that the western scene is the homosocial scene *par excellence*, the corollary to this homoerotica is an auto-eroticism of the self-sufficient loner. The elusive westerner needs and wants no man, preferring the company of his horse." Gaines and Herzog, "The Fantasy of Authenticity," 179.

61. Pye, "Introduction," 15. Pye goes on to suggest that this idea of a utopia is one that the western cannot really believe in.

62. Charles Ford, *Histoire du Western*, 34.

63. Susan LoBello, who very generously gave this chapter a thorough reading and made several crucial suggestions for its improvement, points out that Pat, who obviously knows Doc is the better shot, hopes, or assumes, that Doc will kill him. The complexities of Pat's (unconscious) motives notwithstanding, the fact that Doc refuses to kill Pat in the shoot-out is a form of proof of Doc's enduring love for his old friend. Likewise, moments earlier, during their cuckoo-clock standoff, Doc may have hoped that Billy would kill *him*. The implications of these

possibilities are darkly erotic, to say the least, linking *eros* and *thanatos* in a way that is fairly common in the western.

64. Ford, *Histoire du Western*, 36. For a nuanced reading of Doc Holliday's character in *My Darling Clementine*, see also Corey K. Creekmur, "Acting Like a Man: Masculine Performance in *My Darling Clementine*," in Creekmur and Doty, eds., *Out in Culture: Gay, Lesbian, and Queer Essays on Popular Culture*, 167–82.

65. Cf. John Gray, "The Trusting Self: Is Moral Agency on the Wane?" *Times Literary Supplement*, March 27, 1998, 5–6.

66. While I would agree with Thomson that *The Outlaw* is the first American film to suggest that homosexuality might be pleasant, I must also agree with Andrew Sarris that the film remains one of the most misogynistic ever made. It is really only from the point of view of the treatment of Russell's character, however, that I can agree with Sarris's assessment that *The Outlaw* "stands as one of the coldest, most callous, and most cynical films made up to its time" (Andrew Sarris, "Jane Russell Rides Again with the Bust That Shook the World," *Village Voice*, July 19, 1976, 101).

5. Looking for the "Great Whatsit": *Kiss Me Deadly* and Film Noir

1. Rewritten for the screen by A. I. Bezzerides and directed by Robert Aldrich in 1955, from the novel of the same title by Mickey Spillane.

2. Immediately this look, this scenario, reminds me of a passage in Derek Jarman's *Dancing Ledge*: "[Caravaggio] gazes wistfully at the hero slaying the saint. It is a look no one can understand unless he has stood till 5 a.m. in a gay bar hoping to be fucked by that hero. The gaze of the passive homosexual at the object of his desire, he waits to be chosen, he cannot make the choice" (22).

3. Jake La Motta in *Raging Bull*, quoted by Robin Wood, "Cat and Dog: Lewis Teague's Stephen King Movies." *CineAction!* 2 (Fall 1985): 41.

4. This question of whether the film is reactionary or progressive is a complex one. For a discussion of the structure and function of the ironic/pessimistic/progressive text, see Barbara Klinger, "'Cinema/Ideology/Criticism' Revisited: The Progressive Text," *Screen* 25.1 (January-February 1984): 30–44.

5. Irigaray, *This Sex Which Is Not One*, 171.

6. Sedgwick, *Between Men*, 1.

7. Wood, "Cat and Dog," 41.

8. Foster Hirsch, *The Dark Side of the Screen: Film Noir*, 186.

9. "What is at stake," Stephen Heath has written, "is never the immediacy of a meaning directly expressed from the sex but always the terrain of representation

and representing in which meanings are formed and instituted, offered and possessed, in which 'man' and 'woman,' 'male' and 'female,' 'masculine' and 'feminine' are defined, implicated." Heath, "Difference," *Screen* 19 (Autumn 1978): 103.

10. Irigaray, *This Sex Which Is Not One*, 193.

11. *Note*: The title of the novel includes a comma: *Kiss Me, Deadly*.

12. Carol Flinn, "Sound, Woman, and the Bomb: Dismembering the 'Great Whatsit' in *Kiss Me Deadly*." *Wide Angle* 8.3–4 (1986): 115, 116, and 118.

13. According to Jacques Lacan, the phallus "is chosen because it is the most tangible element in the real of sexual copulation" (*Écrits*, 287). While the phallus is a signifier, not necessarily a penis, its "symbolic usage is possible because it can be seen, because it is erected. There can be no possible symbolic use for what is not seen, for what is hidden" (*The Seminar, Book II*, 272).

14. It is disappointing to discover that in August 1997 a new video edition of *Kiss Me Deadly* was released in the United States with "the restored ending" (recovered from the director's own print of the film and adding some 80 seconds of screen time), in which Mike and Velda do not die in the fire but can be seen dragging themselves on the beach toward the camera with the house behind them. According to the Internet Movie Data Base, Ltd., Mike and Velda are then "seen from behind, walking from the camera towards the surf, lightened by the flames projecting long shadows on the sand; and finally Mike and Velda huddled together, kneeling in the water and watching the house burn down as 'The End' is superimposed on the screen" (http://us.imdb.com/AlternateVersions?0048261 [April 5, 2001]). (My thanks to John Belton for alerting me to this edition of the film.)

This ending, of course, is an attempt to save the film from the queer implications of Mike's quest for the "great whatsit." For better or worse, Mike and Velda "huddled together," etc., strongly suggests (to this viewer, at least) that heterosexuality is a compromise formation. (Cf. Nancy J. Chodorow, "Heterosexuality as a Compromise Formation," in *Femininities, Masculinities, Sexualities: Freud and Beyond*, 33–69. Chodorow's essay challenges the homophobia of psychoanalytic assumptions that take as given a psychosexuality of normal heterosexual development "in which deviation from this norm needs explanation but norm-following does not.")

15. Again, I would refer the reader to Carol Flinn's essay. Although I agree with her that the film (and its finale most conclusively) critiques, or undermines, "the traditional privileging of the rational over the irrational, and . . . sight over sound," Flinn pays more attention to the film's sound track in her reading.

16. Mickey Spillane, *Kiss Me Deadly*, 38. Subsequent page numbers will be cited in the text.

17. Jane Gallop, *The Daughter's Seduction: Feminism and Psychoanalysis*, 66.

18. Mitry, quoted by Affron, *Cinema and Sentiment*, 5.

19. The phallus, according to Lacan, "can play its role only when veiled" (*Écrits*, 288).

20. Noël Burch, *To the Distant Observer: Form and Meaning in the Japanese Cinema*, 113.

21. The content of Pat's announcement speaks of Mike's "castration," which inflects the image (of the embrace) with the suggestion that, for Mike Hammer, the heterosexual embrace itself is castrating. But to be more precise, it is men who have the power to castrate (men like Pat, for example), and so Mike is better off being with, being like, or being one of them. He should be where the boys are—the ones with the guns.

22. Gallop, *The Daughter's Seduction*, 59.

23. Michael Friday's function in the film, apparently, is to make it clear that her brother and probably his henchmen are all gay, and to give Mike a chance to *claim* that he is heterosexual (by saying he's not her brother's "friend": to which she responds with, "Ooh wonderful! Then maybe you can be *my* friend"). (My thanks to Roy Thomas for this observation.)

Here's the actual tongue-in-cheek dialogue when Friday and Mike first meet at Evello's mansion estate:

> *Friday (as Mike gets out of his car and they start walking toward Evello and his henchmen beside the pool):* Who are you?
> *Mike:* Who am I? Who are *you*?
> *Friday (matter-of-factly):* I'm Friday. I'd have been named Tuesday if I had been born on Tuesday. I'm Carl's sister . . . half-sister—same mother, different father. [*She pauses and gives Mike an approving once-over*] You know, you're not like the others . . . Carl's friends, I mean.
> *Mike:* Maybe that's because I'm not his friend.
> *Friday (cooing as she embraces him):* Ooh wonderful! Then maybe you can be *my* friend. All mine . . . nothing to do with Carl. [*They start to kiss but get distracted by the racetrack announcer over the blaring radio by the pool*] They [Carl's friends] chew long black cigars and talk loud. I don't like them.
> [*A few minutes later, over drinks, they toast.*]
> *Friday:* To friendship . . . [*They clink glasses*] I have *lots* of friends.
> *Mike (with a sly grin):* I'll bet you have!

24. For example, the hero (Philip Marlowe/Dick Powell) in Edward Dmytryk's outrageously homoerotic *Murder My Sweet*, blacks out with humorous frequency.

25. In a curious note on substitutions in the face of prohibitions, John Richardson quotes Pablo Picasso in "The Catch in the Late Picasso," (*New York Review of Books*, July 19, 1984, 22): "As Picasso admitted to Brassai, 'Whenever I see you, my

first impulse is to . . . offer you a cigarette, even though I know very well that neither of us smokes any longer. Age has forced us to give it up, but the desire remains. It's the same thing with making love. We don't do it any more but the desire is still with us!'"

26. Cawelti, *Adventure, Mystery, and Romance*, 184.

27. It is sensed as an impossibility. What is required is a fantastic leap over to the field of the other. As Peter Baxter observes: "Born in the wake of biological satisfaction, desire is from the beginning a matter of autoeroticism; subjectivity itself comes into being with the fantasy of an object. Most important of all the autoerotic fantasy which poses the relation of subject and object poses also the distance that it is the very task of fantasy to overcome." Desire is founded in pain, and the nature of human sexuality is "essentially traumatic." Baxter, "The One Woman," *Wide Angle* 6.1 (1984): 35–36.

28. Again, I am reminded of a passage in Jarman's *Dancing Ledge*: "Until I was in my thirties I avoided passive sex. Inhibition and social conditioning made it a traumatic and painful experience. This was hard to overcome. But now I know that until I'd begun to enjoy it I had not reached balanced manhood. You must make the sacrifice to bury the centuries. When you overcome yourself you understand that gender is its own prison. When I meet heterosexual men I know that they have experienced only half of love" (246).

6. MIDNIGHT COWBOY'S BACKSTORY

1. The embedded subversive intent of Joe's choice of phrase becomes more apparent when we hear the lyrics of the film's theme song ("I'm goin' where the sun keeps shining . . ."), an introduction—following the shot of Joe in the shower reaching for the fallen bar of soap—to the theme of homosexuality (as sodomy)/as Joe's unconscious protest against normative sexuality: i.e., Joe is "man enough" to put those dishes "where the sun don't shine." (My thanks to Susan LoBello for this observation.)

2. Juliet Mitchell, *Psychoanalysis and Feminism*, 396.

3. Robert McKee, *Story: Substance, Structure, Style, and the Principles of Screenwriting*, 340–41.

4. Maureen Turim, *Flashbacks in Film: Memory and History*, 149. Subsequent page numbers will be cited in the text.

5. Ibid., 40. Turim's book is comprehensive in its analysis of the wide range and frequently complex significations of flashback forms used in the cinema, and I highly recommend it as a useful supplement to my own, very modest consideration here of the formal properties of *Midnight Cowboy's* flashbacks.

6. The young woman is called "crazy Annie" by the local boys because she will have sex with them—more or less indiscriminately, it seems—to gratify her nymphomania.

7. Cf. Michael Moon's essay, "Outlaw Sex and the 'Search for America'": Representing Male Prostitution and Perverse Desire in Sixties Film (*My Hustler* and *Midnight Cowboy*)," in *A Small Boy and Others: Imitation and Initiation in American Culture from Henry James to Andy Warhol.*

8. McKee, *Story*, 376. Cf. Elizabeth Cowie's discussion of fantasy as "the *mise-en-scène* of desire," in which she uses Freud's essay, "A Child Is Being Beaten," to illustrate what McKee, in effect, is saying works well as a screenwriter's device for the creation of multiple interpretations of characters' motives. Cowie, "Fantasia," 71–104.

9. Moon, "Outlaw Sex," 131.

10. The party scene—for which director John Schlesinger very knowingly uses several of Andy Warhol's "superstars," and in which we see "characters" playing "themselves," as Gastone Rossilli and Viva film guests, who perform for their camera (and Schlesinger's camera)—is the most self-conscious example in *Midnight Cowboy* of this theme of (post)modern subjectivity as performance.

11. We might also remember how Pee-wee in *Pee-wee's Big Adventure* (1985) travels to Texas in search of his stolen bicycle, which he believes he will find in the basement of the Alamo, only to discover that the Alamo does not have a basement. The historical story of the Alamo offers a further, important intertext: In 1836, Colonel William Travis and 187 Texans and others defended the Spanish mission and fortress in San Antonio, Texas, during a thirteen-day siege by the Mexican General Antonio Lopez de Santa Anna and his army of five thousand. The fortress was taken, and all inside perished. As Edward Buscombe summarizes the significance of this event: "Texans cried 'Remember the Alamo' as they went into subsequent battles against the Mexicans, who were defeated within two months. The ruined fort, a potent symbol of a defeat that was turned into a victory, is now preserved as a national shrine" (Buscombe, ed., *The BFI Companion to the Western*, 57).

12. One could argue that Los Angeles or any number of other American cities are more "modern" than New York, but the point here is that the film designates New York, with its density and variety of street life, as the richest site for Joe's hustling fantasy.

13. Richard Dyer, "Getting Over the Rainbow: Identity and Pleasure in Gay Cultural Politics," in Bridges and Brunt, eds., *Silver Linings: Some Strategies for the Eighties*, 61.

14. Dyer, quoted by Moon, "Outlaw Sex," 118–19.

15. The ideal man is impossibly heroic. Like Joe's ideal, this woman's "idea of a man" is finally fantasmatic—not only is Gary Cooper dead, he is/was an actor (i.e., a man who performed manliness—that is, played the role of an ideal man).

16. Among the many, perhaps less obvious, reasons for the homoerotic resonances of this image of Newman in *Hud* are those deriving from details of *Hud*'s narrative, and Brandon de Wilde's presence/performance in the movie, which also refers to his performances in other films, most notably *Shane* (1953).

17. Theoretically speaking, whatever interpellates him and "speaks to" his desire "returns Joe's gaze," and Newman's image in *Hud* certainly does. But who is Joe? And how may we characterize his desire?

18. Moon, "Outlaw Sex," 120.

19. Ethel Spector Person, "Sexuality as the Mainstay of Identity: Psychoanalytic Perspectives," *Signs* 5.4 (1980): 605.

20. The film is basically Joe's "story," although, as Stanley Kauffmann noted in his review, Schlesinger occasionally slips up: "Ratso's fantasies, visualized for us, mar the viewpoint of the film, which is generally and rightly Joe's; and the fantasies themselves are trite." Kauffmann, "*Midnight Cowboy*," *New Republic*, June 7, 1969.

21. Jonathan Lear, in "Discussion" following John Forrester's "Psychoanalysis: What Kind of Truth?" in Brooks and Woloch, eds., *Whose Freud?*, 329.

22. Daniel Lagache, "La psychanalyse et la structure de la personnalité," *La Psychanalyse* VI (1958), cited in Laplanche and Pontalis, *The Language of Psycho-Analysis*, 202.

23. Silverman, "The Language of Care," 150.

24. Quite obviously, the mirror stage precedes any stage or moment of psychosexual development that could be characterized as "oedipal." I am suggesting that Joe's childhood trauma of abandonment has resulted in a partial regression to an earlier phase in the formation of his subjectivity.

25. Lear, "Truth in Psychoanalysis," in Brooks and Woloch, eds., *Whose Freud?*, 308.

26. Ibid., 305. See also Susannah Radstone's wide-ranging and fascinating essay, "Screening Trauma: *Forrest Gump*, Film, and Memory" (in Radstone, ed., *Memory and Methodology*, 79–107), for the way in which psychoanalysis understands memory—and most particularly traumatic memory—as "inevitably interweaved with the determining agency of the inner world and its fantasies" (92). Arguing that psychoanalytic approaches to memory focus on both temporality and symbolization, Radstone calls for "the integration of cinepsychoanalysis' foregrounding of the cinema's relation to fantasy, with an approach which foregrounds the cinema's place in the constitution of history and memory" (103). She argues that the quest for the "cause" of "trauma" is a symptom of contemporary malaise, rather than a form of analysis, and that the "cinepsychoanalysis" of the journal *Screen* during the 1970s overemphasized the opposition between fantasy and memory and therefore has difficulty with analyzing "memory films" other than by operating a history/memory opposition, when an approach that links memory/fantasy/history and the subject might be more productive.

27. I should point out, if it is not obvious already, that I have no moral objections to prostitution. (I am grateful to Susan LoBello for urging me here to make it clear that I am referring to the possible attitude of the text, not making a judgment of my own about hustling as a pathology.)

28. Austin, quoted in Forrester, "Psychoanalysis: What Kind of Truth?" in *Whose Freud?*, 318.

29. Leo Bersani, "Is the Rectum a Grave?" *October* 43 (Winter 1987): 197.

30. Calvin Thomas, "Straight with a Twist: Queer Theory and the Subject of Heterosexuality," in Thomas, ed., *Straight with a Twist*, 33.

31. Silverman, "The Language of Care," 151.

32. Judith Butler, "Quandaries of the Incest Taboo," in Brooks and Woloch, eds., *Whose Freud?*, 40.

33. Kaplan, *Female Perversions*, 10.

34. Mitchell, *Psychoanalysis and Feminism*, 377.

35. Juliet Mitchell, "The Vortex Beneath the Story," in Brooks and Woloch, eds., *Whose Freud?*, 48.

36. Turim, *Flashbacks in Film*, 149.

37. Mitchell, "The Vortex Beneath the Story," 48.

38. Kaplan, *Female Perversions*, 10.

39. A significant difference between the novel and the movie is identified by Penelope Gilliatt in her *New Yorker* review: "Probably the best thing about the book, except for the title, was Herlihy's tenderness toward Joe Buck—his confidence that the thinness of Buck's brave-cowboy disguise would evoke a similar protective feeling in the reader. Again, tenderness isn't the only possible attitude toward Buck, but Schlesinger crushes him with sophisticated condescension. Buck's fantasy collapses quickly, but the camera hangs in there. Intentionally or not, Schlesinger operates like a muckraker going after an unusually cagey malefactor." Gilliatt, "The Current Cinema: Life, Love, Death, Etc.," *The New Yorker*, May 31, 1969, 80.

There is an interesting intertext in the fact that Schlesinger would direct *Sunday, Bloody Sunday* (1971) from Gilliatt's original screenplay. Leonard Maltin remarks that while Gilliatt's script is "very good" and "adult," Schlesinger's direction is "less forceful than usual, also less effective" (*Leonard Maltin's Movie and Video Guide, 2000 Edition*, 1349).

40. James Leo Herlihy, *Midnight Cowboy*, 96. Subsequent page numbers will be cited in the text.

41. Townie complains that some of his friends think it is "sick" that he still lives with his mother.

42. This line of dialogue occurs in the movie. In the novel, Herlihy has Perry ask the question. (See discussion above.)

7. *INNERSPACE*: A SPECTACULAR VOYAGE
TO THE HEART OF IDENTITY

1. Carroll, "When Boy Meets Boy, What's a Girl to Do?" *New York Daily News* (*Sunday News*), February 3, 1974, 7. The piece is remarkably similar to an article by Aljean Harmetz published a few days earlier in the *New York Times* (January 20, 1974) entitled, "Boy Meets Boy—Or Where the Girls Aren't." Some answers to Carroll's question ("Why, all of a sudden . . . ?") can be found in Michael Ryan and Douglas Kellner, *Camera Politica: The Politics and Ideology of Contemporary Hollywood Film*, 149–51.

2. Andrew Sarris, "The Male Mystique: To Be or Not to Be?" *Village Voice*, September 13, 1976," 16.

3. This crisis of self-consciousness has a correspondence in the hysteria that surrounded Bill Clinton's proposal to lift the ban on openly gay men and women serving in the American armed forces. Cf. David Gelman, "Homoeroticism in the Ranks: The Clinton Administration's Compromise Covers Up an Uncomfortable Truth," *Newsweek*, July 26, 1993.

4. Vincent Canby, "Male-Bonding? Now Wait a Minute!" *New York Times*, February 4, 1979, 17.

5. Molly Haskell, "Hers," *New York Times*, February 11, 1982, C2.

6. Walter Goodman, "Prankster Pals: The Appeal Never Ages," *New York Times*, August 16, 1987," H19.

7. Molly Haskell, "The Odder Couples: Is Being a Misfit the New Precondition for Male Friendship?" *Vogue* (May 1988): 66.

8. Wood, *Hollywood from Vietnam to Reagan*, 227.

9. *Innerspace*. Directed by Joe Dante. Written by Jeffrey Boam and Chip Proser. Produced by Michael Finnell. A Steven Spielberg Presentation of a Guber-Peters Production. An Amblin Entertainment Film. A Warner Brothers Release; Summer 1987.

10. Wayne Koestenbaum, *Double Talk: The Erotics of Male Literary Collaboration*, 3.

11. I put the word *unconscious* in quotation marks here because the filmmakers both know and do not know what ideological and narratological imperatives structure the film. They know, for example, why Tuck drinks too much, and we are expected to figure out the cause, but *the filmmakers share the characters' anxieties* (about homosexuality); they are hardly in control of the moral difficulties that they seek to transcend by making their film hip, fast, and funny.

12. Laplanche and Pontalis, *The Language of Psycho-Analysis*, 211. Diana Fuss observes that Freud elaborates his theory of identification through three principal figures: gravity, ingestion, and infection. Obviously, *Innerspace* turns primarily on the figure of identification as ingestion. (See Fuss, *Identification Papers*, 13.)

13. Laplanche and Pontalis, *The Language of Psycho-Analysis*, 211.

14. The casting of Dennis Quaid in the role of Lt. Tuck Pendleton serves this end well, most especially because of the intertext of his earlier role in *The Right Stuff* (Philip Kaufman, 1983), in which he undergoes a grueling physical and psychological training to condition him to perfect masculinity—for the ultimately phallic identity (within the context of the film) of "astronaut." The intent of *Innerspace* is essentially the same: to affirm an ideal of masculinity that is resilient, disciplined, aggressive, *and* heterosexual.

15. This scene recalls Marlon Brando as Stanley Kowalski in *A Streetcar Named Desire*, crying out, "*Stella!*" It functions as one of the film's contradictory efforts to give Tuck a convincing heterosexual identity.

16. "The use of and traffic in women subtend and uphold the reign of masculine hom(m)o-sexuality, even while they maintain that hom(m)o-sexuality in speculations, mirror games, identifications, and more or less rivalrous appropriations, which defer its real practice. Reigning everywhere, although prohibited in practice, hom(m)o-sexuality is played out through the bodies of women, matter, or sign, and heterosexuality has been up to now just an alibi for the smooth workings of man's relations with himself, of relations among men." Irigaray, *This Sex Which Is Not One*, 172.

17. Cf. John Boswell, *Christianity, Social Tolerance, and Homosexuality*. Rabbits (or rather, hares) have been at various times in history also associated with promiscuity and hermaphroditism.

18. The references to the "pod" in which Tuck is miniaturized are probably a homage to *The Invasion of the Body Snatchers* (1956, which also stars Kevin McCarthy), in which the inhabitants of a small town must resist being "taken over" by the pod people. It is a fight against the lure of complete passivity.

19. Freud, "Some Neurotic Mechanisms in Jealousy, Paranoia, and Homosexuality," *SE* 18:230.

20. Freud's sequence of phases in the genesis of object-choice is proposed thus: autoeroticism → narcissism → homosexual object-choice → heterosexual object-choice.

21. Jean Baudrillard, *Simulations*, 42.

22. Laplanche and Pontalis, *The Language of Psycho-Analysis*, 205.

23. Brown, quoted in Vito Russo, *The Celluloid Closet: Homosexuality in the Movies*, 70.

24. The circumstances of the death of director F. W. Murnau in 1931 have entered Hollywood lore. As Kenneth Anger wrote in his famous book, *Hollywood Babylon*: "Murnau had hired as valet a handsome fourteen-year-old Filipino boy named Garcia Stevenson. The boy was at the wheel of the Packard when the fatal accident occurred. The Hollywood *méchantes langues* reported that Murnau was going down on Garcia when the car leaped off the road" (172).

25. A vast amount of fascinating work has been done on the metaphor of the mirror in theories of the subject. The original essay, of course, is Jacques Lacan's "The Mirror Stage as Formative of the Function of the I as Revealed in Psychoanalytic Experience" (Lacan, *Ecrits*, 1–7). For our purposes, a more useful essay is Mary Ann Doane's historical overview and discussion of the ways in which film theory has appropriated notions of identification from psychoanalysis: "Misrecognition and Identity," in Ron Burnett, ed., *Explorations in Film Theory*, 15–25.

26. Lacan said, "In the scopic field, everything is articulated between two terms that act in an antinomic way—on the side of things, there is the gaze, that is to say, things look at me, and yet I see them" (*The Four Fundamental Concepts of Psycho-Analysis*, 109). And, "What determines me, at the most profound level, in the visible, is the gaze that is outside. It is through the gaze that I enter light and it is from the gaze that I receive its effects" (106).

27. Baudrillard, *Simulations*, 42.

28. For a sociohistorical account of the way the image in the West is coded, see Stephen Heath's essay, "Narrative Space," in *Questions of Cinema*, 19–75. As Heath notes, "Spaces are born and die like societies; they live, they have a history" (29).

29. This Deleuzian pun was suggested to me by Lesley Stern.

30. Baudrillard, *Simulations*, 25.

31. "The movie is structured as an *odyssey* (there's no place like home, i.e., being full-size); it has a *ticking clock* (Pendleton's oxygen will run out at 9 a.m. the next morning); its characters are in *jeopardy* (bad guys, led by Kevin McCarthy, chase Putter because they want the miniaturization device to sell to foreign agents); and there is a *moral* (Pendleton teaches Putter to be a man, not a wussy). You get *fish out of water* (dork plays superspy), dandy *car chases*, and *special effects*. Good laughs with the *action,* [and] *romance*." Edelstein, "Adventures in Blockbusting," *Village Voice*, July 7, 1987, 60.

32. Laplanche and Pontalis, *The Language of Psycho-Analysis*, 205.

33. Irigaray, *This Sex Which Is Not One*, 193 (emphasis in original).

34. As if to confirm the existence of a subtext of repressed homosexual desire, the film ends with Rod Stewart on the sound track, now singing suggestive alternate lyrics to "Twisting the Night Away" (". . . New York way/Where the people are so gay" *and* "a fellow in blue jeans/Dancing with an older queen," and so on).

35. Maitland McDonagh, "Innerspace: Entretien avec Joe Dante," *Mad Movies* 49 (September 1987): 46.

36. Parveen Adams, "Per Os(cillation)," *Camera Obscura* 17 (May 1988): 28.

37. Adams, "Per Os(cillation)," 28.

38. Maltin, ed., *Leonard Maltin's Movie and Video Guide*, 668.

39. Sarris, "The Male Mystique," 16.

40. Canby, "Male-Bonding?" 17.

8. BATMAN AND ROBIN: A FAMILY ROMANCE

1. The Batman character first appeared in the pages of *Detective Comics #27* in May 1939, and "The Origin of Batman" was presented almost a decade later, in *Batman #47* in 1948. All Batman stories cited in this essay, unless indicated otherwise, have been reprinted in Mike Gold, ed., *The Greatest Batman Stories Ever Told* (1988).

2. Mike W. Barr and Jerry Bingham, *Batman: Son of the Demon* (1987).

3. Frank Miller and David Mazzucchelli, *Batman: Year One* (1988); originally published in four issues in magazine form, 1986–87.

4. Constance Penley makes a good point in connection with Pee-wee Herman that is worth considering in light of Batman's obsessive return to the scene of his parents' murder: "The adult fantasy of childhood simplicity and happiness is a founding fantasy, one that offers the possibility of innocence to those who need to retain the idea of innocence itself. As long as this fantasy remains unexamined, so too will the fantasy of masculinity." Penley, "The Cabinet of Dr. Pee-wee: Consumerism and Sexual Terror," *Camera Obscura* 17 (1988): 151.

5. Freud, "Family Romances," *SE* 9:238–39.

6. Danny Peary, "Mark of the Beast: A New Screen Batman Resurrects Old Nightmares," *New York Daily News Magazine*, June 4, 1989," 14.

7. Ed Neumeier, quoted in Howard A. Rodman, "They Shoot Comic Books, Don't They?," *American Film* (May 1989): 36. Neumeier cowrote the script for *Robocop*, a film Rodman describes as "cartoonish."

8. Freud, "Family Romances," *SE* 9:240–41 (emphasis in original).

9. Freud, "Group Psychology and the Analysis of the Ego," *SE* 18:105.

10. John Munder Ross, "In Search of Fathering," in Cath, Gurwitt, and Ross, eds., *Father and Child*, 29.

11. Freud, "Group Psychology and the Analysis of the Ego," *SE* 18:105.

12. Freud, *Moses and Monotheism: Three Essays, SE* 23:12. In 1921 Freud wrote in the postscript of "Group Psychology and the Analysis of the Ego" that the poet who invents the heroic myth disguises the truth with lies "in accordance with his longing. . . . The hero was a man who by himself had slain the father—the father who still appeared in the myth as a totemic monster. Just as the father had been the boy's first ideal, so in the hero who aspires to the father's place the poet now created the first ego ideal" (*SE* 18:136).

13. Freud, "A Special Type of Choice of Object Made by Men," *SE* 11:172. Subsequent page numbers will be cited in the text.

14. Freud's phrase, borrowed from *Hamlet*, to describe Leonardo da Vinci's "compulsion to copy and to outdo his father." Freud, *Leonardo da Vinci and a Memory of His Childhood, SE* 11:121.

15. Freud, "Group Psychology and the Analysis of the Ego," *SE* 18:106.

16. To put it another way, "The hero should always be interpreted merely as a collective ego." Otto Rank, *The Myth of the Birth of the Hero* (1914), 72.

17. Jennifer Stone, *Pirandello's Naked Prompt: The Structure of Repetition in Modernism*, 98 and 166. Stone invokes her "pipistrello principle" in a discussion of Pirandello's unpublished screenplay for an unrealized German film version of his play—both based on his published novella, "The Bat" (*Il pipistrello*). Generally in agreement with Jean Spizzo, another psychoanalytic critic of Pirandello, Stone notes that when Pirandello, in his writing, processes his early childhood sexual trauma (of observing a couple making love on a mortuary floor), he "was alert to the sounds of the lovers' bodies moving against each other"—a point she confirms with the observation that "in the primal scene, that 'posthumous action of sexual trauma' [Freud], it is not the unforgettable sight but the uncanny sound that most affects the innocent voyeur." According to Stone, "Spizzo identifies this perturbing noise of the lovers' 'bizarre, uninterrupted movement' with the 'unforgettable whirring' of bats' wings," and in a suggestive analysis, "[Spizzo] locates Pirandello's preoccupation with bats as phallic symbol in this early trauma" (106).

18. William Veeder makes this same observation about Robert Louis Stevenson's *Strange Case of Dr. Jekyll and Mr. Hyde*. See Veeder, "Children of the Night: Stevenson and Patriarchy," in Veeder and Hirsch, eds., *Dr. Jekyll and Mr. Hyde after One Hundred Years*, 107–60.

19. Freud, *Three Essays on the Theory of Sexuality*, SE 7:226n.

20. "The Death of a Boy Wonder: An Introduction by Dr. Socrates S. Rodor, Professor Emeritus of Twentieth Century History, Gotham University," in *Batman: A Death in the Family* (1988); originally published as "Batman: A Death in the Family," by Jim Starlin, Jim Aparo, and Mike DeCarlo, in *Batman #426* through *#429*.

21. Peary, "Mark of the Beast," 14.

22. Bridwell, *Batman from the 30's to the 70's*, 12.

23. Giordano, "Growing Up with the Greatest," in Gold, ed., *The Greatest Batman Stories Ever Told*, 11.

24. In "The First Batman" (*Detective Comics #235*, 1956), we learn that Thomas Wayne wore a Batman costume once to a masquerade ball at which, suddenly, he found himself called upon to perform a heroic act.

25. Freud, "Group Psychology and the Analysis of the Ego," *SE* 18:139.

26. The circumstances in which Dick Grayson/Robin leaves Bruce Wayne/Batman, and how Batman finds Jason Todd and takes him in, are recounted in Jim Starlin, Jim Aparo, and Mike DeCarlo, "White Gold and Truth" (*Batman: The New Adventures #416*, 1988). The story is quite touching in its preoccupation with Batman and Robin's love for each other and with the kind of sibling rivalry and affection between the two Robins.

27. Jason Todd/Robin, introduced in 1983, "was an interesting, and somewhat spooky, case of a fictional character seizing control of his own character. . . . [He] evolved into a disturbed and sometimes disagreeable problem child" (Dennis O'Neil, "Sidekicking: A Brief History of Robins" (introduction), *Robin: Tragedy and Triumph*, 4). Readers voted to have him "retired" from the series, and the result was "Batman: A Death in the Family" by Starlin, Aparo, and DeCarlo.

28. Alan Moore, "The Mark of Batman" (introduction), in Frank Miller's *Batman: The Dark Knight Returns*, iii. Moore observes that Gotham City "becomes something much grimmer in Miller's hands," and Batman himself "is seen as a near-fascist and a dangerous fanatic by the media." This Batman also recognizes that "time passes and that people grow old and die" (iii–iv).

29. Warner Home Video's summary on the box of the videotape of *Batman Beyond: The Movie* (1999, 41 min.).

30. Ibid.

31. Bridwell, *Batman from the 30's to the 70's*, 12–13.

32. For example, in "Half an Evil" (*Batman #234*, 1971), the key to a "coded clue to a fortune" is decided by the flipping of a coin, one face of which is whole, and the other of which is ruined. The coin is owned by Two-Face, who says, "The coin has decided! The evil part of my nature wins." Then the story turns on a series of pivots—at midnight (between one day and the next); on a "mammoth bridge" (between two land masses); on a pier "fronting one of Gotham's twin rivers!" and so on. Throughout the story, the narrator cuts back and forth between Batman in the dark city and Bruce Wayne at Wayne Manor.

33. Jonathan Rutherford, "Who's That Man?" in Chapman and Rutherford, eds., *Male Order: Unwrapping Masculinity*, 47.

34. A brilliant version of the Joker's origins is offered in Alan Moore, Brian Bolland, and John Higgins, *Batman: The Killing Joke* (1988).

35. "The Case of the Joker's Crime Circus," *Batman #4*, 1941; reprinted in Gold, ed., *The Greatest Joker Stories Ever Told* (1988).

36. "Batman vs. The Joker" (*Batman #1*, 1940), reprinted in Gold, ed., *Greatest Joker Stories*.

37. An excellent description of Gotham City—too good not to quote at length—can be found in "Death Strikes at Midnight and Three" (*DC Special Series #15*, 1978): "It is a monster sprawled along 25 miles of eastern seaboard, stirring and seething and ever-restless. Eight million human beings live on the streets that, if laid end-to-end, would stretch all the way to Tokyo, crammed into thousands of neighborhoods from the fire-gutted tenements of Chancreville, where rats nestle in babies' bedclothes and grandmothers forage in garbage cans, to the penthouses of Manor Row, where the cost of a single meal served by liveried servants would support an immigrant family for a year. It is countless chambers and crannies and cor-

ners in bars, boats, houses, hotels, elevators, offices, theaters, shacks, tunnels, depots, shops, factories, restaurants, newsstands, hospitals, junkyards, cemeteries, buses, cars, trains, trams, bridges, docks, sewers, parks, jails, mortuaries—the shelters of the living and the dead, millionaires and bums, fiends and saints. Napoleon's armies could search for a lifetime and leave places unseen."

38. That Crime Alley used to be Park Row—in a neighborhood that was "the dwelling place of the rich and the soon-to-be rich . . . a place of gourmet restaurants and fashionable theaters . . . of elegant women and suave men"—is indicated in "No Hope in Crime Alley" (*Detective Comics #457*, 1976). Gotham City may be an apocalyptic place, but Batman is possessive and nostalgic about it. In many stories it is Batman's sense that Gotham City belongs to him that makes him fight an archcriminal with extra energy. As he says of an art thief in the opening panel of "Le Salon de Crime," *Batman-Poche #52* (Paris: Sagédition-Paris/DC Comics, 1984): "Avant son arrivée, la nuit m'appartenait et je dois la revendiquer!" In "A Caper a Day Keeps the Batman at Bay" (*Batman #312*, 1979), there is a panel in which he is described as "a night-clad guardian [who] stands vigil over the city that he *loves*."

39. Peary, "Mark of the Beast," 12.

40. Greenberger, in Gold, ed., *Greatest Batman Stories*, 347.

41. Susan Sontag, *Styles of Radical Will*, 141.

42. Stone, *Pirandello's Naked Prompt*, 175.

43. Of course, on the narrative level, removing their masks would "completely destroy their value as ace crimefighters"—as Commissioner Gordon says in the 1966 *Batman* movie. When Catwoman (disguised as a reporter) remarks on their curious costumes, Robin replies: "Don't be put off by them, ma'am. Under this garb we're perfectly ordinary Americans!" The exchange hints at an erotic subtext, especially when Catwoman goes on to say, "You're like the masked vigilantes in the westerns, no?" and Commissioner Gordon replies emphatically, "Certainly not! Batman and Robin are fully deputized agents of the law!" (i.e., they are phallic, not fetishistic).

44. The story of how Selina Kyle and Bruce Wayne marry is recounted in "The Autobiography of Bruce Wayne" (*The Brave and the Bold #197*, 1983). In a moving and psychologically acute conclusion, Selina takes off her Catwoman mask and urges Batman, "Look! The cat is gone. There is nothing to be afraid of anymore. Now . . . it's *your* turn, my darling. Take away *my* fear . . ." In an agony of indecision, Batman thinks to himself, "I knew what had to be done . . . but a lifetime of inhibition stayed my hand. I couldn't—I couldn't—I *had* to." He removes his cowl. "Selina! Oh God, Selina, I almost lost you . . . !" They embrace.

In *Batman: Son of the Demon*, another such moment expresses the profundity of Batman's sexual fears: Talia takes off his cowl and draws him to bed, saying, "Forego your *control*, your *discipline* . . . just once, let yourself go . . ."

45. Roland Barthes, *A Lover's Discourse: Fragments*, 41.

46. Starlin, Aparo, and DeCarlo, "White Gold and Truth" (1988).

47. The villain in the 1926 movie version of Mary Roberts Rinehart's *The Bat* was also, apparently, a significant inspiration for Batman's costume.

48. The vampire element in Batman's mythos is extraordinarily explicit in "Man-Bat Over Vegas" (*Detective Comics #429*, 1972). In this story, a beautiful woman turns into a monstrous bat with grasping claws and sharp teeth. Eventually, in a bizarre, unconsciously sexual gesture, Batman is able to subdue the frightening creature by swinging forward with his legs apart and wrapping his legs tightly around it while "swiftly twirling the trailing Batrope into restraining loops . . ." In the 1995 movie, *Batman Forever*, which appeared during a wave of media debate about the ethics of "outing" closeted gays who are in the public eye, Bruce Wayne feels pressured to tell his new girlfriend, Chase Meridian, that he is Batman. Initially, Chase is infatuated by Batman; but she begins to find Bruce Wayne at least as interesting. One night, at her invitation, Batman appears at her bedroom window at midnight—like Nosferatu visiting Lucy, in the vampire story by Murnau or Herzog, or in any number of *Dracula* films—whereupon Chase, standing in the moonlight in her silk nightdress, informs Batman that she has "met someone" else (i.e., Bruce Wayne), and hopes he will "understand."

49. Rank, *The Myth of the Birth of the Hero*, 77.

50. Otto Rank observes that it cannot be stated with certainty that the child's "conflict with the father arises from the sexual rivalry for the mother, but is apparently suggested that this conflict dates back primarily to the concealment of the sexual processes (at childbirth), which in this way became an enigma for the child" (*The Myth of the Birth of the Hero*, 85).

51. "To Kill a Legend" is a postmodern time-warp story, not unlike *Back to the Future*, *Peggy Sue Got Married*, *The Terminator*, and other science fiction movies of the 1980s.

52. *Batman* was written by Sam Hamm and Warren Skaaren, and directed by Tim Burton. *Batman Returns* was written by Daniel Waters and Sam Hamm, and directed by Tim Burton. *Batman Forever* was written by Lee Batchler, Janet Scott Batchler, and Akiva Goldsman, and directed by Joel Schumacher. *Batman and Robin* was written by Akiva Goldsman and directed by Joel Schumacher.

53. Schumacher, quoted in Les Daniels, *Batman: The Complete History*, 186.

54. Goldsman, "I Don't Know Exactly When Batman Came into My Life," 7.

55. Daniels, *Batman: The Complete History*, 187.

56. Benjamin, *The Bonds of Love*, 107.

57. Cf. Freud, "A Special Type of Choice of Object Made by Men," *SE* 11:172.

58. Françoise Vergès, "Dialogue," in Read, ed., *The Fact of Blackness*, 139. Vergès's comments are addressed to the question of why sodomy, or anal rape,

come to acquire such an overdetermined and intolerable emotional significance in representations of colonization in the work of Frantz Fanon.

59. I explore this idea further—of the childhood trauma that is offered as an explanation for desire that deviates from socially sanctioned norms—in "Choosing to Be 'Not a Man': Masculine Anxiety in Nouri Bouzid's *Rih Essed/Man of Ashes* (1986)," in Lehman, ed., *Masculinity: Bodies, Movies, Culture*, 81–94.

60. This fantasy is precisely the one Fredric Wertham identified in his famous attack (in *Seduction Of the Innocent*) on the queerness of Batman and Robin's relationship as an underminer of the nation's morals. Cf. Andy Medhurst's on-target commentary on this episode in the history of the reception of comic books in the United States ("Batman, Deviance, and Camp," in Pearson and Uricchio, eds., *The Many Lives of Batman*, 149–63).

61. Dick's brother is also killed in this tragedy—as if in acknowledgment of recent psychoanalytic studies suggesting that siblings (and/or other peers in the small child's world) can play as important a role as parents are thought to play in the oedipal scenario. It is interesting that when Dick looks down through the opening at the top of the tent and sees his family dead on the circus floor, the countershot is a close-up of Bruce looking up at him. Dick appears to return Bruce's gaze and, as if to confirm that a kind of transference has taken place, the camera cuts back again to Bruce looking intently into Dick's eyes.

We should note, moreover—as an embedded "rescue fantasy"—that Dick takes the name "Robin" because, as he explains to Alfred: "My brother's wire broke, once. I swung out and grabbed him. My father said I was 'his hero.' I 'flew in like a robin.'"

62. The journal turns out to be one kept by Bruce's father: "He'd written in it every day of my life. But now he'd never write in it again. At that moment, I knew ... my life would never be the same." *Batman* has always been self-reflexive in this manner—always a *narrated* story, and often told with flashbacks and memories of traumatic incidents from childhood. In *Batman Forever*, the presence of Dr. Meridian institutionalizes the trope, when she repeatedly urges Bruce: "Your memories are trying to break through, don't fight them." Occasionally, *Batman*'s postmodernity declares itself in a text that is overtly about textual production, as in *Batman* #35 (1946), which contains the story, "Dick Grayson, AUTHOR!" The cover of the comic book shows Dick at a typewriter. Behind him, Batman is punching a villain in the jaw, as Dick is saying: "No, no, Batman! Your *left* fist! I've already *written* it that way!"

63. For no discernible reason, Jim Carrey calls him "*Fatman*" here.

64. Miller, quoted by Christopher Sharrett, "Batman and the Twilight of the Idols," in Pearson and Uricchio, eds., *The Many Lives of Batman*, 38.

65. Medhurst, "Batman, Deviance, and Camp," 162.

66. Dorothy Hammond and Alta Jablow, "Gilgamesh and the Sundance Kid: The Myth of Male Friendship," 245.

67. Ibid., 247. Some of the more striking parallels between Gilgamesh and Enkidu's story and that of Batman/Bruce and Robin/Dick are worth noting. For example, not only does the lonely Bruce take in Dick as his ward, but Dick, as an acrobat, whom we first see in the lofty reaches of a circus tent—flying gracefully, in slow motion, *defying death*—is like an artifact of the gods. An accident of fate, or an act of the gods, makes him an orphan—without kin or community. There is also a sense in which Dick's appearance in Bruce's household, and his passionate plea to be made Batman's "partner," which he supports by eagerly demonstrating his value to Batman as a crime-fighter, wins Bruce's heart and prevents him from marrying either Chase or Julie.

68. Marina Warner, *Six Myths of Our Time*, 70.

69. Hammond and Jablow, "Gilgamesh and the Sundance Kid," 247.

70. Of course there are other indications by the film that such an interpretation can be supported: Poison Ivy makes her entrance at the Costume Ball benefiting Gotham's Botanical Gardens disguised as a gorilla—an allusion to that famous image of dangerous, feminine allure, Marlene Dietrich emerging from her monkey suit in the voodoo number of *Blonde Venus* (Josef von Sternberg, 1932). Poison Ivy then does a turn that alludes to Jane Russell's musical number, "Is There Anyone Here for Love?" in Howard Hawks's *Gentlemen Prefer Blondes* (1953), which has Russell surrounded by nearly naked, muscular men who seem less interested in her than in themselves and each other.

9. *My Own Private Idaho* and the New Queer Road Movies

1. Caryn James, "Today's Yellow Brick Road Leads Straight to Hell," *New York Times*, August 19, 1990, B1+.

2. Two non-American queer road movies that deserve special mention are Wong Kar-Wai's somewhat ironically titled *Happy Together* (1997) and Olivier Ducastel and Jacques Martineau's *The Adventures of Felix* (*Drôle de Félix*, 2000). *Happy Together* is about the troubled relationship of a Hong Kong gay couple in Buenos Aires, and *Drôle de Félix* is about a French-born Arab in search of the father he has never known. Both films—although very different from each other—are marked by a kind of grace in their frank attitude toward their protagonists' homosexuality, which the American films, with their more "loaded," or self-conscious, approach to the problem of being queer in a straight world, tend to lack.

Drôle de Félix is a particularly inspiriting film—probably the only queer road movie made to date (in any language) with a genuinely happy ending.

3. Thomas Waugh, "The Third Body: Patterns in the Construction of the Subject in the Gay Male Narrative Film," in Gever, Greyson, and Parmar, eds., *Queer Looks*, 145.

4. Stephen Holden, "Outraged Autobiographies Make a Collage of Gay Life," *New York Times*, October 8, 1994, 14.

5. Godfrey Cheshire, "*My Own Private Idaho*" (review), *New York Press*, October 9–15, 1991.

6. Waugh's sympathetic and perceptive article, "The Third Body," makes this point forcefully.

7. "Both in my life and in my films, gayness and sexuality have never really been an issue, something to 'come to terms with,' or overcome, or struggle with. It's just sort of there. In a way that's how I view race too. That it's just part of people's makeup" (Araki, quoted in Bill Oliver, "L.A.'s Bad Boy Gregg Araki," *Off-Hollywood Report* (1992): 28.

8. Araki, quoted in ibid., 28. Some of the dangers Araki alludes to appear to have plagued *Even Cowgirls Get the Blues* (1994), the film Van Sant made after *Idaho*. The film is an interesting failure and deserves an analysis—not possible here—of "what went wrong" when Van Sant followed the Hollywood "carrot."

9. Van Sant, quoted in Sean Elder, "Young Actors Go Wild with Gus Van Sant," *Elle* (October 1991): 132.

10. Lynne Segal, *Slow Motion: Changing Masculinities, Changing Men*, 154.

11. Waugh, "The Third Body," 145.

12. Mary Ann Doane, "Sublimation and the Psychoanalysis of the Aesthetic," 264.

13. Ibid., 264–65.

14. Irigaray, "Women on the Market," *This Sex Which Is Not One*, 170–91.

15. Cf. Bruce Dunne, "Power and Sexuality in the Middle East," *Middle East Report* 28.1 (Spring 1998): 8–11. Dunne's summary preamble to this "Special Issue" on power and sexuality in the Middle East is usefully succinct: "Sexual relations in Middle Eastern societies have historically articulated social hierarchies, that is, dominant and subordinate social positions: adult men on top; women, boys and slaves below. The distinction made by modern Western 'sexuality' between sexual and gender identity, that is, between *kinds* of sexual predilections [and] *degrees* of masculinity and femininity, has, until recently, had little resonance in the Middle East. Both dominant/subordinate and heterosexual/homosexual categorizations are structures of power. They position social actors as powerful or powerless, 'normal' or 'deviant.' The contemporary concept of 'queerness' resists all such categorizing

in favor of recognizing more complex realities of multiple and shifting positions of sexuality, identity and power" (8).

16. Moon, "Outlaw Sex," 121.

17. In Van Sant's *Mala Noche* (1985), Walt offers Roberto $15 to sleep with Johnny. The pimping scenario, it would seem, preserves (the hustler's) dignity. The idea is that if the john cannot persuade the young man to sleep with him, his best friend can—he'd be doing it for his friend. The motive is doubly displaced (as if sleeping with the john for money were not enough of a motive).

18. In an essay he shared with me after I completed this chapter, Steven Cohan explores the queer dynamics of the Hope and Crosby series; see "Queering the Deal: On the Road with Hope and Crosby," in Hanson, ed., *Out Takes*, 23–45.

19. Gini Sikes and Page Powell, "River Phoenix," *Interview* (November 1991): 88.

20. For further intertexts, especially in light of the references below to *Flesh*, consider that *Interview*'s publisher was Andy Warhol, who in a sense created Joe Dallesandro's ambiguous hustler image. It is not without relevance, either, that Van Sant had plans to make a long film about Warhol, and that Phoenix hoped to get the Warhol role.

21. Araki, quoted in Steven Rea, "Gay Lovers on the Run from the Law and Illness," *Philadelphia Inquirer*, September 6, 1992, H1.

22. Van Sant, quoted in Gary Indiana, "Saint Gus: From Portland to Hollywood, the Director and His Camera Remain Candid," *Village Voice*, October 1, 1991, 62.

23. Reeves, quoted in David Román, "Shakespeare Out in Portland: Gus Van Sant's *My Own Private Idaho*, Homoneurotics, and Boy Actors," in Siegel and Kibbey, eds., *Eroticism and Containment*, 318.

24. Van Sant, quoted in Lance Loud, "Shakespeare in Black Leather," *American Film* (September-October 1991): 35. There is an interesting intertext in having Lance Loud do the interview, as he was in the famous documentary, *An American Family* (Craig Gilbert, 1973), which is not unlike certain Warhol films in the way it raises questions about authenticity and the extent to which the presence of a camera will affect the subjects being filmed. In *An American Family*, Lance—who is seen to be undergoing a troubled adolescence—eventually comes out as gay.

25. Van Sant, quoted in Indiana, "Saint Gus," 57.

26. Taubin, "Trials and Tribulations," 28.

27. Mainstream cinema, it's worth pointing out, when it treats the issue of hustling at all, prefers to figure the hustler as heterosexual—as in *Midnight Cowboy*, *American Gigolo* (1980), and *The Basketball Diaries* (1995)—but since *My Own Private Idaho* and *Postcards from America*, the independent cinema has returned to the theme of gay hustler, with *Frisk* (1996), *Hustler White* (1996), and *johns* (1996).

28. Waugh, "The Third Body," 151.

29. Van Sant, quoted in Loud, "Shakespeare in Black Leather," 35–36.

30. "There is a joking saying that 'Love is home-sickness,'" wrote Freud, "and whenever a man dreams of a place or a country and says to himself, while he is still dreaming: 'this place is familiar to me. I've been here before,' one may interpret the place as being his mother's genitals or her body" ("The 'Uncanny,'" *SE* 17:245).

31. Richard T. Jameson, "Gus Van Sant Country," 2.

32. Gus Van Sant, *"Even Cowgirls Get the Blues" and "My Own Private Idaho,"* 186–87.

33. My reading of the end of the film is perhaps too optimistic. Consider Maurizia Natali's observation (in *L'Image-paysage: Iconologie et cinéma*, 95), that "the scenic horizon always appears to designate a cultural terminus for the American imaginary, a limit continually fixed and displaced by a cinema that seeks to contain the society's lines of flight." Where the classical western, she notes, "fixes a map and a horizon which the heroes traverse before arriving at the tableau shots of the happy ending" (95), the road movie—a genre that came into its own after the collapse of classical cinema—puts into play "a regressive force, a desire for a wilderness that has historically disappeared in an era of highways and national parks . . . the desire for flight without a name" (95). The road movie hero, writes Natali, moves along a trajectory "toward a scenic terminus that reveals itself to be in reality an immobilizing and catastrophic tableau, an indifferent space that is impossible to catch up to [*rejoindre*] without confronting death there, and which is really an emblem of the past, dangerously fooling the eye" (95) (my own translation).

34. Salman Rushdie, *The Wizard of Oz*, 17.

35. Dennis W. Allen, "Homosexuality and Narrative," *Modern Fiction Studies* 41.3–4 (Fall-Winter 1995): 609–34.

36. Rushdie, *The Wizard of Oz*, 57 (emphasis in original).

37. Ron Eyerman and Orvar Löfgren, "Romancing the Road: Road Movies and Images of Mobility," *Theory, Culture, and Society* 12 (1995): 54.

38. Timothy Corrigan, *A Cinema Without Walls: Movies and Culture After Vietnam*, 145.

39. Félix Guattari, "A Liberation of Desire," in Stambolian and Marks, eds., *Homosexualities and French Literature*, 68.

40. As the reader will have noticed, I generally restrict my discussion of the queer road movie to its male variants, but my comments often apply equally to female queer road movies, like *Faster, Pussycat! Kill! Kill!* (1965; aka *The Leather Girls, The Mankillers*) or *Even Cowgirls Get the Blues*.

41. Cf. Kathleen M. Kirby, *Indifferent Boundaries: Spatial Concepts of Human Subjectivity*.

42. Paul Schmidt, "Visions of Violence: Rimbaud and Verlaine," in Stambolian and Marks, eds., *Homosexualities and French Literature*," 235.

10. "The Things We Think and Do Not Say": *Jerry Maguire* and the Business of Personal Relationships

1. Gilles Deleuze and Félix Guattari use this term ("daddy-mommy-me") throughout *Anti-Oedipus* to refer to the Freudian family (Freud's "tripartite formula—the Oedipal, neurotic one"). Deleuze and Guattari, *Anti-Oedipus*, 23.

2. Krin Gabbard and Glen O. Gabbard, *Psychiatry and the Cinema*, 205.

3. Simpson, *Male Impersonators*, 244.

4. Daniel Dervin, "Guy Films: A New Subgenre?" *Psychoanalytic Review* 84.3 (June 1997): 459.

5. Martin Connors and Jim Craddock, eds., *VideoHound's Golden Movie Retriever: The Complete Guide to Movies on Videocassette, Laserdisc, and CD*, 448.

6. Bech, *When Men Meet*, 72.

7. Anthony Giddens, *Modernity and Self-Identity: Self and Society in the Late Modern Age*, 12.

8. Stephen Frosh, *Identity Crisis: Modernity, Psychoanalysis, and the Self*, 187.

9. Giddens, *Modernity and Self-Identity*, 14.

10. Anthony Giddens, *The Transformation of Intimacy: Sexuality, Love, and Eroticism in Modern Societies*, 60.

11. Ibid.

12. Giddens, *Modernity and Self-Identity*, 15.

13. Ibid. Giddens takes industrialism to refer to "the social relations implied in the widespread use of material power and machinery in production processes."

14. Leo Charney and Vanessa R. Schwartz, eds., *Cinema and the Invention of Modern Life*, 3.

15. Leo Charney, "In a Moment: Film and the Philosophy of Modernity," in Charney and Schwartz, eds., *Cinema and the Invention of Modern Life*, 282.

16. Ibid.

17. Frosh, *Identity Crisis*, 31.

18. Charney and Schwartz, eds., *Cinema and the Invention of Modern Life*, 3.

19. Frosh, *Identity Crisis*, 187.

20. Charney, "In a Moment," 281.

21. Frosh, *Identity Crisis*, 111.

22. Giddens, *Modernity and Self-Identity*, 94–95.

23. Bensman and Lilienfeld, quoted in ibid., 94.

24. Giddens, *Modernity and Self-Identity*, 95.

25. Thomas, "Straight with a Twist," 33.

26. Wexman, *Creating the Couple*, 170.

27. Ibid., 171.

28. Tyson's psychotic episode in Jerry's office, smashing everything he can lay his hands on, is explained by Frosh's observation that "narcissism is almost universally theorized as a defensive response to the inability to construct a secure and stable self, this in turn being a result of 'environmental deficiencies'—notably the inability of the parents themselves, permeated by the infidelities of modernity, to contain the infant's destructiveness or support her or his demands for validation." Frosh, *Identity Crisis*, 113–14.

29. Jack Mathews, "Chemistry with Cruise Carries the Ball," *Newsday*, December 13, 1996, B2.

30. Aaron Gell, "*Jerry Maguire*," *Time Out*, December 12, 1996, 62.

31. Cf. Freud, "A Special Type of Choice of Object Made by Men," *SE* 11:165–75). See also my discussion of rescue fantasies in chapter 8, "Batman and Robin: A Family Romance."

32. Russell Gough, "On Ethics, Money, and the Ending of *Maguire*," *Los Angeles Times*, January 1997; reprinted in Murray and Covell, eds., *Living in America: A Popular Culture Reader*, 216–18.

33. Cf. Ehrenreich, *The Hearts of Men*.

34. Frosh, *Identity Crisis*, 187–88.

35. Henry Louis Gates Jr., "The End of Loyalty," *New Yorker*, March 9, 1998, p. 44.

36. Jessica Benjamin, "Sameness and Difference: Toward an 'Over-inclusive" Theory of Gender Development," In Elliot and Frosh, eds., *Psychoanalysis in Contexts*, 114.

37. Chesler, *About Men*, 236.

38. Charney and Schwartz, eds., *Cinema and the Invention of Modern Life*, 3.

39. Julia Kristeva, *Tales of Love*, 26.

40. As this book tries to reveal, certain cinematic genres, or subgenres, in this sense "authorize" a search for love between men. The most obviously homoerotic of these is perhaps the vampire film, which frequently permits explorations of male-male emotional and sexual intimacy in a way that is unique in popular cinema. Far from being an aberration in Tom Cruise's career, *Interview with the Vampire: The Vampire Chronicles* (1994) is a logical culmination of the theme of the main character trying to find enduring intimacy with another man, which we find in almost every film Cruise has made. See Andrew Schopp, "Cruising the Alternatives: Homoeroticism and the Contemporary Vampire," *Journal of Popular Culture* 30.4 (Spring 1997): 231–43. See also Gaylyn Studlar's take on "the obvious lack of heterosexuality-as-something-that-matters in Cruise's films," in "Cruise-ing into the Millennium: Performative Masculinity, Stardom, and the All-American Boy's Body," in Pomerance, ed., *Ladies and Gentlemen, Boys and Girls*, 171–83.

41. Chesler, *About Men*, 214.

42. Richard Dyer, *White*, 24.

43. Benjamin, "Sameness and Difference," 117.

44. Dyer, *White*, p. 150.

45. Ibid., 147.

46. Barthes, *A Lover's Discourse*, 147.

47. Cf. Chesler, *About Men*, 243–44.

48. John Seabrook, "The Many Lives of David Geffen," *The New Yorker*, February 23–March 2, 1998, 108–119.

49. My "David Geffen" in this section is derived entirely from the text of John Seabrook's article and should be understood therefore as a sort of character, who may or may not bear significant resemblance to the real David Geffen.

50. Seabrook, "The Many Lives of David Geffen," 108.

51. Geffen, quoted in Seabrook, "The Many Lives of David Geffen," 108.

52. Freston, quoted in ibid., 110.

53. Geffen, quoted in ibid., 116.

54. Ibid., 111.

55. Geffen, quoted in Seabrook, "The Many Lives of David Geffen," 111.

56. Oseary, quoted in ibid.

57. Rosenman, quoted in ibid.

Concerning Happiness: An Afterword

1. Vidal, *Screening History*, 1.

2. Freud, *Civilization and Its Discontents*, SE 21:83. The editors of the *Standard Edition* note that the allusion is to a saying attributed to Frederick the Great, King of Prussia, 1740–1786: "In my State every man can be saved after his own fashion."

3. Michael Warner, *The Trouble with Normal: Sex, Politics, and the Ethics of Queer Life*, 11.

4. Ethel Spector Person, *By Force of Fantasy: How We Make Our Lives*, 6.

5. Freud, *Civilization and Its Discontents*, SE 21:77. Subsequent page numbers will be cited in the text.

6. The editors of the *Standard Edition* note that Freud further develops his ideas on these different types in his paper on "Libidinal Types," *SE* 21:215–20.

7. Person, *By Force of Fantasy*, 6.

8. Cf. Metz, *The Imaginary Signifier: Psychoanalysis and the Cinema*, ch. 9 ("Film and Phantasy"), 129–37. Metz ends his chapter with the observation that "the dream belongs to childhood and the night; the film and daydream are more adult and belong to the day, but not midday—to the evening, rather" (136).

9. Person, *By Force of Fantasy*, p. 38.

10. Laplanche and Pontalis, "Fantasy and the Origins of Sexuality," 5–34. Constance Penley provides a useful summary of their essay in "Feminism, Psychoanalysis, and Popular Culture," in Grossberg, Nelson, and Treichler, eds., *Cultural Studies*, 493n2. In her own essay, Penley describes K/S fans (female readers and writers of *Star Trek* fanzines preoccupied with a romantic, sexual relationship between Capt. James T. Kirk of the USS *Enterprise* and his first officer, Mr. Spock), whose philosophy of IDIC, Infinite Diversity in Infinite Combination, is clearly comprehended by Laplanche and Pontalis's psychoanalytic account of fantasy.

11. Cf. Elisabeth Lyon, "The Cinema of Lol V. Stein," *Camera Obscura* 6 (Fall 1980); Elizabeth Cowie, "Fantasia" (1984); Constance Penley, "Feminism, Film Theory, and the Bachelor Machines," *m/f* 10 (1985), reprinted in Penley, *The Future of an Illusion: Film, Feminism, and Psychoanalysis*, 57–80; Steve Neale, "Sexual Difference in Cinema—Issues of Fantasy, Narrative, and the Look," *Oxford Literary Review* 8.1–2 (1986): 123–32.

12. Penley, quoted in Neale, "Sexual Difference in Cinema," 123–24.

13. *Being John Malkovich* is not really what we would call a Hollywood movie. It is a quasi-mainstream film, and as such begs a question that haunts this book: what about mainstream reception of mainstream films? What happens there? When I write that the films I have chosen to analyze inspire resistance to culturally ingrained notions of romance, marriage, and family, I realize that, generally speaking, they do not. It is up to the reader to read "against the grain" and so on, to produce readings that consider Hollywood films in ways that point toward the subjective and sexual freedom that has been our project.

14. Freud, "Hysterical Phantasies and Their Relation to Bisexuality," *SE* 9:159.

BIBLIOGRAPHY

Adams, Parveen. "Per Os(cillation)." *Camera Obscura* 17 (May 1988): 7–29.

Adelman, Janet. "'Man and Wife Is One Flesh': *Hamlet* and the Confrontation with the Maternal Body." In Wofford, ed., *William Shakespeare, Hamlet*, 256–82.

Affron, Charles. *Cinema and Sentiment*. Chicago: University of Chicago Press, 1982.

Allen, Dennis W. "Homosexuality and Narrative." *Modern Fiction Studies* 41.3–4 (Fall-Winter 1995): 609–34.

Althusser, Louis. "Ideology and Ideological State Apparatuses (Notes Towards an Investigation)." In *Lenin and Philosophy and Other Essays*, 127–86. Translated by Ben Brewster. New York: Monthly Review Press, 1971.

Altman, Rick. *Film/Genre*. London: British Film Institute, 1999.

Anger, Kenneth. *Hollywood Babylon*. New York: Bell, 1981.

Barbaro, Nick. "*The Outlaw* (1943)." *CinemaTexas Program Notes* 13.3 (November 15, 1977): 61–66.

Barr, Mike W. and Jerry Bingham. *Batman: Son of the Demon*. New York: DC Comics, 1987.

Barthes, Roland. *A Lover's Discourse: Fragments*. Translated by Richard Howard. New York: Hill and Wang, 1978.

——. *The Pleasure of the Text*. Translated by Richard Miller. New York: Hill and Wang, 1975.

Baudrillard, Jean. *Simulations*. Translated by Paul Foss, Paul Patton, and Philip Beitchman. Foreign Agents Series. New York: Semiotext(e), 1983.

Baxter, Peter. "The One Woman." *Wide Angle* 6.1 (1984): 34–41.

Bech, Henning. *When Men Meet: Homosexuality and Modernity*. Translated by Teresa Mesquit and Tim Davies. Chicago: University of Chicago Press, 1997.

Bellour, Raymond (interviewed by Janet Bergstrom). "Alternation, Segmentation, Hypnosis: Interview with Raymond Bellour." *Camera Obscura* 3–4 (Summer 1979): 71–103.

Benjamin, Jessica. *The Bonds of Love: Psychoanalysis, Feminism, and the Problem of Domination*. New York: Pantheon, 1988.

———. *Like Subjects, Love Objects: Essays on Recognition and Sexual Difference*. New Haven: Yale University Press, 1995.

———. "Sameness and Difference: Toward an 'Over-inclusive' Theory of Gender Development." In Elliott and Frosh, eds., *Psychoanalysis in Contexts*, 106–22.

Bensman, Joseph and Robert Lilienfeld. *Between Public and Private*. New York: Free Press, 1979.

Berenstein, Rhona J. "Attack of the Leading Ladies: The Masks of Gender, Sexuality, and Race in Classic Horror Cinema." Ph.D. diss., University of California, 1992.

———. *Attack of the Leading Ladies: Gender, Sexuality, and Spectatorship in Classic Horror Cinema*. New York: Columbia University Press, 1996.

Bergman, David, ed. *Camp Grounds: Style and Homosexuality*. Amherst: University of Massachusetts Press, 1993.

Bergstrom, Janet. "Alternation, Segmentation, Hypnosis: Interview with Raymond Bellour." *Camera Obscura* 3–4 (Summer 1979): 71–103.

Bersani, Leo. "Is the Rectum a Grave?" *October* 43 (Winter 1987): 197–222.

Blume, Mary. *Côte d'Azur: Inventing the French Riviera*. New York: Thames and Hudson, 1994.

Bly, Robert. *Iron John: A Book About Men*. New York: Vintage, 1992.

Boswell, John. *Christianity, Social Tolerance, and Homosexuality: Gay People in Western Europe from the Beginning of the Christian Era to the Fourteenth Century*. Chicago: University of Chicago Press, 1981.

Bridges, George and Rosalind Brunt, eds. *Silver Linings: Some Strategies for the Eighties*. London: Lawrence and Wishart, 1981.

Bridwell, E. Nelson. *Batman from the 30's to the 70's*. New York: Crown, 1971.

Britton, Andrew. "Blissing Out: The Politics of Reaganite Entertainment." *Movie* 31–32 (Winter 1986): 1–42.

Brod, Harry, ed. *The Making of Masculinities: The New Men's Studies*. Boston: Allen and Unwin, 1987.

Brooks, Peter. "Freud's Masterplot: A Model for Narrative." In *Reading for the Plot: Design and Intention in Narrative*, 90–112. New York: Knopf, 1984.

———. *The Melodramatic Imagination: Balzac, Henry James, Melodrama, and the Mode of Excess*. New Haven: Yale University Press, 1976.

Brooks, Peter and Alex Woloch, eds. *Whose Freud? The Place of Psychoanalysis in Contemporary Culture*. New Haven: Yale University Press, 2000.

Buchen, Irving, ed. *The Perverse Imagination: Sexuality and Literary Culture*. New York: New York University Press, 1970.

Burch, Noël. *To the Distant Observer: Form and Meaning in the Japanese Cinema*. Berkeley: University of California Press, 1979.

Burgess, Anthony. "If Oedipus Had Read His Lévi-Strauss." In *Urgent Copy: Literary Studies*, 258–61. New York: Norton, 1968.

Burgin, Victor. "Man–Desire–Image." In Lisa Appignanesi, ed., *Desire*, 32–34. London: Institute of Contemporary Arts, 1984.

Burgin, Victor, James Donald, and Cora Kaplan, eds. *Formations of Fantasy*. London and New York: Routledge, 1989.

Burke, Nancy, ed. *Gender and Envy*. New York and London: Routledge, 1998.

Buscombe, Edward, ed. *The BFI Companion to the Western*. New York: Atheneum, 1988.

Buscombe, Edward and Roberta E. Pearson, eds. *Back in the Saddle Again: New Essays on the Western*. London: British Film Institute, 1998.

Butler, Judith. *Bodies That Matter: On the Discursive Limits of "Sex."* New York and London: Routledge, 1993.

——. *Gender Trouble: Feminism and the Subversion of Identity*. New York and London: Routledge, 1990.

——. "Quandaries of the Incest Taboo." In Brooks and Woloch, eds., *Whose Freud?*, 39–46.

Cameron, Ian and Douglas Pye, eds. *The Book of Westerns*. New York: Continuum, 1996.

Canby, Vincent. "Male-Bonding? Now Wait a Minute!" *New York Times*, February 4, 1979, 17.

Carroll, Kathleen. "When Boy Meets Boy, What's a Girl to Do?" *New York Daily News (Sunday News)*, February 3, 1974, 7.

Cawelti, John G. *Adventure, Mystery, and Romance: Formula Stories as Art and Popular Culture*. Chicago: University of Chicago Press, 1976.

Chapman, Rowena and Jonathan Rutherford, eds., *Male Order: Unwrapping Masculinity*, 21–67. London: Lawrence and Wishart, 1988.

Charney, Leo and Vanessa R. Schwartz, eds. *Cinema and the Invention of Modern Life*. Berkeley: University of California Press, 1995.

Chasseguet-Smirgel, Janine. *Creativity and Perversion*. New York and London: Norton, 1984.

Cheshire, Godfrey. "*My Own Private Idaho*" (review). *New York Press*, October 9–15, 1991.

Chesler, Phyllis. *About Men*. New York: Simon and Schuster, 1978.

Chodorow, Nancy J. *Femininities, Masculinities, Sexualities: Freud and Beyond*. Lexington: University Press of Kentucky, 1994.

Cohan, Steven and Ina Rae Hark, eds. *Screening the Male: Exploring Masculinities in Hollywood Cinema*. London and New York: Routledge, 1993.

Connell, Richard. "The Most Dangerous Game." In *O. Henry Memorial Award Prize Stories of 1924*, 71–92, chosen by the Society of Arts and Sciences, with an introduction by Blanche Colton Williams. Garden City, N.Y.: Doubleday, Page, 1925.

Connors, Martin and Jim Craddock, eds. *VideoHound's Golden Movie Retriever: The Complete Guide to Movies on Videocassette, Laserdisc and CD*. Detroit, Mich.: Visible Ink Press, 1998.

Cook, Pam. "Women and the Western." In Kitses and Rickman, eds., *The Western Reader*, 293–300.

Corrigan, Timothy. *A Cinema Without Walls: Movies and Culture After Vietnam*. New Brunswick, N.J.: Rutgers University Press, 1991.

Cowie, Elizabeth. "Fantasia." *m/f* 9 (1984): 71–104. Reprinted in *Representing the Woman: Cinema and Psychoanalysis*, 123–65. Minneapolis: University of Minnesota Press, 1997.

Creed, Barbara. "Dark Desires: Male Masochism in the Horror Film." In Cohan and Hark, eds., *Screening the Male*, 118–33.

Creekmur, Corey K. "Acting Like a Man: Masculine Performance in *My Darling Clementine*." In Creekmur and Doty, eds., *Out in Culture*, 167–82.

Creekmur, Corey K. and Alexander Doty, eds. *Out in Culture: Gay, Lesbian, and Queer Essays on Popular Culture*. Durham, N.C.: Duke University Press, 1995.

Daniels, Les. *Batman: The Complete History*. San Francisco: Chronicle Books, 1999.

DC Comics. *Batman: The New Adventures #416*. New York: DC Comics, 1988.

Dean, Tim. "On the Eve of a Queer Future." *Raritan* 15.1 (Summer 1995): 116–34.

Deleuze, Gilles and Félix Guattari. *Anti-Oedipus: Capitalism and Schizophrenia*. Translated by Robert Hurley, Mark Seem, and Helen R. Lane. Minneapolis: University of Minnesota Press, 1983.

——. *A Thousand Plateaus: Capitalism and Schizophrenia*. Translated by Brian Massumi. Minneapolis: University of Minnesota Press, 1987.

Dervin, Daniel. "Guy Films: A New Subgenre?" *Psychoanalytic Review* 84.3 (June 1997): 459–67.

Dinnerstein, Dorothy. *The Mermaid and the Minotaur: Sexual Arrangements and Human Malaise*. New York: Harper and Row, 1977.

Doane, Mary Ann. "Misrecognition and Identity" (1980). In Ron Burnett, ed., *Explorations in Film Theory: Selected Essays from CinéTracts*, 15–25. Bloomington: Indiana University Press, 1991.

——. "Sublimation and the Psychoanalysis of the Aesthetic." In *Femmes Fatales: Feminism, Film Theory, Psychoanalysis*, 249–67. New York and London: Routledge, 1991.

Dollimore, Jonathan. *Sexual Dissidence: Augustine to Wilde, Freud to Foucault*. New York: Oxford University Press, 1991.

Doty, Alexander. *Making Things Perfectly Queer: Interpreting Mass Culture*. Minneapolis: University of Minnesota Press, 1993.

Dunne, Bruce. "Power and Sexuality in the Middle East." *Middle East Report* 28.1 (Spring 1998): 8–11.

Dyer, Richard. "Getting Over the Rainbow: Identity and Pleasure in Gay Cultural Politics." In Bridges and Brunt, eds., *Silver Linings*. London: Lawrence and Wishart, 1981.

———. "Rejecting Straight Ideals: Gays in Film." In Peter Steven, ed., *Jump Cut: Hollywood, Politics, and Counter-Cinema*, 286–95. New York: Praeger, 1985.

———. *White*. London and New York: Routledge, 1997.

Edelstein, David. "Adventures in Blockbusting." *Village Voice*, July 7, 1987, 60.

Ehrenreich, Barbara. *The Hearts of Men: American Dreams and the Flight from Commitment*. Garden City, N.Y.: Doubleday Anchor, 1983.

Eisner, Michael D. with Tony Schwartz. *Work in Progress*. New York: Random House, 1998.

Elder, Sean. "Young Actors Go Wild with Gus Van Sant: A Search for Family and Freedom, from *Drugstore Cowboy* to *Idaho*." *Elle* (October 1991): 130+ (3 pp.).

Elliott, Anthony and Stephen Frosh, eds. *Psychoanalysis in Contexts: Paths Between Theory and Modern Culture*. London and New York: Routledge, 1995.

Eyerman, Ron and Orvar Löfgren. "Romancing the Road: Road Movies and Images of Mobility." *Theory, Culture, and Society* 12 (1995): 53–79.

Faludi, Susan. *Stiffed: The Betrayal of the American Man*. New York: Morrow, 1999.

Fenin, George N. and William K. Everson. *The Western: From Silents to the Seventies* (1962). Rev. ed. New York: Grossman, 1973.

Fiedler, Leslie A. *Love and Death in the American Novel*. New York: Criterion, 1960.

Fiske, John. "British Cultural Studies and Television." In Robert C. Allen, ed., *Channels of Discourse: Television and Contemporary Criticism*, 254–89. Chapel Hill: University of North Carolina Press, 1987.

Flinn, Carol. "Sound, Woman, and the Bomb: Dismembering the "Great Whatsit" in *Kiss Me Deadly*." *Wide Angle* 8.3–4 (1986): 115–27.

Ford, Charles. *Histoire du Western*. Paris: Pierre Horay, 1964.

Forrester, John. "Psychoanalysis: What Kind of Truth?" In Brooks and Woloch, eds., *Whose Freud?*, 311–23.

Foucault, Michel. *The History of Sexuality*. Vol. 1, *An Introduction*. Translated by Robert Hurley. New York: Random House, 1978; pbk., New York: Vintage, 1980.

French, Philip. *Westerns*. New York: Viking, 1973.

Freud, Sigmund. *The Standard Edition of the Complete Psychological Works*. Edited by James Strachey. Translated by James Strachey, and others. London: Hogarth Press and the Institute of Psycho-Analysis, 1953–1974.

Frosh, Stephen. *Identity Crisis: Modernity, Psychoanalysis, and the Self*. New York: Routledge, 1991.

Fuss, Diana. *Identification Papers*. New York and London: Routledge, 1995.

Gabbard, Krin and Glen O. Gabbard. *Psychiatry and the Cinema*. Chicago: University of Chicago Press, 1987.

Gaines, Jane Marie and Charlotte Cornelia Herzog. "The Fantasy of Authenticity in Western Costume." In Buscombe and Pearson, eds., *Back in the Saddle Again*, 172–81.

Gallop, Jane. *The Daughter's Seduction: Feminism and Psychoanalysis*. Ithaca: Cornell University Press, 1982.

Garber, Marjorie. *Vested Interests: Cross-Dressing and Cultural Anxiety*. New York and London: Routledge, 1992.

Garner, Shirley Nelson. "Freud and Fliess: Homophobia and Seduction." In Hunter, ed., *Seduction and Theory*, 86–109.

Gates, Henry Louis, Jr. "The End of Loyalty." *The New Yorker*, March 9, 1998, 34–44.

Gell, Aaron. "*Jerry Maguire*" (review). *Time Out*, December 12, 1996, 62.

Gelman, David. "Homoeroticism in the Ranks: The Clinton Administration's Compromise Covers Up an Uncomfortable Truth." *Newsweek*, July 26, 1993, 28–29.

Gelman, Woody and Len Brown. *The Maxfield Parrish Poster Book*. Introduction by Maurice Sendak. New York: Harmony/Crown, 1974.

Giddens, Anthony. *Modernity and Self-Identity: Self and Society in the Late Modern Age*. Stanford, Calif.: Stanford University Press, 1991.

——. *The Transformation of Intimacy: Sexuality, Love, and Eroticism in Modern Societies*. Stanford, Calif.: Stanford University Press, 1992.

Gilliatt, Penelope. "The Current Cinema: Life, Love, Death, Etc." *The New Yorker*, May 31, 1969, 80.

Giordano, Dick. "Growing Up with the Greatest." In Gold, ed., *The Greatest Batman Stories Ever Told*, 6–11.

Gold, Mike, ed. *The Greatest Batman Stories Ever Told*. New York: DC Comics, 1988.

——, ed. *The Greatest Joker Stories Ever Told*. New York: DC Comics, 1988.

Goldner, Orville and George E. Turner. *The Making of King Kong: The Story Behind a Film Classic*. New York: Ballantine, 1975.

Goldsman, Akiva. "I Don't Know Exactly When Batman Came into My Life" (introduction). In *Batman: The Movies. The Official Comics Adaptations of the Warner Bros. Motion Pictures*. New York: DC Comics, 1997.

Goodman, Walter. "Prankster Pals: The Appeal Never Ages." *New York Times*, August 16, 1987, H19.

Gough, Russell. "On Ethics, Money, and the Ending of *Maguire*." *Los Angeles Times*, January 1997. Reprinted in Patricia Y. Murray and Scott F. Covell, eds.,

Living in America: A Popular Culture Reader, 216–18. Mountain View, Calif.: Mayfield, 1998.

Grant, Barry Keith, ed. *Film Genre Reader*. Austin: University of Texas Press, 1986.

Gray, John. "The Trusting Self: Is Moral Agency on the Wane?" *Times Literary Supplement*, March 27, 1998, 5–6. (A review of *The Problem of Trust* by Adam B. Seligman [Princeton: Princeton University Press, 1997].)

Guattari, Félix. "A Liberation of Desire" (an interview by George Stambolian). In Stambolian and Marks, eds., *Homosexualities and French Literature*, 56–69.

Gutmann, David. "Male Envy Across the Life-Span." In Burke, ed., *Gender and Envy*, 269–76.

Hammond, Dorothy and Alta Jablow. "Gilgamesh and the Sundance Kid: The Myth of Male Friendship." In Brod, ed., *The Making of Masculinities*, 241–58.

Hanson, Ellis, ed. *Out Takes: Essays on Queer Theory and Film*. Durham, N.C.: Duke University Press, 1999.

Harmetz, Aljean. "Boy Meets Boy—Or Where the Girls Aren't." *New York Times*, January 20, 1974.

Haskell, Molly. *From Reverence to Rape: The Treatment of Women in the Movies*. 2d ed. Chicago: University of Chicago Press, 1987.

——. "Hers." *New York Times*, February 11, 1982, C2.

——. "The Odder Couples: Is Being a Misfit the New Precondition for Male Friendship?" *Vogue* (May 1988): 66.

Heath, Stephen. "Difference." *Screen* 19 (Autumn 1978): 50–112.

——. "Narrative Space." In *Questions of Cinema*, 19–75. Bloomington: Indiana University Press, 1981.

Heller, Agnes. "The Beauty of Friendship." *South Atlantic Quarterly* 97.1 (Winter 1998): 5–22.

Herlihy, James Leo. *Midnight Cowboy*. New York: Simon and Schuster, 1965.

Hirsch, Foster. *The Dark Side of the Screen: Film Noir*. San Diego: A. S. Barnes, 1981.

Hoberman, J. "On How the Western Was Lost." *Village Voice*, August 27, 1991. Reprinted in Jameson, ed., *They Went Thataway*, 51–56.

Hocquenghem, Guy. *Homosexual Desire* (1972). Translated by Daniella Dangoor. Rpt., Durham, N.C.: Duke University Press, 1993.

Holden, Stephen. "Outraged Autobiographies Make a Collage of Gay Life." *New York Times*, October 8, 1994, 14.

Hunt, Lynn. *The Family Romance of the French Revolution*. Berkeley: University of California Press, 1992.

Hunter, Dianne, ed. *Seduction and Theory: Readings of Gender, Representation, and Rhetoric*. Urbana: University of Illinois Press, 1989.

Indiana, Gary. "Saint Gus: From Portland to Hollywood, the Director and His Camera Remain Candid." *Village Voice*, October 1, 1991, 57+ (3 pp.).

Irigaray, Luce. *This Sex Which Is Not One*. Translated by Catherine Porter, with Carolyn Burke. Ithaca: Cornell University Press, 1985.

Jacobson, Harlan. "Gus Van Sant Travels His Own Uncomfortable Route." *Boston Sunday Globe*, October 13, 1991, A11.

James, Caryn. "Today's Yellow Brick Road Leads Straight to Hell." *New York Times*, August 19, 1990, B1+ (3 pp.)..

Jameson, Richard T. "Gus Van Sant Country." Essay in Fine Line Features press kit. Clippings Archive, Museum of Modern Art Film Study Center, New York.

Jameson, Richard T., ed. *They Went Thataway: Redefining Film Genres*. San Francisco: Mercury House, 1994.

Jarman, Derek. *Dancing Ledge*. London: Quartet Books, 1984.

Jeffords, Susan. *Hard Bodies: Hollywood Masculinity in the Reagan Era*. New Brunswick, N.J.: Rutgers University Press, 1994.

——. *The Remasculinization of America: Gender and the Vietnam War*. Bloomington: Indiana University Press, 1989.

Johnston, Claire. "Towards a Feminist Film Practice: Some Theses." In Nichols, ed., *Movies and Methods* 2:315–27.

Kantrowitz, Barbara and Claudia Kalb. "How to Build a Better BOY: The 'Crisis Points' in Development and What Parents Can Do." *Newsweek*, May 11, 1998, 54–60.

Kaplan, Louise J. *Female Perversions: The Temptations of Emma Bovary*. New York: Doubleday, 1991.

Kauffmann, Stanley. "*Midnight Cowboy*" (review). *New Republic*, June 7, 1969.

Kawin, Bruce. "Children of the Light." In Grant, ed., *Film Genre Reader*, 237–41.

King, Neal. *Heroes in Hard Times: Cop Action Movies in the U.S.* Philadelphia: Temple University Press, 1999.

Kirby, Kathleen M. *Indifferent Boundaries: Spatial Concepts of Human Subjectivity*. New York: Guilford Press, 1996.

Kitses, Jim. *Horizons West*. Bloomington: Indiana University Press, 1969.

Kitses, Jim and Gregg Rickman, eds. *The Western Reader*. New York: Limelight, 1998.

Kleinhans, Chuck. "Notes on Melodrama and the Family Under Capitalism." *Film Reader* 3 (February 1978): 40–47.

Klinger, Barbara. "'Cinema/Ideology/Criticism' Revisited: The Progressive Text." *Screen* 25.1 (January-February 1984): 30–44.

Koestenbaum, Wayne. *Double Talk: The Erotics of Male Literary Collaboration*. New York and London: Routledge, 1989.

Krips, Henry. *Fetish: An Erotics of Culture*. Ithaca: Cornell University Press, 1999.

Kristeva, Julia. *About Chinese Women*. Translated by Anita Barrows. New York: Urizen, 1977.

———. *The Powers of Horror: An Essay on Abjection.* Translated by Leon S. Roudiez. New York: Columbia University Press, 1982.

———. *Tales of Love.* Translated by Leon S. Roudiez. New York: Columbia University Press, 1987.

Krutnik, Frank. *In a Lonely Street: Film Noir, Genre, Masculinity.* London and New York: Routledge, 1991.

Kuntzel, Thierry. "The Film-Work, 2." *Camera Obscura* 5 (Spring 1980): 6–69. "The Film-Work, 2" was published in French as "Le travail du film, 2" in *Communications* 23 (Paris: Seuil, 1975).

Lacan, Jacques. *Écrits: A Selection.* Translated by Alan Sheridan. New York: Norton, 1977.

———. *The Four Fundamental Concepts of Psycho-Analysis.* Edited by Jacques-Alain Miller. Translated by Alan Sheridan. New York: Norton, 1978.

———. "The Mirror Stage as Formative of the Function of the I as Revealed in Psychoanalytic Experience." In *Écrits: A Selection,* 1–7.

———. *The Seminar of Jacques Lacan, Book I: Freud's Papers on Technique, 1953–1954.* Edited by Jacques-Alain Miller. Translated with notes by John Forrester. New York and London: Norton, 1988.

———. *The Seminar of Jacques Lacan, Book II: The Ego in Freud's Theory and in the Technique of Psychoanalysis, 1954–1955.* Edited by Jacques-Alain Miller. Translated by Sylvana Tomaselli. With notes by John Forrester. New York and London: Norton, 1988.

Lagache, Daniel. "La psychanalyse et la structure de la personnalité." *La Psychanalyse* 6 (1958).

Lang, Robert and Maher Ben Moussa. "Choosing to Be 'Not a Man': Masculine Anxiety in Nouri Bouzid's *Rih Essed/Man of Ashes* (1986)." In Lehman, ed., *Masculinity: Bodies, Movies, Culture,* 81–94.

Laplanche, Jean and Jean-Bertrand Pontalis. "Fantasy and the Origins of Sexuality" (1964). *International Journal of Psycho-Analysis* 49, part 1 (1968). Reprinted in Burgin, Donald, and Kaplan, eds., *Formations of Fantasy,* 5–34.

———. *The Language of Psycho-Analysis.* Translated by Donald Nicholson-Smith. New York: Norton, 1973.

Lear, Jonathan. "Truth in Psychoanalysis." In Brooks and Woloch, eds., *Whose Freud?,* 304–10.

Leff, Leonard J. and Jerold L. Simmons. *The Dame in the Kimono: Hollywood, Censorship, and the Production Code from the 1920s to the 1960s.* New York: Grove Weidenfeld, 1990.

Lehman, Peter, ed. *Masculinity: Bodies, Movies, Culture.* New York and London: Routledge, 2001.

Leverenz, David. *Manhood and the American Renaissance.* Ithaca and London: Cornell University Press, 1989.

"*The Lion King*: Fact Sheet." Clippings Archive, Museum of Modern Art Film Study Center, New York City.

Loud, Lance. "Shakespeare in Black Leather." *American Film* (September-October 1991): 32–37.

Lurie, Susan. "Pornography and the Dread of Women: The Male Sexual Dilemma." In Laura Lederer, ed., *Take Back the Night*, 159–73. New York: Morrow, 1980.

Lyon, Elisabeth. "The Cinema of Lol V. Stein," *Camera Obscura* 6 (Fall 1980): 7–41.

MacInnes, John. *The End of Masculinity*. Buckingham, Eng.: Open University Press, 1998.

Maltin, Leonard, ed. *Leonard Maltin's Movie and Video Guide, 2000 Edition*. New York: Signet, 1999.

Mathews, Jack. "Chemistry with Cruise Carries the Ball." *Newsday*, December 13, 1996, B2.

May, Larry and Robert A. Strikwerda. "Fatherhood and Nurturance." In May and Strikwerda, eds., *Rethinking Masculinity: Philosophical Explorations in Light of Feminism*, 75–92. Lanham, Md.: Rowman and Littlefield.

McDonagh, Maitland. "Innerspace: Entretien avec Joe Dante." *Mad Movies* 49 (September 1987).

McKee, Robert. *Story: Substance, Structure, Style, and the Principles of Screenwriting*. New York: HarperCollins, 1997.

Medhurst, Andy. "Batman, Deviance, and Camp." In Pearson and Uricchio, eds., *The Many Lives of Batman*, 149–63.

Meehan, Eileen R. "'Holy Commodity Fetish, Batman!': The Political Economy of a Commercial Intertext." In Pearson and Uricchio, eds., *The Many Lives of Batman*, 47–65.

Metz, Christian. *The Imaginary Signifier: Psychoanalysis and the Cinema*. Translated by Celia Britton, Annwyl Williams, Ben Brewster, and Alfred Guzzetti. Bloomington: Indiana University Press, 1982.

Miller, Frank and David Mazzucchelli. *Batman: Year One*. New York: DC Comics, 1988. Originally published in four issues in magazine form, 1986–87.

Miller, Frank, with Klaus Janson and Lynn Varley. *Batman: The Dark Knight Returns*. New York: DC Comics, 1986 (originally published in four issues by DC Comics).

Mitchell, Juliet. *Psychoanalysis and Feminism*. New York: Vintage, 1975.

——. "The Vortex Beneath the Story." In Brooks and Woloch, eds., *Whose Freud?*, 47–50.

Mitchell, Lee Clark. *Westerns: Making the Man in Fiction and Film*. Chicago: University of Chicago Press, 1996.

Modleski, Tania, ed. *Studies in Entertainment: Critical Approaches to Mass Culture*. Bloomington: Indiana University Press, 1986.

Moon, Michael. "Outlaw Sex and the 'Search for America'": Representing Male Prostitution and Perverse Desire in Sixties Film (*My Hustler* and *Midnight Cowboy*)." In *A Small Boy and Others: Imitation and Initiation in American Culture from Henry James to Andy Warhol*, 117–32. Durham, N.C.: Duke University Press, 1998.

Moore, Alan, Brian Bolland, and John Higgins. *Batman: The Killing Joke*. New York: DC Comics, 1988.

Mulvey, Laura. "Afterthoughts on 'Visual Pleasure and Narrative Cinema' Inspired by *Duel in the Sun* (King Vidor, 1946)." *Framework* 15–16–17 (1981): 12–15.

Murphy, Peter. "Friendship's Eu-topia." *South Atlantic Quarterly* 97.1 (Winter 1998): 169–85.

Natali, Maurizia. *L'Image-paysage: Iconologie et cinéma*. Paris: Presses Universitaires de Vincennes, 1996.

Neale, Stephen. *Genre*. London: British Film Institute, 1980.

——. "Sexual Difference in Cinema—Issues of Fantasy, Narrative, and the Look." *Oxford Literary Review* 8.1–2 (1986): 123–32.

Nichols, Bill, ed. *Movies and Methods*, vol. 2. Berkeley: University of California Press, 1985.

Norris, Chuck with Joe Hyams. *The Secret of Inner Strength*. Boston: Little, Brown, 1988.

Oliver, Bill. "L.A.'s Bad Boy Gregg Araki." *Off-Hollywood Report* (1992): 28.

O'Neil, Dennis. "Sidekicking: A Brief History of Robins" (introduction). *Robin: Tragedy and Triumph*. New York: DC Comics, 1993.

Pearson, Robert E. and William Uricchio, eds. *The Many Lives of Batman: Critical Approaches to a Superhero and His Media*. New York: Routledge, 1991.

Peary, Danny. "Mark of the Beast: A New Screen Batman Resurrects Old Nightmares." *New York Daily News Magazine*, June 4, 1989.

Penley, Constance. "The Cabinet of Dr. Pee-wee: Consumerism and Sexual Terror." *Camera Obscura* 17 (1988): 133–53.

——. "Feminism, Psychoanalysis, and Popular Culture." In Lawrence Grossberg, Cary Nelson, and Paula A. Treichler, eds., *Cultural Studies*. New York and London: Routledge, 1992.

——. *The Future of an Illusion: Film, Feminism, and Psychoanalysis*. Minneapolis: University of Minnesota Press, 1989.

——. "Time Travel, Primal Scene, and the Critical Dystopia." *Camera Obscura* 15 (Fall 1986): 67–84.

Person, Ethel Spector. *By Force of Fantasy: How We Make Our Lives*. New York: Penguin, 1995.

——. "Sexuality as the Mainstay of Identity: Psychoanalytic Perspectives." *Signs: Journal of Women in Culture and Society* 5.4 (1980): 605–30.

Petric, Vlada. "Psychological Evolution of the Pop Film Hero: From Tarzan to Superman." *Film/Psychology Review* 4.2 (Summer-Fall 1980).

Phillips, Adam. *On Kissing, Tickling, and Being Bored: Psychoanalytic Essays on the Unexamined Life*. Cambridge: Harvard University Press, 1993.

Polan, Dana. "Brief Encounters: Mass Culture and the Evacuation of Sense." In Modleski, ed., *Studies in Entertainment*, 167–87.

Pollitt, Katha. "Subject to Debate." *The Nation*, July 3, 1995, 9.

Poster, Mark. *Critical Theory of the Family*. New York: Seabury Press, 1978.

Propp, Vladimir. *Morphology of the Folktale*. Translated by Laurence Scott. Austin: University of Texas Press, 1968.

Pumphrey, Martin. "Why Do Cowboys Wear Hats in the Bath? Style Politics for the Older Man." In Cameron and Pye, eds., *The Book of Westerns*, 50–62.

Pye, Douglas. "Introduction: Criticism and the Western." In Cameron and Pye, eds., *The Book of Westerns*, 9–21.

Radstone, Susannah, ed. *Memory and Methodology*. New York and Oxford: Berg, 2000.

Rank, Otto. *The Myth of the Birth of the Hero* (1914). New York: Vintage, 1964.

Rea, Steven. "Gay Lovers on the Run from the Law and Illness." *Philadelphia Inquirer*, September 6, 1992, H1.

Read, Alan, ed. *The Fact of Blackness: Frantz Fanon and Visual Representation*. London: Institute of Contemporary Arts/Seattle: Bay Press, 1996.

Rich, Adrienne. "Compulsory Heterosexuality and Lesbian Existence." *Signs: Journal of Women in Culture and Society* 5.4 (1980): 631–60.

Richardson, John. "The Catch in the Late Picasso." *New York Review of Books*, July 19, 1984.

Rodman, Howard A. "They Shoot Comic Books, Don't They?" *American Film* (May 1989): 34–39.

Román, David. "Shakespeare Out in Portland: Gus Van Sant's *My Own Private Idaho*, Homoneurotics, and Boy Actors." In Carol Siegel and Anne Kibbey, eds., *Eroticism and Containment: Notes From the Flood Plain*, 311–33. New York: New York University Press, 1994.

Roof, Judith. *Come As You Are: Sexuality and Narrative*. New York: Columbia University Press, 1996.

Ross, John Munder. "In Search of Fathering: A Review." In Stanley H. Cath, Alan R. Gurwitt, and John Munder Ross, eds., *Father and Child*, 21–32. New York: Blackwell, 1988.

Roth, Marty. "Homosexual Expression and Homophobic Censorship." In Bergman, ed., *Camp Grounds*, 268–81.

Roth, Matt. "A Short History of Disney-Fascism: *The Lion King*." *Jump Cut* 40 (March 1996): 15–20.

Rudnytsky, Peter L. *Freud and Oedipus*. New York: Columbia University Press, 1987.

Ruprecht, Louis A., Jr. "Homeric Wisdom and Heroic Friendship." *South Atlantic Quarterly* 97.1 (Winter 1998): 29–64.

Rushdie, Salman. *The Wizard of Oz*. London: British Film Institute, 1992.

Russo, Vito. *The Celluloid Closet: Homosexuality in the Movies*. Rev. ed. New York: Harper and Row, 1987.

Rutherford, Jonathan. *Men's Silences: Predicaments in Masculinity*. London and New York: Routledge, 1992.

——. "Who's That Man?" In Chapman and Rutherford, eds., *Male Order: Unwrapping Masculinity*, 21–67. London: Lawrence and Wishart, 1988.

Ryan, Michael and Douglas Kellner. *Camera Politica: The Politics and Ideology of Contemporary Hollywood Film*. Bloomington: Indiana University Press, 1990.

Sarris, Andrew. "Cruise Plays the Underdog and, Hey, Guess What? He Wins." *New York Observer*, December 9, 1996, 33.

——. "Jane Russell Rides Again with the Bust that Shook the World." *Village Voice*, July 19, 1976, 101.

——. "The Male Mystique: To Be or Not to Be?" *Village Voice*, September 13, 1976, 16.

Schatz, Thomas. *The Genius of the System: Hollywood Filmmaking in the Studio Era*. New York: Pantheon, 1988.

Schmidt, Paul. "Visions of Violence: Rimbaud and Verlaine." In Stambolian and Marks, eds., *Homosexualities and French Literature*, 228–42.

Schopp, Andrew. "Cruising the Alternatives: Homoeroticism and the Contemporary Vampire." *Journal of Popular Culture* 30.4 (Spring 1997): 231–43.

Seabrook, John. "The Many Lives of David Geffen." *The New Yorker*, February 23–March 2, 1998, 108–119.

Sedgwick, Eve Kosofsky. *Between Men: English Literature and Male Homosocial Desire*. New York: Columbia University Press, 1985.

——. *Epistemology of the Closet*. Berkeley: University of California Press, 1990.

Segal, Lynne. *Slow Motion: Changing Masculinities, Changing Men*. New Brunswick, N.J.: Rutgers University Press, 1990.

Sendak, Maurice. "Introduction." In *The Maxfield Parrish Poster Book*, 4–5. Project Planning by Woody Gelman and Len Brown. New York: Harmony/Crown, 1974.

Sharrett, Christopher. "Batman and the Twilight of the Idols: An Interview with Frank Miller." In Pearson and Uricchio, eds., *The Many Lives of Batman*, 33–46.

Sikes, Gini and Page Powell. "River Phoenix." *Interview* (November 1991): 83+ (2 pp.).

Sikov, Ed. *Laughing Hysterically: American Screen Comedy of the 1950s*. New York: Columbia University Press, 1994.

Silver, Alain and James Ursini. *The Vampire Film: From Nosferatu to Bram Stoker's Dracula* (1975). 3d ed. New York: Limelight Editions, 1997.

Silverman, Kaja. "The Language of Care." In Brooks and Woloch, eds., *Whose Freud?*, 150–53.

Simpson, Mark. *Male Impersonators: Men Performing Masculinity*. New York: Routledge, 1994.

Sinfield, Alan. *Faultlines: Cultural Materialism and the Politics of Dissident Reading*. Berkeley: University of California Press, 1992.

Smith, James L. *Melodrama*. London: Methuen, 1973.

Sontag, Susan. "Fascinating Fascism." *Under the Sign of Saturn*. New York: Farrar, Straus, and Giroux, 1975. Also, reprinted in Nichols, ed., *Movies and Methods*, vol. 2.

——. *Styles of Radical Will*. New York: Farrar, Straus, and Giroux, 1969.

Spillane, Mickey. *Kiss Me, Deadly*. New York: Dutton, 1952.

Stambolian, George and Elaine Marks, eds. *Homosexualities and French Literature: Cultural Contexts/Critical Texts*. Ithaca: Cornell University Press, 1979.

Starlin, Jim, Jim Aparo, and Mike DeCarlo. *Batman: A Death in the Family*. New York: DC Comics, 1988.

——. "White Gold and Truth." *Batman: The New Adventures #416*. New York: DC Comics, 1988.

Stewart, Suzanne R. *Sublime Surrender: Male Masochism at the Fin-de-Siècle*. Ithaca: Cornell University Press, 1998.

Stimpson, Catherine R. "Foreword." In Brod, ed., *The Making of Masculinities*, xi–xiii.

Stone, Jennifer. *Pirandello's Naked Prompt: The Structure of Repetition in Modernism*. Ravenna: Longo Editore, 1989.

Strychacz, Thomas. "Trophy-Hunting as a Trope of Manhood in Ernest Hemingway's *Green Hills of Africa*." *Hemingway Review* 13.1 (Fall 1993): 36–47.

Studlar, Gaylyn. "Cruise-ing into the Millennium: Performative Masculinity, Stardom, and the All-American Boy's Body." In Murray Pomerance, ed., *Ladies and Gentlemen, Boys and Girls: Gender in Film at the End of the Twentieth Century*, 171–83. Albany: State University of New York Press, 2001.

Tasker, Yvonne. *Spectacular Bodies: Gender, Genre, and the Action Cinema*. London and New York: Routledge, 1993.

Taubin, Amy. "Fallen Angels." *Village Voice*, December 17, 1996, 78.

——. "Trials and Tribulations." *Village Voice*, May 24, 1994, 28.

Thomas, Calvin. "Straight with a Twist: Queer Theory and the Subject of Heterosexuality." In Thomas Foster, Carol Siegel, and Ellen E. Berry, eds., *The Gay '90s: Disciplinary and Interdisciplinary Formations in Queer Studies*, 83–115. New

York: New York University Press, 1997. Reprinted in Thomas, ed., *Straight with a Twist*, 11–44.

Thomas, Calvin, ed. *Straight with a Twist: Queer Theory and the Subject of Heterosexuality*. Urbana: University of Illinois Press, 2000.

Thomas, Tony. *Howard Hughes in Hollywood*. Secaucus, N.J.: Citadel, 1985.

Thomson, David. *A Biographical Dictionary of Film*. 3d ed. New York: Knopf, 1994.

Tompkins, Jane. *West of Everything: The Inner Life of Westerns*. New York: Oxford University Press, 1992.

Turim, Maureen. *Flashbacks in Film: Memory and History*. New York and London: Routledge, 1989.

Tyler, Parker. "The Horse: Totem Animal of Male Power—An Essay in the Straight-camp Style." In *Sex Psyche Etcetera in the Film*, 27–36. New York: Horizon Press, 1969; Harmondsworth, Eng.: Penguin, 1971.

Van Sant, Gus. *"Even Cowgirls Get the Blues" and "My Own Private Idaho."* London: Faber and Faber, 1993.

Veeder, William. "Children of the Night: Stevenson and Patriarchy." In Veeder and Gordon Hirsch, eds., *Dr. Jekyll and Mr. Hyde after One Hundred Years*, 107–60. Chicago: University of Chicago Press, 1988.

Vergès, Françoise. "Dialogue." In Read, ed., *The Fact of Blackness*, 132–41.

Vidal, Gore. "Notes on Pornography." In *Reflections on a Sinking Ship* (Boston: Little, Brown, 1966). Reprinted in Irving Buchen, ed., *The Perverse Imagination: Sexuality and Literary Culture*, 125–38. New York: New York University Press, 1970.

——. *Screening History*. Cambridge: Harvard University Press, 1992.

Warner, Marina. *Six Myths of Our Time*. New York: Vintage, 1995.

Warner, Michael. *The Trouble with Normal: Sex, Politics, and the Ethics of Queer Life*. Cambridge: Harvard University Press, 1999.

Warshow, Robert. "Movie Chronicle: *The Westerner*" (1954). Reprinted in *The Immediate Experience*, 135–54. New York: Atheneum, 1979.

Waugh, Thomas. "The Third Body: Patterns in the Construction of the Subject in the Gay Male Narrative Film." In Martha Gever, John Greyson, and Pratibha Parmar, eds., *Queer Looks: Perspectives on Lesbian and Gay Film and Video*, 141–61. New York and London: Routledge, 1993.

Wertham, Fredric. *Seduction of the Innocent*. New York: Rinehart, 1953.

Wexman, Virginia Wright. *Creating the Couple: Love, Marriage, and Hollywood Performance*. Princeton, N.J.: Princeton, 1993.

Willemen, Paul. "Anthony Mann: Looking at the Male" (1981). Reprinted in Kitses and Rickman, eds., *The Western Reader*, 209–12.

——. "Voyeurism, the Look, and Dwoskin." *Afterimage* 6 (Summer 1976): 40–50.

Wodiczko, Krzysztof. "Public Projections." *October* 38 (Fall 1986): 3–21.

Wofford, Susanne I., ed. *William Shakespeare, Hamlet.* Case Studies in Contemporary Criticism. Boston and New York: Bedford Books of St. Martin's Press, 1994.

Wood, Robin. "Cat and Dog: Lewis Teague's Stephen King Movies." *CineAction!* 2 (Fall 1985): 39–45.

——. *Hollywood from Vietnam to Reagan.* New York: Columbia University Press, 1986.

——. "The Murderous Gays: Hitchcock's Homophobia." *Hitchcock's Films Revisited*, 336–57. New York: Columbia University Press, 1989.

Zaretzky, Eli. *Capitalism, the Family, and Personal Life.* New York: Harper and Row, 1972.